READING THE LITERATURES OF ASIAN AMERICA

In the series

Asian American History and Culture

edited by Sucheng Chan

READING THE LITERATURES OF ASIAN AMERICA

EDITED BY

Shirley Geok-lin Lim

and Amy Ling

TEMPLE UNIVERSITY PRESS

Philadelphia

Temple University Press, Philadelphia 19122

Published 1992
Printed in the United States of America

♾ The paper used in this publication meets the minimum requirements of American National Standard for Information Sciences—Permanence of Paper for Printed Library Materials, ANSI Z39.48-1984

LIBRARY OF CONGRESS CATALOGING-IN-PUBLICATION DATA
Reading the literatures of Asian America / edited by Shirley Geok-lin Lim and Amy Ling.
p. cm. — (Asian American history and culture)
Includes bibliographical references.
ISBN 0-87722-935-X (cloth). — ISBN 0-87722-936-8 (paper)
1. American literature—Asian American authors—History and criticism. 2. Asian Americans—Intellectual life. 3. Asian Americans in literature. I. Lim, Shirley. II. Ling, Amy. III. Series: Asian American history and culture series.
PS153.A84R43 1992 92-16844
810.9'895—dc20

CONTENTS

ACKNOWLEDGMENTS

We thank *PMLA* and Professor King-Kok Cheung for permission to reprint her essay, "'Don't Tell': Imposed Silences in *The Color Purple* and *The Woman Warrior*," and TriAm Press, Inc. for permission to quote from *Blue Dragon, White Tiger*.

This volume of essays owes much to Professor Sucheng Chan, University of California, Santa Barbara, whose encouragement and keen mind guided it through completion; to Professor Elaine H. Kim for her pioneering model and foreword; to Carrie Waara for her cheerful assistance; and to our husbands, Charles Bazerman and Gelston Hinds, Jr., whose patience and support have seldom wavered.

FOREWORD

Elaine H. Kim

It is an honor to be asked to write the foreword for this groundbreaking collection of critical essays, penned by seasoned as well as promising new scholars on topics that span decades and genres, cross oceans and continents, and explore the interstice of gender and ethnicity. Ten years ago, I would not have thought such a book possible: as recently as a decade ago, there were few scholars interested in Asian American literature, and most publishers, believing the subject "unmarketable," would not even have looked at a manuscript such as this.

At the moment, we are experiencing the start of a golden age of Asian American cultural production. Beginning around 1983 and continuing into the present, Asian American writers of diverse ancestries have burst onto the U.S. cultural scene with novels, poetry, plays, short stories, and book-length critical studies written from a wide array of perspectives that reflect the increasing heterogeneity of contemporary Asian American communities.

In the late 1970s, I attempted to define Asian American literature as published work in English by writers of Chinese, Japanese, Korean, and Filipino ancestry about the experiences of Asians in America. I sought delimitations, boundaries, and parameters because I felt they were needed to establish the fact that there was such a thing as Asian American literature at a time when most Americans were still insisting that all Asians, regardless of ancestry and nativity, were alike, bound together by their cultural otherness.

To stuggle against this kind of erasure, many Asian Americans sought an alternative identity to what was being offered in the dominant culture—the nonchoice between being either different and inferior or the same and invisible, between eternal alien and assimilated mascot. That is why cultural nationalism has been so crucial in Asian

Americans' struggles for self-determination: insisting on a unitary identity seemed the only effective means of opposing and defending oneself against marginalization. This strategically constructed unitary identity, a closed essence sharply dividing "Asian American" from "Asian," was a way to conjure up and inscribe our faces on the blank pages and screens of America's hegemonic culture and was necessarily exclusive rather than inclusive, leveling such critical differences as gender, nationality, and class. Asian American literature produced in those years centered Chinese and Japanese American male perspectives and valorized Chinatown and Little Tokyo as source, root, and geographical center of Asian America.

Yet, Asian American identities have never been exclusively racial but are tied as well to other things—class, gender, sexual orientation, national origin, nativity, place of residence, generation, age, and so forth—even though historically Asian American voices have been muted by the dominant culture's denial of Asian American heterogeneity and insistence that "Asian" and "American" are incompatible. Thus it was necessary to assert political unity against this binarism and its implicit hierarchy of values. The congealed Asian American identity that emerged, though limited because it itself was a product of hegemony, has been a critically important weapon. Constructed in response to racial oppression that we yet face, albeit in continually altering forms, it is still needed as mantle and armor, like the coat Naomi can put on at the end of Kogawa's *Obasan* or the shawl the narrator of Kingston's *The Woman Warrior* wraps around her when she needs it.

It is within this context that the pioneering work of the members of the Combined Asian Resources Project (CARP)—Frank Chin, Jeffery Paul Chan, Lawson Fusao Inada, Nathan Lee, Benjamin R. Tong, and Shawn Hsu Wong—takes on such importance. In the 1970s, it was immensely difficult for Asian Americans to find venues for their writings, particularly if this work challenged the dominant culture. It is no coincidence that *Aiiieeeee! An Anthology of Asian-American Writers* (1974) was published by Howard University Press or that many Asian American writings of the 1970s were brought out by presses like Third World Communications, Kearny Street Workshop, and Bamboo Ridge. Members of CARP pressed for the revival and reprinting of Asian American classics, including works by Carlos Bulosan, Louis Chu, John Okada, Bienvenido N. Santos, and Monica Sone. They established an archive of materials based on interviews of Asian American actors and writers, organized literature conferences in Oakland and Seattle, and breathed life into Asian American theater.

Despite the critical importance of the stance taken by the CARP writers, we must keep in mind how the terms of our cultural negotiations have changed and are changing over time because of differences in historical circumstances and needs. The new receptivity to Asian American voices that became evident in the 1980s was brought into being by a variety of factors, only one of which was the efforts of groups like CARP. Other, more powerful factors include the changing political relationships between the United States and such Asian nations as the People's Republic of China, Japan, the Republic of Korea, and the Philippines—relationships that have always reached into the lives of Asian Americans—as well as changes in U.S. immigration policy, the dramatic effects of which began to be vividly apparent only in the mid- to late 1970s.

New communities have sprung up across the country as Hmong refugees settled in Minneapolis and Korean immigrants moved into Flushing, New York. Even San Francisco's Chinatown is giving way to "new Chinatowns" in the Richmond and Sunset districts of San Francisco and across the bay in Oakland. Not all of the new communities are territorial. Asian Americans are not necessarily moving along a teleological continuum from "segregation" to "integration." I am continually struck with the existence of geographically dispersed cultural communities that exist along asymptotic lines, side by side but never quite touching. For example, events widely publicized through Korean American community networks and attracting thousands of Korean-speaking participants—such as elections in community organizations, fundamentalist religious revivals, and Korean national reunification efforts—are often totally opaque to the dominant culture and to members of other Asian American communities.

At the same time, the days of forced racial segregation can never be brought back. As the world has changed, so have our conceptions of Asian American identity. The lines between Asian and Asian American, so important in identity formation in earlier times, are increasingly being blurred. Within one family, there may be some siblings whose first language is an Asian one and others whose native language is English, depending on their ages at the time of immigration. Transportation to Asia is no longer daunting, and communication between cities in the United States and many parts of

Asia has become easy and inexpensive. As material and cultural distances diminish, middle-class Asian American youths can spend the summer in Seoul or Taipei almost the way middle-class American youths of yore went to summer camp.

Within the rapid expansion and diversification of Asian populations in the United States, the intercourse between cultural communities becomes ever more complex. We need to acknowledge and celebrate the dynamic nature of our communities, the humanizing valences of differences among us, and the vast interstitial spaces we occupy. As Trinh T. Minh-ha has aptly pointed out, "There is a Third World in every First World and vice versa."[1] The notion of either as monolithic and homogeneous dissolves when placed against the multiplicitous identities and experiences of contemporary Asian Americans.

From these shifting fields of power and cultural change, new writers of many ancestries and persuasions have emerged. Established "longtime Californ'" writers like Frank Chin have been joined by poets like Li-Young Lee, son of a Chinese refugee from Indonesia who settled in the Midwest. "Highway 99 Buddha Bandit" poet Lawson Inada has been joined by novelist Cynthia Kadohata of Arkansas and New York and by poet and essayist David Mura of Minnesota. Chinese and Japanese American literary works may no longer predominate: South Asian American writers like Chitra Divakaruni and Bharati Mukherjee and Filipino American writers like Jessica Hagedorn and Jeff Tagami have produced works of great beauty and significance during the past decade. The relentlessly male and compulsorily heterosexual claim on Asian American identities is being destabilized by new writers and new writing: previously unquestioned political and artistic borders and boundaries are being challenged every day. The activities of Asian American visual artists and film makers are flourishing from coast to coast: Yong Soon Min's powerful installations, Lenny Limjoco's riveting photographs, and Valerie Soe's provocative films are changing the Asian American cultural terrain.

In the midst of rejoicing about these works and about the possibilities created by new social realities, we should remind ourselves that boundary crossing must not be merely an aesthetic and intellectual exercise: we must beware lest our texts cross boundaries that a majority of our people still cannot. Yong Soon Min has put it well: as an artist of color, she teeters high on a tightrope, acutely aware of how easily she can be led astray from her efforts to "change the order of things" by tokenistic misappropriations:

> I'm wary of the inevitable commodification effect in which my racial difference is constantly spotlighted for any number of purposes and interests, not my own. It's not that I want to evade my racial identity—I'm understandably proud of and obsessed with it—I just don't want it predigested and packaged for someone else's profit. Especially when I know how voracious yet fickle their consumerist appetite is. I may be their exotic minority of the day only to be replaced by the next minority who gets "discovered."[2]

Min's weapon of choice in the battle for a self-determined self and subjectivity is a new definition of cultural pluralism that incorporates the immigrant legacies of Asian Americans in creating a sense of "Third World solidarity"—a solidarity that frees them from "minority status," endowing them, instead, with an empowering global identity. Her strategy invokes Cornel West's discussions of the "new cultural politics of difference," which, according to him, requires people of color to be open with one another and to the mainstream while remaining firmly and consciously "rooted in nourishing subcultures that build on the grand achievements of a vital heritage."[3] It is this rootedness, in my view, that keeps us in touch with who we are and prevents us from succumbing to either of the pitfalls West warns us of—"ethnic chauvinism" or "faceless universalism." Thus grounded, we can work toward transforming hegemony, revising the very notions of culture and identity.

I want to end with a passage from Theresa Hak Kyung Cha's *Dictée*, a book that brings us vivid new ways of thinking about Asian Americans, culture, and identity.[4] The first time I glanced at *Dictée*, I was put off by the book. I didn't think that Theresa Cha was talking to me. Instead, it seemed that she was addressing her haunting prose to someone so distant from myself that I could not recognize "him." The most I could hope for, I thought, was to be permitted to stand beside her while she addressed "him." I was struggling at that time to recuperate what I though was "my" Korean American identity—fixed, closed, and ready-made—a desperate attempt to render myself voiced and visible. I was accustomed to thinking in mutually exclusive polarities, according to a logic many of us had learned from the dominant discourse and elaborated on in our own communities:

whatever was interior, personal, emotional, and imaginative was diametrically opposed to whatever was exterior, public, rational, and factual. We learned to think in terms of inner and outer selves, "self" as opposed to "society," poetry as opposed to political economy, and love as opposed to work and politics.

Later, when I was ready to read *Dictée* more closely, I came to see it quite differently. I came to love the book for many reasons, not the least of which is that it expands the possibilities of Korean American female identity by establishing the centrality of that identity as multiple and shifting—racial, colonial, female, mother, and daughter selves, crafted and forged from encounters with French culture and language, Roman Catholicism, Japanese colonialism, U.S. imperialism, and Korean American immigrant experiences. I also find in *Dictée* a passionately *personal* polemic about Korean politics and history that I feel is more fiercely pertinent than ever at this moment, when Korean students and workers are sacrificing their lives to express their wish for peaceful national reunification and democracy and when North Korea, now considered by U.S. military and government leaders to be the country most dangerous to U.S. hegemony, is in imminent danger of being the next victim of a preemptive "surgical strike." The political *is* personal in *Dictée*, where the "imaginary borders" and "Un imaginable boundaries" that divide Korea also divide the narrator against herself: "SHE opposes Her. SHE against her."[5] The pitting of blood against blood, nation against nation, threatens worldwide destruction and holocaust and is a direct and personal "violation of *her*" as a Korean and as a member of the human race:

> *her* fraction *her* invalid that inhabits that rise
> voluntarily like flint
> pure hazard dead substance to fire.
> Others anonymous *her* detachments take her place.
> Anonymous against *her*. Suffice that should be
> nation against nation suffice that should have been
> divided into two which once was whole.[6]

Like *Dictée*, the essays in this volume demonstrate through literature how we can traverse the boundaries of unity and diversity, how our rootedness enables us to take flight, and how we can "have it all" by claiming an infinity of layers of self and community:

> *She says to herself if she were able to write she could continue to live. Says to herself if she would write without ceasing. To herself if by writing she could abolish real time. She would live. If she could display it before her and become its voyeur.*[7]

NOTES

1. Trinh T. Minh-ha, *Woman, Native, Other* (Bloomington, Indiana: Indiana University Press, 1989), 98.
2. Yong Soon Min, "Territorial Waters: Mapping Asian American Cultural Identity," *New Asia: The Portable Lower East Side* 7, 2 (1990): 5.
3. Cornel West, "The New Politics of Cultural Difference," in *Out There: Marginalization and Contemporary Cultures* (New York: New Museum of Contemporary Art, and Cambridge, Mass.: MIT Press, 1990), 33 and 36.
4. Theresa Hak Kyung Cha, *Dictée* (New York: Tanam Press, 1982).
5. Ibid., 87.
6. Ibid., 88.
7. Ibid., 141.

READING THE LITERATURES OF ASIAN AMERICA

INTRODUCTION

Shirley Geok-lin Lim and Amy Ling

In the past twenty years, Asian American literature has burgeoned into a recognized body of texts that must be taken seriously as a rich contribution to the pluralistic culture of the contemporary United States. While this body of texts grows steadily, research in Asian American literature is extending historically backwards as scholars uncover and recuperate neglected texts. The traditions of these historically significant texts also include writings in Asian languages, numerous accounts by Asian visitors to the United States, autobiographies by privileged and educated first-generation Asian Americans, work songs by Chinese immigrant laborers, poems by Angel Island detainees, and the writings of Japanese Americans published during their internment in the 1940s.

Simultaneously with the recuperation of overlooked texts is the ongoing interpretation and evaluation of the productions of fiction, poetry, drama, essays, and works in experimental genres by Asian American authors since the 1970s. In the decade since Elaine H. Kim introduced Asian American literature in her ground-breaking book *Asian American Literature: An Introduction to the Writings and Social Context* (1982), Asian American writers have been extremely productive, often garnering national awards and international recognition. Scholars of Asian American literature have been raising important questions—concerning immigration history, assimilation and acculturation, the model minority status, stereotypes, gender conflicts, the relations between Asian American and other ethnic texts, and those between Asian American and mainstream American literature—that provide historical and cultural contexts and problematize the entire notion of an Asian American canon.

The term "Asian American" implies a homogeneity of people and of purpose; in fact, it elides highly disparate peoples of different races and with diverse languages, religions, and cultural and national backgrounds. "Asian American" generally designates people whose countries of origin may be found within the geographical triangle formed by Japan, Indonesia, and Pakistan. The histories of particular nations within Asia may be filled with intense and long-standing rivalry and even armed conflict, yet once inside the borders of the United States, different Asian nationals share common experiences of immigration, discrimination, acculturation, conflict, and generational strains. Their originating cultures set them apart from the dominant Euro-American ones and become the basis for a sense of community both with each other and with other peoples of color. National, historical, and even class distinctions recede in the light of the experience of difference within a white-dominated society. Although the larger society identifies them by their general Asian origins, what often brings these various peoples together in the United States is the American half of the identifying term: their responses to United States culture and society.

The Pacific Islands, including Hawaii, are commonly included in the larger rubric "Asian-Pacific Islander American." Since theirs is the fiftieth state of the union, Hawaiian natives stand in a different relation to the dominant culture than do immigrants from Asian countries. Hawaiian literature has its own history and tradition, bearing some similarity to that of indigenous American Indian literatures in that both emerge from oral traditions. We have also included Asian Canadians as a gesture toward a more inclusive North American identity.

To speak of opportunities present in Asian American critical studies, we turn to a historical moment, that period in 1848–49 when rumors that gold had been struck at Sutter's Creek in California reached the villages of Guangdong Province. It was a story that first brought the early Chinese immigrants across the Pacific to the United States, a narrative of welcoming plenty that the experiences of discrimination, hard labor, poverty, and deprivation exposed as a figment, an Imaginary. But as a "founding myth," the trope of the "Gold Mountain"—Gum San—is perhaps as powerful as that original founding myth of the new world—a city on a hill—that brought the Puritans across the Atlantic.

The difference in founding myths already predicts differences in literary traditions between Euro-American and Asian American literatures: differences in the kinds of ideals, controlling metaphors, conditions for discourses, and imagined worlds that produce and are represented in novels, short stories, poems, plays, and other cultural forms. The Asian immigrants of the early nineteenth century came to an already populated continent, yet one which was vacant in representations of themselves. Euro-American images of Asians in the United States were frequently degrading, racist, or ignorant—influenced by fear, xenophobia, and economic competition. But these Asians did not arrive tabula rasa. First-generation Japanese Americans, the Issei, wrote letters, diary entries, haiku, and tanka in *kanji*, or characters, and some of these have been translated. Despite, or perhaps in response to, strategies of exclusion, immigrant Chinese inscribed their identities literally on the wooden walls of the Angel Island Detention Center. One anonymous poet wrote:

> Instead of remaining a citizen of China, I willingly
> became an ox.
> I intended to come to America to earn a living.
> The Western styled buildings are lofty; but I have not
> the luck to live in them.
> How was anyone to know that my dwelling place
> would be a prison?[1]

Asian Americans moving into the twenty-first century have a wider, more diverse range of media on which to inscribe themselves, as evidenced in this volume. These essays on Asian American literature are the first such collection to be gathered, a pioneering feat that underlines both the newness of the concept of an Asian American literature and, paradoxically, its crucial belatedness. We have assembled the work of scholars from diverse parts of the United States and Canada, who themselves represent a variety of backgrounds and perspectives: male and female, Asian and non-Asian, immigrant and American-born, theoretical and historical/cultural. Many of these essays were originally delivered at sessions organized by the Asian American Literature Discussion Group, which we cofounded, at the Modern Language Association's annual conventions. Others were solicited to round out the volume. The chronological range of the essays goes as far back as the eighteenth and nineteenth centuries, with Sumida's and Ling's essays, and as far forward as Westfall's discussion of a contemporary experimental dramatist, Ping Chong. In making our selections, we do not intend to create an official "canon" of

Asian American literature. Instead, we wish to illustrate the range of Asian American literary texts, their diverse subtexts, the formation of traditions, the evolution of canonical criteria, the recuperation of neglected texts and writers, and the proliferation of commentary on all these. These essays are themselves cultural representations that demonstrate the shift of Asian American culture from margin to center, from neglect or peripheral and localized significance to national attention and reputation.

The volume falls into four sections. They cover questions of identity of the Asian American subject, issues of race and gender, problems of borders and boundaries (national and cultural), and interpretations of textual representations.

Shirley Geok-lin Lim's essay opens the section "Ambivalent Identities" with an examination of the "paradoxical, difficult, contradictory" texts of first-generation Asian American writers attempting to insert their discourses into dominantly Eurocentric conversation. George Uba's study of "postactivist" Asian American poetry argues that, while the issue of identity continues to demand attention, contemporary poets such as Marilyn Chin, David Mura, and John Yau recognize "problematics of language and event both as a way of approaching identity and of renouncing its stability." In his examination of Filipino American literature, Oscar V. Campomanes focuses on exilic experience, identity, and language as its central determinants, while Chung-Hei Yun, in a parallel gesture, reads Korean American literature as shaped by the loss of the homeland, with the trope of "re-membering" as its centrifugal creative force. Closing this section, Cheng Lok Chua's reading of a single text, *Obasan*, by Japanese Canadian Joy Kogawa, offers an instance of mnemonic communication, leading to the "aggregation" of an ethnic self dismembered by World War II internment. The five essays remind us that the identity of the Asian American is itself heterogeneous, multinational, multiracial, and multicultural—a site of contestation, of shifting, unstable, discontinuous boundaries and of straining limits.

Sau-ling Wong's study of sexuality as sign opens the second section on race and gender. Wong convincingly revises the gender-ethnicity nexus in her reading of the assignment of "Chineseness" or "Americanness" along a spectrum of gender appropriateness in Chinese immigrant literature. Stan Yogi's essay, which reads four stories by Wakako Yamauchi and Hisaye Yamamoto, traces the tragic consequences of the collision of Issei (first-generation Japanese American) women's aspirations with the patriarchal norms of their Issei culture. Similarly, Ruth Hsiao reads Louis Chu's novel *Eat a Bowl of Tea* as representing an attempt to shake the foundations of patriarchal power within the Chinese immigrant community. King-Kok Cheung's "'Don't Tell': Imposed Silences in *The Color Purple* and *The Woman Warrior*" focuses on the central characters in both texts and demonstrates how their breaking the silence imposed on them is not only an act of self-affirmation but a transformation of "liability into asset." Donald Goellnicht reads Maxine Hong Kingston's *China Men* both as ethnic protest against the emasculation and humiliation of Chinese men by discriminatory American laws and as a feminist protest against the patriarchal Confucian order which these men enforce within the Chinese society. These essays, concentrating on Japanese American and Chinese American works, cross ethnic and gender boundaries in their negotiations of race and gender categories. They demonstrate that these categories are never unitary and separate but that as historically and socioculturally embedded constructions, they must be understood as interlocking and provisionally predicated terms.

The section "Borders and Boundaries" begins with Stephen Sumida's essay, which argues that "in Hawaii's island culture, place is conceived as history—that is, as the story enacted on any given site." Into this history Sumida weaves discussions of a native Hawaiian poetic form, the *mele*, as well as an analysis of the work of contemporary poets Cathy Song and Wing Tek Lum. Gayle Fujita Sato's essay analyzes Okada's *No-No Boy* as a text in "binary opposition between two subtexts"—the American Loyalty Oath and "Momotaro," a Japanese folk tale. Renny Christopher's essay reads Tran Van Dinh's novel *Blue Dragon, White Tiger* as refugee literature in which the subject matter is "the negotiating of two cultures." Biculturality is both the predicament and the strategy for the historical condition of the colonized resistance fighter whose nationalism rejects the totalitarianism of communist ideology and the corruption of Western capitalist intrusions. Qui-Phiet Tran, working with the Vietnamese-language fiction of Tran Dieu Hang, discusses the thematic concerns of Vietnamese émigré literature, in which the American haven is critiqued as a penal colony and the native culture is revered and held up as a model against "the shock" of American material circumstances.

The section concludes, fittingly, with Craig Tapping's analysis of the interrogations of Canadian "multiculturalism" in the works of two South Asian American/Canadian writers, Bharati Mukherjee and Rohinton Mistry. Tapping contrasts their different responses to multicultural tensions, concluding that Mistry and his protagonist have chosen to swim with the currents (in Canada), while Mukherjee, like her immigrant characters, has chosen to migrate again (to the United States). These essays reveal that national borders are no longer—perhaps have never been—sealed, that individuals and characters transverse nationality at will but often involuntarily, and that much of the energy in Asian American literature is released through the political disjunctures of identity.

The final section on representations and self-representations begins with Amy Ling's study of the Eaton sisters (the Eurasian pioneers of Asian American fiction) and their ethnic identities as constructed selves. Her essay reads Onoto Watanna as a literary trickster, together with two notable contemporary allies, Gray Owl and Long Lance. Pat Lin's essay on Maxine Hong Kingston's *Tripmaster Monkey: His Fake Book* deconstructs the novel as a postmodernist indigenous ethnographic text. She argues that the novel's strategies enable the central act of retrieval of self-as-subject and that the "authenticity" of the text "lies in comprehending its re-presentation, rather than representation, of reality." David Leiwei Li's essay outlines the "American orientalist discourse" resulting from American trade and diplomatic and missionary contacts with China, and the Chinese American discourse that the Chinese immigrants in the United States produced. Li reads the works of Frank Chin and Maxine Hong Kingston as displacements of American orientalist discourse and creations of a distinct Chinese American literary tradition. James Moy traces the history of the representation of Asians as spectacle in American fiction, drama, and film from 1808 to 1991. Despite the attempts of Asian American playwrights to correct the stereotypes, Moy notes that the "requirement of self-destruction" in representations of Asians and Asian Americans persists, for it affirms "the [white] audience members' privileged look." Suzanne Westfall's concluding essay on postmodern dramatist Ping Chong asserts that in defamiliarizing his subjects—the "distorted mirrors of monsters, creatures, outsiders"—Ping Chong provides "psychic release for people who ignore or cannot recognize their needs" or their fears.

These twenty essays evolved as particular, separate readings, each with a different position and text or texts in mind. The aim of this collection is not simply to allow Asian American writers and critics to voice themselves and make themselves visible—goals that suggest an unproblematic, homogeneous ethnic identity that can be inserted into United States discourse in a continuous or seamless manner. Instead, the diversity and range of subjects, critical stances, styles, concerns, and theoretical grids compellingly demonstrate the heterogeneous, multiple, divergent, polyphonic, multivocal character of Asian American cultural discourse. Reading these essays, the reader will find not more of the same but intellectual pluralism operating in the service of community and literature.

NOTE

1. Him Mark Lai, Genny Lim, and Judy Yung, eds. and trans., *Island: Poetry and History of Chinese Immigrants on Angel Island, 1910–1940* (San Francisco: HOC DOI, 1980), 40.

PART I

Ambivalent Identities

1

The Ambivalent American: Asian American Literature on the Cusp

Shirley Geok-lin Lim

WHEN A colleague at the institution in which I was teaching heard I would be speaking at Brown University, he asked, "So what group do you represent?"[1] His question struck at the heart of the occasion for me, for I was conscious that the invitation to speak was addressed not just to me as an individual but also to the group I represent. I am a representative, I suppose, by virtue of my origin and appearance, my yellow-brown skin and black hair, my birth in an Asian country, and my coming of age in the United States of America.

It is difficult to be a representative. One must always be more than one is, and in like manner one is always less than one is. No wonder my unsubtle colleague caught the taint of tokenism on me and snagged the conclusion that I had been invited because of my minority status. The lingering, unspoken question he posed is, Would I have been invited if I were not Asian American and a woman—in short, if I did not represent a group whom a white mainstream America must make a conscious effort to include? The answer to this question is, to my mind, irrelevant, for I believe there is a more proper question to be asked: Should I have been invited? The taint of tokenism is actually the transmuted stain of racism so long embedded that we no longer see it. No one asks if a William Buckley would be invited to speak at such an institution if he did not represent a white male elitist conservative group each time he opens his mouth. The question of tokenism is actually a question of power. Who has the indubitable power to speak, to insist on being heard, the power to join in the debate? Those on the margins or outside the circles of power will always be questioned on their credentials to participate in inner-circle conversations and will be made to wear identification tags to authenticate their authority to be present.

As a scholar and writer, I have been fortunate to find myself a naturalized citizen of the United States and an equal inhabitant in the domain of the English language. Through my equal access to the English language, I have access to sociocultural, intellectual resources which resist being legislated, commodified, or phantomized into specious consumer items with limited shelf lives. Language gives indiscriminately to every human inherent abilities to shape, manipulate, express, inform; to protest, to empower one's self in the world. So my response to the oppressiveness I felt in my colleague's intimated accusation of tokenism is to hold fast to the First Amendment of the Constitution; I represent that freedom of speech guaranteed to every United States citizen, where freedom of speech is defined not solely as a political right but as a metaphysical condition: the inalienable human condition of access to language.

But the condition of freedom constituted by our human access to language has another dimension; the freedom inherent in speech, even when accompanied by political freedom of speech, which is always and everywhere constrained, means nothing if access to an audience is absent. Thus the human birthright of speech can be made mute, silenced by sociopolitical structures. Language achieves little if it is denied listeners. One may express, create, discover, but how does one move, inform, persuade, protest without an audience? How can speech give the speakers access to social power without social permission?

So I write with an ambivalent mind: resisting the aura of tokenism and the unspoken assumption that I should write for a minority group, yet acknowledging the implication that I will claim access on behalf of a muted social group to a public conversation.

Let me give two illustrations of what I mean by access to the power to be heard, a process which is subtly corrupted and always weighted against a minority voice. I was at the East-West Center in Hawaii in 1988 as a writer-in-residence. When I returned home, two incidents occurred which struck me forcefully. I received in the mail offset copies of an article I had written on Asian American novels that had just appeared in an issue of a journal that had been scheduled for publication some years before. I should have been pleased to receive these copies; after all, I am not such a widely published scholar that my publications have ceased to provide me with a glow of achievement. But what I felt was an actual repulsion, a shudder of disgust and fear; for between the writing of the article and its publication, seven years had elapsed. I had begun the year-long research on twelve Asian American fictionists in 1981 for a graduate colloquium on ethnic American literature at Rutgers University. I presented a paper on the research at the 1982 Modern Language Association Convention and submitted the expanded paper to a journal in early 1983 when it was immediately accepted. In the years it had taken the essay to appear in print, I have read Asian American, ethnic American, and feminist writing much more widely; I am no longer the same person or the same reader I was when I wrote that essay. A critic who reads continuously is continuously revising; Stanley Fish begins with that unapologetic statement in his book *Is There a Text in This Class?* Any critic who is not dead from the neck up will have left some of her ideas behind in a decade or so. But to have an essay one has already outgrown appear as if a fresh statement just made is damaging to both the critic and the discourse to which the essay is supposed to contribute. It is damaging to the critic in that she is publicly presented in a false light, as a newcomer in a field in which she has already revised many early concerns. Many minority scholars, because of such lack of access and opportunity to publish, find that their work is even further marginalized. This publication marginalization is especially damaging for the discourse of minority literary criticism because the delayed appearance of such ethnic-related criticism creates the false appearance of belatedness, a crucial disadvantage in a profession where originality in the sense of newness or novelty is a primary asset. Moreover, such delayed publication of ideas allows the minority discourse to be appropriated by mainstream critics who, because they have access to more immediate publication resources, succeed with such appropriation in reaffirming their positions of power and gaining increased access to even more publication resources. In criticism, as in capitalism, those who have more publication resources publish more—that is, make more intellectual property—while those who have less continue to be impoverished.

The second anecdote concerns a letter and response in the *New York Review of Books*, which may be viewed as among the pinnacles of language power access in the United States. As an observer of the spectacle of publication power in the nation, I spent the first few days after my return from Hawaii reading the back issues of the *New York Review of Books*, to which I have been subscribing uneasily but steadily for the past decade and more. And as any sane reader who reads the funny pages would do, I turned to the personals first, before reading the letters to the editors and finally the articles themselves. I was intrigued to find a letter from Czeslaw Milosz protesting a poor review of his *Collected Poems*. Milosz had always struck me as a modest, nonperforming writer, someone I could read without asking how much of his writing has been tuned on stage and amplified to reach the maximum audience. In his letter he bitterly expressed his "dissatisfaction" with the review, a public denunciation which I felt must have been torn out of him by a very unfavorable reception (Alvarez, "Replies," 42). What struck me even more was the casual and amused response of Alvarez, the reviewer, a critic and scholar whom I had long admired for his acuity of insights into the workings of poetry as deeply personal utterance. His unfazed reply was even slightingly reproving, like that of a Victorian patriarch morally smug at the sight not of Oliver Twist asking for more but of a much-loved spoiled child throwing a greedy tantrum: "Dear, dear," writes Alvarez, "I thought I had written an enthusiastic and sympathetic review of a poet whose work I greatly admire. I am sorry that Professor Milosz has felt impelled to provide proof, if proof were needed, that in the world of letters there is no pleasing anybody" (Alvarez, "Replies," 42). Alvarez expressed regret, not at his deficient review, which he viewed as amply enthusiastic and sympathetic, but at the sorry sight of an eminent man making a pig of himself.

Yet a close reading of his review and of Milosz's letter reveals that he had misunderstood the poet's grievance. Milosz takes exception not to the tone but to the substance of the review. Alvarez's review approached Milosz's *Collected Poems*, the product of a lifetime of writing, from the fixed view of an insider who is speaking for an outsider (Alvarez, "Witness," 21–22). Sympathetic to the poet's political and historical position in the 1930s and 1940s, he grants the poet the special status of witness to the horrors resulting from Nazi and Soviet war policies. To Alvarez, Milosz is the quintessential "Central European man" who is also the ultimate poet-in-exile: "This need for the beauty and order of poetry as an alternative to the disorder of homelessness has been Milosz's constant theme," he declares (Alvarez, "Witness" 22). But Milosz rejects that description; he reads in Alvarez's *idée fixe* of his origin an appalling kind of ethnocentrism (although he does not use that word himself). "With our planet shrinking and distances becoming smaller every year, how does it happen that people continue to be provincial, or, worse, to grow more and more provincial?" he asks in his letter (Alvarez, "Replies," 42). And again, "Am I really so exotic an animal that I deserve to be exposed in a separate cage bearing the label: 'Far away'?" (42). Can it be possible that we hear in Milosz's complaint the same protest against the stereotyping of exoticism, the same anger against a deeply engrained Anglocentrism as has been expressed by black Americans, Chicanos, Asian Americans, Latinos, and other ethnic minorities in the last three decades?

But what could a successful poet, a Nobel prize winner, find so threatening in Anglocentric praise of his work? Let us listen to Milosz explain himself: "My struggle as a writer-in-exile has consisted in liberating my neck from those dead albatrosses; in fact for a long time my name was connected with my books in prose available in translation, while the poetry that I have been publishing since 1931 only slowly made its way to the reading public abroad thanks to its English versions. I am grateful to America and proud of being now one of its poets, reaching young audiences who treat me primarily as a poet" (42).

Now, an astonishing thing has happened in the gap between two sentences. From the first sentence, where Milosz presents himself as a "writer-in-exile" still caught in the struggle to liberate himself from dead albatrosses, cursed like the Ancient Mariner to repeat the same old story to the reluctant listener, to the second sentence, he has become simultaneously an American poet, "reaching young audiences who treat me primarily as a poet." Is Milosz making an ingenious or disingenuous distinction between the writer and the poet? Is he in exile as a writer, that is, as an essayist and prose writer, but naturalized as an American poet, "proud" even of "being now one of its poets"? How is "being" to be construed here? As a shallow idea resulting from legal documents? Or as a more complicated process of coming into being, through poetry which is above all the language of existentialist phenomenology? Is Milosz claiming that he is now (as opposed to an original period) an American poet, and on what does he base this claim? If not a status based on citizenship papers, could he be claiming one conferred by that other power of language and confirmed by the audience—in this case "young audiences" whose very existence assures him of a future in this other place, a future as an American poet, in the American canon?

Milosz takes exception to Alvarez's placement of him in a long ago and far away: "He was born," Alvarez writes, "in Lithuania, a country that has vanished utterly into the Soviet maw" (Alvarez, "Witness," 22). Milosz protests against this false mythologizing of himself as a historical witness, a frozen poet, because he wants to validate his American present to ensure his future in the American canon: "After all," he argues, "a poet repeatedly says farewell to his old selves and makes himself ready for renewals" (Alvarez, "Replies," 42). We can read in Milosz's discontentment an echo of the struggle between descent and consent that Werner Sollors outlines in his book, *Beyond Ethnicity*. Milosz, a first-generation American immigrant, will not permit Alvarez to constrain his writerly identity in simple terms of descent; he will not consent to being only a "Central European man," even one as heroic and fabulous as Alvarez had mythologized in his review; for, in his American present, he has made a new, and to him more powerful, myth, the myth of Milosz the American poet.[2]

This brief account of a minor tussle over books is to provide an example of the paradoxical, difficult, contradictory, anxious, suspicious, struggling creative position of the first-generation minority writer in Anglo-American society. The immigrant and minority writer who is identified as such is immediately suspicious as to the intentions of that identification. The historical fact of foreign birth, once it is in your hands, can be used for all kinds of purposes, many of them perhaps pernicious. This knowledge of my other-origin allows you to deny me entry into your society except on your terms, brands me as an exotic, freezes me in a geographical mythology.

Yet I am proud of my origin. Should you proceed to treat me as if I were not different, as if my historical origin has not given to me a unique destiny and character, I would also accuse you of provincialism, of inability to distinguish between cultures.

In a nation of immigrants, however, origin is only half or less-than-half of destiny. An immigrant, no matter how reluctant an exile, usually undergoes a process of naturalization. The naturalized American—and what an ironically inept term that is, for there is nothing natural about the process of Americanization—is proud to be an American now, just as simultaneously there is in him those other selves that will always escape being only an American. In a nation of immigrants, there must therefore always be already that straining against the grain, the self that is assimilated and the self that remains unassimilatable. This self that escapes assimilation, I believe, renews American culture, making it ready for the future. Even as each new generation of immigrants casts away its old selves in the fresh American present, so American culture casts away its old self in the presence of new Americans. This political and cultural dialectic has presented to the modern world many of its models of dynamism and continues to invigorate despite its many corruptions and oppressions every other nation and culture in the world.

The process of renewal, of the remaking of American civilization, is not easy and not without conflict, and the conflicts have changed in nature from generation to generation. In an earlier generation of immigrants than Milosz's, the paradigm for the American, as numerous cultural historians have reminded us, was that of the melting pot, that tremendous stewing machine into which all the ingredients are combined and fused into a futuristic alloy.[3] The trope of melting differences into a homogeneous whole is still one of enormous persuasive power to the majority of Americans today and was perhaps first used by Crèvecoeur: "Here individuals of all nations are melted into a new race of men, whose labours and posterity will one day cause great changes in the world" (55). But when Crèvecoeur's *Letters from an American Farmer* first appeared in 1782, the notion of all nations was limited to Europe; Africa was not even a dark continent in his consciousness, and Asia was beyond his imagination. To Crèvecoeur the pot contained only the culinary from Europe. "What then is the American, this new man?" he asked, struck by the audacious commingling of origins. "He is either an European, or the descendent of an European; hence that strange mixture of blood, which you will find in no other country" (54). Of course, what to Crèvecoeur was "that strange mixture of blood" is now in twentieth-century America the mainstream, the heartbeat of its presidents and those a heartbeat away from the presidency; it is the norm—what conservatives would preserve from the decadent revisionism of "politically correct" faculty—now enshrined as Western Civilization or the Great Books. The new man has become the grand old man.

But what about those *new* new Americans who, despite restrictive immigration policies, continue to flock to the United States? The national ambivalence toward admitting immigrants, especially those who do not conform to the original European type, can be read in the literature produced by these other Americans—peoples Crèvecoeur did not identify as Americans because they were not yet here, or were here as livestock were here, as slaves, without human and national identity.[4] "[The new Americans] are a mixture of English, Scotch, Irish, French, Dutch, German, and Swedes" (51), Crèvecoeur tells his French audience, omitting the Spanish who had their own colonies on the continent, African Americans, and the native Americans who were not, after all, new on the continent. But the list has greatly expanded since then to include not only Greeks, Italians, Jews—people who by their color blend into a cream stock—but also African Americans, West Indians, Colombians, Nigerians, Ethiopians, Arabs, Samoans, Chinese, Japanese, Vietnamese, Filipinos, Indians, Turks, and others. The racial mixture is probably as broad as the global community's, a kind of species gene pool.[5]

Nevertheless, the original model of the melted nationality, a European or the descendent of one, is still held in place, not only by governmental and institutional bodies whose function, after all, is to rigidify and encode living processes but also by some who count themselves among the nation's intellectual elite.[6] The early definition of American civilization as Western civilization appears as comfortable and comforting as the pair of old boots that the cowboy is supposed to die in; never mind that the definition erases an even earlier origin for American civilization, among the numerous tribal nations of the Navajo, Apaches, Shoshonees, Cherokees, and so on.

Lynne Cheney's 1988 *Humanities in America*, a report of the National Endowment for the Humanities, equates the humanities in American culture with the great books of European and Euro-American culture. "Vast majorities" of the nation's seventeen-year-olds, it complains, "demonstrated unfamiliarity with writers such as Dante, Chaucer, Dostoevsky, Austen, Whitman, Hawthorne, and Melville" (4). Humanity, in Cheney's version, despite what global and national demographics indicate, does not wear a black, brown, or yellow face. Cheney elides the humanities with Western tradition, and Western tradition or European civilization with American civilization. More dangerously, she equates all these with absolute value: "What gives them their abiding worth are truths that pass beyond time and circumstance; truths that, transcending accidents of class, race, and gender, speak to us all" (14).

If we accept Cheney's vision of the European in the humanities, and of American civilization as a more highly evolved European civilization, it follows then that there is no reason to revise the canon. Why admit books from Asia, Africa, or South America, or books written by Americans of non-European descent—except when they specifically claim kinship to Eurocentric culture, as in the passage she quotes from Maya Angelou's autobiography (14–15)—when American civilization is built on ideals arrived at from European civilization? Her argument has a dangerous simplicity, for it asserts partisan national values as undebatable truths and denigrates humanists who do not uncritically accept these valuations.

To sum up Cheney's position, since Western tradition contains both truth and beauty, it follows that "the study of Western Culture should be central to a college education" (13). But culture is a human product; humankind has wandered all over the earth and left its compounded imprint in the most unlikely places. In the United States, humankind insists on wandering still, despite immigration officials and border guards. Imprints of the non-European, non-Western American are found everywhere in American civilization, including American literature. Asian Americans, for example, form less than 3 percent of the population, yet they are producing literature and criticism at a tremendous rate, as evidenced in the recent bibliography of Asian American literature published by the Modern Language Press. A similar situation exists for African American, Hispanic American, and Native American literatures. Every time we come across a minority American writer, we expect an American who is outside that Crèvecoeuran, Cheneyan model of a "European descendent." Should not the cultures of these non-European minorities also be studied in the high schools and universities?

The debate has been more acutely felt recently, for these non-European Americans may be a minority only for the present. The Census Bureau has predicted that by the year 2100, the United States will be a minority-majority nation, with 10 percent Asian Americans, 17 percent black Americans, 27 percent Hispanic Americans, and 46 percent white Americans. New York City, we know, is no longer a majority white city: by the year 2030, only 15 percent of the city's population will be white; Asian Americans will form 14 percent of the population, black Americans 29 percent, and Hispanic Americans 41 percent.[7] What the census projections tell us is that a new American civilization is already here, one of greater ethnic variety, of global representation rather than of European descent. The projections indicate an intraethnic, interethnic new world of interlayered cultures, a product not of a melting pot but of interracial, interethnic marriages whose progeny will claim "America" as their own, in their own rainbow images, with European as only one beautiful hue among the dazzling array (that is, if this new world is not riven by racial and ethnic wars and ruled by a fascist state).

As usual, American business is one of the first on the scene. Even as conservatives are fighting a rearguard action to preserve the monocultural face of Western tradition in American civilization, American corporations are acknowledging that the United States will very soon be a different ethnographic mix. According to "Workforce 2000," a study by the Hudson Institute for the United States Labor Department, of the 25 million people expected to join the labor force in the next dozen years, 85 percent will be women, minorities, and immigrants (Schmidt, 25, 27). The director of Work-force Diversity for Honeywell, Barbara Jerich, has said that her program "emphasizes the importance of understanding and valuing differences" (Schmidt, 25). "The changing labor force," according to Roosevelt Thomas, director of the American Institute for Managing Diversity, "is forcing employers to realize that diversity is a fundamental management issue" (Schmidt, 27). This "fundamental management issue," the management of difference, is perhaps what will manage the transition in the changing face (and traditions) of American civilization.

The ambivalence I alluded to earlier is, I repeat, a dialectic; minority writers, especially first-generation immigrant writers, the ones straight off the boat or the Boeing 747, contain within themselves this double perspective; as in an optical illusion, their identities encompass more than one figure simultaneously, like the figure that is both the image of a delectable young female and the horrid witchy profile of an old woman. This double, even triple or multiple perspective exists simultaneously for the same figure, but we cannot see both simultaneously; only through a switch in focus can one envision one or the other figure. Though we know both figures exist in this optical illusion, we can only see one at a time. Human sight cannot hold both contradictory visions in one glance. So too with the identity of alien and American. For while immigrants are both simultaneously alien and American, they are conscious of only one or the other at any one time.

We can read much of early Asian American writing from this double perspective. Take, for example, Jon Shirota's *Lucky Come Hawaii*, published in 1965 but never seriously taken up either by mainstream or Asian American critics. The novel begins with the bombing of Pearl Harbor on December 7, 1941. This event, signaling Japanese military superiority over the United States, is also the decisive point where vision is focused or refocused on the Asian American figure. For Kama, who has lived in the Hawaiian islands for thirty-five years, the event marks the refiguring of his Japanese identity: "He was as much a part of the valley, he felt, as the Kanakas that had lived there for generations. . . . He knew that in his own way he had been playing an important role in the valley" (15). Kama appears at first sight to be the very model of an assimilated Issei. But on second glance, Kama represents the unreconstructed Japanese national; Pearl Harbor signifies for him the salvation of the Niseis, the second-generation Japanese Americans. "They would learn the true ways of Japan and would be educated under a better system," he fantasizes wildly. "Eventually, everyone in Hawaii would be speaking Japanese" (16).

The second chapter moves to Niro, Kama's second son, a student at the University of Hawaii. Niro is "part-time servant-chauffeur-houseboy" for the rich Mr. and Mrs. Whittingham. He is watching the aerial bombardment with the elderly gardener Kato-san and Mr. Wittingham, when Kato-san recognizes that the airplanes are Japanese and begins "waving a mucous-stained handkerchief at the plane miles away. 'Did you see that!' he screamed into Niro's face. 'Japanese airplanes bombing all the ships in Pearl Harbor. Banzai! Banzai! Banzai!'" (21). Unsurprisingly, Mr. Wittingham responds with patriotic spleen, "Why you goddamn little Jap. . . . You sonofabitch! I'm going to kill you!"

The discovery of this national/racial "ambivalence" in a supposedly loyal servant can be unsettling. But what is more unsettling to my mind is how this sudden change in focus, like a powerfully distorting lens, once used to discover this second perspective, begins to take on a social life of its own. Thus, Niro, who attempts to stop Mr. Wittingham from killing Kato-san, is also suddenly perceived by Mr. Wittingham in this second glance. As Kato has proven himself a disloyal American, having cheered the murderous Japanese planes, so too Niro, because he shares Kato's ethnicity, must be in reality a Japanese. "I'm gonna get my shotgun and blast you two Jap bastards," Mr. Wittingham screams (22).

For Japanese Americans, Pearl Harbor marked that point in their history when ambivalence, the ambivalence in their own community toward Americanization and the ambivalence in the larger American society toward assimilating these Asian immigrants, became visible. Not that both ambivalences were not already there, as they have been there for all immigrant, especially non-European, groups. For Asians, the history of legislated injustices has been clearly documented; the riots, expulsions, and other forms of violent discriminations are a matter of public record. (The psycho-political effects of these events on the Asian minority groups, however, have not been as clearly or fully recorded, or even where recorded fully apprehended.)[8] What makes the treatment of Japanese Americans during the early 1940s different from other forms of racism in the nation, as slavery was and is a different form of racism in American history, is that for the first time the powers of the federal government were deliberately and explicitly used to pervert the Constitution of that government itself. Significantly, also, this historical overruling of the Constitution can be traced back to that single event. It is no wonder, therefore, that Pearl Harbor, for Japanese American writers, has the anarchic resonances of a demonic creation story. "As of that moment," John Okada tells us in the preface to his novel *No-No Boy*, "the Japanese in the United States became, by virtue of their ineradicable brownness and the slant eyes which, upon closer inspection, will seldom appear slanty, animals of a different breed. [At that] moment . . . everything Japanese and everyone Japanese became despicable" (vii). Okada describes the shift in perspective for Japanese Americans thus: "The Japanese who were born Americans and remained Japanese because biology does not know the meaning of patriotism no longer worried about whether they were Japanese-Americans or American-Japanese. They were Japanese, just as were their Japanese mothers and Japanese fathers and Japanese brothers and sisters. The radio had said so" (ix).[9]

In *Beyond Ethnicity*, Sollors argues that in contemporary America, ethnicity takes the form of "voluntary or multiple-choice ethnicity"; he is sympathetic to the position that there are few cultural differences among ethnic groups, quoting with approval Parsons's revised position that "however strongly affirmative these ethnic affiliations are, the ethnic status is conspicuously devoid of 'social content'" (Sollors, 35). Sollors bases much of his thinking on ethnicity in the United States on Gans's work on symbolic ethnicity; according to Sollors, Gans posits that "modern ethnic identification works by external symbols rather than by continual activities that make demands upon people who define themselves as 'ethnic'" (35). "American ethnicity" therefore, "is a matter not of content but of the importance that individuals ascribe to it" (35). But Executive Order 9066 and the experience of 120,000 Japanese Americans in the internment camps in Manzanar, Lake Tule, Poston, Gila River, Lordsburg, Fort Sill, and so on would provide the exception to this theory. In this instance, ethnicity had sociopolitical content. Stripped of their homes, possessions, livelihoods, and dignity, herded into substandard housing, for these Americans their Japanese identity was a problematic that made demands upon their daily activities. (I would argue that the same kind of negative sociopolitical content applies today in the lives of many Americans of color. What lies *beyond* Sollors' definition of ethnicity, in fact, is more ethnicity, and an increasing political strain in "ethnicities," at that, in twenty-first–century American culture.)

In *No-No Boy*, the character of Kenji represents one means of incorporating his ethnicity into his American identity. Kenji was

> the one who had come to [his father] to say calmly that he was going into the army. It could not be said then that it mattered not that he was a Japanese son of Japanese parents. It had mattered. It was because he was Japanese that the son had to come to his Japanese father and simply state that he had decided to volunteer for the army instead of being able to wait until such time as the army called him. It was because he was Japanese and, at the same time, had to prove to the world that he was not Japanese that the turmoil was in his soul and urged him to enlist. (121)

Kenji's actions say "both . . . and"—yes-yes.

In contrast, Ichiro's refusal to serve in the army and to take the pledge of loyalty brands him a "no-no boy," someone as deeply despised by his Japanese American community as by white Americans, perhaps more deeply despised, because by refusing to submit himself to white American hegemony, Ichiro threatens those very Japanese Americans who desperately wish to assimilate into American society. Here is how Okada's satirizes these doubly loyal assimilationists:

> Please, judge, said the next one. I want to go in your army because this is my country and I've always lived here and I was all-city guard and one time I wrote an essay for composition about what it means to me to be an American and the teacher sent it into a contest and they gave me twenty-five dollars, which proves that I'm a good American. Maybe I look Japanese and my father and mother and brothers and sisters look Japanese, but we're

> better Americans than the regular ones because that's the way it has to be when one looks Japanese but is really a good American. We're not like the other Japanese who aren't good Americans like us. . . . We can be Chinese. We'll call ourselves Chin or Yang or something like that. (33)

The passage offers a fictionalized instance of what Sollors terms "voluntary or multiple ethnicity"; in the 1940s, many Japanese Americans would rather have been any other race than Japanese!

The major thrust of Okada's novel, however, is exactly how involuntary, unerasable, full of burden—that is, of content—Japanese ethnicity was at that moment in American history; and the novel's power lies in its reminder to us that for people of color—whose external (biological) features are not simple external symbols that we can shuffle around in a free play of interpretation but are perceived, or are capable of being perceived, by others as irreducible content of our selves—this occasion of sociopolitical ambivalence is always possible. (Testifying before a congressional subcommittee, General DeWitt, prime mover of the Japanese Americans' internment, said in support of his position, "A Jap is a Jap" [Hershey, 5]. Despite what Sollors and Gans would indicate, ethnicity as a marker of difference—containing already and always the possibility of sociopolitical content (as in discriminatory acts, violence, prejudices, unequal treatment, whether positive or negative, enacted legislation, and so on)[10]—was and remains an active cultural yeast, virus if you will, in American civilization, producing these split images, this ambivalence toward and within certain American ethnic groups.

This ambivalence is rooted in the immigrant experience; when the internal subjectivized ambivalence is confronted by the sociopolitical, seemingly "objectivized" ambivalence, the yeast of ethnicity or the virulence of racism takes place. Asian American writers, recording their experiences of America, reinscribe this ethnic energy and lunatic racism. Hisaye Yamamoto, who was incarcerated in Lake Tule, says of her ethnic identity:

> I'm sure the Japanese tradition has had a great influence on my writing since my parents brought it with them from Japan and how could they not help but transmit it to us? I even wonder if I would have been a writer at all without this tradition to go by, since most of the stories seem to deal with this interaction of the Japanese tradition with the American experience. And even while I have come to look upon the American experience with a jaun-

> diced (yellow) eye, I appreciate being able to communicate in the English language. (Quoted in McDonald, 23).

For many immigrant minority writers such as Yamamoto, Richard Rodriguez, and Carlos Bulosan, the English language gives them the means by which they can begin to affirm an American identity. Bulosan's autobiography, *America Is in the Heart*, begins with a Filipino childhood (the first twelve chapters of part one), traces a difficult immigrant experience of poverty, rootlessness, and illness along the West Coast (part two), and culminates in Bulosan's remaking of self through the act of writing in English (part three).[11] The second part of the autobiography draws to an affirmative conclusion with the narration of the emergence of the English language writer:

> I bought a bottle of wine when I arrived in San Luis Obispo. I rented a room in a Japanese hotel and started a letter to my brother Marcario, whose address had been given to me by a friend. Then it came to me, like a revelation, that I could actually write understandable English. I was seized with happiness. I wrote slowly and boldly, drinking the wine when I stopped, laughing silently and crying. When the long letter was finished, a letter which was actually a story of my life, I jumped to my feet and shouted through my tears: "They can't silence me any more! I'll tell the world what they have done to me!" (180)

For many ethnic writers, writing is frequently a writing of "the story of my life" (or "of my people's lives"), whether it takes the form of poetry, fiction, or autobiography. This writing of and from life can be read for those slippages of selves—national, racial, existential—which, I would argue, form a pattern in what we call the American experience. In Bulosan's autobiography, these slippages recur frequently. For example, Bulosan provides us with his reading list, his own great books library, as he was lying sick with tuberculosis in the hospital for two years. Among the American proletarian and socialist writers he reads, Whitman figures prominently: "And from him, from his passionate dream of an America of equality for all races, a tremendous idea burned my consciousness. Would it be possible for an immigrant like me to become part of the American dream?" (251). A little while later, however, Bulosan discovers "with amazement that Philippine folklore was uncollected, that native writers had not assimilated it into their writings. This discovery gave me the impetus to study the common roots of our folklore. . . . Now I must live and integrate Philippine folklore in our struggle for liberty!" (260). This ambivalence of cultures, biculturalism if you will, the simultaneous existence within the same mind of the Utopian American future and the Golden Past of Filipino nativistic folk, it can be argued, is what creates the dialogics of identity for the immigrant American writer.

In Bulosan's case, this ambivalence, while further negotiated, is never completely resolved. By the end of the autobiography, Bulosan is working for legislation that would give citizenship to Filipinos in the United States. Bulosan speaks here as an American to other Americans:

> We who came to the United States as immigrants are Americans too. All of us were immigrants—all the way down the line. We are Americans all who have toiled for this land, who have made it rich and free. But we must not demand from America, because she is still our unfinished dream. Instead we must sacrifice for her. (312)

Speaking thus to Filipino workers, he discovers community and a new faith. The common cause for citizenship fuses his life and writings into a meaningful purpose: "This was what I had been looking for in America! To make my own kind understand this vast land from our own experiences" (312). In this cause the American ideals of individual worth and liberty and his own yearnings to serve his Filipino community can cohere to infuse the brutality and meanness of his immigrant experiences with purpose. But Bulosan himself never became a United States citizen. Just as his writing demonstrates the difficult, paradoxical, contradictory negotiations of ambivalent American identity in an American civilization ambivalent toward the Asian immigrant, so too his life and his legal papers show identity on the cusp.

I would like to believe that with the inexorable shift of the United States from a white majority nation to a multiethnic nation of minorities, the paradigm of conflict and ambivalence reflected in these early Asian American texts, which finds expression in internalized alienations and in external racial discrimination and violence, will be transformed into a productive multivalence. "Valences" speak for the abilities to integrate, combine, fuse, and synthesize different elements. Conflict is almost always a product of dualities; perhaps synergistic commonalities will be the product of pluralities of ethnic figures, a pluralism which we know is already on its way.

NOTES

1. The occasion for this essay was a public lecture funded by the Mellon Foundation for the Department of American Civilization at Brown University in the fall of 1988. In preparing the paper for publication, I refer to the occasion as it provides the context for the paper.

2. Milosz's position in American literature is perhaps being shaped in the direction that literature teachers such as Leonard Deutsch are indicating. In an interview for the local paper when Milosz spoke to students of Marshall University, Deutsch expressed the view that "the position of Milosz in American literature exemplifies the thesis of the Society of the Multi-Ethnic Literature of the United States that American literature is the literary expression of all Americans, regardless of language or content." Noted in *MELUS News Notes*, November 1984, 5.

3. Milton M. Gordon offers three "philosophies" of assimilation at work in American history: that of "Anglo-conformity," of the "melting pot," and of "cultural pluralism" (85). The work of later immigrant scholars such as Robert Blauner, Lucie Cheng and Edna Bonacich suggests these paradigms are inadequate.

4. According to Gordon, at the time of the American Revolution, African Americans made up nearly one-fifth of the total U.S. population (86).

5. This argument is not new. The case for cultural democracy or diversity was made by Horace M. Kallen in 1924 (Gordon 142).

6. See, for example, the books that defend Western civilization humanities in the early eighties and that have their antecedents in the recent university-bashing polemics of "political correctness"; e.g., Allan Bloom, *The Closing of the American Mind*; Roger Kimball, *Tenured Radicals: How Politics Has Corrupted Our Higher Education*; Page Smith, *Killing the Spirit: Higher Education in America*; and Bruce Wilshire, *The Moral Collapse of the University: Professionalism, Purity and Alienation*.

7. The figures were culled from Roger Sanjeck's presentation, "Race and Ethnicity in 21st Century U.S. of A.: Historical Possibilities," delivered at the American Studies Association Conference, Miami, 1988. The 1990 census figures indicate that "as the proportion of white Americans dwindles, the percentage of minorities, led primarily by growth among Asians and Pacific Islanders, is increasing" (Fulwood A3). The national percentage of Asians increased in 1990 to 2.9 percent from 1.5 percent in 1980, and the number of Latinos rose from 6.4 percent in 1980 to 9 percent in 1990.

Blacks continue to be the largest minority group, increasing to 12.1 percent. American Indians rose to 0.8 percent (Fulwood A30).

8. See, for example, the case of Joe Kurihara, a Nisei born in Hawaii, which demonstrates how this ambivalence functions upon the subject. Kurihara was a veteran of the United States Army and had been wounded in World War I. "He swore, after he was put behind barbed wire, 'to become a "Jap" a hundred percent.'. . . [Kurihara] greatly influenced many other Nisei to oppose the government in its recruitment efforts to enlist Nisei volunteers" (Chuman 249).

9. In 1924 a federal law had forbidden all Japanese immigration and naturalization; thus, many of the parents of the nisei were never able to take citizenship in the United States. This law was not rescinded until 1952 (Hershey 59, 73–76, 120). These issei were treated as enemy aliens during the Pacific war, and many were pressured into repatriation to Japan. There are many untold stories of such "ambivalent Americans" and their fate after they returned to their countries of origin (including Chinese and Filipinos who decided to return to Asia).

10. There have been numerous sociological, historical, and testimonial volumes on the Japanese American internment. See, for example, Weglyn, *Years of Infamy*; the Japanese American Citizens League, *The Japanese American Incarceration*; and Chuman, *The Bamboo People*. It might surprise the average American reader to learn that "at first 15 temporary detention camps were constructed scattered throughout Arizona, California, Oregon, and Washington. They were mostly county fairgrounds, race tracks, and livestock exhibition halls hastily converted into detention camps with barbed wire fences, search lights and guard towers. . . . The vast majority of Japanese Americans were moved from the temporary detention camps near their hometowns to the permanent camps several hundred miles away after the threat of invasion had vanished. Each of the permanent camps held some 12,000 Japanese Americans, and a total of about 120,000 Japanese Americans were ultimately detained" (*The Japanese American Incarceration* 14–15).

11. Marilyn Alquizola argues against a reading of *America Is in the Heart* as straight autobiography, citing approvingly Morantte's formulaic breakdown of the text as "thirty percent Bulosan's autobiography, forty percent histories of the first-generation Filipino workers in America and thirty percent fiction" (211). The text is clearly composed of constructions that resist a simple reading as factual experience. In its blurring of genre boundaries, it is another instance of the collapse of distinct generic boundaries that James Olney discusses in his study of the autobiography and that is generally accepted in postmodern interpretations of literary works (Olney 4). Even so, I use the term "autobiography" here as the least contestable generic signifier; whatever the text has been called, it has not been classified as a novel.

WORKS CITED

Alquizola, Marilyn. "The Fictive Narrator of *America Is in the Heart.*" In *Frontiers of American Studies*, ed. Gail M. Nomura et al. Washington: Washington State University, Pullman, 1989.

Alvarez, A. "Witness." *The New York Review of Books*, June 2, 1988, 21–22.

———. "A. Alvarez Replies." *The New York Review of Books*, July 21, 1988, 42.

Blauner, Robert. *Racial Oppression in America*. New York: Harper & Row, 1972.

Bloom, Allan David. *The Closing of the American Mind*. New York: Simon and Schuster, 1988.

Bulosan, Carlos. *America Is in the Heart: A Personal History*. 1953. Seattle: University of Washington Press, 1981.

Cheney, Lynne V. *Humanities in America*. National Endowment for the Humanities: Washington, D.C., September 1988.

Cheng, Lucie, and Edna Bonacich, eds. *Labor Immigration Under Capitalism: Asian Workers in the United States before World War II*. Berkeley: University of California Press, 1984.

Chuman, Frank F. *The Bamboo People: The Law and Japanese-Americans*. Del Mar, Calif.: Publisher's Inc., 1976.

Crèvecoeur, St. John de. *Letters from an American Farmer*. 1782. London: Chatto & Windus, 1905.

Deutsch, Leonard. *MELUS News Notes*, November 1984, 5.

Fish, Stanley. *Is There a Text in This Class? The Authority of Interpretive Communities*. Cambridge, Mass.: Harvard University Press, 1980.

Fulwood, Sam, III. "California Is Most Racially Diverse State." *Los Angeles Times*, June 13, 1991, A3, A30.

Gordon, Milton S. *Assimilation in American Life: The Role of Race, Religion, and National Origins*. New York: Oxford University Press, 1964.

Hershey, John. "Behind Barbed Wire." *New York Times Magazine*, September 11, 1988, 57–59, 73–76, 120.

The Japanese American Incarceration: A Case for Redress. National Committee for Redress, Japanese American Citizens League, 1978.

Kallen, Horace M. *Culture and Democracy in the United States*. New York: Boni and Liveright, 1924.

Kimball, Roger. *Tenured Radicals: How Politics Has Corrupted Our Higher Education*. New York: Harper & Row, 1990.

McDonald, Dorothy Ritsuko, and Katharine Newman. "Relocation and Dislocation: The Writings of Hisaye Yamamoto and Wakako Yamauchi." *MELUS* 7, no. 3 (Fall 1980): 21–38.

Milosz, Czeslaw. "A Poet's Reply." *The New York Review of Books*, July 21, 1988, 42.

Morantte, P.C. *Remembering Carlos Bulosan*. Quezon City, Philippines: Manlapaz, 1971. 61–76.

Okada, John. *No-No Boy*. 1957. Seattle: University of Washington Press, 1979.

Olney, James. "Autobiography and the Cultural Moment: A Thematic, Historical, and Bibliographical Introduction." In *Autobiography: Essays Theoretical and Critical*, ed. James Olney. Princeton: Princeton University Press, 1980.

Rodriguez, Richard. *Hunger of Memory*. Boston: Godine, 1985.

Sanjeck, Roger. "Race and Ethnicity in 21st Century U.S. of A.: Historical Possibilities." Paper presented at the American Studies Association Conference, Miami, October 30, 1988.

Schmidt, Peggy. "Women and Minorities: Is Industry Ready?" *The New York Times*, October 16, 1988, F25, 27.

Shirota, Jon. *Lucky Come Hawaii*. 1965. Honolulu: Bess Press, 1988.

Smith, Page. *Killing the Spirit: Higher Education in America*. New York: Viking, 1990.

Sollors, Werner. *Beyond Ethnicity: Consent and Descent in American Culture*. New York: Oxford University Press, 1986.

Weglyn, Michi. *Years of Infamy: The Untold Story of America's Concentration Camps*. New York: Morrow, 1976.

Wilshire, Bruce. *The Moral Collapse of the University: Professionalism, Purity and Alienation*. Albany: State University of New York Press, 1990.

2

Versions of Identity in Post-Activist Asian American Poetry

George Uba

THE RAW energy of Asian-Pacific American "activist" poets of the late 1960s and early 1970s gave impetus to a literature in the process of self-discovery. By refereeing unexplored spaces of Asian American existence, these poets helped preside over an emerging ethnic consciousness and helped plot the sociopolitical vectors of the age. Seeking to "unmask" poetry by removing it from the elitest academy (which had sealed meanings in the esoteric and the arcane, renounced plainness of speech, and conferred shamanistic status on university professors), the activist writers sought to deliver poetry to the People, who, apprehending its "essentials," would renew it in the spirit of emerging political freedom. The activist spirit survives in the bristling warning contained in Janice Mirikitani's "We, the Dangerous":[1]

> We, the dangerous,
> Dwelling in the ocean.
> Akin to the jungle.
> Close to the earth.
>
> Hiroshima
> Vietnam
> Tule Lake
> And yet we were not devoured.

And yet we were not humbled.
And yet we are not broken.

(*Ayumi*, 211)

Not uncommonly, activist poems resorted to linguistic shock tactics as well, as in these lines from Merle Woo's "Yellow Woman Speaks":

Yellow woman, a revolutionary speaks:

"They have mutilated our genitals, but I will
 restore them
. . . .
 I will create armies of . . . descendants.

And I will expose the lies and ridicule
the impotence of those who have called us
 chink
 yellow-livered
 slanted cunts
 exotic
in order to abuse and exploit us.
 And I will destroy them."

(*Bruchac*, 286)

Woo's poem eschews the conventional finesse of Euro-American poetry in an effort to confront directly the oppressors who have developed and perpetuated racist stereotypes. The revolutionary's vow is to multiply and to "destroy." Less confrontational, Mirikitani's approach is to assert the vitalizing power to endure. Nevertheless, she too warns that "we" are "dangerous." The impetus behind these poems is not only politics in the conventional sense but also the politics of poetry. Both poems align themselves self-consciously with an oral tradition. Woo's poem demands that it be spoken aloud ("a revolutionary speaks"); in the process it also contests standard Euro-American definitions of poetry by embracing polemic. Mirikitani's poem violates the contemporary "rules" of poetry by relying heavily on political slogans and the rhetoric of abstraction. Her poem aligns itself not with a theory of poetry as written inscription but with an oral tradition that blurs the distinction between poem and chant, and privileges performance over inscription. Moreover, the poem's paratactical linking of "Hiroshima / Vietnam / Tule Lake" reflects Russell Leong's notion of a "tribal" impulse common to poets of the late

1960s and early 1970s, an impulse that highlighted the "shared experience[s] of subjugation" among people of color and that actively sought to "unlock the . . . keys to memory and to provide a base for unity" (166).

This tribalism was a common way of negotiating identity, especially valuable as an ethnographic signifier of resistance to an oppressive, well-armed, and thoroughly entrenched dominant culture. It was a means of resisting the assimilationist ethic for so long spreading insidiously across the American ethnic landscape by focusing on and celebrating differences between whites and people of color, while acknowledging both similarities and differences among the latter as well.[2] To some degree, much of contemporary Asian American poetry presupposes this activist base.

The situation has altered, however, in the sense that many of today's poets express at once an affinity for and a sense of distance from the activist tradition. In the wake of the profound demographic changes affecting Asian America, changes which have resulted in a diversity unimaginable twenty years ago, the reification of the "tribal" has become increasingly problematic.[3] The dimensions of the effort to achieve a communal or "tribalistic" connection have multiplied, even as the results of such effort have grown less certain. Keenly aware of heterogeneity, as well as the absence of geographical centers, today's poets may yearn for a connection they can only ratify in a compromised form. They have been thrust back upon their sense of an individual self, an alteration implying the forfeiture of oral traditions. Joined with a loss of faith in the efficacy of language as an agent of social reform and as a reliable tool of representation, this individualizing tendency has redirected poets toward Euro-American poetics.

But with a difference. Today's poets tend to appropriate such poetics for their own ethnographic purposes. If, in acknowledging the provisional conduct of poetry, post-activist poets hold that identity, whether tribal or otherwise, is always in doubt, it is not that the issue of identity has ceased to demand their attention. Indeed, the post-activist poem tends to recognize problematics of language and event both as a way of approaching identity and of renouncing its stability. Although these recognitions extend to an increasing number of poets, recent works by Marilyn Chin and David Mura and the special case of John Yau reveal some of the distinct contours that Asian American poetry currently describes. For Chin and Mura—

although in different ways—conceiving identity is only possible by foregrounding its partialities, while for Yau every version of identity is radically contestable because of the unstable nature of the tools used to conceptualize it.

In dedicating her book *Dwarf Bamboo* to the Communist poet and revolutionary Ai Qing, Marilyn Chin reveals an affinity with the collectivist politics of the activist poets. However, her skepticism toward unificatory gestures and her intense recognition of identity as process rather than as cultural preserve lead her to question the very impulses toward which she is otherwise drawn. The poem "Segments of a Bamboo Screen," for example, conjoins the centrifugal tendencies of world politics with the inability to negotiate pictorial unity out of the "segments" of the bamboo screen. The speaker questions the bamboo screen artist's ability to "sit there on top of the world" and gain a perspective "that I cannot"(18)—a centrist position around which all others supposedly revolve. For this speaker, the partial replaces the whole: "The moon is gibbous. Just say / She shall no longer pay you her full attention" (17).

Chin is also acutely aware of how historical contingencies intrude upon every version of identity. Rather than stabilizing a connection to her "Parent Node," Chin's frequent use of historicized personae reveals the provisional nature of all identity. The poems "The Landlord's Wife" and "Untrimmed Mourning" offer contrasting portraits of the widows of two Chinese men, one a wealthy landlord slain in the course of political ferment in 1919 and the other a poor man who had "only small pink babies / and one good hog" (14). Years later in post-revolutionary China, the landlord's wife, who still regrets her loss of status as "the wealthiest woman in Guang Dung," nevertheless repudiates her husband's memory and proclaims her allegiance to Chairman Mao. "'I never loved him, never. / The only man I love now, the only man I believe—/ The man from above, from Yenan'" (12). For the impoverished widow remaining in pre-revolutionary China, however, who for ten years has "gulped down / this loneliness," the continuing pressures of survival have forced her to drag the hog to market where she will proclaim in broken dialect, "'Rich man, have you no / dollars to taste?'" (14). The "Chinese" identity of these two survivors is self-consciously multiple, deriving from no acknowledged center but negotiated among historical contingencies. In severing her allegiance to her landlord husband's estate, the rich widow responds to a far-reaching alteration in political circumstances, while the poor widow responds to an immediate change in her personal environment. At the same time, it is evident that each woman's sense of identity is subject to further internal shift, depending on forces beyond her control.

As history destabilizes identity, so can ideology. The poem "After My Last Paycheck from the Factory . . . " takes as its epigraph, "For the Chinese Cultural Revolution and all that was wrong with my life" (21)—a satirical thrust at the notion that Mao's Cultural Revolution conferred a stable identity upon everyone of Chinese descent. And, indeed, in the poem a youthful Chinese American expatriate working in a Communist factory experiences a profound revulsion when she invites an elderly Chinese man for an afternoon meal. The sight of old Liu eating dog and smacking "his greasy lips" is enough to make the woman yearn for "home" and her "lover's gentle kisses" (21). Although the sight of two girls wearing uniforms, bandanas, and armbands and "shouting slogans and Maoish songs" momentarily reminds her of why she has come to China in the first place, "the realist Liu" disrupts this "mirage" by revealing that the raw conditions of life have not changed for him, for as he declares, " 'It's the dog I ordered and am eating still!' " (21). The dog has spots, "rampant colonies of scabies and fleas," and a forehead that "bled with worms" (21-22). The woman says, "I rubbed my eyes, readjusted the world" (22). But through Chin's lenses, the world must be readjusted yet again. For a neighboring patron, a "stout provincial governor" who dines for free on fine "Chinese pug, twenty-five yuan a leg" and who afterwards flaunts his wealth, is destined, according to Liu, to pay a drastic penalty for his reactionary ways: " 'and he as dead as the four-legged he ate / two short kilometers before home' " (22).

By setting itself skeptically on the shifting borders of ideological rectitude, the poem complicates the leftist political identification that constitutes the radical base of an "authentic" Asian American identity. Obviously, though, it also prohibits the retreat into bourgeois complacency. At the end of the poem, the woman is given no firm ideological hold on her own identity. Whatever she thought it was is now called into question; whatever it may become remains in a state of flux.

If history and ideology move toward the destabilization of identity, their "absence" exacts a similar price. Originally from Hong Kong, Chin has spent most of her life in America. In the poem "Repulse Bay," the "dead and swimming creatures of the sea" are images of the speaker herself, struggling to remain culturally afloat in a defamiliarized locale, a part of "the country I have lost" (64). In the poem "A Chinaman's Chance," Chin acknowledges the special difficulties faced by the American-born Chinese attempting to recover the Chinese American past when only its fragments remain. The inability to pattern oneself after Chinese ancestors in America is stated succinctly in the lines "The railroad killed your great-grandfather / His arms here, his legs there. . . . / *How can we remake ourselves in his image?*" (29). That is, how can a connection be forged with an image that has been rent, scattered, and left unpreserved? With an ancestor who can only be recalled—both physically and otherwise—in pieces? Such a dilemma can be exacerbated by alienation from traditional systems of belief, an alienation manifested in the sardonic question posed at the poem's start:

> If you were a Chinese born in America, who would you believe
> Plato who said what Socrates said
> Or Confucius in his bawdy way:
>   "So a male child is born to you
>   I am happy, very very happy." (29)

The repudiation of traditional beliefs further problematizes the effort to recover a "lost" identity.

Yet, despite their instabilities, it is wrong to assume that Chin's views of identity inevitably testify to loss. In the poem "I confess . . . " the speaker expresses a dialogic relationship between cultures by reading alternately Bachelard's "The Poetics of Space" and chapters from "The Compassionate Buddha." She pens ironic "letters of progress":

> one day I am filial
> monkey, practicing reading
> and writing. Next day
> I wear ink
> eyeliner, open up
> Mandarin frock for the boys. (53–54)

The speaker's mischievous "confession" regarding her obsessive movement between cultures is partly an acknowledgment of the intellectual tradition of the West, which she willingly inherits. But more to the point, it is simultaneously a defense of an identity kept vital by its own instability. For Chin, the question of identity is engaging precisely because it is never still. The alternative—to snatch "a quick decision—/ to marry Chinese, / to succeed in business, / to buy that slow boat" (54)—is to avoid the vexations and rewards of self-examination by impulsive marriage to convention. Attending only to "business" means boarding a "slow boat" bound for a cultural nowhere.

Like Marilyn Chin, David Mura, author of the book *After We Lost Our Way*, acknowledges how activist poets serve as his literary ancestors, even as he insists upon his necessary differences from them. As a third-generation Japanese American, Mura feels a particular connection with the activists of twenty years ago of whom so many were also at least third-generation Asian Americans. The anger, outrage, and alienation they shared are especially manifest in Mura's poems dealing with racism, internment camps, and assimilation. Like Chin, Mura operates from outside the earlier oral tradition, even though he remains attracted to the aural (as is evidenced by several poems bearing the words "suite," "song," and "argument" in their titles). But whereas Chin remains skeptical of the communalistic impulse as a basis for identity, even as she yearns for its retrieval, Mura campaigns at once to recover and expand the impulse by embracing other marginalized lives—the oppressed, wretched, and suffering in all stations and cultures, including (in a singularly bold stroke) the homosexual Italian film director and writer Pasolini. By embracing even a white male European, Mura testifies to the impossibility of containing identity along purely racial and ethnic lines. Identity may also be conceived in the presence of lives outwardly removed from one's own.

Pasolini, as Mura explains in a series of eleven poems strategically placed at the center of his book, frequented the brutal Italian demimonde of "punks, pickpockets, whores," even as he directed brilliant, controversial films—nearly all of them censored, denounced, or involved in lawsuits—that assure his place in film history. From the peasant son of a father devoted to Mussolini to the adult "crazy about Marx and *terza rima*" (25) and from his compassion for slum dwellers to his autocratic desire "to subjugate, to block / his [lover's] ego's light with the shadow of mine" (30), Pasolini was a figure steeped in contradictions. Refusing to abjure "the ambiguous life"

(25), Pasolini was persecuted in the popular press and prosecuted in a series of demeaning public trials.

In the majority of these poems Mura assumes a mask, usually that of Pasolini himself—Pasolini describing his seduction at the hands of his young lover Ninetto, Pasolini describing his ambivalence toward Roland Barthes or writing a letter from Nepal to Alberto Moravia, Pasolini transcribing a stunning apologia for his promiscuous, risk-filled life—while interspersing these subjective accounts with neutral ones of his brutal murder by a teenager, a "two-bit thief" (44). Although Pasolini seems as remote from conventional Japanese American experience as humanly imaginable, Mura identifies him as a sort of presiding spirit, joined to the author by his powerful sense of alienation from bourgeois culture, by his artistry, and by his human frailty. Despite the apparent modesty of the title, the centrally placed poem "Intermission: Postcard from Rome" elucidates the nature and depth of the connection between the two artists. In a cemetery in Casarsa the American wife, a descendant of the Mayflower Pilgrims, discovers Pasolini's simple stone marker. It lies "next to the stone of Susanna," his mother; coincidentally, the American wife's name is "Susie" (37). Here, at the grave, the Japanese American poet stares at the stone of the Italian filmmaker and begins to weep, apologizing once because "it seems so predictable." Later, the speaker acknowledges that "in my country, // it's customary to ask why, why Pasolini?" (38). That is, why should a Japanese American poet be drawn so powerfully to Pasolini? The speaker answers, "We are young. We believe in the unconscious, an emotional life" (38). A stream of connection, unconscious and emotional, underlies and proceeds from the two lives despite surface discontinuities. The speaker affirms, "It's no good to say my genes are Japanese" (38), as though that simple biological accident somehow accounts for an entire identity. The speaker acknowledges, "We will never be intimate. Will always be the same" (38). They will always be the same in their lack of intimacy; their distance will never be completely bridged. Their identities are acknowledged as conjunctural, not identical. But at the same time the speaker reaffirms at the end the initiating connection: "Dear ghost, do not go to another house" (38). Only in this one poem is the issue of the speaker's Japanese American identity directly raised. But the affirmation of the connection to Pasolini suggests the plural possibilities of identity within the framework of opposition, rage, and outrage.

Elsewhere, Mura offers a gallery of portraits of the infirm and dying, the lost and the as-good-as lost. The range itself is remarkable—an architect's five-year old son dying, a Cambodian refugee bound for France, a Viet Cong recalling the men he has slain, a man in a pornographic bookstore, another turned informer in South Africa, a brutally beaten woman lying in a hospital emergency room. The nearly unbearable cry of pain, so heterogeneous in its sources yet so alarmingly unified in its despair, contributes to Mura's idea of identity expanded beyond its customary limits.

Ostensibly, then, Mura merely expands what the activist tradition had all along pointed in the direction of—a synthetical identity of the oppressed that resolves all the competing elements of experience. But the difference between him and the activist writers is pronounced, starting with the fact that he acknowledges linguistic limitations, admitting that language can result in "dangling rantings" (71) and averring that even at its best, its value in a world marked by profound suffering remains problematic. Like Marilyn Chin, Mura also acknowledges that all ideas about identity are in some way inadequate, partial, and contradictory, even as he asserts that it is these very properties that help us to install identity at any moment in history. So imperfect, partial, and inherently contradictory is any expressed notion of identity that it cannot be known through any concrete instance; yet these same partialities and contradictions necessarily point in the direction of identity. As Fredric Jameson so succinctly puts it in describing Adorno's *Negative Dialektik* (Adorno is one of Mura's intellectual affiliations), "a negative dialectic has no choice but to affirm the notion and value of an ultimate synthesis, while negating its possibility and reality in every concrete case that comes before it" (56).

It is in this light that Mura's continual yearning for reconciliation, wholeness, and the unification of identity must be understood. The opening lines of his book's first poem, "Grandfather and Grandmother in Love," elucidate the poet's charge: "Now I will ask for one true word beyond / betrayal" (3). This word should be as true, as authentic, as the speaker takes the sex act between his grandparents in love to have been. Taking this "one true word," the speaker will "crack it, like a seed / between the teeth, spit it out in the world" (3), where, it is hoped, it may take root. The effort seemingly reflects what Adorno describes as "neo-romantic" poetry's endeavor "to recover some of the substantiality of language" (*Aesthetic Theory*, 23).

For Mura, to substantialize language would be to resubstantialize his grandparents' pasts, to negotiate identity with an instrument made reliable and whole once again.

But Mura's poetry does not actually suggest either that language can be resubstantialized or identity stabilized in this way. In investigating identities within a given group, Mura repeatedly uncovers contradictions. In "A *Nisei* Picnic: From an Album" he describes an uncle, a veteran of the war, who eventually "ballooned like Buddha, / over three hundred pounds"; an aunt who tried vainly to raise minks instead of children; and the speaker's father who "worked . . . hard to be white" (14). The use of the family photograph to inscribe these disparate selves in a version of unity serves as reminder of how such family presentations constitute a lie collectively assented to, functioning to conceal rather than reveal differences. The speaker, still a young boy in the old photo, sees through the imposture in a burst of helpless sympathy: "Who are these grown-ups? / Why are they laughing? How can I tear / the bewilderment from their eyes?" (14).

Such self-awareness joins with vituperation in "Song for Uncle Tom, Tonto, and Mr. Moto," where Mura savages the unitary mask that racial stereotyping assumes by proclaiming a declaration of war to be waged by the obsequious yes-men of popular culture. These oppressed—African American, American Indian, Hispanic, Asian American—who have been forced to "live in the monstrous sarcophagi" of a "white cultivated heart" (15), have forged an alliance of the oppressed out of their hurt and rage. Here Mura self-consciously aligns himself with the tribal impulse and comes closest to connecting with an oral tradition of song. The creature orchestrating this rage is "Kitsune, the fox," a trickster figure with a "sneaky inscrutable body" (15) who reveals not only the inadequacy of racial stereotypes but also the yearning for an authentic identity. But himself a polymorphous figure, Kitsune cannot help but represent the uncertain nature of the identity aspired to. Linked by a shared outrage over oppression, the identities behind the mask of Kitsune nevertheless are never wholly revealed. By use of Kitsune, the poem necessarily acknowledges its own partialness.

Mura offers no enduring consolation in the form of language or event, no "true word beyond / betrayal" (the poem "The One Who Tells, The One Who Burns" describes a black South African watching the brutal murder of the black man he has informed on). Indeed, the poem "Hope Without Hope" contests the value of writing at all:

"Words on the page, prayers, even shouts of rage, / What do they count against tanks, missiles, guns?" (61). Alternating lines of the poem rhyme, often conventionally ("rage"/"wage"; "guns"/"one"), as if to point up the futility of poetry against the unrhymed brutalities of existence. One's "poems are like roses," we are told, "Washed in the gutter by a dozen hoses" (61). Throughout there persists the feeling that language, no matter how powerfully expressed, changes nothing. And even though the despair is sometimes countered by "moments of release" (76) and affirmation, it is always with the sense of the temporal, with the acute knowledge that every brief burst of "clarity" contains as well the threat of its own extinction.

Only in the poem "The Natives" is an image of perfect unification offered. It is here where "time disappeared" (22), here where soldiers are absorbed into a mysterious, pacifistic "native" culture and gradually transformed into peaceful beings, "like soft-eyed virgins" (22). Gradually, the speaker of the poem says, "our names / fell from our mouths, never heard again" (21). But this note of reconciliation and transcendence recognizes at the same time its own unreality. Indeed, the markedly "unreal" conditions are what allow such a note to sound at all. Thus, the unificatory identity is negated as an actuality even as it is affirmed as an ideal.

Unlike both Chin and Mura, John Yau poses the special instance of the writer who not only eschews communalistic connections and oral traditions of poetry but affiliates with decidedly Western traditions of modern art (he doubles as an art critic). Author of *Corpse and Mirror*, along with at least six other volumes of poetry, Yau utilizes many of the elements associated with experimental writing, including discontinuous narrative, suspended logic, blurred distinctions between animate and inanimate objects, and a network of private symbols. His effort primarily is to disconnect rather than connect, to project a world cut off from certitude—a world in which human beings exist in perpetual exile, their lives an amalgam of absurdity, banality, and insufficiency, and in which politics are the ephemerae of a provisional reality. By contesting myths and other structuring devices as coherent stewards of meaning, as well as language as a reliable epistemological tool, Yau posits a world of disorder in which the unstable traces of identity threaten to dissolve as quickly as they appear.

Evidence of such instability can be found in the prose poem "Two Kinds of Story-Telling," which describes an immigrant woman for whom the China of her childhood is recalled as a fairy tale, "a kind of Eden she could never return to" (72). Yet in the second telling of her story, she focuses on "how the present is better, and how the future will be better still." Behind this second version, the narrator asserts, lies the indigenous narrative of "the passage of the *Mayflower* to the New World," even though the names *Mayflower*, *Pilgrim*, and *Plymouth Rock* are associated in the woman's mind only with a moving van and insurance ads (72). The point is that the woman's sensibility has been incidentally conditioned by things she has come into contact with in America, and in the process she has become more thoroughly imbued with an American myth than even she is aware. The line of demarcation between the exile longing for her Chinese home and the immigrant at home in America becomes hopelessly blurred by such subconscious activity, as does the identity such demarcations are intended to reveal.

Behind the problematics of identity lies Yau's skepticism regarding the organizing properties of myth and other forms of narrative. Consistently foregrounding how writer and readers together create meaning, his poems acknowledge "the human urge to make order while pointing out that the orders we create are just that: human constructs, not natural or given entities" (Hutcheon 41–42). "Missing Pages," which describes an unidentified resort island whose featured attraction is a pair of "jeweled towers" rising out of a bay—"symbols of the miraculous"—parodies one type of mythmaking (33). The creation legend surrounding these towers begins "in daylight and desire" (33), which means that "anyone can add whatever they like to the story, or take some chunk of it away" (34). The precise details are later settled upon by vote of the city council at the beginning of the tourist season, and the story is passed on to the inhabitants' children as the "basis for the entire [school] curriculum" (34).

Yau also challenges language as a reliable epistemological tool. The poem "Persons in the Presence of a Metamorphosis," whose title pays homage to Mirò, demonstrates his method. It begins thus:

> The porcelain bayonet of noon scrapes the face
> of a man who has forgotten why he started
> to spit. A uniformed girl,
>
> tiny and tireless, memorizes words
> she believes make accurate mirrors.
> A nun felt damp and gray. . . . (19)

Just as Mirò attempts simultaneously to quicken and release a flux of energies through his biomorphs, Yau disturbs and liberates the individual word from its "inert" positioning within syntax. Words mysteriously appear and reappear, behaving like linguistic particles capable of leaving and reentering this created universe at random points. The "porcelain" reappears as a "porcelain glaze of noon," which then reappears as "porcelain rooms" (19). Likewise, the "bayonet" reappears, as do the man and the girl and the mirrors. And so on. Despite the girl's belief that words "make accurate mirrors," the evidence of the poem is otherwise. In vain the poem, like the plumber, "looks for a word / with none of its pages missing" (19). If the words cannot be trusted as representations of reality, neither can their meanings be managed. So a young Catholic girl in her uniform who earnestly memorizes words (perhaps her catechism) suddenly may "spit" out a different kind of word or be transformed into a different type of person—a woman warrior polishing bayonets (19). Identity, then, is immediately contested by the very means used to construct it. Because these basic units of syntax are subject to almost instantaneous change (metamorphosis), this poem and others like it defy adequate summarizing. Their meanings change in the process of decoding.

"Shanghai Shenanigans" is a poem whose title seems to promise a negotiation between a recognizably Chinese setting and a recognizably non-Chinese set of behaviors. Instead, it is a poem whose lines depend on conjunctures as accidental as the alliterative "sh" sounds that apparently determined the poem's title. Here is how the poem begins:

> The moon emptied its cigarette over a row of clouds
> whose windowsills tremble in the breeze
>
> The breeze pushed my boat through a series
> of telephone conversations started by perfume
>
> Perfume splashed over the words of a nomad
> who believed it was better to starve than to laugh (57)

The concluding word of each stanza instigates each succeeding stanza. The connections between stanzas are purely linguistic, however, not logical. Clearly the poem could proceed indefinitely. Closure is possible, but the illusion of inevitability is forfeited. Under such conditions, the geographical bearings implied in the word "Shanghai" fail to assist in the formulation of meaning. Since the poem suggests that language is in some sense always a series of linguistic accidents, then the adequacy of language in formulating identity must always remain problematic. Yau writes at the farthest possible remove from the assumptions of the activist poets.

Nevertheless, in maintaining that identity as a construction of language and myth is always insecure, Yau does not dismiss such constructing activities as useless; on the contrary he serves as an example of the directions these activities may take. His identity formation involves the dissolving of the more apparent evidences of the "ethnic" but not a denial that such evidences, on some level, persist. The poem "Two Kinds of Language" recalls the exclusion that a Chinese American boy felt whenever his immigrant parents spoke Chinese in his presence. As an adult traveling along "the back roads through North Carolina," his radio tuned to, presumably, country music, the Chinese American senses how "all the songs seemed to tell a similar story, and yet the words and music never quite seemed to fit together" (82). In other words, for the Asian American there must always be a recognition of difference, no matter how deeply he or she penetrates into the heart of America. At the same time, what was forfeited by virtue of becoming American may be recovered on some unannounced level. Although the boy did not understand the words of his parents, he realized that "if he listened hard enough, what he thought he understood was the intonation and the voice" (82). Below the level of the conscious and beyond our ability to report, these vestiges persist.

Occasionally, Yau even acknowledges the ability to construct moments of alignment among disparate selves. In his poem "Parallel Lives," he arrives at an astonishing connection between Alexander Pope and a mythological Aztec, a figure who arrives "In the guise of a postcard / Depicting a grim-faced Aztec deity." This god is "bent beneath / A disc meant to represent the sun" (3). Yau recollects that Pope was ravaged by polio in his youth, "And the memory of it grew out of his back / Until he resembled a squat reptile" (4). By the end of the poem, Yau affirms the unexpected "parallel" between the poet and the Aztec god as messengers: "Joined together in their deformity / And the need to deliver something / To its correct destination" (4). To be sure, the parallel is presented provisionally, depending on a momentary agreement to suspend all the disqualifying factors which another moment may restore, but the impetus behind it would be easily recognizable to David Mura and ultimately to the activist poets.

Together, the writings of Marilyn Chin, David Mura, and John Yau reveal some of the depth, range, and sophistication of Asian American poetry today. From the social ferment of the 1960s arose an intense concern over the nature of Asian American identity and the instruments of a new socioeconomic policy. Such concern manifested itself valuably in challenging racial stereotypes and literary conventions alike. Attuned to the increasingly heterogeneous nature of Asian America as well as to the problematics of language, today's poets acknowledge the conditionalities that shape identity without stabilizing it and the provisionality of poetry itself. At the same time, their writings recognize a tradition to which, even in departure, they ultimately refer back.

NOTES

1. Janice Mirikitani is probably the best-known of the Asian American activist poets. For additional background, see, for example, her editing of *Time to Greez!* See also Bruce Iwasaki's introductions to the sections on literature in the anthologies Tachiki, ed., *Roots* and Gee, ed., *Counterpoint*.

2. As a corollary to the attack on the assimilationist ethic, Frank Chin, though not an activist writer per se, has long served as the most outspoken opponent of the concept of the "dual identity," i.e., "half" (white) American, "half" Asian. See, for example, *Aiiieeeee!*, p. viii and passim.

3. A fairly typical anthology of the period, Hsu's 1972 *Asian-American Authors* limited itself to Chinese American, Japanese American, and Filipino American authors. Wand's 1974 *Asian-American Heritage* added Korean Americans and an indigenous Polynesian oral poetry in translation.

WORKS CITED

Adorno, T. W. *Aesthetic Theory*. Trans. C. Lenhardt. Ed. Gretel Adorno and Rolf Tiedemann. London: Routledge, 1984.

———. *Negative Dialektik*. Frankfurt: Suhrkamp Verlag, 1966.

Bruchac, Joseph, ed. *Breaking Silence: An Anthology of Contemporary Asian American Poets*. Greenfield Center, N.Y.: Greenfield Review Press, 1983.

Chin, Frank, et al., eds. *Aiiieeeee! An Anthology of Asian-American Writers*. Washington, D.C.: Howard University Press, 1975.

Chin, Marilyn. *Dwarf Bamboo*. Greenfield Center, N.Y.: Greenfield Review Press, 1987.

Gee, Emma, ed. *Counterpoint: Perspectives on Asian America*. Los Angeles: Asian American Studies Center, University of California, 1976.

Hsu, Kai-yu, and Helen Palubinskas, eds. *Asian-American Authors*. Boston: Houghton Mifflin, 1972.

Hutcheon, Linda. *A Poetics of Postmodernism*. New York: Routledge, 1988.

Jameson, Fredric. *Marxism and Form: Twentieth-Century Dialectical Theories of Literature*. Princeton, N.J.: Princeton University Press, 1971.

Leong, Russell. "Poetry within Earshot." *Amerasia Journal* 15.1 (1989): 165–193.

Mirikitani, Janice, ed. *Time to Greez!: Incantations from the Third World*. San Francisco: Glide Publications, 1975.

———, ed. *Ayumi*. San Francisco: The Japanese American Anthology Committee, 1980.

Mura, David. *After We Lost Our Way*. New York: Dutton, 1989.

Tachiki, Amy, et al. *Roots: An Asian American Reader*. Los Angeles: Continental Graphics, 1971.

Wand, David Hsin-Fu, ed. *Asian-American Heritage: An Anthology of Prose and Poetry*. New York: Washinton Square Press, 1974.

Yau, John. *Corpse and Mirror*. New York: Holt, Rinehart and Winston, 1983.

3

Filipinos in the United States and Their Literature of Exile

Oscar V. Campomanes

IS THERE a "Filipino American" literature? Current and inclusive notions of Asian American literature assume the existence of this substratum without really delineating its contours. There is no sustained discussion of how "Filipino American" literature, if shaped as such a substructure, problematizes some of the claims of Asian American literature as a constitutive paradigm. Although developed unevenly as a category and distinctive body of writing,[1] "Asian American" literature now commands a significant presence in the American academy and the movement to revise the national literary canon. The imperative, then, is to test the descriptive and explanatory powers of this general paradigm in light of its as yet undetermined but nominally acknowledged tributary formation of "Filipino American" writing. To leave this area unmapped is to create exclusion, internal hierarchy, and misrepresentation in the supposedly heterogeneous field of Asian American cultural production.[2]

The informal but long-standing directive to align "Filipino American" literature with the Chinese and Japanese American mainstream of Asian American literature has had its own consequences. When asked to construct "a literary background of Filipino-American works" for a founding Asian American anthology, the writers Oscar Penaranda, Serafin Syquia, and Sam Tagatac declared: "We cannot write any literary background because there isn't any. No history. No published literature. No nothing" (49). Their statement proved not only to be quite precipitate but also uncritical of the limiting assumptions foisted on their project by the anthologists.[3] Already implicit in this view was their disconnection from the exilic literature created by N.V.M. Gonzalez and Bienvenido Santos or, in more recent times, by Ninotchka Rosca and Linda Ty-Casper. Perhaps, rather than the veracity of its claim, what remains compelling is how this declaration expresses the incommensurable sense of nonbeing that stalks many Filipinos in the United States and many Americans of Filipino descent.

WITHOUT NAMES: WHO ARE WE?

Indeed, one cannot discuss the (non)existence of "Filipino American" literature without interrogating the more decisive issues of self and peoplehood, of invisibility. This combined problematic certainly shapes the available expressions. For example, the Bay Area Filipino American Writers titled their first collection of poetry after Jeff Tagami's historically textured piece, "Without Names" (in Ancheta et al.). "Who are we? / What are we?" (230) asks public historian Fred Cordova in his picture book and oral history on Filipino Americans. In a 1989 essay, the journalist Cielo Fuentebella pointedly observes that even with the group nearing the one-million mark, "our numbers don't add up to visibility in business, media and the cultural field. And all these at a time in history that is being dubbed as the Asian/Pacific Century" (17).

From these various expressions, one detects some hesitance to claim the name "Filipino American" unproblematically. The term "Filipino American" itself seems inadequate, if oxymoronic. "The Filipino American cannot be defined without elucidating what the problematic relationship is between the two terms which dictates the conditions of possibility for each—the addition of the hyphen which spells a relation of subordination and domination" (San Juan, "Boundaries" 125). There is some recognition, in other words, of the irreducible specificity of the Filipino predicament in the United States and, corollarily, of the literary and cultural expressions that it has generated. Although one finds many self-identified Filipino Americans and Filipino American works (the preferred term is "Pilipino American"), their relationship to this provisional term seems to be ambivalent and indeterminate, shored up only by its roots in 1960s ethnic identity politics.[4] Hence, I choose the formulation "Filipinos in the United States" for this discussion while also tactically deploying the conditional but meaningful category "Filipino American."

The task of my essay is to characterize the available writings by Filipinos in the United States and Filipino Americans in light of community formation and Philippine-American (neo)colonial relations. I seek to describe a literary tradition of Filipino exilic writing and an exilic sensibility that informs both the identity politics and the cultural production of this "community-in-the-making" (San Juan, "Filipano Artist" 36).

As does any preliminary account, this essay has several limitations. Because of the urgency of the task and space considerations, the survey of some of the available writings is only suggestive, if incomplete, and the arguments of propositions (along with the bases) for constituting them as a tradition are abbreviated. That the writings and the history of the group codify their own theoretical claims is a question to which I pay the most attention, for "each literary tradition, at least implicitly, contains within it an argument for how it can be read" (Gates xix–xx). I concentrate on the older writers whose works have reached a certain consolidation and then suggest some beginning orientations with which to steer future readings of the work of the younger writers who are in several stages of emergence.

Motifs of departure, nostalgia, incompletion, rootlessness, leave taking, and dispossession recur with force in most writing produced by Filipinos in the United States and by Filipino Americans, with the Philippines as either the original or terminal reference point. Rather than the United States as the locus of claims or "the promised land" that Werner Sollors argues is the typological trope of "ethnic" American writing (40–50), the Filipino case represents a reverse telos, an opposite movement. It is on this basis that I argue for a literature of exile and emergence rather than a literature of immigration and settlement whereby life in the United States serves as the space for displacement, suspension, and perspective. Exile becomes a necessary, if inescapable, state for Filipinos in the United States—at once susceptible to the vagaries of the (neo)colonial U.S.-Philippine relationship and redeemable only by its radical restructuring.

The intergenerational experience will certainly dim this literary/historical connection to the Philippines for many Filipino Americans. But the signifiers "Filipino" and "Philippines" evoke colonialist meanings and cultural redactions which possess inordinate power to shape the fates of the writers and of Filipino peoples everywhere. These considerations overdetermine their dominant sense of nonbelonging in the United States, the Philippines, and other places. The word "overdetermine" adequately describes the complex of historical inscriptions, developments, processes, interventions, and accidents in which their present predicament is embedded.

For Filipinos in the United States and their history of community formation, it is not enough to examine immigration policies (symptomatic of a U.S.-centric approach to which most sociologists/historians are prone) that by themselves fail to account for the diversity of immigration patterns. "The historical, economic, and political relationships between the United States and the country of origin, as well as the social and economic conditions in the source country, have to be examined to explain the major differences in immigration streams" (Carino and Fawcett 305). Robert Blauner's point that the status of any Asian American group should roughly equal the status of its country of origin in relation to the United States bears remembering (Takaki, *Race and Ethnicity* 159). Conceptually useful for the Philippine case, both of these views also expand American immigration, ethnic, and cultural studies beyond their parochial purviews of American nation building, acculturation, and settlement.[5]

INVISIBILITY AND (NON)IDENTITY: THE ROOTS IN HISTORY

Among the various Asian countries of origin, the Philippines holds the sole distinction of being drawn into a truly colonial and neocolonial relation with the United States, and for this reason it has been absorbed almost totally into the vacuum of American innocence. It was the founding moment of colonialism, "a primal loss suffered through the Filipino-American War (1899–1902) and the resistance ordeal of the revolutionary forces of the First Philippine Republic up to 1911 that opened the way for the large-scale transport of cheap Filipino labor to Hawaii and California [and inaugurated] this long, tortuous exodus from the periphery to the metropolis" (San Juan, "Boundaries" 117). Hence, while rooted in the earlier period of Spanish rule, the spectre of "invisibility" for Filipinos is specific to the immediate and long-term consequences of American colonialism.

The invisibility of the Philippines became a necessary historiographical phenomenon because the annexation of the Philippines proved to be constitutionally and culturally problematic for American political and civil society around the turn of the century and thereafter. (A consequent case in the point was the anomalous status of migrant workers and students for much of the formal colonial period when they were considered American "nationals" but without the basic rights of "citizens.") To understand the absence of the Philippines in American history, one faces the immense task of charting the intense ideological contestation that developed in the United States around the Philippine question at the point of colonial conquest, and the active rewriting of American historical records from then on that articulated and rearticulated the verities of "American exceptionalism."[6] As Amy Kaplan suggestively notes, "The invisibility of the Philippines in American history has everything to do with the invisibility of American imperialism to itself."[7]

Discursively, the unbroken continuity of this historic amnesia concerning the Philippines has had real invidious effects. Note the repetitious and unreflective use of the modifier "forgotten" to describe, even renew, this curse of invisibility which may be said to have been bestowed on the Philippines as soon as the bloody war of conquest and resistance began to require stringent official/military censorship in the United States around 1900. No one has bothered to ask some of the more unsettling questions: Who is doing the forgetting? What is being forgotten? How much has been forgotten? Why the need to continue forgetting?

Contemporary examples abound. An essay by the American historian Peter Stanley bears the title "The Forgotten Philippines, 1790–1946" and sticks out in a retrospective survey of American–East Asian studies, a field which has always revolved around China and Japan (May and Thomson 291–316). Quoted in Russell Roth's journalistic account of the long and costly Filipino-American War, one writer admits that "our movement into the Philippines is one of the least understood phases of our history, one of those obscure episodes swept under the rug, and forgotten" (1981). In a truthful exemplification of the workings of hegemony, a chapter of Takaki's

Strangers from a Different Shore is devoted to "The Forgotten Filipinos" (314–54), and one Filipino American documentary work itself, *Filipinos: Forgotten Asian Americans*, finds the term as unproblematic and adequate (Cordova 1983).

GENEALOGIES OF EXILE AND THE IMAGINED COMMUNITY

So it is that "in the Philippine experience, History has provided its own despotism" (Gonzalez, *Kalutang* 32). It is in the various forms and manifestations of this despotism that one can locate the productive conditions of possibility for Filipino writing and the making of Filipino identities. For something as specific as Filipino writing in the United States, the banishment of the Philippines and Filipinos from history, the global disperal of Filipinos, the migrant realities of Pinoy workers and urban expatriates, and "the alienation of the English-speaking intellectuals from workers and peasants speaking the vernacular" (San Juan, *Ruptures* 25) must constitute the set of tangled contexts. They amount to a common orientation of the experiences, writings, and identity politics toward a "national mythos," following the creation of a "Filipino diaspora . . . the scattering of a people, not yet a fully matured nation, to the ends of the earth, across the planet" by the colonial moment (Brennan, "Cosmopolitans" 4; San Juan, "Homeland" 40).

Through a coordination of the expressive tendencies and impulses of Filipino and Filipino American writers in the United States, a "literature of exile and emergence" can be constructed from the normally separated realms of the old and new countries. I see the obsessive search for identity that marks Philippine literature in the colonial language (and in the vernacular, which is not possible to cover here), and the identity politics articulated by first- and second-generation Filipino American writers (after the social and ethnic movements of the 1960s and 1970s) as specific streams with certain points of confluence.

In recognizing the intimate connection between Filipino nation building and the problematics of Filipino American community formation and, hence, the radical contingency of both processes, the seeming scarcity of "published literature" (sometimes attributed to the smallness of the Filipino American second generation) ceases to be a problem. That "we still don't have anyone resembling Maxine Hong Kingston for the Filipino immigrant community here"[8] begins to make sense and points us to the many writers who write about the situation in the Philippines and the Filipino American writers who may be U.S. grounded yet articulate this same ancestral focus. The orientation toward the Philippines prevents prevailing notions of Asian American literature from reducing Filipino writing in the United States to just another variant of the immigrant epic, even if this in itself must be seen as an ever-present and partial possibility as time passes and Philippine-American relations change.

In what follows, I examine some expressions of exile and gestures toward return—either explicit or latent—that typify the available writings. How do they characteristically respond to, or even embody, the experience of exile and indeterminacy and the question of redemptive return? Put another way, what are the intersections between historical experience and literary history, between subjection and subject positions? I organize my review around several interrelated issues: exilic experience and perspective, exilic identity and language, and exilic sensibility and attitude toward history and place, all of which account for the forms of indeterminacy and visionary resolutions in the writings.

The writers may be clustered into three "cohorts" that need not necessarily coincide with the migration and immigration patterns or cycles documented by historians and sociologists (see, for example, Carino and Fawcett 305–25; and Pido). There is the pioneering generation consisting of Bienvenido Santos, N.V.M. Gonzalez, José García Villa, and Carlos Bulosan for the period of the 1930s to the 1950s; a settled generation that matures and emerges by the 1960s who, after Penaranda, Tagatac, and Syquia, may be called the "Flips";[9] and the politically expatriated generation of Epifanio San Juan, Linda Ty-Casper, Ninotchka Rosca, and Michelle Skinner from the 1970s to the present. These writers whom I have specifically mentioned must be taken as demarcating, rather than definitive, figures for each group.

This periodization has obvious limits. Bulosan died in 1956 and Villa ceased to write nearly three decades ago, while Santos and Gonzalez continue to be prolific and have exhibited significant shifts in their perspectives and writings after extended residence in the United States as professors. Bulosan, with the intervention of U.S. cultural workers, has earned some critical attention and student readership in ethnic studies courses, yet to be matched in the cases of Santos and Gonzalez, whose exilic writing did not fit with the immigrant ethos. Villa has languished in self-selected obscurity even as Sollors recently and curiously recuperated him as an "ethnic modernist" (253–54).[10] My concern here is much more in comparison than in contemporaneity, since these writers' works are uneven in quality, their developments divergent in pattern, and their influence diffuse in reception. By "comparison" I mean their styles of coping with the experiential reality of exile—given their initial and subsequent ties with, or alienation from, each other—and their relevant self-definition and development of certain forms of writing on this basis.

I also make the Flips assume a kind of corporate existence, although this is suggested itself by their self-designation as "Bay Area Pilipino American Writers" and their networks that are rooted in the ethnic movements of the late 1960s and 1970s. Of these writers (mostly poets), I find a few who exhibit tendencies to outgrow the agonized temporizings associated with that historic juncture, namely Jeff Tagami, Virginia Cerrenio, and Jaime Jacinto. What concerns me here is their search for kinship with their predecessors in the pioneering generation and their symbolic appropriations of Philippine history and identities from the perspective of a second, or consciously American, generation (hence, "Pilipino American").

Not all those who may belong to the "politically expatriated" were literally so, by the yardstick of martial law politics and the sensibility of nationalism that grew out of the social and political turmoil of the late 1960s and the subsequent period of authoritarian rule in the homeland. It is the peculiar elaboration of the theme of exile from a more troubling historical moment and its consequent suspension of Filipinos within a more ideologically and politically bounded sphere that distinguish the actions and predicament of this group. San Juan shifted to Philippine and Third World literary and historical studies from traditional literary scholarship and creative writing in the conjuncture between his initial residence in the United States as an academic, and the politicizing movements in the United States and the Philippines in the early 1970s. Skinner came to the United States with the sensibility of her martial law generation back home but did not exactly flee from political persecution as Rosca did. And yet again, their relationships of affinity and alienation as a group, and with the other two, may be divined in what they have written and how they have defined themselves.

My groupings are not chronological but synchronic, concerned with what Benedict Anderson has called "the deep horizontal comradeship" that enables profoundly dispersed populations to imagine peoplehood and community, to overcome historically disabling differences, and to occupy new spaces of historical, literary, and cultural possibility (15–16). Writers can find a home in the relevant pattern or cohort of affinity specific to their own origins in any of these three historical moments of colonial generation, ethnic identity politics, and political expatriation. The groupings need not be rigid, since certain movements between them are possible, within defensible bounds, and depending to some extent on the stronger sentiment of the writer or reader.

EXILE AND RETURN: LITERARY AND EXPERIENTIAL PARALLELS

In looking at the plurality of Filipino experiences, positions, and writings in the United States as a generalized condition of exile, I refer to the ensemble of its many relations, degrees, and forms, and not to its easy reduction to a single thematic. One cannot succumb to the homogenizing assertion that "immigration is the opposite of expatriation" (Mukherjee 28) or the tendency to construe the West as only a base for "cosmopolitan exiles" and not a place "where unknown men and women have spent years of miserable loneliness" (Said 359). The need is to "map territories of experience beyond those mapped by the literature of exile itself" (Said 358) and, if I might add, the areas of exile and writing overlap.

Sam Solberg notes that "if there is one indisputable fact about Filipino-American writing nurtured on American shores that sets it apart from other Asian American writings, it is that it is inextricably linked with indigenous Filipino writing in English" (50). He adds that Carlos Bulosan, José García Villa, Bienvenido Santos, and N.V.M. Gonzalez did not find the distinction between writing in the Philippines and the United States meaningful. Yet, also, their common experiences of migration to the United States and the vicissitudes of their careers in this setting consigned them to the same state of indeterminacy and limbo of invisibility as their less noted kinfolk.

Bharati Mukherjee posits that "exiles come wrapped in a cloak of mystery and world-weariness [and in] refusing to play the game of immigration, they certify to the world, and especially to their hosts, the purity of their pain and their moral superiority to the world around them" (28). Aside from making exile sound like a choice, this view fails to consider that there is nothing to romanticize about this condition even if it might sometimes generate romantic visions of one's origins. "Exile is a grim fate and its recourses equally grim" (Seidel x). Although exile gives birth to varieties of nationalist sentiment, even imagined communities and unlikely kinships among peoples with enduring differences, "these are no more than efforts to overcome the crippling sorrow of estrangement . . . the loss of something left behind forever" (Said 357).

Just as it has been for similarly situated peoples, the exilic experience for Filipinos and Filipino Americans has engendered such "enormously constructive pressures" (Gurr 9) as self-recovery and the critical distance from a putative homeland whose outlines are sharpened from the perspective of their new or "other" home in the metropolis. More, for Filipinos as "colonial exiles," the "search for identity and the construction of a vision of home amount to the same thing" (Gurr 11). In turn, this "identity" (now in the sense of specular experiences and visions), condenses itself in the institution of creative genealogies, mythic reinterpretations of colonial history, and reevaluations of the linguistic and cultural losses caused by colonialism. These may be seen as notations of redemptive return to a "home" in the imagination, with specific inflections for Filipinos and Filipino Americans.

When Bienvenido Santo declares that "in a special sense I, too, am an oldtimer" ("Pilipino Old Timers" 89) and a Flip poet like Jeff Tagami (1987) memorializes these migrant workers (also called Pinoys" or Manongs") in his work, there is already this particular reciprocity of self-representations among unlikely "allies." Distances are being bridged here among generational locations, social classes, and particular experiences, from the pioneering experiences and enduring ties to the native territory of such workers in the Pacific Coast states as the privileged point of origin. Documentary works have described the exilic conditions of these Pinoys in paradigmatic terms because of the complexity of their displacements: "Between themselves and their homeland, between themselves and their children who have known only America, and between themselves and recent arrivals whose Philippines is in some ways, drastically different from their own" (Santos, *Apples* xiv).

Santo's claim of affinity with the "survivors of those who immigrated in the 1920s or even earlier, through the 1940s" ("Pilipino Old Timers" 89) may seem ill-considered because of the large wedge in class, migratory pattern, and education between this former "pensionado" or colonial government scholar and resident writer of a Kansas university and the faceless, nameless "Manongs." Carlos Bulosan—valorized as the supreme chronicler of the Pinoy story and claimed as an immigrant writer even while moved to state once that "I think I am forever an exile" (*Falling Light* 198)—particularly lamented this great divide. Regarding the pensionados of his time (and the ruling/middling classes they helped form in the Philippines) with suspicion and contempt, Bulosan foregrounded his shared peasant origins with the oldtimers in his identity as a writer. Among many expressions of affiliation with them are his controversial letter to a friend concerning his critique of Filipino writers in English and their "contrary feelings" for him (*Falling Light* 228) and his narrator Allos's discovery of the estranging and demarcating stance of this social class in regard to the Philippine peasantry in *America Is in the Heart* (1946), in the humiliating encounter between the narrator's mother and a middle-class girl (37–38).

This great wedge partly originated in the institution of education as a form of social hierarchy in the Philippines during the colonial period (the pensionados were sent to the United States to train in government and cultural administration) and threatened Bulosan's own close kinship with the migrant workers as his writing career took off in the 1930s and 1940s. He obviated this successfully with a symbolic return to their ranks and their lives in his writing and by articulating a Pinoy critique of upper/middle-class conceit: "There is no need for Filipino writers to feel that . . . they are educated because they went to colleges, nor should they think that I am ignorant because I lack formal education" (*Falling Light* 228). If Bulosan's "return" to the oldtimers is warranted by an original class affinity, this makes Santos's gesture from the other side toward this group striking.

The sense of indeterminacy conveyed by Santos in his many stories and essays, and in interviews, resonates with the Pinoy's suspension in eternal time and alien place, "deracinated and tortured by the long wait to go home" (Gurr 18). Like Bulosan, he has codified this linkage in his work, as in the symbolic kinship between the Michigan farmworker Celestino Fabia and "the first class Filipino" in the moving story "A Scent of Apples" (*Apples* 21–29). Especially revealing is Santos's juxtaposition in an essay of his fictional transfiguration of the oldtimers's characters and lives with their documentation in oral and social history to illustrate his point—when asked "to explain the difference between the old timer as character in fiction and in real life"—"that there is nothing to explain because there is no difference" ("Pilipino Old Timers" 91).

These heroes with all their little triumphs and tragic losses as exiles but "survivors" populate Santos's tightly crafted stories, endowing his identity as a writer and his writing with a pointed specificity. One detects the origin of Santos's notion of the struggling exilic writer as a "straggler"—doomed into irrelevance and hermitage for writing in English—in the condition of the migrant worker as a "survivor [who] lives through years of hiding [and waits] until a miracle of change happens in the homeland and in this, our other home" ("Personal Saga" 404, 399, 405). That the construction of kinship and identity among Filipinos is fraught with difficulty and paradox is also in the foreground of much of the writing, but especially as emblematized in Santos's "The Day the Dancers Came." While Santos finds common cause with his Pinoy subjects, he also confronts the tensions of this affiliation on the level of symbolism.

Like "Scent of Apples," this story concerns the re-encounter of the Pinoy with the other-self, a representative of one's time-bound vision of home, in visitors from the islands. "Identity," as in similitude, in mutual recognition as Filipinos, is sought by the oldtimer Fil in the young members of a dance troupe from the Philippines who stop by Chicago for a visiting performance. But just as the middle-class girl reduces Allos's mother to humiliation in Bulosan's *America Is in the Heart*, the visiting dancers reduce Fil to an "ugly Filipino" (Santos, *Apples* 116), subtly spurning his attempts to communicate with them and his offer to entertain them in his humble abode (an eventuality foreseen by his fellow oldtimer and roommate Tony, who is dying of cancer). There is none of the natural affinity that develops between Fabia and the visiting lecturer in "Scent of Apples," only the edge of class hierarchy and generational or experiential difference. While making his overtures to the dancers in the Chicago hotel lobby where they milled after the performance, "All the things he had been trying to hide now showed: the age in his face, his horny hands. . . . Fil wanted to leave, but he seemed caught up in the tangle of moving bodies that merged and broke in a fluid strangle hold. Everybody was talking, mostly in English" (120).

The frequent impossibility of "identity" (as similitude) between Filipinos expatriated by colonialism, placed in different social/historical rungs, and separated by transoceanic timelines, is figured by this story in specular instances. Focused on the predicament of Fil, these compounded mirrorings of the other-self reflect the many dimensions of Filipino exilic identity and perspective. A memory that Fil associates with one of his many jobs—as "a menial in a hospital [where] he took charge . . . of bottles on a shelf, each shelf, each bottle containing a stage of the human embryo in preservatives, from the lizard-like fetus of a few days, through the newly-born infant, with its position unchanged, cold, and cowering and afraid"—is of "nightmares through the years of himself inside a bottle" (114). This reflection of himself in these aborted, disowned, and arrested lives, mediated by the figure of the "bottle" that both exhibits and encloses them, is a powerful statement on the utter disconnection of the old-timer from the flow of time and from a Philippines whose birthing as a nation itself has been aborted by American colonialism. (Perhaps it is significant that his name is "Fil," almost "Filipino," but attenuated into an American nickname).

The relationship between Fil and Tony also takes this form of allegorical doubling. When Fil castigates Tony in one of their playful spats: "You don't care for nothing but your pain, your imaginary pain," Tony retorts: "You're the imagining fellow. I got the real thing." Tony's skin not only "whitens" from the terminal ailment that is inexplicably but slowly consuming him, but he also feels "a pain in his insides, like dull scissors scraping his intestines" (115). Yet, if Tony's pain is indeed excruciatingly physical, it only seems to be the correlative for Fil's pain which, in a sense, is more real. For after being denied his last few memories of home by the dancers's disavowal, the pain that guts him is similar but more keen: "Was it his looks that kept them away? The thought was a sharpness inside him" (121); and then again, in recounting their rebuff to Tony, "The memory, distinctly recalled, was a rock on his breast. He gasped for breath." (124)

The identity between Fil and Tony (they are both oldtimers wrapped in pain and warped in time) stands for the singular problem of constructing Filipino American identity in light of colonialism. The doubling of colonizer and colonized, its conflictedness, is signified in Fil's specular but contrastive relationship with Tony, even as this is also kinship forged by their history of shared banishment. Tony stands for one's translation into a colonial: "All over Tony's body, a gradual peeling was taking place. . . . His face looked as if it was healing from severe burns. . . . 'I'm becoming a white man,' Tony had said once" (114). Note also that Tony is figured as looking young. "Gosh, I wish I had your looks, even with those white spots," Fil says to him (116)—Fil, who feels and looks old and ugly in the company of the *young* dancers. Where Tony "was the better speaker of the two in English," Fil displayed "greater mastery" in the dialect (117), although Fil's prepared speeches for inviting the dancers "stumbled and broke on his lips into a jumble of incoherence" in their presence (120). If Tony is his other-self, a desired ideal of being, then even turning to him for identity is unsuccessful as the reader knows that Tony will die to signify Fil's own rebirth.

As the dancers board their bus for the next destination and Fil imagines or sees them waving their hands and smiling toward him, Fil raises his hand to wave back. But wary of misrecognition one more time, he turns to check behind him but finds "no one there except his own reflection in the glass door, a double exposure of himself and a giant plant with its thorny branches around him like arms in a loving embrace" (122). Here, the reader is being alerted to the strength of an identity that is reflected in and by the constituted self, the spectral but appropriate figure being a "a giant plant with its thorny branches."

In vowing to commit the performance and memory of the dancers to a tape recording in what he calls "my magic sound mirror" (he loses the "record" by accidentally pushing the eraser near the end, symbolizing the fragility of his "memories" of home), Fil wonders if the magic sound mirror could also keep "a record of silence because it was to him the richest sound?" (117) This implicit recognition of himself as the supreme record, the actual referent of his identity, is brought to the fore at the conclusion of the story when he exclaims: "Tony! Tony! . . . I've lost them all." The last glimpse the reader has is of Fil "biting his lips . . . turn[ing] towards the window, startled by the first light of dawn. He hadn't realized till then that the long night was over" (128). Looking through the bottle at "frozen time" early in the story, Fil looks through a window at "time unfolding" by the end. Fil is somehow restored to history, to the sufficiency of his silence and resilience.

The interposition of "English" in the story (Tony speaks better English, he is turning into a "white" man; the dancers talk mostly in English, they are all beautiful) as the radical mode of difference for and among "Fils" (Filipinos) implies the organizing relation between exilic identity and language. Recall the symptomatic link or parallelism in Solberg's argument between the exile experienced by Filipino writers of English in the Philippines and that expressed by the "writing nurtured on American shores"—or between literary and experiential exile, generally. But this historically interesting nexus, this "inextricable link," is usually disarticulated in universalizing formulations like "the human condition" or the "alienation of the soul" (Gonzalez, *Kalutang* 64–65). Language has a historical specificity in relation to the development of "indigenous writing," "writing nurtured on American shores," and the migratory movements of writers and laborers to/in the United States that these careless oversimplifications flatten out. The result has been to compound these literatures and experiences imperceptibly or to explain them away in terms of the inescapable alienations that afflict the dislocated, as if there were nothing more to say about their historic concurrence or recurrence.

As Santos's work suggests, writing in English, the colonizer's language, and migrating to the United States, the colonizing country, are analogous and fundamentally imbricated processes, or are parallel while related forms of cultural translation and historical exile. Carlos Bulosan's consummate piece "The Story of a Letter" starkly embodies such relationships in aesthetic form and supplies another paradigm for beholding these various writings and experiences together. In this allegory of the epic of migration and expatriation, the narrator is a peasant son who finds himself heading for the United States with the migratory waves of workers in the late colonial period, partly as a consequence of a letter to his father written in English—a language alien in history and social class to his father and his people—by the narrator's brother Berto who had migrated earlier. Simply, the letter remains unread until the narrator himself has gone through the linguistic, cultural, and historical translation necessary for him to decode the letter for his father and himself. The letter reads: "Dear father . . . America is a great country. Tall buildings. Wide good land. The people walking. But I feel sad. I am writing to you this hour of my sentimental. Your son.—Berto" (*Bulosan Reader* 44). It is an attempt by an exiled son to bridge the distance between him and his origins in truncated language that aptly mirrors Berto's and his family's truncated lives.

The narrator's voyage is propelled by various developments (climaxed by the loss of the family's small landholding), and prefigured by the father's plea to the narrator "to learn English so that [he] would be able to read [the letter] to him" (41). After landing in the United States and being whirled into the vortex of displacement, labor exploitation, and fragmentation of Pinoy life, he accrues the experience needed to make sense of the letter and develops some mastery of the language that it speaks. In this process of personal translation (experientially and symbolically), he sustains a series of losses, for one always risks losing the original matter substantially in the historic passage from one experiential/cultural realm to another. The father dies before the narrator reaches the point of linguistic and historical competence and therefore before he can read his son's translation; the narrator himself experiences the deep-seated removal from origin and the past that acquiring such a competence entails; and he is only able to glimpse (not to reunite with) Berto in the United States.

With the letter returned to him after a series of disconnected deliveries, the narrator muses: "It was now ten years since my brother had written the letter to Father. It was eighteen years since he had run away from home. . . . I bent down and read the letter—the letter that had driven me away from the village and had sent me half way around the world. . . . I held the letter in my hand and, suddenly, I started to laugh—choking with tears at the mystery and wonder of it all" (44). Being able to decode the simple message of the letter (couched in his brother's fractured English) endows him with an expansive consciousness, agency, renewed memory, and the sign of redemptive return to his moorings.

The story of the letter then can be read allegorically, whereby one's search for self or identity is enabled and simultaneously codified in the trans-Pacific voyage to the United States, condensed here primarily in the demarcating and analogic role ascribed to "English." But particular stress must be placed on the symbolic weight of language in the story and in cultural history itself. By viewing English as a material and symbolic mode of alienation and transformation, one can account for the inextricable link as well as the great wedge among various classes, generations, and experiences of Filipino peoples. In surveying the thematic landscape of contemporary writing, David Quemada concludes that the recurrent themes of rootlessness indicate "a spiritual dislocation which is nurtured by the act of writing in a foreign language" (428). "Spiritual" here suggests that one's translation and transformation *through* the colonial language is fundamental and all-encompassing.

Albert Memmi refers to this phenomenon as "colonial bilingualism," describing it also as a "linguistic drama" because it is the struggle between the colonizer's and colonized's cultures in and through the linguistic sphere (108). The "possession of two languages" means immersion in "two psychical and cultural realms" that, because "symbolized and conveyed in the two tongues" of the colonizer and colonized, generates an irremediably conflicted and complicated condition for the colonial subject. Memmi qualifies that most of the colonized are spared this condition since their native tongue is not given the same level of circulation and status in the colony itself (108). This can be extended to mean that not every Filipino can be allowed through the gates of immigration or his/her impossible dream of statehood for the Philippines. Yet, English becomes a mechanism of social hierarchy and thinking that ensnares the colonial/neocolonial natives or immigrants/citizens into the same circuit of exilic suspension while also segmenting them from each other in class or experiential terms.

In his many creative and scholarly works, N.V.M. Gonzalez has dwelt extensively on the linguistic alienation of Filipino English writers from their people and what he calls its "national and historical dimension" ("Drumming" 423). He specifies the period "when English was adopted as a national language" in the Philippines as the inaugural moment for the complicated American reconstruction of the Filipino, recalling Frantz Fanon's metaphor of consequent "changes in the flesh, even in the composition of the body fluids" of the colonized (*Kalutang* 32, 34). Quoting the writer Wilfrido Nolledo, Gonzalez avers that with the "receiving" (the term he uses to reckon with the American imposition) of English, the Filipino writer was converted into a "domestic exile, an expatriate who has not left his homeland" ("Drumming" 418–19).[11] Yet this also locates the writer at a particular remove from his subject since, as Raymond Williams argues, "To be a writer in English is already to be socially specified" (193).

For Gonzalez, writing in English about the *kaingineros*, the peasant folk of Mindoro and the other islands of his imagination, "separated each actuality from me at every moment of composition. . . . Rendered in an alien tongue, that life attained the distinction of a translation even before it had been made into a representation of reality through form. . . . The English language thus had the effect of continually presenting that life as non-actual, even as it had affirmed the insecurity of its making" (*Kalutang* 40–41). Like Santos, however, Gonzalez shortcircuits these multiple determinations of linguistic/cultural exile and seeks identity with and in the "poor folk going from clearing to clearing, island to island, working in the saltwater sweat of their brows for whatever the earth will yield" (Guzman 111). Consequently, his writing has been critiqued for creating a literary brand of nativism and ethnography about a "bygone rural Philippines . . . no longer mapped by American anthropologists . . . but by insurgents (San Juan, *Ruptures* 31). But like Santos, Gonzalez has also reflected upon the contradictions of his identity claims and codified several important categories of the exilic sensibility.

From *Seven Hills Away* (1947) to his most recent writings, Gonzalez has lyrically valorized the people of the "backwoods, barrio, and town," graphing their lifeways and folk culture in styles, rhythms, and forms of storytelling that express a pointed fidelity to this point of origin. Like Santos in his oldtimers, Gonzalez mirrors his exilic condition in the patterns of migration, dispersal, and selfhood of these people who populate the past that he re-members: "Although they might become city folk, I seem to see them at their best against the background to which they eventually return" (*Kalutang* 66). In a parallel vein, Gonzalez re-turns to this life and place by the power of a language that renders his gesture always already imaginative. A very early piece, "Far Horizons" (Mindoro 23–26), harbors the beginnings of Gonzalez's model and vision of exile. As in his other stories that feature the sea, voyaging/sailing, and the island-hopping lifestyle of his past as metaphors for exilic distances, departures, and arrivals, this piece involves characters who find themselves ineluctably separated from their habitat by seafaring as a way of life.

Juancho, the surviving crew member of a sailboat sunk off Marinduque island recalls that among the casualties is Gorio, a sailor from a remote barrio in Mindoro. Juancho surmises that the news of Gorio's death will not have reached his village at all, and this worries him until he meets a fellow sailor, Bastian, who turns out to be Gorio's brother. Bastian finds himself making an unintended homecoming after so long, but as a bearer of sorrowful news for his mother and kinfolk. When the sailboat (suggestively called *Pag-asa* or "hope") bound for southern Mindoro comes to lie at anchor off the coast leading to his village, Bastian convinces Ka Martin, the *piloto*, to let him ashore for one night to make this important visit.

What sets off this story is a classic scene in exilic writing: the actual and transient return and the first glimpse of home after an absence of many years. When Bastian sees the first familiar landmarks of home, "A strange feeling swept over him. There came some kind of itching in the soles of his feet and his heart began to throb wildly as though trying to get out of his mouth. . . . Then it occurred to him that it was some seven or eight years since he had left home" (*Mindoro* 24).[12] Yet mindful of the tragic news that he brings with him and the grief it may cause his mother, Bastian reflects: "Perhaps it would be better to tell her nothing at all. Should she learn of his brother's death, it might prove difficult for him to go to sea again. And how he loved the sea although it might claim him too" (24). Bastian loses his nerve and, at the call of Ka Martin's horn, stealthily heads out to sea. He entrusts the news of his brother's death to the boatman who ferries the villagers across the river and trusts him to spread it after he, Bastian, is gone. The mother, Aling Betud, receives the news of the death of one son and the sudden departure of another with a curious response. It occurs to her that "it must have been Bastian himself who had died and what had come was his ghost" (26).

In this act of substitution, Aling Betud nurses her "hope" for her other son's apparition and return, and she irritatedly responds to the villagers's disbelief: "We shall know all, we shall know all. For my other son Gorio will come—and we shall ask him, and he will tell us" (26). In this instance of "identity" (as similitude), the dream of return as formed from the site of departure reflects back the idea of exile's loss and gain—signified here in the dialectic between sorrow and hope, when the mother represents to herself the incalculable transience yet worth of her sons' "imagined" and imaginable returns.

Indeed, "the sea might claim him too," and it is the idea of homecoming as ever deferred for the pleasure and curse of voyaging (miming the ever-deferred nature of representation of loss and gain in language) that Gonzalez suggests here. Still, for Gonzalez, it is place as the locus of rootedness, the islands from which sailboats and sailors flee and to which they return, and the clearings between which peasant folk shuttle, that supply the coordinates and the orientations for these movements.

In many stories, including "Children of the Ash-Covered Loam," "Seven Hills Away," and "Hunger in Barok" (*Mindoro* 49–61, 32–42, 27–31), Gonzalez also foregrounds the tensions of Philippine social relationships, the difficulties of mutuality and kinship. He maps this historical geography by paraphrasing John Kenneth Galbraith's description of India as not a country but a continent: "Understanding the Philippines begins in the realization that it is one nation made up of three countries. . . . Manila is the capital of the first country of the City. The second country—the Barrio—has a capital known by many names: Aplaya, Bondok, Wawa, whatever. . . . the third country—the Mountain—by its very nature needs no capital or center, although it shares with the Barrio a calculated distance from the city" (*Kalutang* 29). Whether concerned with the calibrated frictions between the citified and the folk or the benign feudal paternalism of landlords over their tenants and its illusion of reciprocity, Gonzalez recognizes the problems of constructing a unitary notion of national identity.

The movements of the folk are defined by the location of gain and loss in the oppositional relationship between places of power and disenfranchisement: "We of the Barrio—for it is to that country that I belong . . . trudged in the direction of the country of the City" (*Kalutang* 32). By figuring his expatriation as always already determined by the uneven development of the colonized homeland, Gonzalez restores a dimension of internal conflict that gets lost in the accustomed antinomy between colony and metropole. His memorialization of "the country of the Barrio" (a particular re-vision of the Philippines) constitutes what Said calls a "cartographic impulse," since "for the native, the history of his or her colonial servitude is inaugurated by the loss to an outsider of the local place, whose concrete geographical identity must thereafter be searched for and somehow restored" (Eagleton et al. 77). Yet the dispossession creates a rhetoric of placelessness, nostalgia, and wandering, and in Gonzalez's case, one drawn from the "local place," the *kaingin*: "It is enough that solid ground, whether illusory or real, lies under our feet, and that not too far away is the next clearing, and the next, and the next" (*Kalutang* 74).

These pioneering writers have constructed literary analogues of the national mythos that are not without their dangers. The mythic tropes of native and native territory in Gonzalez's work, like the sense of suspension endemic to the oldtimers of Santos or Bulosan's uneven idealization of peasant folk, stop short of becoming "demagogic assertions about a native past, history, or actuality that seems to stand free of the colonizer and worldly time itself" (Eagleton et al. 82). What these gestures sketch is a "new territoriality" that recovers or repossesses the colonized land imaginatively, and from which, in turn, the countercolonial "search for authenticity, for a more congenial national origin than provided by colonial history, for a new pantheon of heroes, myths and religions" should emerge (Eagleton et al. 79).

It is to the younger and more recent writers that one must turn for an extension of these suggestive tendencies in the exilic identities and writings of the pioneering writers. Recent writers (nearly all women) are turning their own exilic condition into a powerful stance, an engagement with the reality of invisibility that is doubled by the absence of the appropriation of woman as a metaphorical presence in the historical antecedents and models of the pioneers. (Here I have in mind Bulosan's dualized representations of women characters or even, specifically, the gendering of the homeland as female in Santos's "Scent of Apples," among countless instances.) The Flip poets are writing from an alienation that is double-sided as they address their own historical absence in the United States and remain implicated in the historic invisibility of the nation that permanently identifies them.

With a set of concerns and questions determined by their own historical conjunctures and different from the pioneers, recent writers view "history [as] the rubbish heap in which lie hidden the materials from which self-knowledge can come" (Gurr 10). This is a disposition that the Flips share with politically expatriated writers because their politics of emergence builds from a dialectic between past and present, not "a past sealed off from the vigorously altering effects of contemporary events" (Brennan 17). For example, although the old-timers continue to serve as figures of origin for many Flip poets, there is a re-search into their social history for a stronger genealogical link. It is an attempt to "turn over the rubbish heap of history by studying the past and in that way fixing a sense of identity" (Gurr 10). This is an impulse codified in Virginia Cerenio's "you lovely people": "ay manong / your old brown hands / hold life, many lives / within each crack / a story" (Bruchac 11). History is inscribed in, is an imprint on, the appropriated Pinoy body: "and it is in his hands / cracked and raw / that never heal. / Shotgunned stomach. One-kidney

Franky. / One hot day he revealed / that stomach to me, slowly raising / his T-shirt, and proclaimed it the map of California" (Tagami 13).

The probing of history for Flip poets also takes the form of social analysis, but of the conditions in a country as alien to them as they are to it. Perhaps this critical distance is what allows Jaime Jacinto to dramatize, in measured tones of grief and tension, the enduring inequities of Philippine life as sanctioned by the Church and the semifeudal order, and as symbolized by the burial of a peasant woman's little daughter: "As the blonde Spanish priest / anoints you, touching your / lips and feet with oil, / your mother wonders if ever there was enough to eat or / if only she had given in / to the landlord's whispers, / that extra fistful of rice / might have fattened the hollow / in your cheeks" (Ancheta et al. 48–49).

Nearly all the emergent writers are women, and this amplitude of women's writing is a development observable for other emergent literatures in the United States and the postcolonial world. Compared to the two other groups, it is the women or Filipina writers who recognize that "the relationship to the inherited past and its cultural legacy has been rendered problematic by the violent interference of colonial and imperial history" (Harlow 19). As Filipino historical crises are intensified by the authoritarian rule of Ferdinand Marcos and its aftermath, history and its countermythic writing become their own forms and visions of return, identity building, and self-recovery.

Linda Ty-Casper returned to early colonial Philippine history and showed the way for this group with *The Peninsulars* (1964). The novel has been critiqued for its "ill-advised" revisions of some historical documents but also commended for setting "certain precedents that are bound to subsequent efforts" (Galdon 202). In fact, Ty-Casper went on to handle Philippine historical subjects more boldly, seeking to make material out of the moral atrophy and political intrigues that mark the period of authoritarian rule by Marcos (see, for example, *Wings of Stone*, 1986; *Fortress in the Plaza*, 1985). One can profit from examining the intertextuality between Ty-Casper's and Ninotchka Rosca's ventures, specifically as borne out by Rosca's historical novel *State of War* (1988). This novel alerts the reader to Rosca's indebtedness to Ty-Casper's pioneering efforts, establishing certain genealogical links between both writers on the narrative level.

In *The Three-Cornered Sun* (1979), Ty-Casper turns to the Philippine Revolution of 1896 against Spain, creating a somewhat indecisive picture of national identity through the members of the Viardo family, whose individual traits are unevenly endowed with allegorical weight. As N.V.M. Gonzalez notes, the call is for "a depiction of private lives that would encompass Philippine experience within living memory," and as Rosca herself qualifies, "The problem is how to tell a story that was not anybody's story yet was everybody's story" (Gonzalez, "Filipino and the Novel" 962; Mestrovic 90). In *State of War*, Rosca re-visions the whole stretch of colonial history in the context of the period of Marcos's dictatorship through a mélange of dreamy sequences, historical vignettes, and hyperrealized characters and events. She balances allegory with personal history in the triadic relationship of her main characters, Anna Villaverde, Adrian Banyaga, and Eliza Hansen, whose genealogies and symbolic stories intertwine in a series of historical wars and developments that are symbolized by a 24-hour period of festivity and political conspiracies. The interrelated carnivalesque of merrymaking and political conflict is emphasized by narrative pattern and design, as supremely exemplified by the three-part structure of the novel ("Acts," "Numbers," "Revelations . . .").

An obvious footnote to the triangulated characteristic of Ty-Casper's *Awaiting Trespass* as "a small book of hours about those waiting for their lives to begin . . . a book of numbers about those who stand up to be counted . . . a book of revelations about what tyranny forces people to become; and what, by resisting, they can insist on being" (author's preface, n.p.), Rosca's organizing stratagem also directs the reader to incremental and interreferential layers internal to the work of either author. In Rosca's case, for example, Eliza and Anna (along with Colonel Amor, incarnated as the Loved One in *State of War*, symbol of the authoritarian and military reign of terror) first make their appearance as character sketches in the piece "Earthquake Weather" (see *Monsoon Collection* 129).

This movement continues outward as Michelle Skinner packs her extremely short stories in *Balikbayan: A Filipino Homecoming* (1988) with powerful allusion and subtexts concerning the life under dictatorial rule as it was subtended by American neocolonial support for Marcos; or as Cecilia Manguerra-Brainard compresses into a story ("The Black Man in the Forest," in *Woman with Horns* 21–25) the many historical ramifications of the Filipino-American war, which had concerned Ty-Casper in *Ten Thousand Seeds* (1987).

Experientially, these writers create from the same sense of expatriation from the past and their history that stems quite immediately from the founding moment of American colonization and the cultural translocation through the master's language. But the distance is not crippling, as they invert its anthropological commonplaces from their perspective as colonized natives or immigrants/citizens who regard from the outside that is also the country of the colonizer the whole spectacle of their transhistorical movements and displacements. Return for them is redefining and rewriting "history" from the perspective of banishment: "Physical departure from the scene of one's personal history provides a break in time and separates the present from the past. History then becomes what preceded departure" (Gurr 10–11).

For these writers, the pioneers serve as stark examples and models. Either one is disabled and "waits for miracles to happen"—as Santos seems to express when recalling how his writing teacher Philip Roth excised his desired ending image for a short story, that, significantly enough, of "floating in a shoreless sea" (Fernandez and Alegre 245)—or one is enabled, moving on, as the narrator in Bulosan's story does, to tell the "story" (history) of the "letter" (one's transcription or codification of the self-in-history) through the language and experience of one's subjection.

NOTES

Many thanks to Epifanio San Juan, Jr., Robert Lee, Roland Guyotte, Barbara Posadas, and Neil Lazarus for their comments and suggestions, and to Yuko Matsukawa for suggesting some important references.

1. Asian American literature is remarkably undertheorized when compared to African American, Chicano, and Native American literatures. Yet one can intuit from existing anthologies, bibliographies, and prevailing notions of Asian American literature a pronounced but unacknowledged focus on Chinese and Japanese American writings and their telos of immigration and settlement, to the unintended exclusion of other Asian American writings and their concomitant logics. The *Aiiieeeee!* group (1974), David Hsin-fu Wand (1974), Elaine Kim (1982), and many others reflexively include Filipinos or Filipino Americans as part of the Asian American triad of major communities, but because of their preoccupation with Chinese and Japanese American writings, they are hard-pressed to list "Filipino American" writers other than Carlos Bulosan, the "Flip" writers who figured prominently in the identity politics of the 1960s, or the younger California poets. A singu-

lar exception to this is Kai-yu Hus and Palubinskas (1972). Cheung and Yogi (1988) recognize the problems with this implicit theoretical center of Asian American literature when they note that "the influence of overseas Asians—be they sojourners or immigrants with American-born offspring—cannot be ignored" and that there are "authors who may regard themselves as expatriates or as regional writers rather than as Asian American"(v).

2. There has been a similar but related "neglect" or "invisibility" of Filipinos and Filipino Americans in the sociology of American immigration, ethnicity, and communities (Posadas, "Filipino American History" 87–88).

3. The anthology featured a short excerpt from Carlos Bulosan's *America Is in the Heart* (1946) and two short pieces by Penaranda and Tagatac. The writers themselves went on to construct a "literary background" from the history of Philippine literature in English, choosing Carlos Bulosan and Bienvenido Santos from "five authors [who] left the Philippines and wrote about Filipinos in America" even as this extremely limited pool consisted of "already mature men whose psychology and sensibilities were Filipino". Compare the essay by Penaranda et al. (44-47) with Bienvenido Santos, "The Filipino Novel in English" (634–38).

4. Here, I certainly do not wish to subsume, even to reduce, the identity and community politics of immigrant and native-born Filipino Americans into a totalizing structure. The historians Roland Guyotte and Barbara Posadas warn against the dangers of this facile move ("Unintentional Immigrants," 26). Rather I am interested in how Filipino Americans and exiled Filipinos are caught in a web of mutual implication with each other and with their groups of affinity in the Philippines when faced with the question of American colonialism within a U.S. context.

5. Recent efforts in various fields recognize the need to coalesce around such possibly comparative issues as American imperialism and Orientalism. Mazumdar (1991) calls for a dialogue between Asian American studies and Asian studies on this score and many others, while Cheng and Bonacich (1984) have initiated a parallel dialogue of these fields with studies in political economy. Hunt has called the attention of diplomatic historians to the centrality of the immigration question. He also urges increased attention to "the intellectual currents among the elite and popular views in the regions intimately involved in trans-Pacific contacts" to any fresh work in American–East Asian international relations (Cohen 18, 20–30).

6. In historiographical terms, this doctrine was codified in many ways, but most relevant for us here, through the "aberration thesis" of Samuel Flagg Bemis in diplomatic history—the notion that American imperialism was merely a blot in an otherwise spotless and incomparable political tradition. This dominated the literature for many years and (although debunked by subsequent paradigms) continues to assume many lives in different

works and cultural expressions. Some prior but exemplary incarnations include the notion of Manifest Destiny, which naturalized the expansive thrust of American nation and empire building, and "benevolent assimilation," which distinguished American imperialism as "humanitarian" and "tutelary." For a critique of the historiography, see San Juan, *Crisis* (1986), esp. 3–5, and Miller (1982), 1–12, 253–67. For recent renewals of this sacrosanct view of American imperialism, see Welch (1979), chap. 10; May, *Social Engineering* (1980), 170–83, and the Pulitzer Prize-winning book by Karnow *In Our Image* (1989), 12–15, 227ff, 323ff.

7. Letter to the author, October 10, 1989. Kaplan's work on American imperialist discourse announces a much-awaited cultural turn in the study of American imperialism; see, for example, "Romancing the Empire" (1990). Rydell (1984) preceded Kaplan with his ground-breaking work on American world fairs and their focus on the Philippines. Institutional developments that indicate the wholesale submergence of the Philippines in various American historiographies include its erratic and tokenistic positioning in East Asian and Southeast Asian studies and the absence of a strong Philippine studies tradition in the United States. See May's half-hearted critique of this benign (or active?) academic neglect of the Philippines in *Past Recovered* (1987); 175–89, but also Alice Mak, "Philippine Studies in Hawaii" (6, 9), which notes that in instituting a formal Philippine studies program at the University of Hawaii in 1975, the university faculty observed that no other U.S. institution "had a program focusing on the Philippines." Mak adds: "After many decades of [so-called] close political, historical and social ties, it seemed odd that no American university had made an effort to encourage research on the Philippines."

8. Letter to the author from Epifanio San Juan, Jr., April 24, 1990.

9. Penaranda et al. use this term to refer to Filipino Americans born and/or rasied in the United States (Chin 49).

10. San Juan critiques Sollors's uninformed and ahistorical appropriations of Villa in the "Cult of Ethnicity." For an account of Villa's autocanonization and self-obsolescence see San Juan, "Reflections on U.S.-Philippine Literary Relations," 47–50.

11. Or as Memmi describes the situation unambiguously, "The entire bureaucracy, the entire court system, all industry hears and uses the colonizer's language. . . . highway markings, railroad station signs, street signs and receipts make the colonized feel like a stranger in his own country" (106–7).

12. Compare with Bulosan, "Homecoming," where the protagonist Mariano's first glimpse of his hometown and the family hut after twelve years in the United States evokes a quickness of step and powerful emotions (*Bulosan Reader* 64).

WORKS CITED

Ancheta, Shirley, et al., eds. *Without Names*. San Francisco: Kearny Street Workshop, 1985.

Anderson, Benedict. *Imagined Communities: Reflections of the Origins and Spread of Nationalism*. London: Verso, 1983.

Brennan, Timothy. "Cosmopolitans and Celebrities." *Race and Class* 31.1 (1989): 1–19.

Bruchac, Joseph, ed. *Breaking Silence: An Anthology of Contemporary Asian American Poets*. Greenfield Center, N.Y.: Greenfield Review Press, 1983.

Bulosan, Carlos. *If You Want to Know What We Are: A Carlos Bulosan Reader*. Minneapolis: West End, 1983.

———. *America Is in the Heart*. 1946. Seattle: University of Washington Press, 1973.

———. *Sound of Falling Light: Letters in Exile*. Ed. Dolores Feria. Quezon City, Phils.: University of Philippines Press, 1960.

Carino, Benjamin, and James Fawcett, eds. *Pacific Bridges: The New Immigration from Asia and the Pacific Islands*. New York: Center for Migration Studies, 1987.

Cheng, Lucie, and Edna Bonacich, eds. *Labor Immigration Under Capitalism: Asian Workers in the United States before World War II*. Berkeley: University of California Press, 1984.

Cheung, King-kok, and Stan Yogi. *Asian American Literature: An Annotated Bibliography*. New York: Modern Language Association, 1988.

Cordova, Fred. *Filipinos: Forgotten Asian Americans*. Dubuque, Iowa: Kendall Hunt, 1983.

Eagleton, Terry, et. al. *Nationalism, Colonialism and Literature*. Minneapolis: University of Minnesota Press, 1990.

Fuentebella, Cielo. "What is Filipino American Culture?" *Philippine News Magazine*, August 9–15, 1989.

Fernandez, Doreen and Edilberto Alegre. *The Writer and His Milieu*. Manila: De La Salle University Press, 1982.

Galdon, Joseph, ed. *Philippine Fiction*. Quezon City, Phils.: Ateneo de Manila University Press, 1972.

Gates, Henry Louis. *The Signifying Monkey: A Theory of African-American Literary Criticism*. New York: Oxford University Press, 1988.

Gonzalez, N.V.M. *Kalutang: A Filipino in the World*. Manila: Kalikasan Press, 1990.

———. *Mindoro and Beyond: Twenty-One Stories*. Quezon City, Phils.: University of Philippines Press, 1979.

———. "Drumming for the Captain." *World Literature Written in English* 15.2 (November 1976): 415–21.

———. "The Filipino and the Novel." *Daedelus* 95.4 (Fall 1966): 961–71.
———. *Seven Hills Away*. Denver: Alan Swallow, 1947.
Gurr, Andrew. *Writers in Exile: The Identity of Home in Modern Literature*. Atlantic Highlands, N.J.: Humanities Press, 1981.
Guyotte, Roland and Barbara Posadas. "Unintentional Immigrants: Chicago's Filipino Foreign Students Become Settlers, 1900–1941." *Journal of American Ethnic History* 9.2 (Spring 1990): 26–48.
Guzman, Richard. "'As in Myth, the Signs Were All Over': The Fiction of N.V.M. Gonzalez." *Virginia Quarterly Review* 60.1 (Winter 1984): 102–18.
Harlow, Barbara. *Resistance Literature*. New York: Methuen, 1987.
Hsu, Kai-yu, and Helen Palubinskas, eds. *Asian American Authors*. Boston: Houghton Mifflin, 1972.
Hunt, Michael. "New Insights But No New Vistas: Recent Work in 19th Century American–East Asian Relations." In *New Frontiers in American–East Asian Relations*, ed. Warren Cohen. New York: Columbia University Press, 1983.
Kaplan, Amy. "Romancing the Empire." *American Literary History* 3 (December 1990): 556–90.
Karnow, Stanley. *In Our Image: America's Empire in the Philippines*. New York: Random, 1989.
Kim, Elaine. *Asian American Literature: An Introduction to the Writings and Their Social Context*. Philadelphia: Temple University Press, 1982.
Mak, Alice. "Development of Philippine Studies in Hawaii." *Philippine Studies Newsletter*, October 1989.
Manguerra-Brainard. *Woman with Horns and Other Stories*. Quezon City, Phils.: New Day, 1988.
May, Ernest, and James Thomson, Jr., eds. *American–East Asian Relations: A Survey*. Cambridge, Mass.: Harvard University Press, 1972.
May, Glenn. *A Past Recovered*. Quezon City, Phils.: New Day, 1987.
———. *Social Engineering in the Philippines*. Westport, Conn.: Greenwood, 1980.
Mazumdar, Sucheta. "Asian American Studies and Asian Studies: Rethinking Roots." In *Asian Americans: Comparative and Global Perspectives*. ed. Shirley Hune, et al. Pullman, Wash.: Washington State University Press, 1991.
Memmi, Albert. *The Colonizer and the Colonized*. Boston: Beacon, 1965.
Mestrovic, Marta. "Ninotchka Rosca." *Publishers Weekly*, May 6, 1988.
Miller, Stuart Creighton. *"Benevolent Assimilation": The American Conquest of the Philippines, 1899–1903*. New Haven: Yale University Press, 1982.
Mukherjee, Bharati. "Immigrant Writing: Give Us Your Maximalists!" *New York Times Book Review*, August 28, 1988.

Penaranda, Oscar, et al. "An Introduction to Filipino American Literature." In *Aiiieeeee! An Anthology of Asian American Writers*, ed. Frank Chin et al. Washington, D.C.: Howard University Press, 1974.

Pido, Antonio. *The Pilipinos in America: Macro/Micro Dimensions of Immigration and Integration*. New York: Center for Migration Studies, 1986.

Posadas, Barbara. "At a Crossroad: Filipino American History and the Old Timers' Generation." *Amerasia* 13.1 (1986–87): 85–97.

Quemada, David. "The Contemporary Filipino Poet in English." *World Literature Written in English* 15.2 (November 1976): 429–437.

Rosca, Ninotchka. *State of War*. New York: Norton, 1988.

———. *Monsoon Collection*. New York and Sta. Lucia: University of Queensland Press, 1982.

Roth, Russell, *Muddy Glory: America's "Indian Wars" in the Philippines 1899–1935*. West Hanover, Mass.: Christopher Publishing House, 1981.

Rydell, Robert. *All the World's a Fair: Visions of Empire at American International Expositions, 1876–1916*. Chicago: University of Chicago Press, 1984.

Said, Edward. "Reflections on Exile." In *Out There: Marginalization and Contemporary Cultures*, ed. Russell Ferguson et al. Cambridge, Mass.: MIT Press, 1990.

San Juan, Epifanio, Jr. "Mapping the Boundaries, Inscribing the Differences: The Filipino in the U.S.A." *Journal of Ethnic Studies* 19.1 (Spring 1991): 117–31.

———. "The Cult of Ethnicity and the Fetish of Pluralism." *Cultural Critique* 18 (Spring 1991): 215–29.

———. "Farewell, You Whose Homeland is Forever Arriving As I Embark: Journal of a Filipino Exile." *Kultura* 3.1 (1990): 34–41.

———. "Reflections on U.S.-Philippine Literary Relations." *Ang Makatao* (1988): 43–54.

———. *Ruptures, Schisms, Interventions: Cultural Revolution in the Third World*. Manila: De La Salle University Press, 1988.

———. "To the Filipino Artist in Exile." *Midweek*, August 19, 1987.

———. *Crisis in the Philippines*. South Hadley, Mass.: Bergin and Garvey, 1986.

Santos, Bienvenido. "Pilipino Old Timers: Fact and Fiction." *Amerasia* 9.2 (1982): 89–98.

———. *Scent of Apples*. Seattle: University of Washington Press, 1979.

———. "The Personal Saga of a 'Straggler' in Philippine Literature." *World Literature Written in English* 15.2 (November 1976): 398–405.

———. "The Filipino Novel in English." In *Brown Heritage: Essays on Philippine Cultural Tradition and Literature*, ed. Antonio Manuud. Quezon City, Phils.: Ateneo de Manila University Press, 1967.

Seidel, Michael. *Exile and the Narrative Imagination*. New Haven: Yale University Press, 1987.
Skinner, Michelle Maria Cruz. *Balikbayan: A Filipino Homecoming*. Honolulu: Bess Press, 1988.
Solberg, Sam, "Introduction to Filipino American Literature." In *Aiiieeeee! An Anthology of Asian-American Writers*, ed. Frank Chin et al. Washington, D.C.: Howard University Press, 1983.
Sollors, Werner. *Beyond Ethnicity: Consent and Descent in American Culture*. New York: Oxford University Press, 1986.
Tagami, Jeff. *October Light*. San Francisco: Kearny Street Workshop, 1987.
Takaki, Ronald. *Strangers from a Different Shore: A History of Asian Americans*. Boston: Little, Brown, 1989.
———, ed. *From Different Shores: Perspectives on Race and Ethnicity in America*. New York: Oxford University Press, 1987.
Ty-Casper, Linda. *Ten Thousand Seeds*. Manila: Ateneo de Manila University Press, 1987.
———. *Wings of Stone*. London: Readers International, 1986.
———. *Awaiting Trespass*. London: Readers International, 1985.
———. *Fortress in the Plaza*. Quezon City, Phils.: New Day, 1985.
———. *The Three-Cornered Sun*. Quezon City, Phils.: New Day, 1979.
———. *The Peninsulars*. Manila: Bookmark, 1964.
Wand, David Hsin-fu, ed. *Asian American Heritage*. Boston: Houghton Mifflin, 1974.
Welch, Richard. *Response to Imperialism: The United States and the Philippine-American War, 1899–1902*. Chapel Hill: University of North Carolina Press, 1979.
Williams, Raymond. *Marxism and Literature*. New York: Oxford University Press, 1977.

4

Beyond "Clay Walls": Korean American Literature

Chung-Hei Yun

ASIAN AMERICAN literature is a child born of uprootedness and transplantation. The pain of dislocation is followed by nostalgia for the lost home, for in many instances there is no more "homeland" one can return to (*The Woman Warrior* 125). This nostalgia often haunts the psyche and imagination of the exiled like a hungry ghost that refuses to be appeased (*The Woman Warrior* 19).

The Puritan exodus from England and subsequent entry into America is one example of the journey-quest for the Holy Grail/the New Canaan. Woven into this teleological matrix is a spiritual struggle and a typology consonant with Western metaphysical dualism. The Puritans' journey was not an ordinary sea voyage; it was a spiritual pilgrimage through the sea of faith to fulfill Providence as God's instrument in the unfolding of the grand design and telos of human destiny. Taming the wilderness, therefore, became an external counterpart of the Holy War: conquest of the wilderness and wild men was a struggle between good and evil, the ultimate triumph of "The City of God" over "The City of Man."

Unlike Puritan Americans, the impetus for the Asian exodus-emigration is rooted mainly in economic, political, and social reality. Although Asians also came on a quest for "a New Canaan full of milk and honey," it is a Canaan that exists within an earthly kingdom without Moses. An earthly "manna" embodied in money, education, and success lured and beckoned Asian immigrants to the "Gold Mountain" with a vision of streets cobbled with "gold nuggets" (*China Men* 41).

Often economic necessity is accompanied by political conditions in the nation that spurred emigration. Such was the case for the Korean immigrants depicted in the four works by three Korean American authors that this chapter examines: Younghill Kang's *The Grass Roof* (1931) and *East Goes West* (1937), Theresa Hak Kyung Cha's *Dictée* (1982), and Ronyoung Kim's *Clay Walls* (1986). All three authors share the same dark tragedy of the Korean past, which they narrate from various angles of vision.

The centrifugal force shaping the Korean American literary imagination is generated from the loss of homeland through Japanese annexation, the mutilation of the land when it was divided into North and South Korea following the liberation from Japan after World War II, the Korean War, and the post-1965 exodus.

Although *The Grass Roof* is about Kang's early experience in Korea under the "grass roof" recollected in nostalgia, it serves as a necessary psychological bridge to *East Goes West*, the record of his experience in America and Canada as a displaced person. Not long after the Japanese annexed Korea, Chung-Pa Han, the narrator-author of the novel-autobiography, departs for America in quest of "New Knowledge." Han recalls his first encounter with the West: "I thought them [the Arabic numerals, 1, 2, 3, etc.] beautiful, fascinating and a little bit black magic. This was my first taste of the Western learning" (31). Han enlarges his knowledge of the West through Japanese translations of works by various Western authors, including Shakespeare, Shelley, Coleridge, Arnold, Schopenhauer, Goethe, Poe, and Whitman. Ideas from these authors largely shape the contours of Han's vision of the West. For him, "Shakespeare and Michael Angelo [*sic*] . . . were heroes" (258).

Han perceives that enlightened Western ideology and its scientific advancements are externally manifest in the political strength of Japan, for "Japan has conquered Korea by Western Science. We [Koreans] must regain our freedom by a superior knowledge of that Science" (185). Park Soo-San, Han's history teacher, asserts that Korea must emulate Japan and master the entire learning of the West. Thus, Han's odyssey begins with his journey to Japan, his first great leap. He makes this leap first by cutting off his topknot (sang-too), the traditional hairstyle for Korean men, "something like a baptism"

(186) before he "takes the solitary pilgrimage" (235). For Han, the act is "a symbol . . . of breaking away from the bondage of tradition, [his] oath, that [he] had set [himself] toward Western learning and all the West had to give and to teach" (186).

Though Japan serves as a bridge to the West, his sojourn in Japan is a brief one. Restless and disenchanted, Han returns to Korea with an altered perspective on his village and his own people: "My people now seemed the foreign element in their own country, still in top knots and white clothes wandering around in the market place with perplexed expression, faces wrinkled and ghost-like with worry, wondering what was to happen tomorrow!" (299). With his altered vision, he can no longer see his village Song-Dune-Chi (the Village of the Pine Trees) nestled in "the Valley of Utopia" with its "delicious taste of the first frost" and the brilliance of chrysanthemums nodding in the breeze, sending forth their "pungent aroma under the grass roof" (17). Instead, he sees "the round shaggy roofs clustered close to the ground on the wide floor of the valley, [he] had an illusion that every soul in [his] childhood village was dead, swept away by a plague, and that the spot was abandoned" (306). This bleak landscape aptly corresponds to the oppressive political reality of Korea under Japanese colonialism. Yet the passion of the March 1, 1919 uprising, the Korean "Declaration of Independence," fails to touch or inspire Han. The only action he takes is that of flight to Manchuria and then, once more, return, thus ending his second abortive odyssey.

Han's passionate and desperate yearning for Western civilization in all its glory and grandeur is not without conflict. Western civilization, as manifested in its arts, its achievements in the practical spheres of life, politics, and war, is ultimately the external embodiment of a weltanschauung shaped by Judeo-Christian ideology. To comprehend the West, then, one must comprehend Christianity. Han observed that Mr. Park "had become a liberal Christian, wishing to turn his back on the past, and his face toward the future, he made me see that the road of a scholar's future prominence lay toward America like the shortest distance between two points . . . in a straight line" (186). Again, Han resolves to flee from Korea, and he approaches Mr. Parker, an American missionary, only to be rejected with the words, "We only take care of Christians! We don't take care of heathens" (226). Mr. Parker adds that he does not think it a good idea for Koreans to come to America, although it is the native home of missionaries, for there they will forget all the good that they learned from missionaries while in Korea (227).

The disparity between Western ideology and its practice is succinctly articulated in light of the existing social and political reality:

> The War . . . So the West didn't act what they said! They were just as bad as the East,—or worse, for the East didn't send out missionaries, saying "Our Christianity has the superior righteousness. You are heathen and your sages are no good. Why don't you follow our example?" . . . [Japan] became more powerful than China, since she learned rapidly from the West whatever the West had to teach in the way of skillful homicide. Then Japan tested that art out on China and defeated her in 1894. (259)

Han sees the ultimate contradiction in the disparity between an increased quality of life and decreased humanity, for "the West . . . makes life better, because it reduces death, and adds to the refinements of life by inventions and mechanical improvements. But now they were killing in wholesale business the life that was saved. It seemed to [him] that the refinement was all in warfare, not in high superiority of mind, or in scholarship" (261). Nevertheless, with these conflicting attitudes towards the West still unresolved, Han crosses the Pacific.

On his voyage to America, Han encounters a young girl who reminds him of another girl whose fleeting form he had seen at the station on his way to Seoul from Japan. The girl in the past voyage had seemed to balance "in her two hands the Eastern and Western world" (276). Recollecting the vision of the girl from the past, Han says of the girl before him:

> She seems isolated like myself, a woman with no nationality. Is she of West or East? Is she a Chinese or a Japanese? Is she European or American? Now she alone touches the chord to which my heart dances, because of how she stands and looks into the night. Her eyes are on the far off stars. And from the milky way they move to look at me. . . . Is it possible that the Princess Immortality is in the same boat going with me to America? (377)

As the embodiment of his desire and dream, the girl is transformed into his Princess Immortality, perhaps the Faustean *Ewigweibliche* befitting his Faustean dream/quest.

The Grass Roof, then, as Elaine Kim remarks in her illuminating account of the work, "is a justification of Han's departure from Korea" (34). The validity of this justification is yet to be substantiated in Kang's next work, *East Goes West*. In the beginning of this second book, Han clearly states why he left Korea and what the book is going to be about:

> I cried for the food for my growth and there seemed no food. And I felt I was looking on death, the death of an ancient planet, a spiritual planet that had been my father's home. . . . In loathing of death, I hurtled forward, out into space, out toward a foreign body . . . and a younger culture drew me by natural gravity. I entered a new life like one born again. Here I wandered on soil as strange as Mars, seeking roots, roots for an exile's soul. . . . It was here in America for me to find. But where? This book is the record of my early search, and the arch of my projectile toward the goal. (4–5)

The strength of the dreams spun in Korea is to be tested through Han's experiences in America. In New York, Han understands for the first time the fear of "the pavement famine, with plenty all around but in the end not even grass to chew" (32). He also comes to a painful realization of "how far [his] little grass-roofed, hill-wrapped village [is removed] from this gigantic rebellion which was New York!" (6). From his solitary, dingy hotel room, Han ventures out to have a glimpse of Harlem, the "Other Kingdom" (19) within the kingdom of exile, where the inhabitants are leading "the plaintive, alluring sadness of life's farthest exile . . . a dimmer, vaster captivity than the Babylonian one" (20). Han identifies himself with these "exiles" in the "Other Kingdom" and, in turn, is identified with them by white American society. Han is told by Mr. Allen, who interviews him for a job at the YMCA, that the vacancy is not to be filled by a "Negro" or an "Oriental."

His first job as a houseboy confirms and further intensifies this initial rejection. When his books fall out of his suitcase, the lady of the house, seeing the dingy Oriental covers of some secondhand books he had bought in Japan, exclaims, "I hope they have no germs" (62). The visible difference—race and color—that signifies separateness and alienation in white American consciousness seems like a vermin invested with the power to contaminate white society.

Han's experience at Maritime College in Canada reinforces his isolation and loneliness in a converse manner. With the exception of the hostile Leslie Robin, one of Han's classmates, everyone is generous and overly kind toward the "poor and humiliated protégé of the right honorable British Canadian theologues [*sic*]" (112). For Han, "there was always special favor, special kindliness, special protection . . . the white man's-burden attitude toward dark colonies" (126). Han summarizes this experience in the following brooding reflection: "Why then did I feel myself so lonely and sad, small, lowly, and unappreciated? Why, in short, did I long once more . . . for escape? The magnificent journey to America, the avid desire for Western knowledge, had it come to this?" (112).

Han's experiences as a displaced person arc interwoven with various portraits of other Korean exiles in New York, all of whom crossed the ocean hoping to realize their separate dreams. George Jum becomes a hedonist who has denounced Confucius, Christ, and Buddha, and found life's meaning only in women's arms, for "life lies with woman, not with the classics or the ancestors" (44). The Westernized and Christianized Dr. Ko, in spite of his belief that he is an earnest Christian, is not able to eradicate his Confucian root: "He had simply changed the letter of his faith" (49). Mr. Pyun learns American pragmatism, efficiency, and the Protestant work ethic fast and becomes a good businessman who can be held up as a model for an Oriental success story. He enjoys food, works hard, and enjoys his night life (57).

Han describes Pak, who accompanies Han to his first job as a houseboy, as a "typical Korean" who is "an exile only in body, not in soul, as if Western civilization had rolled over him as water over a rock" (58). A typical model Korean is a nationalist, a good Christian, a hard worker, and a supporter of all organizations working for Korea's revolutionary cause. Often the immigrant's tenacious hold on his cultural heritage, pride, and identity, juxtaposed against his lurking desire to be rid of the grip of nostalgia, creates resistance and ambivalence. These tantalizing paradoxes and double binds fill the immigrant's imagination, as has been expressed in many Asian American literary works.

Fulchoon Chang's dreams and ambitions are representative of the mental state of contemporary Korean American students. "Chang was studying to be an engineer—and unlike Guru, the Hindoo, overcame all theosophical [*sic*] temptations—he stuck to engineering" (248). Often stifling the whispers of their desires and resisting "temptations," many young immigrants today pursue medicine, engineering, business management, or computer science in hope of translating their dreams into reality in the most efficient, practical, and expedient way. The Muse must be banished; otherwise, she is likely to lead them to despair and nihilism, as we are to see in the fate of To Wan Kim in Greenwich Village.

It is, however, with this Greenwich Village romantic aesthete Kim that Han finds an intellectual and spiritual kinship, as Han discovers in him the mirror wherein are reflected his own dreams, ideals, frustrations, and despair. In a utilitarian civilization where aesthetes are not appreciated, Kim feels that his "life is like the useless tree. [He tries] to plant [his] tree in the land of nonexistence" (233). Unable to transplant his tender roots in the hard concrete pavement of the New World, yet also unable to retransplant them in his native soil, Kim's "roots" slowly wither.

The first formidable task that all immigrants undertake is to "enter into the economic life of Americans" (277). Kim is aware of the socioeconomic reality that Korean immigrants confront in the New World, where "the only goal for a man is money and power. But money and power in New York are not for men of my race. Even if we succeeded, we would not be admired for that, but only hated and feared" (231).

To Kim's lamentation on the state of the arts in America, Han responds: "We do not come to the West for poetry . . . but for man's new way of mastering Nature" (177). In America, the destination of their quest, the urgency of existential choices persists: the old or the new, the "homeland" or the land one stands on, muse or gold? In this ethical battleground, inexorable conditions relentlessly drive one to choose. To the idealistic Kim, who "came to the West to find a new beauty, a new life" (178) only to discover the great void around him, Han remarks: "But tell me, what now is to be our fate? Being unable to go back to that previous existence, being unable to label ourselves in this New World . . . becoming lost within another lost world?" (178).

One ray of light enters the gloom of Kim's exile—his relationship with Helen, a white American girl from a proper New England family. With Helen, Kim no longer feels a lonely exile and is "always happy . . . as with Nature" (240). Although this episode intimates hope, hope that one human heart could emancipate another heart in exile, the flickering light is soon extinguished by the end of their relationship, leaving Kim in darkness and despair. Kim chooses to make Greenwich Village his grave and becomes an exile both in life and death. Lamenting Kim's suicide, Han reflects:

> The greatest loss . . . was himself [Kim], his brain which bore in its fine involutions our ancient characters deeply and simply incised, familiar to me. And over their classic economy, their primitive chaste elegance, was scrawled the West's handwriting, the incoherent labyrinth. . . . To me—to me almost alone—a priceless and awful parchment was in him destroyed. (395)

Han's search in the New World concludes on an inconclusive note. Yunkoo, his childhood friend under "the grass roof," appears in his dream. As Yunkoo is pointing Han toward a never-never-land, things begin tumbling out of Han's pockets: money, contracts, and business letters. He desperately clutches on "to the key to his . . . American car" (401). He dreams that the cellar is attacked and on fire, but he awakes "like the phoenix out of a burst of flames" (401). Also in this dream journey to the grass-roofed village of his childhood, appears Trip, an American girl he met in New York. Han returns to New York and calls Trip early in the morning, for "he had to be saved quickly from going quite empty like Kim. It was real emergency" (401). Perhaps, in Trip, Han is determined to see a fragmented embodiment of the Princess Immortality. With a suggestion of rebirth and the forging of a new identity through community bonds, one chapter in Han's odyssey ends. Its conclusion, I believe, inaugurates his quest for the village without the "grass roof," life "here and now" in America with "the *key* (italics mine) to his American car" (401).

The struggle to nurture and cultivate transplanted roots so that they can survive is the focus of Ronyoung Kim's *Clay Walls*. As with Kang's Han, the increasingly oppressive political reality of Korea after it is annexed by Japan in 1910 is the moving force that drives Chun and Haesu to emigrate. The novel depicts their life in Los Angeles during the mid-twentieth century. Realistic descriptions of their struggle and of life within the Korean "enclave," their initiation into an alien mode of life and culture, their innocence and ignorance, their knowledge gained through experience—these constitute the substance of this novel. It begins with the saga of the first-generation Korean immigrants and ends with the emergence of the second generation. Like "the grass roof," the image of the "clay walls" that surround the thatched-roof houses elicits in many Koreans both nostalgic and ambivalent responses.

The antipodal forces and values manifest themselves in two opposing attitudes toward life, as figured in the characters of Haesu and her husband, Chun. The tentacles of the old tradition encircle both Haesu and Chun, at times threatening to choke their precariously rooted existence. The tradition-clad social hierarchy binds Haesu, causing her to quit her job as a maid and curse her employer Mrs. Randolph as a *sangnyun* (a woman of the lowest class). Haesu feels humiliated at having to clean toilet bowls, for she is from a *yangban* (aristocratic) family in Korea, and no yangban would stoop to clean a toilet, a menial task tended to only by the sangnyun. Deeply conscious of the traditional social rank reserved for the scholar class, Haesu never reconciles herself to her arranged marriage to a mere farmer. For Chun, "just a farmer's son," "any work is good enough" and is "just a job" (10), but for Haesu, Chun's work is a most demeaning and humiliating one. Haesu resorts to reviling him: "How you can remain mute while someone orders you to come here, go there, do this, do that . . . like you were some trained animal. They call you a houseboy. A twenty-five year old man being called 'boy'" (10). Constantly measuring their status as defined by their having to perform menial tasks for a living against traditional values, Haesu perceives her life in America to be utterly meaningless. Haesu repeats the question to herself and to Chun: "What are we doing here? As soon as we make enough money, we are going back to Korea. We don't belong here. Just tell me, what are we doing here?" (10).

Haesu soon discovers that walls, whether of stone or clay, circumscribe the fragile world of the displaced. Many apartments are restricted and not for Orientals; their house has to be bought by Charles Bancroft, an American citizen. Harold, their eldest son born in America, is barred from entering Edward Military Academy because the founders of the Academy desire to accept only white Anglo-Saxon Protestants.

Haesu goes back to Korea with her children, intending never to return, but once in Korea, she realizes that her homeland under Japanese colonialism has ceased to be a home. She feels trapped, for every time she thinks she has a way out, she is up against a stone wall. Feeling "out of sorts in her homeland, homesick in Korea without being homesick for America" (125) and suffering exile in their own homeland, the family decides to return to America, although they are fully aware of the all-too-familiar "walls" that await them there.

After moving to their first home, Chun wants to "put up a fence or a wall of some kind," for he was used "to having a clay wall around [his] house" (28) in Korea. Haesu rejects this suggestion, preferring an open space, and exclaims: "If they can see us, we can see them. No one can hide anything." (28). The Janus-faced wall stands for protection and the security of tradition for Chun, but for Haesu, it represents enervating and paralyzing constraint. Clay walls, like her heritage, are an anachronism in America. These "clay walls" of tradition, indeed, have long confined and sequestered Korean women:

> The higher the woman's rank, the more she was sequestered, and hers was of the upper class. Her country had fought for its own seclusion, struggling against the penetration of eastern invaders and western ideology. A futile struggle, she thought. Korean walls were made of clay, crumbling under repeated blows, leaving nothing as it was before. Chun had wanted a wall around their house in L.A. She remembered, and she had ridiculed him. (103)

Chun's desire to cling to the crumbling and ineffectual "clay walls" also determines his attitude toward life. He believes that to "not contend" is the highest level of human behavior and that if one wants "muddy water to become clean" (163), one has to lie still. When he realizes that he has been cheated on his wholesale produce contract with the government, Chun, to control his rage, recalls his father's Taoist injunction: "Breathe in deep and empty your thoughts. Give play to your feelings and everything will fall into place" (135). Against this quietism Haesu rebels and asks him to "abandon the tenets of his ancestors" (163) in defiance of the ineffectual clay walls of the past.

In the struggle of the displaced, the "clay walls" that Chun refuses to relinquish fail to protect him. Drifting from one place to another in search of work and exhausted from his futile wandering, he dies in a hospital room in Reno, Nevada—an exile and homeless even in death. Left with three children, Haesu grapples with the hard economic reality. Bending over a piece of cloth, squinting her eyes to embroider handkerchiefs, for which she is paid by the piece, Haesu carries the burden of living. Yet, Haesu, together with innumerable displaced people, survives triumphantly. Her children will further cultivate the roots of this heroism, the legacy of the displaced.

In a gesture that seems to symbolize her last effort to cling to the land that she had left and, at the same time, her refusal to embrace the new land as her home, Haesu had bought a piece of land in

Qwaksan, North Korea, a place to which she can no longer return: for "the South Korean government says the KPR is a communist group. We can't get into North Korea either. . . . My land in Qwaksan is gone" (300). At the novel's conclusion, the daughter Faye has a sudden flash of revelation:

> The land was Momma's only holding in her homeland and it had been taken away from her; her only holding in the world. Suddenly, I felt as if I had been stamped with stupidity. That was what I was supposed to understand. She had clung onto Qwaksan as long as she could. (300)

Human desire and the belief that a piece of land would make one's home a homeland turn out to be another human folly and illusion. Letting go of a corner of the remote land to which she has clung not only emancipates Haesu from crippling nostalgia but also impels her to accept the alien land as "my country."

When Faye, Haesu's daughter, meets Daniel Lee, a student at Yale who wants to be a medical doctor, she tells him that she loves to read; she wants to see "how other people live," yet she hasn't "found a book written about the people she knows" (297). Dan responds: "That would be another form of isolation. . . . Unless one becomes part of that 'other world'" (297). Dan's response to Faye's desire to know how "other people" live through books attests to the conflicts he has experienced as a Korean American, the conflicts he acknowledges to Haesu: "Most of my life has not been spent with my 'father's people' but with the other people of this country. I live among one group of people while my commitments are to another. WASP assumptions require that I be one thing and my ancestry demands another" (297). Dan's resolution of this conflict is shown by the choice he makes: "We do live in the United States. You and I do speak English to one another. I do wear the uniform of this country. We are part of this society. Segments of it may not be completely accessible to everyone, but we who live here have something in common." (297–98). Beyond a piece of land and beyond the dichotomy of "others" and "we," Dan perceives that the true meaning of home and homeland is found in the commonality of human experiences.

The novel ends with the arrival of a special delivery letter from Daniel. The unopened letter seems full of promises to Faye. The vision of a daughter marrying a medical doctor—the unequivocal hope of many immigrant parents—is perhaps too pat. Yet, this land is theirs, Dan's and Faye's, to mold, shape, and cherish. Faye, together with all children of the displaced, not only must chart and shape the path of her destiny but also cultivate the path in this new land, freed from sequestration by "clay walls."

Before Dan's departure from Los Angeles, Faye has asked him about New Haven. "White Anglo-Saxon Protestant," Dan replies. "Oh, like Beverly Hills?" she asks, to which he responds, "No, not at all. It's conservative with a Puritan tradition. Morality denuded of imagination. Beverly Hills, on the other hand, strikes me as being based on imagination denuded of morality" (296). One can only hope that a world will emerge from their dreams where aesthetic and ethical visions are harmoniously wedded and realized; where "morality" is adorned by "imagination" and imagination is illumined by morality.

Although its publication precedes Kim's *Clay Walls* (1986), Theresa Hak Kyung Cha's *Dictée* (1982) can be read as the last coda for the "exiles in the kingdom." Cha's vision goes beyond the boundary of historical time and space, blending her aesthetic and religious visions and placing the remembered tragic history of Korea in a mythical context.

The title, *Dictée*, with its connotations and intentional ambiguities, defines that indefinable and ineffable realm of memory. The "dictée" of *Dictée* assumes both an active agent who transcribes the tales told by her mother as well as a passive agent serving as the repository and the vessel for that memory, which in turn is being remembered and shaped by the dictée finally manifesting itself in the pages of *Dictée*.

The very act of dictating through the process of remembering, the process manipulated by the dictée, emerges in the palpable form of the book, *Dictée*, which defies categorization. It encompasses multiple avenues of human communications: language/signs; visual media (pictures of Yu Kwan Soon, Cha's mother, Joan of Arc, Chinese ideograms, and ruins); and semiotic devices (rearrangement and manipulation of the words; juxtaposition of English, French, Korean, and Chinese). The term *dictée* in French also signifies "inspired." The basic structure of the work, which is divided into nine sections "dictated" by the nine Muses, respectively, gives cogency to this inspiration. The dictée's act of remembering by re-membering the dismembered fragments of memory scattered onto the void of the past and the attempt to create an ordered form out of the chaos are to be taken as an act inspired by the Muses.

The dedicatory lines by Sappho placed like an epitaph on the "tomb of the naked and [displaced]" (20), denote an act of resurrecting the "dead dust" from memories: from the mere smear of signs are born "living words" that are "more naked than flesh, stronger than bone, more resilient than sinew, sensitive than nerve." Recording of the past, thus, begins with the birth pang of words, which resemble "bared noise, groan, bits torn from words" (3). Moreover,

> it [speech] murmurs inside. . . . Inside is the pain of speech the pain to say. Larger still. Greater than is the pain not to say. To not say. . . . It festers inside. The wound, liquid, dust. Must break. Must void. (3)

This symbolic act of releasing the speech/words imprisoned within a cold, silent marble is superimposed with the images of Holy Communion, evoking a mystic religious experience (13).

The tragic history of Korea is recollected in a pensive and melancholic prelude to her destiny as well as to the plight of the displaced:

> *From A Far* / What Nationality / or what kindred and relation
> what blood relation / what blood ties of blood / what ancestry /
> what race generation / what house clan tribe stock strain
> what lineage extraction
> what breed sect gender denomination caste
> *what stray ejection misplaced*
> *Tertium Quid neither one thing nor the other*
> *Tombe des nues de naturalized*
> what *transplant to dispel upon.* (20, italics mine)

On the abortive revolution of March 1, 1919, and the martyrdom of a young revolutionary, Yu Kwan Soon, Cha concludes with the following lines: "The decapitated forms. . . . The present form face to face reveals the missing, the absent. Would-be-said remnant, memory. But the remnant is the whole. The memory is entire. The longing in the face of the lost" (38). Cha continues to "re-member" by retelling her mother's story as told to her. The painful memory of the time when her mother and all Koreans became "tongueless" and nameless, when her mother was forced to denounce her mother tongue and even to change her name, blends into the Catholic Mass.

The tragic strain of one nation dissolves into the chorus of humanity carried by the "ebb and tide of echo" (47) toward the "Antiphonal hymn" (46).

Memories of Korea's liberation from Japan in 1945 and those of the Korean War of 1950 fuse and blend together beyond historical time as if Korea's destiny "is fixed on the perpetual motion of search. Fixed in its perpetual exile" (81). This "perpetual motion of search" manifests itself in the section "Erato" (love poetry), where human love and marriage are juxtaposed with the heavenly love represented by Christ as the Bridegroom. Though "only through a glass darkly," this dusky shadow of the Divine Love in and through human love (erato) is all that our darkened vision can "see" here and now, yet it is not without an intimation of the miracle of transubstantiation. Erato's song ascends and blends into the ecstasy of the heavenly song of martyrdom (117).

However, this vision of flight from time and space is not long sustained, and it inevitably returns "to the very memory" (131) of the past in time, whose "stain attaches itself and darkens on the pale formless sheet, a hole increasing its size larger and larger until it assimilates the boundaries and becomes itself formless. All memory. Occupies the entire" (131). To restore memory, one must return to this formlessness; hence the following invocation: "Let the one who is mother Restore memory . . . one who is daughter restore spring with her each appearance from beneath the earth" (133). The mythic figures of Demeter, Persephone, and Pluto are suggested here. The timeless myth finds its counterparts in time through the figures of the Mother, the Daughter, and the Limbo of Memory. The returning emergence of Persephone ushering in the spring of "re-membering" and the rebirth of nature become analogous to the dictée/daughter's act of recording the past through the words, restoring words which had been mere signs and "dead words" "buried in Time's memory" (133) "from beneath the earth."

This rebirth in the eternal cycle of birth/death heralds the celebration and affirmation of life in and through the creative act: "She says to herself if she were able to write she could continue to live. Says to herself if she would write without ceasing. To herself if by writing she could abolish real time. She would live. If she could display it before her and become its voyeur" (141). To write (create through re-membering), then, is to live; to live, to write. In the time-bound reality where there is "only the onslaught of time" (140) obliterating the future, memory and past are all and "entire" (131), a continuum along infinitesimal points of time. Recording what has been re-membered out of the dismembered past becomes a monument chiseled from the stone of oblivion, a monument to the "simulated pasts resurrected in memoriam" (150).

The child exhausted and burdened with the "dead words" of the past is restored and healed by the water given by a woman who drew it from the fountain, so that she can continue her journey toward the flickering "small candle" (170) in spite of the "entering dusk" (170). This vision is followed by an image of a child imploring her mother: "Lift me up mom to the window" (179). To be able to see the vista of the future as well as the present through the window of time, Cha, like the child, has to be lifted up by the arms of her mother who links her to the past, by her mother's memories, which, told to Cha, the dictée re-members.

Without the past, without the dismembered history to be re-membered, the child of the present cannot redeem future or past. In retelling as a dictée/diseuse, the child born of exile is able to speak the words. The very act of retelling and re-membering the past emancipates her from the prison of stony and immobile silence.

All three authors bear the wounds of the past. Kang's works reflect the early Korean immigrants' dreams, a quest-journey accompanied by disillusionment and despair yet not without hope that the immigrant can accept the world he chooses, in spite of the grip of nostalgia. Kim's work depicts the struggle of one Korean immigrant family in Los Angeles. It is also a realistic picture of the Korean community there, an arena for praxis where they realize or fail to realize their dreams, and where, as Lim has phrased it, they can "assay the gold."

The vision offered by Cha's work places the tragic fate of Korea within the concentric circles of human drama and in the luminous light of eternal myth as well as the mystery of religious transfiguration. *Dictée* suggests that a child born in exile with a tragic history can be redeemed only in and through the wounds of the past. Herein lies the profound paradoxical truth of the law of compensation and evaluation: out of dark tragedy, the light of Sacred Poesy; through the agony of dismemberment, the joy and ecstasy of creation through re-membering; through the "Babylonian exile," the shore of "Siloam." Amidst the landscape circumscribed by time and space, the ruins of the past inexorably loom, yet within it one "remains dismembered with the belief that magnolia blooms white even on seemingly dead branches and one must wait" (155) with hope and, Cha would add, with faith.

This intimation of the possibility of transcendence through mystical vision in no way obliterates the immanence of time or "abolish[es] real time" (141). The ruins of the past relentlessly intrude upon the present like the indelible marks chiseled on the wall of the mine in Kyushu, Japan, by a young Korean performing forced labor, a cry that, in the very beginning of the book *Dictée*, invites the reader to participate in the act of re-membering: "I want my mother; I am hungry; I want to go home" (cited in Korean and translated by Yun). In the fugue of *Dictée*, we hear this human "peal to the sky" (179) with its primordial desire and longing for "home" counterposed by the "Antiphonal hymn" that comes after "the Misere" (47).

The Korean American literature discussed in this essay illustrates the life of the displaced in the chiaroscuro of hope and despair, dream and disillusionment, the ideal and the real, life balanced between the weight of the past and that of the present. Each author offers his/her own resolution: Kang, through his effort to inaugurate a quest for his "new life"; Kim, through the children born in exile who would become pioneers in shaping their own destiny; and Cha, through her aesthetic and religious visions that enable her to transcend the tragic past, transforming it into a creative act of re-membering.

ACKNOWLEDGMENTS

Grateful acknowledgment is hereby made for permission to use extracts from the following previously published material:

Ronyoung Kim, *Clay Walls* (Sag Harbor, N.Y.: Permanent Press, 1986).

Theresa H. K. Cha, *Dictée* (Tanam Press, 1982; distributed by McPherson & Co., Kingston, N.Y.). Copyright the Estate of Theresa H. K. Cha.

Younghill Kang, *East Goes West* (New York: Charles Scribners, 1937) and *The Grass Roof* (New York: Charles Scribners, 1931). Copyright Frances Kelly Younghill.

WORKS CITED

Cha, Theresa Hak Kyung. *Dictée*. New York: Tanam Press, 1982.

Kang, Younghill. *East Goes West*. New York: Charles Scribner's Sons, 1937.

———. *The Grass Roof.* New York: Charles Scribner's Sons, 1931.

Kim, Elaine H. *Asian American Literature: An Introduction to the Writings and Their Social Context.* Philadelphia: Temple University Press, 1982.

Kim, Ronyoung. *Clay Walls.* Sag Harbor, N.Y.: The Permanent Press, 1986.

Kingston, Maxine Hong. *China Men.* New York: Alfred A. Knopf, 1980.

———. *The Woman Warrior: Memoirs of a Childhood among Ghosts.* New York: Vintage Books, 1976.

Lim, Shirley Geok-lin. "Assaying the Gold: or, Contesting the Ground of Asian American Literature." Paper presented at the Modern Language Association Convention, 1990.

5

Witnessing the Japanese Canadian Experience in World War II: Processual Structure, Symbolism, and Irony in Joy Kogawa's Obasan

Cheng Lok Chua

LIKE THAT of the United States, Canada's is a multiracial society that is predominantly Caucasian and Christian. Again like the United States, Canada is a nation of immigrants; and both have had a history of antipathy toward immigrants from Asia, a history that has perhaps not been widely witnessed in literary works or literary studies.

That such a history of anti-Asian sentiment exists is easily documented. The evidence exists not only in unofficial anti-Asian actions like ad hoc housing discrimination and spontaneous mob violence but also in official legislation to exclude Asians from rights like naturalization, voting, and employment. For instance, one of the most serious incidents of mob action against Asians in North America took place in 1907 in Vancouver when "a mob of 1,500 Canadians led by store owners and union leaders marched on and destroyed the Chinese quarter . . . and attacked the Japanese ghetto as well" (Lyman 61, also Adachi 63–85). An example of deliberate anti-Asian legislation was Canada's 1923 act excluding Chinese from immigration, an act which, in the two decades between 1925 and 1945, limited the number of Chinese allowed to immigrate to Canada to only eight (Anderson and Frideres 146–51)! Also, Canadian citizens of Asian ancestry were denied the vote until 1947 (Morton 251–52, LaViolette 295–301). And as early as 1878, the provincial legislature of British Columbia enacted the Labour Regulation Act prohibiting Asians from being employed on projects granted by provincial franchise, a regulation enacted despite requests from the Dominion government in Ottawa and the imperial office in London not to do so (Morton 61).

In recent U.S. and Canadian history, the outbreak of World War II in the Pacific stirred up the most massive organized show of resentment against one subgroup of Asians in North America, those Asians of Japanese descent. Canada preceded the United States in declaring the Pacific Coast a strategic military zone from which inhabitants of Japanese ancestry were to be removed. The United States "relocated" 120,000 Japanese Americans from its West Coast into remote "concentration camps"—a term President Roosevelt used during a 1944 press conference (Weglyn 217). Canada "removed" 23,000 British Columbians of Japanese descent, 75 percent of them Canadian citizens. More drastic than the U.S. "relocation," the Canadian removal also split up families because it shunted able-bodied males to labor and "concentration" camps (Kogawa, *Obasan* 77) six weeks before moving all families to ghost towns and abandoned mining communities in the interior (Adachi iv). Unsold property of Japanese Canadians was confiscated and auctioned off to defray the costs of the removal (Weglyn 56–57). Even after World War II ended in 1945, Canada refused to permit Japanese Canadians to return to Vancouver until four more years had elapsed; in fact, Canada attempted to deport as many of them as possible to war-ravaged Japan (Weglyn 190–91). Both the U.S. relocation and the Canadian removal were political and civilian decisions taken despite official recommendations against implementation by the Royal Canadian Mounted Police, the Canadian Army (Major-General Maurice Pope), the Canadian Navy (Vice-Admiral Raustus Reid), and a special U.S. presidential commission (the Munson Report) set up by Roosevelt to investigate the loyalty of Japanese Americans (Weglyn 51, Adachi 203). Obviously, there is no dearth of historical instances to document anti-Asian sentiment in North America.

However, the body of literature that bears witness to this history of antipathy is not large: among American writers, one thinks of the Filipino American Carlos Bulosan's *America Is in the Heart*, the Chinese American Maxine Hong Kingston's *China Men*, and two works by Japanese Americans, John Okada's *No-No Boy* and Jeanne Wakatsuki Houston and Jones Houston's *Farewell to Manzanar*. Among

Canadian writers dealing with this historical experience, Joy Kogawa's *Obasan* stands head and shoulders above all others (Chan 67).[1]

Indeed, *Obasan* is a deeply moving, highly crafted lyrical and meditative account of a Japanese Canadian family's experience of anti-Japanese racism and hysteria in Canada during World War II. The events are seen through the narrative viewpoint of a young Japanese Canadian girl who watches her secure and happy family disintegrate as it undergoes the removal decreed by the Canadian government. But it has not been sufficiently noted that Kogawa employs a subtle irony to tell her story, an irony apparent in the form and the symbolism of the novel. Thus, although the historical experience depicted in *Obasan* is one of disintegration and dislocation, the novel's form parallels the three-stage "processual structure" noted by anthropologists like Victor Turner and Arnold van Gennep in their studies of ritual migration, a ritual that often transforms a society's victim into a hero. For Turner (*Ritual* 94ff.), three phases mark this ritual processual structure: (1) *separation* from a position of security in a highly structured society; (2) *liminality* or *marginality* in a death-like state where one is stripped of "status, property, rank" and accepts "arbitrary punishment without complaint" (*Ritual* 95); and (3) *aggregation* or reintegration into society but ironically with a heightened status ("sacredness") gained during the liminal stage (*Ritual* 96). The irony of this process as it occurs in *Obasan* is reinforced by the way Kogawa uses subtly recurrent leitmotifs drawn from Christian rituals and symbols; these symbols she has "displaced" into an ironic narrative mode (to use Northrop Frye's terminology—136ff.), and this technique in turn puts an ironic question to the Christian ethic professed by Canada's majority culture.

The form of Joy Kogawa's *Obasan* parallels remarkably Victor Turner's analysis of the migratory processual structure. Through a complex series of flashbacks, the first eleven chapters of the novel situate the young protagonist Naomi Nakane in a close-knit, securely placed Japanese Canadian family within the structured society of Vancouver. On her paternal side, the Nakanes are substantial shipbuilders and salmon fishermen, traditional Japanese Canadian occupations (Young et al. 43). On the maternal side, Grandfather Kato is a Cadillac-owning doctor. Both branches of the family are Christians, and both of Naomi's parents are Canadian-born citizens. Kogawa places a special emphasis on the family's unity: "The Nakanes and the Katos were intimate to the point of stickiness, like mochi. . . . My [Naomi's] parents, like two needles, knit the families carefully into one blanket, . . . till the fibre of our lives became an impenetrable mesh" (20).

Chapters 12–32 chronicle the separation and the family's fall into liminality and marginal serfdom after Pearl Harbor. Naomi's family is dislodged from their structural social niche and "removed" from Vancouver. The tightly knit family is torn by the government's separation of them into first-generation isseis and second-generation niseis, into the men for work on road gangs and the women, children, and elderly for exile in ghost towns, and even by the fact that Naomi's mother is trapped in Japan where she had gone to visit her ailing grandmother. Separated from father and mother, Naomi and her brother Stephen must follow their aunt Aya Obasan to the ghost town of Slocan. In Turner's description, liminality resembles "being in a tunnel, a place of hidden, mysterious darkness" (*Dramas* 231) where one undergoes an experience "likened to death, . . . to the wilderness" (*Ritual* 95). The imagery describing Naomi's removal from Vancouver is reminiscent of Turner's description: "I sit . . . within the darkness. . . . Behind us lie our drowning specks of memory. . . . We are going down to the middle of the earth, . . . into the waiting wilderness" (Kogawa 111). And in this wilderness Naomi will witness death and near death by the elemental forces of fire and flood: the death and cremation of Grandmother Nakane (chap. 18) and her own near drowning (chap. 21). Furthermore, during their decade of liminality, the family also suffers the death of Naomi's father. Naomi's family, therefore, falls from a settled place in a structured society and becomes, in Turner's words "temporally liminal and spatially marginal, . . . stripped of status . . . i.e., removed from social structure" (*Dramas* 258).

Turner also observes, however, that the unstructured, status-free condition of liminality is also conducive to the formation of a *communitas* (*Ritual* 96–97) built on relationships resembling Martin Buber's "I-Thou" (*Ritual* 127). And, from their liminal experience in Slocan, Naomi and her brother Stephen do indeed form a *communitas* with the surrogate family of their paternal uncle Isamu and his wife, the "Obasan" of the book's title. This *communitas* nurtures Naomi and Stephen as they develop toward a final integration with society and with self (chaps. 33–39). Stephen achieves reintegration with structured society, if not with self, when he becomes an internationally acclaimed concert pianist; but Stephen's experience as a victim of Canadian racism leaves him uneasy with his own ethnic identity: "He is always uncomfortable when something is 'too Japanese'" (217).[2] As if to contrast with this, Naomi's place in her society is less eminent than her celebrated brother's: she is a rather diffident and alienated spinster schoolteacher; but Naomi achieves a more fundamental integration than Stephen's when she breaks through the personal and cultural screens of silence and secretiveness that have enshrouded her individual, familial, and ethnic past and reintegrates herself with her history through the recuperation of that past. This breakthrough leads her to a perception of the symbols that illuminate and close her narrative, for by breaking through silence into knowledge, Naomi gains a vision of human oneness with universal nature that surpasses societal categories. As Turner has observed, not only is *communitas* a feature of liminality but "secular powerlessness may [also] be compensated by . . . a reception of sacred knowledge. In this no-place and no-time that resists classification, the . . . categories of the culture emerge within the integuments of myth, symbol, and ritual" (*Dramas* 258).

At this point, it is apposite to examine the mythic and symbolic qualities of *Obasan*'s narrative texture. Much of *Obasan* consists of Naomi's meditative recuperation of her experience of marginality during World War II. And into the texture of Naomi's narrative, Kogawa has woven recurrent leitmotifs, some of the most powerful of which derive from Christian rituals and symbols, specifically Easter, Nebuchadnezzar's fire, Eucharist, and stones into bread; these Christian motifs Kogawa has "displaced" (Frye 136ff.) into an ironic narrative mode that makes for a critique of the professed ethics of her structuring majority culture. (In discussion, Kogawa said that she was brought up as a Christian, her father being a pastor and a model for the Reverend Nakayama of *Obasan*; Kogawa also habitually reads a randomly chosen biblical text every morning [Kogawa, tape recording].)

One of the most effective of these Christian symbols is the hoard of toy Easter chicks (67) which Naomi has saved from a previous year's Easter basket. They are intended to be a welcome-back present for her mother when she returns from visiting her dying grandmother in Japan and when she resumes her life in Canada with the new generation. These Christian symbols of new life become ironic because Naomi's Canadian-born mother never does return. Instead, she suffers the horrors of radiation sickness after the bombing of Nagasaki and then is prevented by Canadian authorities from returning to her native land because she has adopted an orphaned niece, also a radiation victim. This ironic reversal negating the hope and rebirth symbolized by these Easter chicks is further heightened by a childhood incident during which Naomi innocently puts some newly bought live Easter chicks into the compound of a mother hen in the belief that the hen would nurture the life of the chicks. Contrary to Naomi's naive expectations, however, the mother hen pecks at the chicks and kills them (58); Kogawa's ironic comment upon the treatment of Japanese by Caucasian Canadians in their own homeland is clear when one notices that the chicks are yellow and the mother hen is white (58).[3]

Kogawa extends this symbol that ought to mean life but that has been ironically displaced into a symbol of death when she imagistically suggests a further breakdown in community relationships in Naomi's nightmares; during her ghost-town years, Naomi is haunted and repulsed by the recollection of an incident in which Japanese boys performed a ritualized killing of a white chicken (154–58). This is certainly a frightening image of hate and reprisal taking precedence over what ought to be love and rebirth in social relationships and rituals.[4]

A more ambiguous Christian symbol is the elemental one of fire, a force that can refine as well as destroy. In the earlier sections of the book, the positive qualities of fire are emphasized, chiefly through the interfusion of Christian allusions with Japanese contexts. Hence, heat is cleansing and bearable in the context of a Japanese hot bath which the child Naomi shares with her Grandmother Kato. To be sure, the bath is described as "a liquid furnace," but one which Grandma is "approving and enjoying"; if the heat is a "torture," it is also "sweet" (48). And even as Naomi undergoes this searing experience, she thinks of the Old Testament miracle of Abednego: "I go into the midst of the flames, obedient as Abednego, for lo, Grandma is an angel of the Lord and stands before me in the midst of fire and has no hurt" (48). Here, fire is an affirming element where faith is tested and rewarded by security and surrounded by love.

In contrast to this affirmation, the full destructiveness of fire is described in the closing chapters of the novel. This description is contained in a letter from Grandma Kato about her daughter, Naomi's mother; both women had gone to Japan to visit Naomi's sick great grandmother in 1941 and had been stranded there after the outbreak of war. The two women happen to be in Nagasaki in August 1945 when it is bombed by the United States and the world enters the age of nuclear warfare. The destructiveness of the fire storm in Nagasaki is of apocalyptic proportions: "An intolerable heat, blood, a mountain of debris. . . . Almost all the buildings were flattened or in flames as far as she [Grandmother Kato] could see. The landmarks were gone. Tall columns of fire rose through the haze and everywhere the dying and the wounded crawled, fled, stumbled like ghosts among the ruins" (237). In the chaos, Naomi's mother and her grandmother are separated, but one evening the grandmother "sat down beside a naked woman she'd seen earlier who was aimlessly chipping wood to make a pyre on which to cremate a dead baby. The woman was utterly disfigured. Her nose and one cheek was almost gone. Great wounds and pustules covered her entire face and body. She was completely bald. She sat in a cloud of flies and maggots wriggled among her wounds. As Grandma watched, the woman gave her a vacant gaze, then let out a cry. It was my mother" (239). In this instance, fire is hardly an element that affirms divine salvation; instead it has been ironically displaced into an element that confirms human destructiveness.

A third, and perhaps the most intricate, symbolic leitmotif of the novel clusters around the Christian ritual of communion. This leitmotif, which is pervasively embedded in the novel's narrative texture, also clarifies the novel's processual structure and is the defining metaphor of the liminal stage where liminality can, as Turner tells us, lead to illumination, where "secular powerlessness may be compensated by . . . a reception of sacred knowledge" (*Dramas* 258). Two chief images, bread and stone, paradoxically constitute this symbolic leitmotif.

The image of bread is associated with Naomi's recently dead Uncle Isamu, the husband of her Obasan. Isamu, scion of a shipbuilding, shipowning family, is forcibly estranged from his accustomed means of earning his daily bread when he is exiled to the prairie. This denial of material bread, signifying Isamu's and his people's secular powerlessness, is accentuated by a parallel denial of spiritual bread. For Isamu, a lifelong Christian, is also denied the communal bread by a Caucasian clergyman after Pearl Harbor (38). The "removal" thus deprives Isamu of his daily bread and symbolically excludes him from his spiritual sustenance. This Eucharist motif is repeated with an ironic variation later in the novel when a Japanese clergyman presides over a farewell communion service just before the Canadian government imposes a second dispersal order after World War II; as the host is served, Reverend Nakayama intones the words: "In the same night that He was betrayed He took Bread" (177).

To the sea-loving Isamu, the time of his exile on the prairie is tantamount to the Israelites' sojourn in the Sinai desert or Jesus' forty days in the wilderness. (In fact, Kogawa had used the image of "wilderness" to describe the removal of the Nakanes—111.) But in the desert the Israelites found manna to sustain their physical selves, while in the wilderness Jesus sustained himself spiritually with the word of God. In a subtle symbolic displacement and fusion, Kogawa tells us that Isamu begins to learn how to bake bread during his forced exile in his desert, a bread so hard that his family jokingly calls it "stone bread" (12). But Isamu's bread is also so delicious ("oishi desu ne") that he becomes famous for distributing and sharing it throughout his community. Significantly, it is this bread that Naomi snacks on throughout Isamu's wake, which occupies about nine-tenths of the novel's actual time, and it is during this time that Naomi recuperates and communes with her memories that flesh out her narrative. Indeed the oxymoronic "stone bread" is an apt symbol for the hardships endured by Japanese Canadians, hardships out of which they must miraculously make something life sustaining and out of which Kogawa has equally miraculously wrought a work of art to sustain the spirit. As Kogawa's biblical epigraph states: "To him that overcometh will I give to eat of the hidden manna and will give him a white stone and in the stone a new name written."

In Kogawa's novel, however, stone is not only a metaphor for hardship endured but also a trope for the attitude of stoical, unspeaking silence adopted by the Japanese Canadians (and Naomi) toward their victimization. Aya Obasan personifies this since she "lives in stone; Obasan's language remains deep underground" (32). Such stony silence, especially in the older generation of isseis like Obasan, comes from a kind of power (14) of self-denial and a strength of love for the younger generation, which needs to be protected from the unspeakable horrors ("Kodomo no tame"—21). This protective silence, however, can stunt the younger generation. Thus Naomi has grown up as a clinging (64), secretive child who is silent about her sexual abuse by a white neighbour (64–65) and whose nickname had been Nomi, a homophone for "no me," no self. Even as an adult,

Naomi's thoughts are "self-denigrating" (7) and "crone-prone" (8). Paradoxically, then, and contrary to the ethic of strength in silence, the younger generation, in order to come into its own, must break the protective but petrifying silence and tell the unspeakable truths; that is why Naomi's activist Aunt Emily urges her to confront her history, saying that "the past is the future" (42) and insisting, "You are your history. If you cut any of it off you're an amputee. Don't deny the past. Remember everything. . . . Denial is gangrene!" (49–50). Hence Naomi's remembering and narrating of her history become the frame as well as the essence of the novel's action: Naomi's confrontation of her past, her voicing of her history, exorcises a personal and ethnic amnesia, thereby allowing her to integrate herself into a stronger, firmer, and more holistic personality cleansed of shame and free of repression.

On the level of symbolic imagery, we note that the mnemonic catalyst for Naomi's recuperation of history and integration of self is the bundle of documents and letters Aunt Emily supplies her; this bundle is imagistically described as a "parcel . . . as heavy as a loaf of Uncle's stone bread" (31). This parcel of history, composed of stone-hard facts, brings Naomi to the heart-chilling recognition of her motherland's abuse of her own people, the suffering and dismantling of her family. But implicit in these hard facts is also the manna of a spiritual sustenance that affirms the toughness and durability of her people and of herself, who have survived and grown beyond their desert experience in their unpromising native land.

Hence Kogawa's *Obasan* draws toward a close on Naomi's vision of a holistic image embracing humanity and nature. It is an image of beauty wrought by the word miracle of imagery and trope that creates a union of contraries: "Above the trees, the moon is a pure white stone. The reflection is rippling in the river—water and stone dancing. It's a quiet ballet, soundless as breath" (247). The first sentence of this passage is an image reminding us of the miraculous and the paradoxical that is a matter of course in nature: it posits a stone (the moon), freed from gravity, floating lighter than air, higher than the trees. The white moon and the dark sky also form a contrastive image and pose another miracle-paradox, that of an object which sheds light without producing any. The succeeding imagistic contraries further reinforce this effect. For instance, the still moon is imagistically made to ripple by the reflecting water; and through personification, the hardness of stone and the yielding of water paradoxically join in a dance. And the dance trope is elaborated in the final paradoxical image, which joins the silence of death with the vitality of breath in a metaphorical ballet.

This image near the end of the novel brings the reader full circle to the book's beginning, where its epigraph, from the Book of Revelation 2:17, had promised that stones could yield a manna and confirm a new identity. And indeed through Kogawa's book, through Naomi's speaking her story, Kogawa transubstantiates the stony silence of the Japanese Canadians' victimization into a speaking manna-bread of communication. This communication, in turn, has drawn her readers through the miracle of the word into a communion with her people's historical and spiritual experience. In this way, the novel has moved its protagonists and its readers from separation, through liminality, toward aggregation.[5]

NOTES

1. Reviewers greeted Joy Kogawa's novel *Obasan* with acclaim when it appeared in 1981 in North America. For instance, Edith Milton, writing in the *New York Times Book Review*, called it "a tour de force, a deeply felt novel, brilliantly poetic in its sensibility" (17). And in Canada, *Obasan* met with a chorus of praise typical of which is Suanne Kelman's review in *Canadian Forum* lauding its "finely honed craft . . . the language alone is almost a sufficient reward . . . [and] makes the novel into an extended poem" (39). The novel went on to win the Canadian Authors Association Award, the American Book Award off the Before Columbus Foundation, a Books in Canada Award, and an American Library Association commendation (Bruchac 111).

Since these early reviews and accolades, Kogawa's novel has consolidated its literary reputation by attracting the scrutiny of an increasing number of scholars and literary historians. For instance, B. A. St. Andrews has hailed Kogawa as "chief among the . . . new voices in the Canadian literary renaissance" (29–30). Gayle Fujita reads *Obasan* as "a stunning first novel" (33), comparable to James' *Portrait of a Lady* or Silko's *Ceremony* and analyzes the artistry with which it "narrates a story of personal apocalypse" (39). Erika Gottlieb ponders in minute detail the novel's "multi-layered texture of . . . narrative" (34) and sees it taking the pattern of three concentric circles woven, like a spider's web, by the shuttling of characters through time (51). Gary Willis focuses on the theme of silence and speech in the novel, seeing them represented in the contrasting characters of Obasan and Emily (241–43), Old Man Gower and Rough Lock Bill (246–49). Touching also on the theme of speech and silence, Shirley Geok-Lin Lim illuminates *Obasan* with an extensive analysis of the "mother-daughter relationship" (294) and demonstrates convincingly that "the daughter's quest/ion for the lost mother is also the political quest/ion that the novel explores" (308). Marilyn Russell Rose terms the Japanese Canadians' relocation experience a "sociopathic rape" (222) and compares the silence of the Japanese Canadian victims to that of rape victims (222–24); she also considers *Obasan* a "remarkably sophisticated" (216) example of narrative rhetoric that "attempts to enact historical experience" (218) through "a journey which takes the form of a descent into [three] ever-deepening circles of hell" (220)—"uncertainty" (220), "hardship" (221), and "exile" (221).

2. In the sequel to *Obasan*, Stephen's denial of his roots even makes him neglect to visit Obasan when she asks for him on her deathbed, and this arouses Naomi's bitterness and ire against him: "It's Stephen from whom I have most learned how not to be. . . . Anger. I began to want him to know the hurt" (Kogawa, "Excerpt from a Sequel to *Obasan*" 122–23).

3. In a penetrating discussion of Kogawa's language, Shirley Geok-Lin Lim also concludes that "*Obasan* carries a bitter critique of Christian discourse. The images offered in the use of biblical language are contextually 'ironized' and depleted of their significance" (304).

4. Willis generalizes the symbolism of the chicks to include the idea "that in all animals there exists, alongside an impulse to nurture, an opposite impulse, to destroy" (244).

5. This essay is a revised version of a paper presented at the conference of the Association for Commonwealth Literature and Language Studies held in Singapore, 1986; the conference theme was The Writer as Historical Witness.

WORKS CITED

Adachi, Ken. *The Enemy That Never Was: A History of the Japanese Canadians*. Toronto: McClelland and Stewart, 1976.

Anderson, Alan B., and James S. Frideres. *Ethnicity in Canada*. Toronto: University of Toronto Press, 1981.

Bruchac, Joseph, ed. *Breaking Silence: An Anthology of Contemporary Asian American Poets*. Greenfield Center, N.Y.: Greenfield Review Press, 1983.

Bulosan, Carlos. *America Is in the Heart*. 1943. Seattle: University of Washington Press, 1973.

Chan, Anthony B. "Born Again Asian: The Making of a New Literature." *Journal of Ethnic Studies* 11.4 (1984): 57–73.

Frye, Northrop. *Anatomy of Criticism*. Princeton: Princeton University Press, 1957.

Fujita, Gayle K. "'To attend the sound of stone': The Sensibility of Silence in *Obasan*." *MELUS* 12.3 (1985): 33–42.
Gottlieb, Erika. "The Riddle of Concentric Worlds in 'Obasan.'" *Canadian Literature* 109 (1986): 34–53.
Houston, Jeanne Wakatsuki, and James D. Houston. *Farewell to Manzanar*. New York: Bantam, 1974.
Kelman, Suanne. "Impossible to Forgive." *Canadian Forum*, February 1982, p. 39.
Kingston, Maxine Hong. *China Men*. New York: Knopf, 1980.
Kogawa, Joy. "Excerpt from a Sequel to *Obasan*: Chapters Nine and Ten." *Seattle Review* 11.1 (1988): 115–25.
———. *Obasan*. Boston: David R. Godine, 1982.
———. Tape recorded class discussion with Joy Kogawa, in C. L. Chua's course, Asian American Studies 146: Asian American Experience in Literature, at University of California, Santa Barbara, 22 May 1986.
LaViolette, Forest E. *The Canadian Japanese and World War II*. Toronto: University of Toronto Press, 1948.
Lim, Shirley Geok-Lin. "Japanese American Women's Life Stories: Maternity in Monica Sone's *Nisei Daughter* and Joy Kogawa's *Obasan*." *Feminist Studies* 16.2 (1990): 289–311.
Lyman, Stanford M. *Chinese Americans*. New York: Random, 1974.
Milton, Edith. "Unnecessary Precautions." *New York Times Book Review*, 5 September 1982, 17.
Morton, James. *In The Sea of the Sterile Mountains: The Chinese in British Columbia*. Vancouver: J. J. Douglas, 1974.
Okada, John. *No-No Boy*. 1957. Seattle: University of Washington Press, 1977.
Rose, Marilyn Russell. "Politics into Art: Kogawa's *Obasan* and the Rhetoric of Fiction." *Mosaic: A Journal for the Interdisciplinary Study of Literature* 21.3 (1988): 215–26.
St. Andrews, B. A. "Reclaiming a Canadian Heritage: Kogawa's *Obasan*." *International Fiction Review* 1311 (1986): 29–31.
Turner, Victor. *Dramas, Fields, and Metaphors*. Cornell University Press: Ithaca and London, 1974.
———. *The Ritual Process*. Chicago: Aldine, 1969.
Van Gennep, Arnold. *The Rites of Passage*. Trans. Monila Vizedon and Gabrielle L. Caffee. Chicago: University of Chicago Press, 1960.
Weglyn, Michi. *Years of Infamy: The Untold Story of America's Concentration Camps*. New York: Morrow, 1976.
Willis, Gary. "Speaking the Silence: Joy Kogawa's *Obasan*." *Studies in Canadian Literature* 12.2 (1987): 239–49.
Young, Charles H., Helen R. Y. Reid, and W. A. Carrothers. *The Japanese Canadians*. 1938. Toronto: University of Toronto Press, 1978.

PART II

Race and Gender

6

Ethnicizing Gender: An Exploration of Sexuality as Sign in Chinese Immigrant Literature

Sau-ling Cynthia Wong

THIS ESSAY postulates a concept, the ethnicizing of gender, to account in semiotic terms for representations of sexuality in Chinese immigrant literature produced since the 1960s[1]—representations that offer intriguing contrasts to those found in the works of American-born, Anglophone Chinese writers of roughly the same period. This inquiry is prompted by the observation that, in many works about immigrant life by both male and female writers from Taiwan and Hong Kong, what appear to be merely self-contemptuous or insensitive gender stereotypes reveal, upon closer scrutiny, an intricate signifying practice at work. An examination of this practice, which I name the ethnicizing of gender, raises potentially far-reaching questions about the comparative study of Chinese American literature by foreign- and American-born writers, about reading strategies appropriate to each corpus of works, and ultimately about the nature of the gender-ethnicity nexus in Chinese (and possibly other Asian) American literature.

The ethnicizing of gender may be thought of as the mirror image of the gendering of ethnicity, familiar to people of color in the United States, whereby white ideology assigns selected gender characteristics to various ethnic Others to create a coherent, depoliticized, and thus putatively self-explanatory mythic account of American social institutions and operations. The stereotypes of the black stud, abnormally libidinous and driven by aggressive sexual appetites, and the black mammy, masculinized in her strength and stripped of sexual allure, are two of the best-known illustrations of this process. Such images, superficially descriptive of gender-specific behavior, serve to maintain power relationships by justifying them in terms of biological nature. In the plantation economy, for instance, slave women had to be given a nonthreatening ideological representation, because their close proximity meant sexual competition to the white mistress. After Emancipation, blacks began to be portrayed as unleashed savages, a social menace instead of an economic asset; belief in the exaggerated and dangerous virility of black males legitimized racial violence against them (as it has indeed continued to do so to this day, albeit in a more urbanized context) (Christian 2; Riggs).

For Asian Americans, of course, the effeminization (which is also to say emasculation) of the Asian man and the ultrafeminization of the Asian woman have long been a source of deep outrage to the community. The skewing of Asian Americans of both sexes toward the female side is an index of the entire group's marginalization and its function as the "good natives" in American cultural myth (Chin and Chan; Kim 18–22). In response to this skewing, Asian American writers have engaged in a wide range of rehabilitative projects in cultural politics to defend Asian American manhood and womanhood (e.g., Chin et al. xv; Kim 173–213; Tajima; Ling). As critics of the Model Minority myth have pointed out, Asian Americans began to be designated the "good natives" only during the racial turmoil of the 1960s, when an ideological weapon to counter minority demands for social justice was needed (Osajima; Yun). The gendering of ethnicity has likewise fluctuated throughout history: Chinese women, for example, used to be considered by white men as repulsive, totally devoid of feminine charms (Yung 17), whereas post-1960s Asian women are frequently fetishized as the embodiment of perfect womanhood (Ling 11; Walsh). Deconstructive analyses of the intersection of gender and ethnicity, such as those undertaken by recent Asian American commentators on David Henry Hwang's controversial play *M. Butterfly* (Alquizola; Pao), have made it clear that the gendering of ethnicity is a historically situated and ideologically motivated process of great complexity.

It seems conceptually plausible that an opposite process of signification—the ethnicizing of gender, or the attribution of allegedly natural ethnic essences such as "Chineseness" or "Americanness" to "masculine" and "feminine" behavior—exists. Such a conjecture is confirmed when we study Chinese immigrant literature, which, being a product of obvious geographical and cultural disruptions, is particularly apt to uncover the constructedness of both gender and ethnicity. When we cross cultural boundaries, the provisionality of previously naturalized, smoothly functioning categories becomes suddenly visible. Further, as the immigrant characters are shown groping for symbolic means to encode, enact, and eventually come to terms with the conflicts generated by relocation, we will be able to note the coalescence of new configurations between gender and ethnicity.

In such a semiotic inquiry, an especially useful focus of attention is sexuality, whose multivalence renders it a potent sign in the immigrant's restless negotiations and renegotiations of meaning. As Snitow, Stansell, and Thompson note in their introduction to *Powers of Desire: The Politics of Sexuality*, sex is "a central form of expression, one that defines identity and is seen as a primary source of energy and pleasure" (9). Though it is common to think of sex as natural force devoid of social meaning, the truth is that even such feelings about sex are "social and socially constructed. There is no escaping it: sex as refuge, or sex as sacrament, or sex as wild, natural, dark and instinctual expression—all these are *ideas* about sex" (11). In Chinese immigrant writing, which by its very nature depicts multiple cultural contexts, the meaning of sexuality is rich and fluid. At once irreducibly private, intensely communicative, and fraught with public implications, sexuality is invoked and endlessly modulated by writers to enact a number of conflicts between private tendencies and social influences—conflicts not peculiar to immigrants but certainly exacerbated by their precarious economic and cultural situation. If any single "idea" about sexuality emerges as central in these fictional couplings and uncouplings, it is that heterosexual fulfillment free of demeaning compromises signals an idealized state of fullness of being—ethnic dignity without practical failure, power without callousness, self-actualization without social irresponsibility—which seems to be the endpoint of the immigrant's recentering efforts.

The concept of the ethnicizing of gender may be explored through a reading of three works of immigrant fiction in Chinese.[2] In all of these, sexuality is represented as far more than a physical fact; rather, it constitutes one of the primary terms through which one's ethnic identity is understood, experienced, and structured. Away from an ethnically homogeneous setting, bewildering new existential and social experiences call for strategies of signification that encompass a hitherto elided category: ethnicity. Gender roles, invested with strong emotions concerning what is "naturally fitting," become a convenient locus for testing out and codifying cultural meaning. Thus the characters' actions, depicted along a spectrum of gender appropriateness, are assigned varying shades of "Chineseness" or "Americanness" to indicate the extent of their at-homeness in the adopted land.

A short story by Yi Li, a woman writer from Hong Kong, entitled "A Date at Age Twenty-eight," serves as an excellent introduction to the concept outlined above, since it contains representations of male sexuality that defy a one-dimensional reading. This story is typical of Chinese immigrant literature since the 1960s in that it exemplifies many situations canonical of the genre. Huang Zhixian, a degree-obsessed physics graduate student from Hong Kong, is faced with the expiration of his student visa and reluctantly decides to court a distant cousin who immigrated years earlier, hoping to engineer a "green card marriage." The story unfolds through descriptions of his preparations for his first date, with flashbacks filling the reader in on his background; it culminates in an apprehension-filled confrontation with cousin Meili, who is at best mildly curious about the entire affair.

The author's descriptions of Huang Zhixian appear to agree perfectly with white stereotypes of Chinese Americans as bespectacled, sexless nerds. In one flashback scene, Huang attends a Christmas party which turns into an orgy; a coed described as "large" approaches him, and he flees in terror. In another, Huang is caught in a skinny-dipping session and has no choice but to strip.

> But when he saw his classmates' bodies—the men with thick, hairy chests, the women with full breasts and hips—he felt inferior. He was cold; he shivered; he was afraid that that well-built redhead would advance on him and claim him. Timidly he backed away and hid. . . . When he got home he came down with a cold and was laid up for a week; for a while he became the laughingstock of his friends. (31)

This seems to be desexing with a vengeance. If the source of this quotation were unknown, one might suspect stereotyping of the most vicious sort. However, since it comes from the pen of a "politically correct" writer like Yi Li (whose favorite subject matter is the life of struggling but undaunted working-class immigrants), such an interpretation would be highly problematic—unless, of course, one also posits an all-eroding American cultural imperialism and an overdose of unconscious self-contempt on Yi Li's part, both of which are strongly contradicted by the story's unabashedly wholesome tenor.

While the influence of the gendering of ethnicity cannot be underestimated—even fairly new immigrants may readily internalize white images of Asian men and women—positing the ethnicizing of gender allows one to see richer dimensions of meaning in the tale of Huang's sexual inadequacy. The skinny-dipping scene does not occur in isolation but functions in an intricate network of signs. It echoes a simile occurring later in the story: Huang "felt like a track star who found himself in water, unable to use his skills to advantage" (33). Huang's underdeveloped sexuality—his sunken chest and gangly limbs, his prolonged celibacy, his phobia of sexually confident women—thus symbolizes the diminishment of self brought on by the disruptions of immigration. Thus the author has chosen to produce the meaning of the immigrant experience in sexual terms. The basis for this reading is the fact that in the story, the Huang Zhixian before immigration, though also inept at sports (24), has been able to assert his sense of "masculine" control and competence by excelling in academics (27–28) and acting in a responsible, quasi-parental manner toward younger relatives (20). Huang's relatively intact sense of manhood in Hong Kong is in keeping with the traditional Confucian emphasis on scholarship as the path to fame, fortune, and family honor (officialdom having been reserved for men, such success is automatically deemed "masculine"), as well as with the values of unquestioning industry encouraged by the competitive British colonial educational system.[3]

For Huang, as for many immigrants, preimmigration life is prelapsarian life. Living among Chinese, one need not be aware of one's ethnicity; living in multiethnic, white-dominated America, one cannot avoid being aware of one's ethnicity. The state of innocence preceding immigration is identified with the security of adolescent psychosexuality, when questions of choosing a sexual partner need not arise or, even if they do arise, are channeled by reassuringly familiar cultural ideals of manhood and womanhood. Neither gender nor ethnicity has impinged upon Huang's conscious map of the world before immigration. Immigration, however, precipitates a spiritual crisis that is epitomized by the vexatious "green card" issue and calls for a comprehensible model of how and why things go wrong. The ethnicizing of gender offers a means to make sense of the troubling, "unnatural" events confronted by the struggling immigrant.

The three women in Huang's life—his mother, his fantasy childhood sweetheart Zhou Yuxia, and his cousin Meili—set up the terms in which Huang understands his life as a reluctant immigrant. All the attributes that used to define a solid, trustworthy, admirable man in Hong Kong society—industry, scholastic achievement, seriousness of purpose, reticence, attachment to family—suffer a severe and irreversible devaluation in a new environment, symbolized by the death of Huang's nurturing mother. Irrevocably lost, too, are Huang's fantasies of an unthreatening, because culturally sanctioned, sexual union. (Zhou Yuxia is described as a child bride, graced with the hallmarks of classical Chinese feminine beauty: "small, straight nose," "delicate mouth," "pointed chin," "long, soft hair," and a body small enough for an unathletic man like Huang to scoop up on the wedding night [31]). Meili, whom Huang must court for survival, is portrayed as being in the same category as the aggressive American females at the orgy and on the beach, almost in betrayal of her Chinese biological origin. Unlike Huang, Meili has grown accustomed to the cold weather in America; for the date, she wears a white tennis outfit that shows off her "dark skin" and "powerful muscles," and she stands beside a "fiery-red" sports car that she has bought with her own money (33). The car not only signifies the material comfort, power, mobility, and independence that an assimilated life can bring but connotes overt libidinal gratification. To Huang, the "Americanized" Meili, who as a little girl used to follow him around like a younger sister (potentially another child bride?), is now like "an experienced [namely, sexually experienced] foreign girl." Intimidated, he stands transfixed in the parking lot, unable to approach her.

The reverses suffered by Huang as a struggling immigrant are translated into a sex-role reversal involving unequally Americanized partners. A series of equivalencies has been tacitly established to make this translation possible. First of all, in both Chinese and Western tradition, the ability to cope has been absorbed into the concept of masculinity, in keeping with the hierarchical ordering of artificially opposed binary terms that makes patriarchy possible. In feeling overwhelmed by the demands of his new environment, therefore, Huang feels his masculinity challenged. Moreover, in the United States, where racial stratification is made possible by, again, a hierarchical ordering of paired terms, the ability to cope has been appropriated by the white majority. Peoples of color are relegated to positions of servitude, their alleged retarded development given as justification for the arrangement. Thus to be less Americanized is to be less masculine. By the same logic, the American or Americanized women in the story are assigned a greater than usual share of "can do" aggressiveness as well as rank, almost shameless, sexuality, both of which are identified with the capacity to survive in America. In Huang's eyes, strength in a Chinese woman is not only unwomanly but tantamount to ethnic betrayal.

That Huang's concept of "Americanness" is a construct rather than a report of objectively existing conditions is corroborated by his parting thoughts on his plight: "This society [American society] does not allow people like him to climb up. Sooner or later, he will be eliminated and destroyed by this ruthless competition, this cult of survival of the fittest, this pragmatism" (33). Of course, as anyone who knows anything about Hong Kong can attest, competitiveness and pragmatism are hardly the monopoly of America. If anything, Hong Kong society, where unbridled capitalism and colonial laissez-faire have combined to create a phenomenally successful economic juggernaut, is even more cutthroat than the United States. It is not the absolute nature of American society, the dictates of its Darwinistic culture, that leads Huang to his current vision of ethnicized gender but an interacting network of cultural forces and actual events activated by immigration.

To recapitulate: in the immigrant's land of origin, gender, observed among people of the same ethnicity, is undestood to be naturally coextensive with the characteristics of biological sex. The disruptions of emigration and resettlement deconstruct the natural: masculinity and femininity prove to be contingent, mutable, provisional—products of historical particularity. Moreover, ethnic traits come to be attached to gender terms. Interestingly, however, the ethnicizing of gender, though initially subversive, may itself come to be naturalized. "A Date at Age Twenty-eight" ends with an intriguing image of renaturalization. Dazzled by her bold, colorful aura of sexuality, Huang sees himself reflected in the dark glasses which hide Meili's eyes. He doesn't like what he sees. Presently he feels himself "immobilized" and "impaled" by "Meili's gaze from behind the sunglasses" (34). But the gaze, of course, is really Huang's own: since Meili's eyes are concealed, her assessment of Huang's potential for sexual conquest remains inaccessible.

A network of signs similar to the one that Huang transforms into his psychosocial landscape governs Cao Youfang's 1986 novel *American Moon*, a comic tale of virility regained strongly reminiscent of Louis Chu's *Eat a Bowl of Tea*. (Cao is a veteran writer active since before her immigration from Taiwan.) While both are, in a sense, parables of community renewal, the concept of Americanization figures comparatively weakly in Chu's treatment of the sexual comedy, published more than two decades before *American Moon*. In contrast, the story of Cao's male protagonist, Tao Minshi, is one of learning to come to terms with the ways of America; his failure to do so condemns him not only to jilting by his college sweetheart, Xueqing, but also to a twelve-year period of hibernating impotence.

The scene in which Xueqing breaks up with Tao Minshi recalls Huang Zhixian's humiliation at the Christmas party and the beach, and the same motifs that define the battle between the sexes in Yi Li's story appear here, with some new twists. Tao pursues Xueqing to the United States, only to find that she has transferred her affections to a more desirable man: someone with a "green card" and a good job in one of the technical fields (the so-called "hard" sciences instead of the "soft" humanities, Tao's area of study). The showdown takes place on a chilly fall day; as in Yi Li's story, the woman is the one who can handle the cold, while the man shivers in misery. The woman is the better driver and knows her way around, literally and figuratively, in this country. Xueqing's newfound self-assurance and independence are amply in evidence as she negotiates turns on the mountain road with happy abandon; Tao, the recent arrival, has little more than a driver's license to his credit. The man's scrawniness is again an issue: whereas Xueqing has never complained about Tao's build when in Taiwan—in fact she has complimented him on being the poetic, melancholic type—in the United States she picks on him constantly and explicitly for being a weakling (12).

At their last meal together in a fancy restaurant, Tao is dismayed by Xueqing's alien tastes in food: a before-dinner margarita, a rare slab of steak, and a slice of cheesecake (15, 18). Tao is nauseated by the meat oozing blood on his plate and secretly longs for Chinese dishes. Xueqing, much to her discredit, relishes every bite. She is described as calmly cutting into her steak with a sharp knife, recalling an explicit reference to castration some pages earlier. Xueqing's Americanized eating habits are read as a violation of the unspoken codes of her gender: "Xueqing's unusually keen appetite terrified him. Such a delicate, frail-looking woman wolfing down such a huge steak! The neat way in which she aligned her knife and fork on the plate, to signal the conclusion of her meal, filled him with a nameless horror" (18). The Amazon-like women in Yi Li's story have turned positively cannibalistic in Cao's. Tao provides the perfect gloss to this scene: "He was the kind of man who can't take blows from life. To survive out here [in the United States], one must acquire the ability to go on eating and sleeping no matter what happens" (18). In the new world, one must either swallow or be swallowed. There is thus nothing inherently unnatural and unfeminine about Xueqing's appetite, in food, sex, or life in general; she looks like a man-destroying devourer simply because Tao has failed to become one.

Like Meili, Xueqing is associated with the color red: blood on the steak, maple leaves on the hills (21). Blood, in turn, is an emblem of ripe female sexuality of the "bad" sort: Tao "had always been afraid of glamor. Not only did he see nothing sexy about it, he even felt revulsion toward it, as toward blood" (16). Tao is soul brother to Huang in that he, too, prefers the sort of "femininity" that is "kind and gentle" (16). Tao's color is pastel blue, the traditional color for baby boys. The pastel blue sweater knit by Xueqing that he has put on—to remind Xueqing of her more dutifully feminine days and their good times together as a properly matched couple—only provokes the outburst: "I don't want to be your older sister or your mother!" (22). Just as, at this point, Tao cannot "swallow" American ways, he cannot conceive of a fulfilling sexual relationship between equals.

Both Yi Li's and Cao Youfang's stories share a symbolic vocabulary in which gender and ethnicity are fused and the meanings of "universal" archetypal symbols (such as blood) are modified by the specificities of American immigrant life. Whereas white ideology characterizes Asians as one of the ethnic Others, Chinese immigrant literature operates on the assumption that the Other is American. The sufferings of the protagonists stem from self-division and privileging of the "Chinese" side. Neither Huang nor Tao (initially) recognizes that "Chineseness" and "Americanness," much like "masculinity" and "femininity," are not essences but historically conditioned, communally shared, and psychologically motivated constructs. Both men lead Westernized lives—wear Western-style shirts and pants, ride in airplanes, use the telephone, all quite free of qualms—except in those aspects which they (and their peers) invest with cultural (as opposed to merely utilitarian) meaning. Both men fail to see that the insouciance of Meili and Xueqing—a composite of practical adaptability, sexual confidence, and flexibility in ethnic identification—is in fact the implicit end point of their quest for at-homeness in American. There seems no way out of binary oppositions.

American Moon being a romantic comedy, deliverance is eventually provided for Tao in the form of a wife who is, so to speak, illiterate in the sign system that has governed his life for so long. This system dictates that the ideal wife should be, like Huang's childhood girlfriend, sweet, virginal, ethereal, and above all, un-Americanized. The woman whom Tao chooses from among the many applicants to his newspaper advertisement, Qifeng, qualifies on minimal technicalities: she is physically small, fair-skinned, young, and a virgin. In every other way she seems to violate the net prescriptions of the code and promise disaster: she hungers for material comforts, loves foreign fads, and is, if anything, even more shrewd and enterprising than Xueqing. These are all putatively "American" qualities. Yet the marriage works out because Qifeng is totally oblivious to the possibility of such a reading. A creature of her sociohistorical environment, she lives instinctually, driven by an animal-like energy to improve her lot. To gender and ethnicity issues her responses are unreflecting. She never challenges Tao's male supremacist views, since on a conscious level she subscribes to them herself; but she wields great power over him through so-called feminine wiles, thereby accomplishing a sex-role reversal without either partner perceiving it as such. Her sense of ethnic identity is virtually nonexistent; in running Tao's restaurant, she refuses to share his scruples about catering to American tastes and socializing with American customers. Simply by ignoring it, she induces Tao, by example, to drop the elaborate web of signification woven by him and his fellow immigrants. True to the wish-fulfilling nature of its genre, *American Moon* undoes the ethnicizing of gender and restores its protagonist to innocence. When, at the end of the story, Qifeng becomes pregnant, we are made to understand that the old binary oppositions have outlived their usefulness in codifying and interpreting the American experience, and the Chinese immigrants who have been living by them are ready to settle down into an integrated life.

Finally, "Excursion to Fire Island," a story by Bai Xianyong (whose American name is Kenneth Pai) in his *New Yorkers* collection, when read in conjunction with "A Date at Age Twenty-eight" and *American Moon*, illustrates the manifold and sophisticated ways in which a writer can draw on a language of figuration to embody his American experience. The "American experience" in Bai's account differs considerably in its sociological details from that portrayed in Yi Li's and Cao Youfang's stories. Lin Gang in "Excursion to Fire Island" is a highly educated professional enjoying what would now be called a yuppie lifestyle; in "real life" he would probably be one of the patrons in Tao Minshi's restaurant, separated from the waiter by social class and degree of assimilation. Unlike the struggling Huang Zhixian, Lin is successful, does not suffer from the language barrier, and has a busy social life. From a narrowly deterministic materialist point of view, there may seem to be little binding all these male protagonists together. However, if responding to the stresses of dislocation is taken to mean more than acquiring the practical knowhow of survival in American society or the trappings of assimilation but is seen to encompass a spiritual self-reckoning and reorientation, we will find the sign of sexuality functioning in Bai's story in recognizably familiar ways.

Lin Gang, a gregarious bachelor with a high-paying engineering job and an expert New Yorker who can guide his visitors to the best restaurants and shows in town, seems at first sight to be the antithesis of the morose, socially inept Huang Zhixian further pinched by meager means. Interestingly, though, Lin too is described as being physically stunted and desexed. Not scrawny but chubby, Lin, in his thirties, is short and "cute": "His plump face was like the baby face of a teenaged kid, a pinkish glow showing through his fair skin, as if he would never suffer the erosions of time" (49). The many Chinese girls who pass through town love him for the "safe," "innocent"—namely, sexless—friendship that he can offer; of course, they always end up marrying someone else.

This loosely plotted short story is set on a sultry day in summer; as usual, Lin is serving as tour guide/host to fun-loving young Chinese women. He takes three visitors to Fire Island for a swim. The sexually aggressive Amazon in Yi Li's story is reincarnated here in triplicate. One woman wears a "fiery-red bikini, revealing her firm, rounded waist and two full, spherical breasts thrusting unscrupulously forward" (55–56). (Red is here again the color of blatant sexuality.) Another, wearing a white suit, is described as "large-boned," her hair in a thick, black ponytail which "swung left and right in an unruly manner." A third wears a pastel blue suit which "squeezes her plump torso into three sections" (56). Their at-homeness in disorderly, uncontained but fertile flesh is contrasted with Lin's tameness and underdevelopment: faced with the waves, he stumbles clumsily about, arms spread apart, "like a toddler who just learned to walk" (58). The three women, sirenlike, taunt Lin by luring him into a fruitless chase in the water. The red-clad woman, a champion swimmer, provokes Lin into a rage and almost causes him to drown. When Lin comes to, he is drenched in cold sweat, the "fireball" sun beating down on him, the three women surrounding but inaccessible to him (60). The story concludes with the party heading back away from the dangerous waters of life to the secure, man-made environment of Radio City shows and Chinese restaurants.

Swimming as a trope of risky but necessary engagement in life, merely touched on in Yi Li's story, has been developed by Bai Xianyong into a wide-ranging if veiled critique of Chinese American existence of a certain kind. The similarities between "Excursion to Fire Island" and "A Date at Age Twenty-eight" on the one hand, and *American Moon* on the other, are obvious: a harking back to preadult security on the male protagonists' part; an ambivalent relationship of pursuit and withdrawal with fully sexed women; prolonged if not entirely voluntary abstinence. Bai's story, however, defies a ready definition of Americanization in terms of observable social behavior, which in the previous two stories is made to correlate with sexuality. The ethnicizing of gender spoken of earlier is oblique, almost abstract, in apparent contradiction to the patterns perceived in Yi Li's and Cao Youfang's stories. For Lin Gang is assimilated in lifestyle, a model of what Huang Zhixian, from a bitter feeling of inferiority, takes pride in not being, but minus the slick, brazen self-salesmanship that Yi Li associates with Americanization. He possesses that resourceful confidence with American ways that Tao Minshi attributes in his imagination to his rival for Xueqing's affections. Lin Gang's Chinese women friends are never labeled as more American than he is. Yet in spite of all this, he is depicted as emasculated. Lin Gang's reduced masculinity can be understood only in a larger context, by placing the class he belongs to—affluent "uptown" Chinese Americans, individually successful but collectively powerless and marginal—within the structure of American society. Only then does it become clear that spiritual privation, signified by desexing, unites otherwise disparate Chinese of the immigrant generation who have not made peace with their own ambivalent decision to become members of American society. Prevented from actively engaging with history and fixed in a static, essentialist notion of "Chineseness," they are, indeed, free from the "erosions of time," as all things ahistorical can be said to be. Only that preservation is a kind of slow death. This reading of "Excursion to Fire Island" can be easily confirmed by pairing it with other stories in the *New Yorkers* collection, such as "Death in Chicago," where male sexual sterility and death feature centrally (and where, one might add, the Amazon/siren/devourer takes the form of a bar girl who sinks her glistening teeth into a chicken leg prior to initiating the virgin protagonist into his first and last sexual act).

The foregoing analysis of sexuality as sign suggests several interesting theoretical possibilities. The first concerns the comparative study of Chinese American literature across generational lines. Explorations of sexuality, particularly adult sexuality in matrimonial context, appear far more frequently in immigrant literature than in the works by American-born writers; the three stories cited above are typical in this sense. Among immigrant writers, Yu Lihua, Nie Hualing (alias Hua-ling Nieh), Chen Ruoxi (alias Chen Jo-hsi), Li Li, Shi Shuqing, and Cong Su (all women, incidentally) are especially interested in issues of heterosexual courtship, marriage, jilting, celibacy, divorce, widowhood, extramarital affairs, and child rearing, a consequence of sexual union. In contrast, American-born authors seem to favor the coming-of-age story in which sexual initiation is conspicuously absent: the canonical pattern shows an adolescent or young adult seeking a healing reconnection to his/her ethnic culture and a viable place in American society.[4] Typically, the tale ends when the protagonist is poised to be launched into adult life; the possibility of sexual engagement, seldom on the protagonist's mind to begin with, is projected into some nebulous future.

This intriguing contrast between the thematic preoccupations of the foreign- and American-born calls for in-depth comparisons; perhaps, when immigrant writings are translated and made accessible to the majority of students of Chinese American literature, such a project can begin in earnest. Tentatively, we may speculate that immigrant writers, arriving in the United States in adulthood, possess an already well-formed sense of self that, even under challenge by a new environment, allows them to envision full, adult participation in society. Even stories harking back to a preadolescent condition of ethnic innocence, such as Yi Li's "A Date at Age Twenty-eight," assume as their reference point a vision of eventual comfort or at-homeness in American society, encoded as heterosexual fulfillment. If it is true that, until very recently, heterosexual union has been considered a prerequisite for procreation and has formed the basis of numerous social institutions of continuance, it stands to reason that the literature of the American-born is so little concerned with sexuality: for the "native son" or "native daughter," prevented by racism from feeling at home in their homeland, the most urgent struggle is that of fashioning a Chinese American selfhood. The effort may be so all-consuming for the American-born writer that it forecloses further imaginative venturing; formulation of a serviceable identity then constitutes the culminating achievement of which subsequent experiences are but applications or variations. As manifested in the literature, this means the predominance of autobiographical or quasi-autobiographical writing in which the protagonist is shown on the verge of adulthood, as yet innocent of the couplings and uncouplings that symbolize various possibilities of involvement with American society.[5]

If, as this hypothesis suggests, first-generation writing focuses on the ethnicizing of gender while works by the American-born are preoccupied with the effects of the gendering of ethnicity, the question then arises as to what reading strategy is most appropriate for each corpus. Thus far, Chinese American critics, whether feminist or masculinist in persuasion, have tended to use stereotyping, in particular sex-role stereotyping, as their primary conceptual instrument for assessing the nature and worth of specific literary works. Since stereotyping rankles more when one is born into a society but not treated as a natural member, concern with stereotyping may find its way more readily and explicitly into American-born writers' works, which are naturally more amenable to stereotype-based readings than immigrant works. On the other hand, if, as shown in this essay, immigrant writing appears to exhibit a distinct understanding of how gender and ethnicity are interrelated, stereotyping may not be such a profitable interpretive grid. In the method chosen for this essay, the concept of the sign system rather than the stereotype is the ordering principle. Terms are given their broadest possible range of signification within the constraints imposed by their relationship to other terms within the system; only through this means can the affinities shared by works within the corpus be captured. Thus if temperature (heat versus cold) is a sign, it is so only in the sense that adaptability to temperature changes symbolizes a certain mode of reaction to one's American existence as explored in the stories. The "American environment" is rendered as cold in Yi Li's and Cao Youfang's stories but hot in Bai Xianyong's; while Huang Zhixian and Tao Minshi are afraid of the cold, Lin Gang cannot stand the heat. Yet the limited physical stamina of all three derives a dimension of meaning from contrast with the women's more flexible, self-sufficing responses. In much the same way, the mapping of "Chinese" and "American" onto "feminine" and "masculine" or "desexed" and "sexed" is not fixed but fluid. (That is why a stereotype-based reading would have little to say about Lin Gang, who is so obviously realized in the same symbolic language as the other male protagonists discussed here; such an approach might even be forced to regard him in a presumably positive, antisterotyping light, when in the story he is clearly not offered as a paragon of unimpoverished being.) By juxtaposing as few as three works of Chinese immigrant literature, we can already discern how sexuality functions as a richly suggestive sign amid other signs (colors, stature, temperature, water, mobility, alimentation, etc.); indeed, sexuality propels the protagonists into diverse relationships whose configurations embody the workings of social forces, especially those of ethnicity.

Such an approach does not preclude the possibility that immigrant writers may be engaging in stereotyping of their own (e.g., oversexing American-born or American-raised women), but unlike Hom's study of intergenerational stereotyping, it is not interested in how laudable or ideologically justifiable a given portrayal is. Rather, it shifts critical attention from content analysis—from determining the presence or absence of stereotypes within a text—to a study of the semiosis whereby both stereotyping and counterstereotyping are made possible. After all, as Cheung points out, it is possible for challengers to white male authority to "remain in thrall to," or even to "unwittingly [uphold]," what they assail (235). Whether a semiotic approach is generalizable at all beyond immigrant writing remains to be investigated, but its potential advantages are obvious. By emphasizing the writer's role as an active sign user and maker of meaning, not just a victim of accidents of nativity who is doomed to a rigged ideological salvage operation, some of the power of definition yielded to the dominant society may be reclaimed. The danger of being entrenched in a reverse essentialism, such as is discernible in the *Aiiieeeee* (Chin et al. group's blatant sexism and inadvertently betrayed self-contempt (see also Chin, "Backtalk" and *Donald Duk*), may also be bypassed.

Finally, the opposite but complementary notions of ethnicizing gender and gendering ethnicity may lead to a revision of how the gender-ethnicity nexus is understood in Chinese American criticism. The *Aiiieeeee* school dismisses the reality of sexism and gender politics for Chinese American women; feminist students of Chinese American literature, such as Ling, favor a "double jeopardy" model that stresses the dual oppression of sexism and racism (Beale). Both these views regard gender and ethnicity as discrete; even the "multiple jeopardy" model proposed by King, which purports to take into account race, gender, and class, retains an additive slant in its "interactive" analysis. However, judging from our analysis of sexuality in Chinese immigrant literature, it could well be that gender and ethnicity are fused to a much greater extent than previously suspected: that in a society like that of the United States, ethnicity is, in some sense, always already gendered, and gender always already ethnicized.[6] Cheung has called for the development of new paradigms that can admit the "crosscurrents" between gender, race, and class (245) and an "alliance between gender studies and ethnic studies" (246). The task is, indeed, an important and urgent one. This essay, speculative as it is in some instances, may be considered a first step toward such a paradigm revision.

NOTES

1. I use the term *Chinese immigrant literature* to refer to all Chinese-language works about American life written by first-generation writers residing permanently in the United States. The 1960s are chosen as a watershed date because these years witnessed the beginning of an influx of immigrants from Taiwan and Hong Kong, which not only made possible a flowering of immigrant writing but also profoundly altered the Chinese American community and contributed to an awakening of ethnic consciousness among the American born.

2. The English titles of the immigrant stories (my translations) are given in the text; the Chinese transliteration of the original titles, in works cited. All quoted passages are my translations.

3. It is true that a martial tradition existed in traditional Chinese society and continues to survive in popular culture; it is also true that the phrase

wen wu shuang quan ("accomplished in both the literary and martial arts") represents a high compliment for a man. However, as ideology the scholarly ideal is definitely dominant in Chinese culture past and present.

4. An exception that comes readily to mind is Maxine Hong Kingston's *Tripmaster Monkey: His Fake Book*, but even there Wittman Ah Sing has barely crossed the threshold of adulthood. Louis Chu's *Eat a Bowl of Tea*, in which sexuality is a central issue, is, of course, written by a first-generation writer. The tradition of initiation into young adulthood continues in recent works such as Frank Chin's *Donald Duk* and Gus Lee's *China Boy*.

5. For the same reason the narrator in Shawn Wong's *Homebase*, though in love with the Chinese American woman in Wisconsin who represents "the myth of the perfect day" (79), must first resolve his entanglement with the blond "dream girl"—the "shadow" or the "white ghost" (78) who holds out an enticing but unattainable assimilationist vision.

6. In this regard, Chow's analysis of "ethnic spectatorship" (3–33)—the way she reads ethnicity in the "feminized space" of films like *The Last Emperor*—may be relevant and instructive, even though her subject is China rather than Chinese America.

WORKS CITED

Alquizola, Marilyn. "*M. Butterfly*: The Mirror Image of Patriarchal Notions on Both Sides." Paper presented at the Association for Asian American Studies convention, Santa Barbara, May 1990.

Bia Xianyong [Kenneth Pai]. *New Yorkers* [*Niuyueke*]. Hong Kong: Wenxue Shuju, 1975.

Beale, Frances. "Double Jeopardy: To Be Black and Female." *The Black Woman: An Anthology*. Ed. Toni Cade. New York: New American Library, 1979. 90–100.

Cao Youfang. *American Moon* [Meiguo yueliang]. Taibei: Hongfan Shudian, 1986.

Cheung, King-Kok. "The Woman Warrior versus the Chinaman Pacific: Must a Chinese American Critic Choose between Feminism and Heroism?" In *Conflicts in Feminism*, ed. Marianne Hirsch and Evelyn Fox Keller. New York: Routledge, forthcoming.

Chin, Frank. "Backtalk." In *Counterpoint: Perspectives on Asian America*, ed. Emma Gee. Los Angeles: Asian American Studies Center, 1976. 556–57.

———. *Donald Duk*. Minneapolis: Coffee House Press, 1991.

Chin, Frank, and Jeffery Paul Chan. "Racist Love." In *Seeing through Shuck*, ed. Richard Kostelanetz. New York: Ballantine, 1972. 65–79.

Chin, Frank, Jeffery Paul Chan, Lawson Fusao Inada, and Shawn Hsu Wong, eds. *Aiiieeeee! An Anthology of Asian American Writers*. Washington, D.C.: Howard University Press, 1974.

Chow, Rey. *Woman and Chinese Modernity: The Politics of Reading Between West and East*. Minneapolis: University of Minnesota Press, 1991.

Christian, Barbara. *Black Feminist Criticism: Perspectives on Black Women Writers*. New York: Pergamon, 1985.

Chu, Louis. *Eat a Bowl of Tea*. 1961. Seattle: University of Washington Press, 1979.

Fuss, Diana. *Essentially Speaking: Feminism, Nature and Difference*. New York: Routledge, 1989.

Hom, Marlon K. "A Case of Mutual Exclusion: Portrayals by Immigrant and American-born Chinese of Each Other in Literature." *Amerasia Journal* 11.2 (1984): 29–45.

Kim, Elaine H. *Asian American Literature: An Introduction to the Writings and Their Social Context*. Philadelphia: Temple University Press, 1982.

King, Deborah K. "Multiple Jeopardy, Multiple Consciousness: The Context of a Black Feminist Ideology." *Signs* 14.1 (1988): 42–72.

Kingston, Maxine Hong. *Tripmaster Monkey: His Fake Book*. New York: Knopf, 1989.

Lee, Gus. *China Boy*. New York: Dutton, 1991.

Ling, Amy. *Between Worlds: Women Writers of Chinese Ancestry*. New York: Pergamon, 1990.

Osajima, Keith. "Asian Americans as the Model Minority: An Analysis of the Popular Press Image in the 1960s and 1980s." In *Reflections on Shattered Windows*, ed. Gary Okihiro et al. Pullman: Washington State University Press, 1988. 165–74.

Pao, Angela. "The Critic and the Butterfly: Sociocultural Context and the Reception of David Henry Hwang's *M. Butterfly*." *Amerasia Journal*. Forthcoming.

Riggs, Marlon, director. *Ethnic Notions*. San Francisco: California Newsreel, 1987.

Snitow, Ann, Christine Stansell, and Sharon Thompson, eds. *Powers of Desire: The Politics of Sexuality*. New York: Monthly Review Press, 1983.

Tajima, Renee E. "Lotus Blossoms Don't Bleed: Images of Asian Women." In *Making Waves: An Anthology of Writings by and about Asian American Women*, ed. Asian Women United. Boston: Beacon, 1989. 308–17.

Walsh, Joan. "Asian Women, Caucasian Men: The New Demographics of Love." *Image*, 2 December 1990, 11–16.

Wong, Shawn. *Homebase*. New York: I. Reed Books, 1979.

Yi Li. "A Date at Age Twenty-eight" [Ershibasui de yuehui]. In *The Soil* [*Nitu*]. Hong Kong: Nanyue chubanshi, 1979.

Yun, Grace, ed. *A Look beyond the Model Minority Image: Critical Issues in Asian America*. New York: Minority Rights Group, 1989.

Yung, Judy. *Chinese Women of America: A Pictorial History*. Seattle: University of Washington Press, 1986.

7

Rebels and Heroines: Subversive Narratives in the Stories of Wakako Yamauchi and Hisaye Yamamoto

Stan Yogi

SOME OF the best and most well-known short stories of Wakako Yamauchi and Hisaye Yamamoto explore how the aspirations of Issei (Japanese immigrant) women collide with the patriarchal norms of Issei culture. Yamauchi's "And the Soul Shall Dance" (1966) and "Songs My Mother Taught Me" (1976) and Yamamoto's "Seventeen Syllables" (1949) and "Yoneko's Earthquake" (1951) depict Issei women striving to realize ambitions that contradict traditional roles. Although marriage afforded Issei men greater control over their lives, for Issei women it meant the transference of obedience from parents to husband.[1] An Issei woman's primary concern was to provide for the well-being of her family. In this context, Issei women's efforts at self-fulfillment outside the boundaries of family and community necessarily become rebellions against cultural standards.

Yamauchi and Yamamoto portray the resistance of Issei women and the consequences of their rebellions in narratives that subvert the strict cultural codes of the Issei family. Told from the perspectives of Nisei (second-generation Japanese American) daughters who view their mothers sympathetically, the narratives temper empathy with objectivity; if the Issei women themselves narrated the stories, melodrama or self-pity could dominate the narratives. Through the first-person narrators who selectively reveal information in the stories of Yamauchi or through the third-person narrators with limited perspectives in the stories of Yamamoto, readers discover the Issei women's defiance in much the same way as do the daughters who observe their mothers: through indirect actions and perceptions that often defy definitive explication. These narratives thus not only quietly subvert the rigid constructs of the Issei family by portraying sympathetically such taboo behavior as women's drunkenness and adultery, they also subtly suggest, through the reactions of Nisei daughters to their mothers, the transformation of the very standards the mothers violate.

Of the four stories, Yamauchi's "And the Soul Shall Dance" is the most straightforward in its presentation of an Issei woman's rebellion.[2] The reminiscence of a Nisei named Masako, the story depicts her childhood fascination with Mrs. Oka, an aloof, disturbed Issei neighbor whose unconventional behavior is both frightening and intriguing. Mrs. Oka, though, is not the only unhappy woman in the story. Through the complex relationships among the four female characters, Yamauchi depicts both resistance and containment among Issei and Nisei women.

Mrs. Oka is the most visibly agitated character. An arranged marriage with her dead sister's husband sparks her frustration.[3] Although Mrs. Oka's marriage does not diverge radically from Japanese custom, it keenly underscores her powerlessness.[4] She does not control her destiny and is coerced into marriage and shipped off to lead a harsh farm life. That she would not defy the marriage may strike readers as odd. The options open to Issei women, however, were few. As Yuji Ichioka points out, "To refuse [a picture-marriage] would have been an act of filial disobedience, a grave moral offense" (166). In addition, once in the United States, Issei women, lacking English-language skills and ignorant of their new environments, were dependent on their husbands.

Mrs. Oka does, however, register her unhappiness by drinking, a habit uncommon among Issei women. As Masako comments, Mrs. Oka's "aberration was a protest of the life assigned her" (196). This protest, although "obstinate," is "unobserved" and "unheeded" (196). The denial of Mrs. Oka's behavior not only reflects the discomfort of confronting disturbing actions, it also becomes a de facto means of punishing her for protesting her circumstances. Consequently, she further distances herself to a point where displaying the "welts and bruises on her usually smooth brown face" (194)—the results of brawls with her husband—becomes a form of resistance;

the injuries attest to her suffering more powerfully than verbal complaints. By exposing her wounds, Mrs. Oka signals she is not ashamed that she defies her husband.

Masako's mother is one of the neighbors who observes but avoids acknowledging Mrs. Oka's dissent. Unlike Mrs. Oka, Masako's mother does not challenge or confront. When Mrs. Oka displays her wounds, for example, Masako recalls that her mother "hurried us home," "murmuring her many apologies" (195). She does not discuss with Mrs. Oka the strife that produces the welts and the troubled thoughts that compel her to show them. Rather, she is a silent witness.

Masako's mother, though, has many words for Mrs. Oka's giggling, awkward stepdaughter, Kiyoko. Masako remembers when Kiyoko first arrives from Japan:

> My mother took her away. They talked for a long time—about Japan, about enrollment in American school, the clothes Kiyoko-san would need, and where to look for the best values. As I watched them, it occurred to me that I had been deceived: this was not a child, this was a woman. The smile pressed behind her fingers, the way of her nod, so brief, like my mother when father scolded her. (197)

That Masako's mother would take on the role of surrogate parent with Kiyoko is understandable given that Mrs. Oka would not share with her stepdaughter such "feminine" concerns as where to shop for clothes. Masako carries the connection further. She directly links her mother and Kiyoko imagistically: Kiyoko's nod reminds Masako of her mother's nod when scolded. This image suggests conflict within Masako's family and hints at the problems that Kiyoko will encounter in her own home.

Kiyoko soon discovers this domestic conflict and responds in the manner of Masako's mother. After a distraught retreat to Masako's home in reaction to the violent bickering at her own house, Kiyoko seldom speaks of the troubles she witnesses. Masako, however, is well aware of her neighbor's unhappiness. She sees evidence of Kiyoko's misery in her eyes which "were often swollen and red." Kiyoko ceases her giggling and routinely presses "her fingers to her mouth" (198), powerfully symbolizing the forced silence she has learned. She no longer hides a "smile pressed behind her fingers" but instead attempts to mask her distress.

While a tie develops between Masako's mother and Kiyoko, Masako to a certain extent identifies and allies herself with Mrs. Oka. Although Masako confesses that "'strange' was the only concession" (196) her family bestowed upon their troubled neighbor, she displays a tender sympathy for Mrs. Oka. About Mrs. Oka's drinking, Masako recalls, "Her taste for liquor and cigarettes was a step in the realm of men; unusual for a Japanese wife, but at that time, in that place, and to me, Mrs. Oka loved her sake in the way my father loved his, in the way of Mr. Oka, the way I loved my candy" (195). As a child, Masako sees nothing morally wrong with Mrs. Oka's enjoyment of liquor and even identifies a double standard that allows men the pleasure of alcohol but denies women the same escape. She links the attraction to liquor with one of the few analogies open to a child: a love for candy. Immediately after this reflection, Masako comments: "That her psychology may have demanded this anesthetic, that she lived with something unendurable, did not occur to me" (195). Informed by age, the adult reveals a more sophisticated sympathy for the troubled woman.[5]

Masako not only expresses sympathy for Mrs. Oka but mirrors her behavior. In her reaction to Kiyoko, for example, Masako acts similarly to Mrs. Oka. Expecting a "soul mate" in her new neighbor, Masako recalls that upon meeting Mr. Oka's daughter her "disappointment was keen and apparent" (197). This lack of concern about showing her feelings subtly mimics Mrs. Oka's display of her welts and bruises; Masako thinks nothing of disrupting the decorum of this initial meeting, just as Mrs. Oka is unconcerned with the discomfort she causes by revealing her injuries. Yamauchi further links the two in one of the story's final images. Both women are drawn to the desert on a particular night, and there Masako witnesses Mrs. Oka's poignant dance of despair.[6] Mrs. Oka's dance becomes a potent and ironic image of both freedom and control. She escapes to the desert and liberates herself through the dance, her flowing movements contrasting with the restrictions she faces in daily life.[7] Dance, however, also implies the control of mind over body—the body executing the mind's visions. The image is ironic, then, in that Mrs. Oka dances as she descends into dejection exactly because she lacks control over her life.

Yamauchi, however, does not portray a simplistic symbiosis between Mrs. Oka and Masako. Indeed, the relationships among the four women are interwoven. Although she cannot openly engage

Mrs. Oka, Masako's mother is sympathetic toward her. She continually asks Kiyoko about her, and when she observes Mr. Oka and his daughter drive off to movies she comments, "'They've left her home again; Mrs. Oka is alone again, the poor woman'" (199).

Part of this sympathy may stem from her own dissatisfaction. We recall that Kiyoko's nod reminds Masako of her mother's nod when scolded. The image implies a strict hierarchy. In addition, Masako comments that it is one of her "mother's migraines" that drives her out of the house the evening she observes Mrs. Oka's dance. The migraines could be manifestations of the suffering she endures and the frustrations she represses. Unlike Mrs. Oka, who physically battles her husband and drinks to escape her problems, Masako's mother suppresses her anger. When Kiyoko, frantic over the violence between her father and stepmother, seeks solace with Masako's family, Masako's mother tells her, "Tomorrow you will return to them; you must not leave them again. They are your people" (198). The mother here expresses a cultural value common among Issei—*gaman*, or the "internalization of, and suppression of, anger and emotion" (Kitano 136). She more explicitly states this principle when telling a resigned Kiyoko, "Endure, soon you will be marrying and going away" (199). Ironically, she may vocalize the *gaman* ideal as much for herself as for Kiyoko.

Masako inherits some of her mother's sympathy for Mrs. Oka but also her mother's reticence. The story opens with a confession of silence in which Masako unyokes herself from the self-censorship that guarded Mrs. Oka's story. "It's all right to talk about it now," she says. "Most of the principals are dead" (193). Breaking the silence, Masako becomes a vindicator, a reporter of wrongs who fleshes out a void into a vivid picture.[8] By telling Mrs. Oka's story, Masako diverges from her mother's legacy of silence and accepts the painful insights she has reaped from Mrs. Oka's life.

Mrs. Oka eventually dies of pneumonia, and Mr. Oka and Kiyoko move from the desert, leaving Masako to speculate that "Kiyoko-san grew up and found someone to marry" (200). Masako's conjecture is ironic and comments on her mother's earlier counsel, "Endure, soon you will be marrying and going away." In the context of Mrs. Oka's troubled marriage and the suggestions of dissatisfaction in the marriage of Masako's parents, the statement hints that matrimony is neither the escape that Masako's mother suggests nor a balm for the trauma Kiyoko has already endured. That the story ends on this ironic note implies the transformation of attitudes toward marriage from the Issei to Nisei generation. Masako's subtle cynicism and unromantic speculation about Kiyoko's marriage indicate that the Nisei daughter acknowledges the constrictions placed on Issei women in marriage and the tremendous ramifications of these limitations whether the immigrant women rebel or conform.

"Songs My Mother Taught Me" operates in much the same manner as "And the Soul Shall Dance." An adult Nisei narrator recalls childhood experiences that she only now understands. Unlike "And the Soul Shall Dance," though, "Songs My Mother Taught Me" is more cryptic in its revelation of an Issei woman's rebellion. The narrative is indirect and suggestive because the narrator, Sachiko Kato, hints at her mother's hidden actions through a series of contrasts that build to intimate the pain of a woman caught in a life of disappointments.

The first of these contrasts develops between Sachiko's parents. Sachiko comments, "My father was a quiet man. . . . He never revealed his dream for us, his children, in America, or permitted his own dreams to articulate" (63). In contrast, her mother "spoke often of returning to Japan, of smelling again the pine forests, tasting the exquisite fruits, hearing the evening flutes, of seeing her beloved sisters" (64). The divisions between articulation and silence, between dreams and reality, not only suggest the mismatched temperaments of husband and wife, they also signify the importance of things unexpressed in words.

After recounting the dream vision of Japan to which her mother wishes to return, Sachiko shatters this image by presenting the stark realities of life in America: "In the Valley the days of summer are unbearable. The sun beats on miles of scrub-covered prairie and the air is deathly still. There are successions of listless days, one running into another without incident, without change" (64). This poignant juxtaposition of the sensual fantasy of a temperate Japan with the harsh truth of desert life provides the context in which to interpret Mrs. Kato's actions. This contrast is more meaningful when we consider the historical experience of Issei women. Many came to America believing that it was a land of milk and honey, some thinking they would return to Japan after becoming rich.[9] Once in America, however, they often were caught in a cycle of poverty and hard work. With the birth of children, the link to America became almost inevitable.[10] Mrs. Kato's situation, then, is ironic, since she might have left Japan dreaming of returning as a wealthy woman (or at least one able to live in comfort) but instead is trapped in a harsh American life.

The contrast between America and Japan continues through the two men in the story: Yamada, a hired hand, and Kato, Sachiko's father. She describes the two:

> [Yamada] was younger than my father, and he was handsome. He came to the dinner table in a fresh shirt, his hair combed back with some kind of good-smelling oil. My father, like most farmers, wore his hair so short that neither comb nor rain nor sun changed its shape. Yamada-san had eyes that looked straight through you. When you talked, he seemed to commit himself to you. My father's eyes were squinty from the sun, and he hardly saw or heard you. (66)

From a child's perspective, the physical differences between the two men are rather innocent, but Sachiko's observations suggest reasons that Mrs. Kato would be attracted to the handsome Yamada, just as her daughter is impressed by him. The division between the two men takes on greater significance because Yamada comes to represent the dream of Japan that Mrs. Kato envisions. As a Kibei, a Japanese born in America but raised in Japan, Yamada is more immediately linked to the island nation. He possesses "a quality of the orient" that Kato does not have, and Sachiko notes that Yamada "was the affirmation of my mother's Japan" (67). This connection is not lost on Mrs. Kato, who alters her behavior when in Yamada's presence: her smile softens; her voice becomes gentler. This change threatens Kato. For a man of few words, he has many when referring to Yamada. Kato complains to his wife that the farmhand, with his fancy clothes and "frivolous" habit of plucking the mandolin, sets a "terrible example" for their young son. Although the employer finds these attributes unappealing, his wife may find them very attractive. Kato, though, has the power to enforce his judgments and announces that after the harvest, when Yamada's assistance is no longer needed, he will dismiss the laborer.

Although it appears that this is just what happens, ambiguity surrounds Yamada, especially his relationship with Mrs. Kato. This uncertainty becomes more pronounced with Mrs. Kato's pregnancy; Yamauchi indirectly suggests that Yamada is the baby's father. Yamada's room, for example, houses Mrs. Kato's sewing machine, an arrangement that would facilitate clandestine meetings. After Yamada's departure, Sachiko finds on the sewing machine an empty jar of pomade. Read symbolically, the image is suggestive. If the sewing machine represents Mrs. Kato and the jar of pomades stands for Yamada, the image subtly conveys their relationship, implying that Yamada leaves part of himself behind with Mrs. Kato. A secretive visit Yamada pays Mrs. Kato when the family vacations in San Pedro also suggests an affair between the two.

Mrs. Kato's sadness during and after her pregnancy is also a clue to her hidden rebellion. If Yamada is the father of the baby, Mrs. Kato's depression is understandable. Trying to cope with unfulfilled dreams and filling a void she feels for her homeland, she takes Yamada, a physical reminder of Japan, as a lover. She thus couples a dream ideal of Japan with an American reality. The result of this affair, ironically, is a child that further ties her to the country in which she suffers.

Perhaps because the child comes from a union that recalls Japan and the impossibility of ever returning, Mrs. Kato does not hide her despondency over the newborn. Sachiko consequently takes on the role of surrogate parent, caring for the baby, "loving him, changing his diapers, picking him up when he crie[s]" (69), rushing home from school to "take care of the baby and play with him" so he will not trigger Mrs. Kato's "terrible, strangled sighs" (70). This contrast between mother and daughter discloses the extent to which Mrs. Kato rebels against her responsibilities. Sachiko cannot understand that her mother does not love the baby because she did not want him, and only realizes this after witnessing her mother place a hatchet blade against the baby's forehead, crying "I didn't want this baby, I didn't want this baby. My children are all grown. I didn't want this baby" (70).

The child drowns, but it is unclear whether Mrs. Kato actually kills him. She wails, "I've killed him, I've killed him, forgive me, I've killed him," after the discovery of her drowned son, but she prefaces these cries with an explanation: "I left him only for a moment and I found him face down in the water!" (72). Whether Mrs. Kato speaks from guilt over murdering the child or guilt over leaving him unattended, the contradictory nature of her utterances shrouds the infant's death in ambiguity. Certainly she did not want the child, but it is impossible to say that she intentionally killed him.

Even though Mrs. Kato's affair and neglect of her child directly violate the norms of the Issei family, Sachiko does not condemn her mother. On the contrary, the final image of the story suggests Sachiko's acceptance of her mother's behavior. Sachiko recalls that at her brother's funeral, "My father helped my mother to her feet. She gripped my hand. It seemed to me if my tears would ever stop, I would never cry again. And it was a long long time before I could believe in God again" (73). The joining of hands between mother and daughter indicates a connection, a sense of mutual support. That Sachiko matures and accepts the troubling events she has witnessed is suggested by the final line of the story, "it was a long long time before I could believe in God again." This statement implies that Sachiko has come to terms with her mother's frustration and her brother's death because she can accept the concept of a force that orders events, no matter how painful. Much like Wordsworth's ideal poet who meditates on intense emotion (435), the narrator of "Songs My Mother Taught Me" looks back at tragic events and attempts to understand them. In so doing, she compassionately remembers her mother, an Issei who violated cultural boundaries in trying to resist the frustrations that seemed to engulf her.

Unlike the mature Nisei first-person narrators of Yamauchi's stories, the young Nisei protagonists of Yamamoto's "Yoneko's Earthquake" and "Seventeen Syllables" lack adult powers of reflection. Although written in the third person, both stories are told from the perspective of young Nisei daughters.[11] As in "Songs My Mother Taught Me," the Issei woman's rebellion in "Yoneko's Earthquake" is offered indirectly through the observations of a Nisei. Told from the perspective of ten-year-old Yoneko Hosoume, the story unfolds specifically because Yoneko discloses significant events she cannot comprehend. Throughout the story, Yamamoto develops parallels between Yoneko and her mother that reveal Mrs. Hosoume's rebellion.

Yoneko's crush on the young Filipino farmhand, Marpo, for example, hints at the relationship Mrs. Hosoume develops with him. Although Yoneko is more interested in Marpo's talents as an athlete, musician, artist, and radio technician, she discloses that he has a "thin mustache like Edmund Lowe's, and the rare, breathtaking smile like white gold" (47). The child's fascination with Marpo suggests reasons that an adult would be attracted to the young Filipino.[12]

The hours Yoneko accompanies Marpo in daily awe of his many charms also foreshadow the time that her mother will spend with the hired hand.

Marpo's qualities take on greater significance after an earthquake that leaves Mr. Hosoume incapacitated, the result of near electrocution caused by his car being "kissed by a broken live wire" (50).[13] Because of Mr. Hosoume's disability, Mrs. Hosoume and Marpo must take on extra responsibilities, including all the field labor and weekly trips for groceries. They consequently spend more time together alone. Mr. Hosoume, on the other hand, if he had a relatively painless day, "would have supper on the stove when Mrs. Hosoume came in from the fields" (51).[14] While these changes initially seem innocent, they have serious ramifications.

The first evidence of dramatic change is Mrs. Hosoume's acceptance of a ring from Marpo and her subsequent gift of it to Yoneko. These actions not only link mother and daughter in their attraction for the hired hand but signal serious changes in the family. Mrs. Hosoume's adultery is a direct violation of partriarchal dominance, and Yoneko's unknowing compliance and silence about the ring's origin suggests generational rebellion against the patriarchy.[15]

An argument erupting between Mr. and Mrs. Hosoume regarding Yoneko's wearing nail polish further discloses Mrs. Hosoume's defiance and the erosion of patriarchal dominance. Believing that his wife brazenly contradicts him, Mr. Hosoume insults her by calling her "nama-iki" ("uppity," "impudent").[16] Mrs. Hosoume fights back, further enraging her already sensitive husband, who then slaps her. The various reactions to this violence are revealing: Mrs. Hosoume is temporarily immobile but resumes ironing as though nothing had happened, only glancing at Marpo, who happens to be in the room reading a newspaper. She then calmly tells her husband, "Hit me again. . . . Hit me all you wish" (53). Mr. Hosoume is about to do just that, but Marpo intercedes. Although Mrs. Hosoume's remark could disclose a latent masochism, more likely it is a challenge. Her reaction could also indicate that she is aware Marpo will come to her defense. The cryptic glance she gives Marpo after the slap indicates some level of communication between the two. Marpo's reaction is telling also. That Marpo would defy his employer by preventing him from slapping Mrs. Hosoume is particularly powerful when we consider that before the earthquake Marpo was "a rather shy young man meek to the point of speechlessness in the presence of Mr. and Mrs. Hosoume" (49).

Soon after this incident, Marpo suddenly leaves the family, without even saying good-bye to Yoneko and her younger brother Seigo. Marpo's abrupt leave-taking wounds Yoneko "more than she would admit even to herself," and her pain mirrors the intense agony that Mrs. Hosoume must feel. Not only has she lost a lover, she loses another reminder of Marpo. The departure of the hired hand occurs the same day that the Hosoume family takes a mysterious trip to the hospital. These two events are inextricably linked in Mrs. Hosoume's mind, because the purpose of the hospital trip is to abort Marpo's child. This is never explicitly stated, and the incident is more powerful exactly because it is never depicted. Rather, Yamamoto offers a symbolic representation of the abortion in the scenes that frame the trip. On the way to the hospital, Mr. Hosoume hits a collie that dashes out of a yard: "The car jerked with the impact, but Mr. Hosoume drove right on and Yoneko, wanting suddenly to vomit, looked back and saw the collie lying very still at the side of the road" (54). On the return from the hospital, Yoneko looks for the collie, "but the dog was nowhere to be seen" (54).

The final parallel between Yoneko and her mother paradoxically distinguishes how far apart mother is from daughter. Seigo suddenly dies, and Mrs. Hosoume is inconsolable, finding comfort only in the Church. She eventually becomes a Christian, and her conversion mirrors Yoneko's earlier acceptance of Christianity. The catalyst for the conversions of Yoneko and her mother is Marpo. With Yoneko, the acceptance of God is straightforward and simple: after a "protracted discussion on religion," Yoneko becomes an "ideal apostle, adoring Jesus, desiring Heaven and fearing Hell" (49). With Mrs. Hosoume, however, the path to Christianity is more twisted. Her embrace of God comes about because of Seigo's premature death, which in turn she links with the abortion. She indicates this causal connection at the end of the story when she tells her daughter, "Never kill a person, Yoneko, because if you do, God will take from you someone you love" (56).

Yoneko and her mother also differ in the depth of their religious feeling: Yoneko lacks the faith in things unseen to which her mother now clings. Yoneko's belief is fleeting. After the fateful earthquake, Yoneko spends "three solid hours [in] silent, desperate prayer," entreating God to make the earth stop rattling. When she sees no results she concludes that "God was either powerless, callous, downright cruel, or nonexistent," finally choosing the last as "the most plausible theory" (51). Yamamoto suggests that Yoneko, in her childlike demands of God, rebels against the patriarchal Christian system and blind faith in a male deity. Mrs. Hosoume, on the contrary, surrenders herself to it. The void once filled by Marpo is now filled by God. The roles of child and adult are reversed. Yoneko expresses adultlike cynicism, while Mrs. Hosoume seems to live out the biblical exhortation "unless you are converted and become like children, you shall not enter the kingdom of heaven."[17]

The story ends with Mrs. Hosoume trying to educate Yoneko in the tragedies of life. The warning that Mrs. Hosoume gives her daughter, "Never kill a person, Yoneko, because if you do, God will take from you someone you love," falls on uncomprehending ears. Yoneko is oblivious to the implications of her mother's words.[18] Instead she rattles off reasons for her rejection of God, and the two talk at cross purposes. Although Yoneko does not understand her mother's advice and its accompanying guilt, it is important to recall the parallels that Yamamoto draws between mother and daughter throughout the story. They hint that once Yoneko matures she may grasp how her mother's violation of cultural standards ultimately led to her retreat into religion. Unlike Sachiko Kato in "Songs My Mother Taught Me," Yoneko may never come to an acceptance of God. She may, however, come to sympathize with her mother's personal tragedies.

Like "Yoneko's Earthquake," "Seventeen Syllables" depicts an Issei trying to teach her daughter about the frustration and pain of adulthood. The story has a double focus: the sexual awakening of the adolescent Nisei, Rosie Hayashi, and the growing obsession of Rosie's mother with the writing of haiku. In observing this literary obsession, Rosie begins to recognize that her mother has ambitions satisfied neither by farm work nor by family. Mrs. Hayashi's pursuit of an identity other than wife, mother, or laborer is a refusal to succumb to the confines of her life. This resistance, however, is not without its price.

Yamamoto introduces Mrs. Hayashi's literary preoccupation as an innocent hobby. Rosie discovers that "her mother had taken to writing poems" after Mrs. Hayashi finishes one and recites it for her daughter's approval. Rosie, however, does not completely understand the poem because she cannot fully translate Japanese, and her mother must explain the poem's meaning. As the story progresses, Rosie echoes this initial instance of incomplete understanding in increasingly serious situations. Although Rosie may not completely comprehend what she encounters, the reader develops a fuller understanding of Mrs. Hayashi's resistance through Rosie's observations.

Yamamoto links Rosie's lack of cognizance with the strain created by her mother's artistic endeavors. When the Hayashis visit the neighboring Hayano family, Rosie observes her mother discussing haiku with Mr. Hayano while her father uncomfortably browses through a magazine, trying in vain to make conversation with the palsied Mrs. Hayano. Rosie is surprised when her father abruptly orders her to leave and stalks out of the house. Through Rosie's offhand observations, the reader gains a better understanding of Mr. Hayashi's behavior. Not only does Mr. Hayano understand literary efforts that Rosie's father cannot appreciate, Rosie notes that Mr. Hayano is "handsome, tall, and strong." Since Rosie has not yet discovered her sexuality, she cannot fathom her father's jealousy or her mother's desire to discuss haiku with the handsome neighbor.[19]

Only after Mrs. Hayashi apologizes to her husband does Rosie begin to apprehend the significance of her father's behavior. Although her mother assumes the subservient behavior of a Japanese wife, Rosie's reaction on the ride home from the Hayanos is more intricate:

> [She] felt a rush of hate for both—for her mother for begging, for her father for denying her mother. I wish this old Ford would crash, right now, she thought, then immediately, no, no. I wish my father would laugh, but it was too late: already the vision had passed through her mind of the green pick-up crumpled in the dark against one of the mighty eucalyptus trees they were just riding past, of the three contorted, bleeding bodies, one of them hers. (12)

Rosie's momentary hatred toward her parents discloses her own dissatisfaction with the hierarchy typical of Issei families. While frustrated because her mother acts submissively, Rosie sees this only in terms of the literary discussion. She is oblivious to the more complex sexual politics underlying the scene. Rosie's fantasy of the car crash, moreover, is disturbing because her adolescent mind cannot initially imagine another alternative to the complete escape suggested by the crash, an escape that annihilates her as well. This response is significant because later in the story Rosie replays this reaction in other uneasy situations that are linked to her mother's rebellion.[20]

Rosie's own sexual awakening brings together the themes of incomplete understanding and escape. Her discovery comes through Jesus Carrasco, the son of seasonal workers hired by the Hayashis, who invites Rosie to meet him in a packing shed because, he tells her, "I've got a secret I want to tell you." The two tease each other, and from their interaction the reader infers that Jesus' secret is a pretense to meet Rosie alone. Rosie, however, is blind to the import of Jesus' invitation. When she arrives at the appointed time, she demands, "Now tell me the secret." Jesus actually fulfills his promise of conveying to Rosie a secret—the mystery of sexual attraction—but Rosie has a mixed reaction: "Kissed by Jesus, Rosie fell for the first time entirely victim to a helplessness delectable beyond speech. But the terrible, beautiful sensation lasted no more than a second, and the reality of Jesus' lips and tongue and teeth and hands made her pull away with such strength that she nearly tumbled" (14). Although Rosie flees the scene, the memory of Jesus preoccupies her. Not only succinctly capturing the confusion generated by a first sexual encounter, the description of Rosie's response also recalls her fantasy of the car crash and foreshadows her desire to evade her mother's confession of thwarted love.

Rosie hears this confession after witnessing devastating events on the hottest and most demanding day of the season, when every available hand is needed to pack tomatoes. In the midst of this tense situation, the haiku editor of a Japanese American newspaper published in San Francisco arrives to announce that Mrs. Hayashi has won a Hiroshige print, first prize in the newspaper's haiku contest. Although she knows that her husband needs her help in the packing shed, she invites the suave editor to the house for tea. By choosing to entertain the editor rather than pack tomatoes, Mrs. Hayashi rebels against the strict roles defined for Issei women. Rosie, moreover, notices that her mother acts differently in the presence of the editor, a "good-looking man" who uses "elegant Japanese." Like Mrs. Kato in "Songs My Mother Taught Me," who alters her behavior in Yamada's presence, Mrs. Hayashi easily falls into the eloquent speech patterns of her guest.

These events do not escape Mr. Hayashi, who sends Rosie into the house to remind her mother that help is needed in the packing shed. When his wife does not return, Mr. Hayashi storms into the house, comes out with the Hiroshige picture, and proceeds to smash and burn it. Mr. Hayashi's anger results from double jealousy: disturbed about his wife's attention to the sophisticated editor, he is also upset because her literary interest is beyond the pale of his understanding. It represents a direct threat not only to his dominance but also to the family's economic survival.[21]

After her father destroys the painting, Rosie runs into the house to find her mother calmly watching the dying fire. Mrs. Hayashi then explains the tragic love affair and premature birth of a stillborn son that prompted her immigration to the United States. As an alternative to suicide, Mrs. Hayashi asked her sister in America to send for her. Yamamoto links Mrs. Hayashi's revelation with Rosie's past behavior. The choice between suicide and fleeing to America is an extreme and crushing version of Rosie's inclination to escape the uncomfortable or unfamiliar. Yamamoto reminds us of this tendency by framing Mrs. Hayashi's story with Rosie's attempts to avoid the burdens her mother shares. When Mrs. Hayashi prefaces her story with the question, "Do you know why I married your father?" Rosie thinks immediately of escape: "Don't tell me now, she wanted to say, tell me tomorrow, tell me next week, don't tell me today" (18). Even before her mother launches into the story, Rosie, sensing its darkness, wants to evade it.

After hearing her mother's history, Rosie still does not want to recognize its more disturbing implications. Rosie focuses on the possibility of a half brother in an attempt to evade a complete recognition of her mother's unhappy sexual past, which might dampen her own budding sexuality. In addition, an acceptance of her mother's story requires that Rosie see Mrs. Hayashi in a new light—as a distinct individual with sexual needs and desires similar to Rosie's own.

The story ends with Mrs. Hayashi kneeling on the floor, grabbing Rosie's wrists and insisting she promise never to marry. In this disturbing image the issue of Rosie's sexuality and that of Mrs. Hayashi's thwarted desires and efforts collide. Although Mrs. Hayashi's menacing demand stems from her attempt to protect Rosie from pain and disillusionment with men, the request subverts her daughter's growing sexual awareness. The demand is another manifestation of the escape response seen earlier in the story. The pledge not to marry is an extreme evasion of life's possibilities—those of happiness in marriage and, by implication, of the pain and the wonder of love.

Rosie, while trying to placate her mother, simultaneously cannot fully understand or capitulate. Rosie's confusion is captured in her thoughts while her mother awaits an answer: "There returned sweetly the memory of Jesus' hand, how it had touched her and where" (19). At the very moment her mother asks her to relinquish the prospect of love, Rosie cannot help remembering the possibility of love, and in so doing unconsciously subverts her mother's demand.[22]

Rosie ultimately gives her mother the affirmation she wants, but Mrs. Hayashi, understanding that her daughter's response is more the result of confusion than assent, looks at her with eyes and twisted mouth that seem to say "you fool."[23] As if as a sign of her arrival into adulthood, Rosie receives an "embrace and consoling hand" from her mother much later than she expects, suggesting the maturity Mrs. Hayashi now expects of her daughter, who has been initiated into the excitement, pain, and disillusionment of adult life. Part of this maturity includes a recognition of her mother's quashed attempt to transcend through art her dissatisfactions and disappointments.

With the exception of Masako's mother in "And the Soul Shall Dance," none of the Issei women depicted in these four stories conforms to the Issei ideal of a good Japanese wife as "quiet, reserved, nonaggressive, and somewhat subservient" "constantly loyal and obedient to her husband" (Yanagisako, 103). In writing about the unfulfilled desires and dreams of Issei women, Yamauchi and Yamamoto not only reveal the painful implications of this ideal but also question and critique the norm itself.

Although the muted rebellions of these women ultimately do not bring them the self-fulfillment they seek, they are not completely unsuccessful. That the Nisei from whose perspective the tales are told view the resistance with compassion indicates that they reject the subjugation of women dictated by Issei culture.[24] Because the narratives sympathetically reveal Issei women's struggles, readers come to respect these unlikely outlaws who violate cultural rules. In these four stories, Yamauchi and Yamamoto transform the rebels of the past into the heroines of the present.

NOTES

I thank Susan Schweik, King-Kok Cheung, Genaro Padilla, Eric Sundquist, and Amy Ling for their helpful comments on earlier versions of this essay.

1. Sylvia Yanagisako explains that Issei men associated their marriages with adult status. It redefined their relationships with family, giving them a greater sense of control. Marriage for Issei women, however, "often brought them greater subordination than they had experienced in their natal families—a subordination that was doubly oppressive if untempered by compassion" (96). Issei marriages were based on the Japanese concept of *giri* (obligation) rather than love.

2. Yamauchi has also written a dramatic version of "And the Soul Shall Dance." See *West Coast Plays* 11/12 (1982): 117–64 and *Between Worlds: Contemporary Asian-American Plays*, ed. Misha Berson (New York: Theatre Communications Group, 1990), 127–74.

3. Readers unfamiliar with Japanese American history may find Mrs. Oka's marriage bizarre, with its violent deviation from notions of romatic love. Viewed in the context of Japanese American history, however, her marriage is not too different from the prevalent practice of "picture-marriages" among Issei. Arranged marriages were traditional in Japan. When Japanese men in the United States sought to marry, this practice was altered to suit their needs. Issei men forwarded to their relatives photographs of themselves along with information about their situation in America. Relatives would then negotiate a marriage, and an Issei man would in turn receive a picture of his betrothed. Women were sent to America where they would meet their husbands for the first time. Although the exact number of picture-brides is unknown, "the majority of wives who entered immigrant society between 1910 and 1920 came as picture-brides" (Ichioka 165).

4. In picture-marriages, a groom did not have to be present for a ceremony; the main action of the marriage was to strike the bride's name from her family register and enter it in her husband's family register. This practice forcefully illustrates the trading of women as property, and the marriage by proxy where Mr. Oka is not even present becomes a potent image for Mrs. Oka's lack of power.

5. Susan Koppelman observes: "'Disgraceful mother' stories portray unconventional mothers and their daughters' struggles to resolve their feelings about their mothers and about themselves as the daughters of such women. Aspects of their character and behavior that violate narrow partriarchal [*sic*] rules for women cause mothers to be labelled 'disgraceful'" (xxviii). Since the narrator identifies Mrs. Oka as a quasi-maternal figure, "And the Soul Shall Dance" is a variation of a "disgraceful mother story."

6. As Dorothy Ritsuko McDonald and Katharine Newman note, Yamauchi often places emotional and earthly landscapes in parallel (35). This scene illustrates the idea well. Mrs. Oka's barren life in America mirrors the desert.

7. My thanks to King-Kok Cheung for alerting me to this possibility.

8. The similarities between the opening of "And the Soul Shall Dance" and Maxine Hong Kingston's *The Woman Warrior* are striking. *The Woman Warrior* begins with the warning, "You must not tell anyone . . . what I am about to tell you." The narrator than proceeds to tell all about an aunt who has been banished from family history (Kingston 3).

9. Many picture-brides were misled by their husbands into believing that they would lead comfortable lives in America. Issei men sometimes exaggerated claims of success. Some sent their future spouses touched-up photographs which made them appear younger than they actually were (Ichioka 168).

10. Yamauchi has said that her mother wanted to return to Japan. However, having boasted to her relatives that she would become wealthy in America, she felt unable to return until she had amassed a respectable sum of money. This never happened, and Yamauchi's mother never returned (interview with the author, 23 November 1987).

11. The stories are thus similar to those in Joyce's *Dubliners*.

12. King-Kok Cheung also notes that "it is through Yoneko's separate admiration for Marpo and for the mother that we learn the likelihood of mutual attraction between the two adults" (xxi).

13. The use of the word "kissed" is ironic because the almost fatal electrocution leaves Mr. Hosoume impotent.

14. This reversal of gender roles is significant when seen in the context of issei culture. Issei divided daily activities and responsibilities along the lines of "inside" and "outside": "Wives took care of everything 'inside' the house, home, or family, and men took care of 'everything else' (Yanagisako 101). Cooking would be considered an "inside" responsibility. So for Mr. Hosoume to perform domestic chores is in itself a major upheaval.

15. Although Yoneko is unaware that in hiding the ring's origin she defies her father, she is more than happy to keep the ring as a "secret revenge on her father," who has upset Yoneko with an annoying display in front of her friends (51–52).

16. "Nama-iki" is used only with women and children, to indicate that they are out of line.

17. Matthew 18:3, *New American Standard Bible*.

18. Charles L. Crow notes that "Yoneko does not pause to ponder the ambiguities of this statement—was the person taken Seigo or Marpo?" ("Home and Transcendence" 202).

19. I owe this observation to King-Kok Cheung, who first noted that Mr. Hayashi would be jealous of his wife's conversation in part because Mr. Hayano is handsome.

20. As Yuri Kageyama points out, Rosie's "fantasy of the bloody accident is an omen of the future—the father's 'murder' of his wife's past as a poet" (36).

21. Charles Crow considers Mr. Hayashi's portrayal as unflattering and as part of a broader "extended quarrel with or perhaps rite of exorcism against [a] generalized *Issei* male" ("*Issei* Father" 34). Yamamoto has responded that Mr. Hayashi was "only acting the way he'd been brought up to act, the way men were supposed to be" (Crow, "A MELUS Interview" 80).

22. King-Kok Cheung observes that the scene "conflates the mother's disenchantment and the daughter's dampened but inextinguishable hopes" (xx). She notes that Mrs. Hayashi's posture and demand are a travesty of a marriage proposal.

23. Elaine Kim suggests that Rosie "might come to comprehend the meaning of her mother's experience in time to benefit from it" (163).

24. Both Yamamoto and Yamauchi have commented on their needs to understand or to tell their mothers' stories. Yamamoto has said of "Seventeen Syllables," "Even though none of the details are true, "Seventeen Syllables" is [my mother's] story. It is the most reprinted of all the stories. Maybe she, wherever she is, guided the writing of it, and, even now, the propagation of it . . . so her story would be known. Or is that too far-fetched to comtemplate?" (Koppelman 162). Yamauchi mentions similar sentiments about the need for generational understanding when she comments, "[Y]ears ago when my mother passed away, she left a diary in Japanese that I was unable to read. I realized I never really knew her nor would I ever know her, and it became important to me to leave something of myself that my daughter could read and perceive the person I really was, so she could know who she was and why" (Chin 192).

WORKS CITED

Cheung, King-Kok. Introduction to *"Seventeen Syllables" and Other Stories* by Hisaye Yamamoto. Latham, N.Y.: Kitchen Table Press, 1988. xi–xxv.

Chin, Frank, et al. *Aiiieeeee!: An Anthology of Asian-American Writers*. 1974. Washington: Howard University Press, 1983.

Crow, Charles L. "Home and Transcendence in Los Angeles Fiction." In *Los Angeles in Fiction*, ed. David Find. Albuquerque: University of New Mexico Press, 1984. 189–203.

———. "The *Issei* Father in the Fiction of Hisaye Yamamoto." In *Opening Up Literary Criticism: Essays on American Prose and Poetry*, ed. Leo Truchlar. Salzburg: Verlag Wolfgang Neugebauer, 1986. 34–40.

———. "A MELUS Interview: Hisaye Yamamoto." *MELUS* 14.1 (1987): 73–84.

Ichioka, Yuji. *The Issei: The World of the First Generation Japanese Immigrants, 1885–1924*. New York: Free Press, 1988.

Kageyama, Yuri. "Hisaye Yamamoto—Nisei Writer." *Sunbury* 10 (n.d.): 32–42.

Kim, Elaine H. *Asian American Literature: An Introduction to the Writings and Their Social Context*. Philadelphia: Temple University Press, 1982.

Kingston, Maxine Hong. *The Woman Warrior: Memoirs of a Girlhood among Ghosts*. 1976. New York: Vintage, 1977.

Kitano, Harry H. L. *Japanese Americans: The Evolution of a Subculture*. 1969. Englewood Cliffs, N.J.: Prentice-Hall, 1976.

Koppleman, Susan, ed. *Between Mothers and Daughters: Stories Across a Generation*. Old Westbury, N.Y.: Feminist Press, 1985.

McDonald, Dorothy Ritsuko, and Katharine Newman. "Relocation and Dislocation: The Writings of Hisaye Yamamoto and Wakako Yamauchi." *MELUS* 7.3 (1980): 21–38.

Wordsworth, William. "Preface to the Second Edition of *Lyrical Ballads*." In *Critical Theory Since Plato*, ed. Hazard Adams. New York: Harcourt, 1971. 435.

Yamamoto, Hisaye. "Seventeen Syllables." 1949. In *"Seventeen Syllables" and Other Stories*. Latham, N.Y.: Kitchen Table Press, 1988. 8–19.

———. "Yoneko's Earthquake." 1951. In *"Seventeen Syllables" and Other Stories*. Latham, N.Y.: Kitchen Table Press, 1988. 46–56.

Yamauchi, Wakako. "And the Soul Shall Dance." 1966. In *Aiiieeeee!*, ed. Chin et al. Washington, D.C.: Howard University Press, 1983. 193–200.

———. "Songs My Mother Taught Me." *Amerasia Journal* 3.2 (1976): 63–73.

Yanagisako, Syliva Junko. *Transforming the Past: Tradition and Kinship among Japanese Americans*. Stanford: Stanford University Press, 1985.

8

Facing the Incurable: Patriarchy in Eat a Bowl of Tea

Ruth Y. Hsiao

CHINESE AMERICAN writers have all had to reckon with patriarchal tradition. Their attitudes range from agreeing with the value of this tradition to designing its collapse with a subversive plot. The earliest questioning of patriarchy exists in nineteenth-century Cantonese folk rhymes, which came into circulation when Chinese laborers immigrated to California. A female speaker challenges, "How can we tolerate the confines of those dated moral conventions" when education has brought equality? Another female speaker declares, "We don't submit ourselves to oppression. . . . What's there to fear?" (*Songs of Gold Mountain* 220–21). The first Eurasian writer to publish in the United States, Edith Eaton, used a subtler means of subverting patriarchal tyranny; her character Mrs. Spring Fragrance couches put-downs of her husband and his fellow male chauvinists in irony (Amy Ling 411–19). These occasional expressions of feminism in Chinese American writings were the exception rather than the rule. Most writings resemble a group of stories in the short-lived New York Chinatown literary magazine, *The Bud* (1947–48), which depicts women as no more than "appendages to men" with little complexity and no inner needs (Sau-ling Wong 71–13).

By the late 1940s, as a result of China's role as an American ally in World War II, the United States lifted some of its anti-Chinese immigration laws to admit Chinese women. Not accidentally, these events coincided with the publication of the two autobiographies, *Father and Glorious Descendant* (1943) by Pardee Lowe and *Fifth Chinese Daughter* (1945) by Jade Snow Wong. Both offspring of stern Confucian fathers, these authors extolled patriarchal precepts; but their defiant behavior, such as Wong's going to college against her father's wish and Lowe's marrying a Caucasian wife, constitutes unintended criticism of their autocratic fathers. Appropriate for their time, they erred on the side of applauding the patriarchal but much-maligned Chinese emigrants, who had come to be associated with opium, coolies, and tong wars. But as hostility lessened toward the Chinese, veiled criticism of patriarchy gave way to more open warfare between generations.

In comparison to these two autobiographies published before the civil rights era of the sixties, Louis Chu's only novel, *Eat a Bowl of Tea* (1961), reveals the uneasy truce between American-born children and their patriarchal elders. The emerging antipatriarchal tradition barely started by Chu's predecessors becomes prominent. The novel depicts male characters subjected to humiliations no healthy patriarchal society would have allowed. When transplanted to America, patriarchy itself became a victim. Discriminatory laws deprived the men of respectability and blighted their lives. Yet, when more liberal laws brought Chinese women to Chinatown, their presence created havoc, which the tragicomic novel uses to great advantage. The novel treats women as an intrusive nuisance that throws the male dominant community out of kilter, but not for long. Not only does the novel restore the ruffled, old-order social hierarchy, but it also suggests the birth of a new age patriarchy.

To be sure, Chu shows the negative effects of an autocratic upbringing. Chu's characters bear the unmistakable marks of patriarchy's sons and daughters: they are dependent, limited, and unfulfilled. At the end of the novel, however, rejuvenation and potency return to the beleaguered young couple Ben Loy and Mei Oi when they move away from the collective control of New York in paternalistic Chinatown and begin a new breed of Chinese Americans.

In the introduction, Jeffery Chan credits Chu with locating the source of Chinese American vitality:

> It is no coincidence that Chu sends Ben Loy and Mei Oi to San Francisco for Ben Loy to reclaim his virility, his paternity, and his wife. His return to San Francisco to make himself anew is not the response of a sojourner. He

> is a Chinese-American remaking a covenant with Gum Sahn, what the first generation called America, the Golden Mountain. He returns to the city where Chinese-America first began. (5)

Ben Loy reclaims in one swoop "his virility, his paternity, and his wife." (Patriarchy reigns *again*.) Ben Loy is cured of the enervating effects of patriarchy and racism that rob him of manhood, but can we purge Chinese American writings of patriarchal views? I think not. A bowl of herbal tea restores Ben Loy's virility only to install him as the new-generation patriarch. If *Eat a Bowl of Tea* is an attempt to purge the patriarchal tradition in literature, it has failed.

Because of his depiction of the twin evils—patriarchy and racism, Chu is widely acclaimed by Asian American writers and critics. His novel has had two revivals, a reissue in 1979 and a film version in 1989. This continued interest also has much to do with his achievement as a herald of the new Asian American sensibility, a sensibility supposedly free of such anachronisms as patriarchy. Since his novel plays a pivotal role in the evolution of the Asian American sensibility, we should first place the novel in its historical context.

By the late 1950s, demographic changes brought on by more liberal immigration laws resulted in the conditions depicted in Chu's novel. The War Bride Act of 1945 finally allowed more Chinese women to enter the United States. This act changed the previously male dominant so-called bachelor society of Chinatown. Set in 1947, *Eat a Bowl of Tea* shows the authoritarian father reduced to a pathetic parody, while the newly arrived women flaunt shocking freedoms. Mei Oi, Ben Loy's wife, even violates the cardinal female virtue of chastity and marital fidelity. Ideologically advanced, Ben Loy accepts her "love child" as his own and thus damages the Confucian image of patrilineal purity. This un-Chinese ending marks patriarchy's first serious fall into disrepute in Chinese American fiction.

The fall begins with the decline of family after decades of male emigration and harsh realities in the new land. Compared to Lowe and Wong's paeans to family life, Chu's fictionalized "family," headed by Wong Wah Gay and barely held together by Ben Loy and Mei Oi, becomes a mockery of Chinese family. Men are reduced to "paper sons," "bachelor fathers," and absent husbands. The circle of Wah Gay's foul-mouthed cronies who meet at lunch counters and basement gambling halls takes the place of family. These "bachelors" cannot return to China because of inertia, lack of money, and immigration restrictions. Their wives, amply represented by the capable and energetic Lau Shee (Ben Loy's mother and Wah Gay's wife), bring up the children in the ancestral village. The "rice cookers," as they are referred to by their "*gimshunhock*" (gold-mountain sojourner) husbands, take on domineering aspects as the husbands' self-esteem diminishes. Left to Wah Gay and Lee Gong, without their wives' goading, their children would not find suitable parentally approved matches. Wah Gay remains a subordinate, accountable to his wife in China, who has been separated from him for over two decades.

The fathers' foibles lend an un-Confucian sensibility to the novel. Chu legitimized this sensibility: he wrote in a salty vernacular, describing the pleasures of the flesh and evoking the raw, harsh life of waiters, barbers, cooks, gamblers, and hangers-on. Consequently Chu became something of a trailblazer in his portrayal of emotionally damaged sons and daughters locked in battles of independence with their fathers or with the tradition that gives the fathers power. Since then, overtly or subversively, the literature has repeatedly attacked the Confucian fathers. Chu's iconoclastic treatment of Chinatown fathers emboldened later writers to express what has now come to be accepted as the Chinese American sensibility. During the postsixties flowering of Asian American literature in general, antipatriarchal and anti-Confucian attitudes colored most of the writings. Indeed Chinatown, the symbol of Chinese America, is now regarded as a culture unto itself, rather than the inauthentic imitation of two mother cultures, forever split by a hyphen. This prevailing sentiment has become so strong in the last decade, in fact, that in writing, the hyphen in "Chinese-American" has disappeared. Chinatown is its own source of language and expression—and these are good enough for high art.

After the consciousness-raising 1960s, many critics and writers held up Chu's book as a model of a realistic portrayal of Chinatown. The current crop of Asian American writers who abandon their characters to alienation, raw anger, patricidal obsessions, self-contempt, and marginality follow in the same tradition as *Eat a Bowl of Tea.* Ben Loy, the emasculated and frustrated son, has many literary descendants in the stories and plays by Asian Americans, as can also be said of Mei Oi, the threatening Chinese female characterized by male writers.

This new sensibility came first from Chu's intimate knowledge of the ossified Chinese traditions that had survived and flourished in

America's Chinatown. Chu shows that while customs changed in China's villages, ethnic culture remained entrenched in the insulated ghetto of cosmopolitan New York City. Ben Loy and Mei Oi's wedding, emblematic of Chinatown's anachronism, is celebrated twice—in the "new generation" style back in Sunwei village and then at a banquet given in New York's Chinatown. The village wedding arranged by the couple's mothers combines East and West: a Christian minister officiates on a day picked by an astrologer. The church wedding reflects the Westernization China was going through and the inroads missionaries had made into the hamlets and villages. In Sunwei, without the *gimshun* fathers, the bride and groom occupy the center of attention and receive their benediction. But in Chinatown, U.S.A., which is cut off from mainstream American society, the banquet—more a stag party than a nuptial feast—is untouched by American custom. Chu describes in detail the customs that the old-time "bachelors" still cling to. The bride and groom's presence is incidental. In keeping with the feudalistic social network of family associations, Wang Chuck Ting, as president and elder statesman, takes over as host and introduces the officers of the organizations. The banquet serves Wah Gay's need to curry their favor rather than celebrating the marriage of his son and daughter-in-law, Ben Loy and Mei Oi.

By depicting the old and new ways, Chu echoes the silencing of women and the young in earlier writings. Jade Snow Wong notes that at the Fourth Older Sister's wedding "hardly anyone talked to the bride; they all talked to the parents," and the bride "was merely a sort of decorative, noneating, nondrinking, nonspeaking accessory to the wedding celebration" (144). In Pardee Lowe's autobiography, as the contrite elder son that he is, he never once mentions his Caucasian wife by name but only as one who adds "luster to the family honor" and is "one of the models for Chinatown's feminine etiquette, a preserver of its ancient traditions of social intercourse" (237). In spite of their implicit criticism of patriarchy, Wong and Lowe acquiesced in its practices. Chu, however, does not allow the bride to be forgotten, and his pivots on Mei Oi's affair with Ah Song. It is a tale of the bride's revenge. Ben Loy becomes a cuckold, and their marital crisis sends the community reeling.

In New York, patriarchy can no longer exert moral influence over the entire community; it contains its own undoing. Among the invited guests at the feast is Mei Oi's seducer, Ah Song, who first sees her there. Although the watchful eyes of the Chinatown fathers follow Ah Song, a notorious wife stealer, he is an outsider with no powerful family associations to kowtow to or to lean on, and he confesses to Mei Oi that he rather enjoys "this bachelor life." He is free to cause trouble. As one scholar of labor and political history points out, the internal structure of village and family associations "was not as functional as it seemed. Its organizational model, after all, was the feudal China of the Ch'ing Dynasty, whose self-sufficient rural economy was scarcely comparable to the urban industrialized setting of New York's Chinatown. The traditional associations were run on strict hierarchical lines; they demanded unquestioning obedience and total control" (Kwong 41). New York's Chinatown has many competing tongs and family associations, plus all kinds of unaffiliated drifters. Thus control cannot be "total." Ah Song sets off a chain of events that humiliate, infuriate, and fragment the family and the community.

Finally, Chu's antipatriarchal portrayal resides in the two fathers' characters. Wah Gay and Lee Gong, gambling partners and now in-laws through Ben Loy and Mei Oi's marriage, are mere shadows of the Confucian father. Wah Gay, proprietor of the gambling shop Money Come, knows all too painfully that his life is far from exemplary and sends Ben Loy to work in a restaurant in Connecticut to keep him out of "harm's way." Lee Gong has been an absent father and has never set eyes on his daughter until the day she arrives in New York as Ben Loy's bride. The pregnant Mei Oi longs to confide in her father about her illicit affair, but they have no father-daughter bond and she gets neither solace nor guidance. In Chinatown, children disgrace their parents as often as fathers fail their children.

Chu places the blame for male inadequacy, however, squarely on the social and historical conditions of the Chinese emigrants in America. Circumstances excuse these failed fathers' and husbands' lack of ambition. They cling to the only tradition they know, which is reflected in Wah Gay's view of Ben Loy's impending marriage:

> He ventured to think that, after the marriage, Ben Loy would work that much harder because he would have a family to support. Instead of having to keep track of his son himself, he would have a daughter-in-law to take over the responsibility. A year or so after the wedding, a grandson, perhaps. Or a granddaughter? A boy first? Our Chinese people always like boys. But what if . . . " (46)

Children exist to propagate future generations, with the daughters-in-law as accessories to the whole process. Patriarchal loyalty also dictates that thc fathers do everything they can to protect the reputation of the family association, which in turn protects their livelihood. They do not care about the suffering of their offspring—Ben Loy and Mei Oi. In fact throughout the family crisis Wah Gay and Lee Gong behave as the wronged party. In a community supposedly dedicated to mutual aid, Ben Loy and Mei Oi stand alone in their crisis. Without the social and family network of a normal community, they have nowhere to turn for advice and solace.

Patriarchy is unyielding and unforgiving in its characteristic sternness. The wrongdoer Ah Song has his ear sliced off in one melodramatic stroke by Wah Gay and is banished. Even the aging fathers, Wah Gay and Lee Gong, must pull up stakes and go elsewhere to rid the community of any trace of shame. Because Chu has made the implacable patriarchy the emotional center of his novel, Wong Chuck Ting's mediation of the incident takes over the plot. In the tense negotiations between Wah Gay and the Wang Family Association (headed by Chuck Ting), the young couple nearly disappears from the plot. In fact there are two plots, with the plot having Ben Loy and Mei Oi as its focus subordinate to the main plot: how Chinatown fathers maintain order. New York's Chinatown remains strangled by the feudalism that has held sway in China for centuries and rules it even now. However benevolent, Chuck Ting and his lieutenants exert their power and influence. They intrude into Chinatown's private lives. The intricate power structure of family associations and tongs still rules supreme in the insulated Chinatown. Its grip is relentless, its judgment swift, and its power unyielding. Under this system, the ruling patriarchs mete out rewards and punishments. Ben Loy and Mei Oi, and even their fathers, live at the mercy of the collective decisions.

In the limited world of Chinatown, failure begets failure. The impoverished old-fashioned males cannot provide the authoritarian guidance a son like Ben Loy is conditioned to need. Coming to New York at the age of seventeen, Ben Loy is a cultural orphan, ill-equipped to handle his new life. His parents dictate what work he should do and when and whom he should marry. Filial obedience makes him passive and dull. The freedom he has stolen—whoring behind his father's back—robs him finally of his manhood. As a character, Ben Loy seems totally acted upon by the social forces Chu describes.

Ben Loy's limitations ar further aggravated by the community's sense of proprietorship over all its sons. He is not only his father's son but also a son of Chinatown. The community's gossip places further strain on the couple's childless state. As the whispered rumor of Mei Oi's affair spreads, Ben Loy sinks deeper into inaction and becomes more susceptible to his elders' maneuverings. Although he moves to San Francisco, the source and cradle of Chinese America, and comes into his own, the cure for his impotence comes appropriately from a bowl of medicinal tea. He finds renewal outside himself. The perfunctory happy ending only underscores the extent of Ben Loy's impotence. Louis Chu's art may be ahead of his time, but he could not conceive of any inner change in the sons of patriarchy.

Unlike the rags-to-riches prototype in many immigrant memoirs, Chu's Ben Loy languishes in indecision and ineptitude. In this respect Ben Loy has many literary descendants in the stories and plays of the next decade. He is reincarnated in Frank Chin's Johnny in "Food for All His Dead" and Tam in *Chickencoop Chinaman* and in Jeffrey Chan's Bill Wong in "Chinese in Haifa." Conditioned by Chinese tradition and the standards of the masculine image in American culture, these Chinese sons and husbands prove defenseless and impotent, mastered by rather than mastering their fate. These schlemiels seem to wallow in their self-emasculation, with no hope of measuring up to either the patriarchal Chinese image of authority or the American model of masculinity. The fathers, dead or alive, remain in control. The frustrated and passive sons rail against what their fathers represent, yet they cannot break out of the confines of tradition. Failed dreams, unfulfilling marriages and relationships, and what they see as a cultural conspiracy to rob them of power plague their lives. By the same token the male authors yearn for the potency the once-powerful patriarchy would have conferred on them.

Chu's greatest achievement lies in his exploitation of the complications created by women who are not prostitutes in the "bachelor society" of Chinatown. The presence of women brings out patriarchy's most ruthless character—its misogny—manifested in the language and attitudes of the bachelor community. The otherwise enfeebled male community joins in a swelling chorus of "Nowadays women are not to be trusted" echoed by "*Gim Peng Moy,*" the Cantonese opera the bachelors listen to in the barber's chair. Despite their own loose morals, the men demand purity and fidelity of their wives and daughters. This double standard is ingrained in the culture. But the feudal code is a thing of the past. Given the education that women now receive and the male-female imbalance in Chinatown, women have freedoms that the bachelors cannot stem. On one level, *Eat a Bowl of Tea* satirizes the "bachelor society's" hollow show of authority.

But Chu's achievement is limited by his depiction of Mei Oi. It shows his ambivalence toward the heroine he both liberates from and imprisons in traditional ideas of womanhood. Although he gives Mei Oi the role of discrediting and humiliating patriarchy, he does not entirely transcend his male view of women. To be sure, he acknowledges the independence of the "new woman" as represented by the middle-school graduate Mei Oi. This educated "school girl" can shake up the rickety patriarchy. Mei Oi has a mind of her own and has already chosen a path for herself: "She knew she wouldn't marry a farmer. A farmer's wife worked from dawn till dusk out in the fields. . . . Marry a school teacher? Not Mei Oi. There was this common observation. Unless you're poor you would not be teaching (66). Yet for all the benefits of a middle school education, Mei Oi must stay home and be economically dependent. Bored and childless, the listless Mei Oi wants to find work outside. Ben Loy turns down her request—but not before he consults his father. Ben Loy says he wants to preserve family dignity, but he really fears that Mei Oi may meet other men. By an ironic twist of fate, Ben Loy's worst fear materializes right in his own house, which is where Mei Oi meets Ah Song. Here as elsewhere Chu's treatment of this pivotal event is ambiguous. He metes out freedoms to Mei Oi with one hand and takes them back with the other.

Not only is Mei Oi's freedom limited, but her character gets scant development. The briefly introduced school-girl image of Mei Oi undergoes a drastic change with her crossing the Pacific. Mei Oi turns into a dangerous seductress overnight—with little preparation by Chu. Abruptly, the innocent village girl discards her loose two-piece suits in favor of clinging gowns. For the Chinatown banquet she wears a "snugly" fitted satin gown, which is appropriately red for a wedding but also portends Mei Oi's subsequent behavior as bordering on that of a scarlet woman. In fact she rather relishes her affair with Ah Song,: "The great pleasures she got from her indiscretions were worth the risk" (124). While Ben Loy is haunted by his past dalliance with prostitutes, no qualms bother Mei Oi. Confronted by Ben Loy, she counterattacks: "'What kind of a husband have you been?'" she declares; "'I didn't do anything wrong . . . but it turns out that I've married an old man . . . an old man who's too old to make love to me'" (145). Here again ambivalence governs Chu's attitude toward Mei Oi's sexuality. Her aggressive role makes Ben Loy all the more a victim of social forces over which he has no control. The author builds up our sympathy for Ben Loy as Mei Oi steps up her pursuit of extramarital gratification. Like the unfaithful wife in *Gim Peng Moy*, Mei Oi has the destructive potential to bring about her husband's downfall—and her destructiveness erodes Ben Loy's self-esteem.

In effect, Mei Oi personifies the proverbial temptress, both to be desired and feared. Male artists and writers have often put their female subjects in such paradoxical light, and Chu is no exception. Chu's narrative, perhaps unconsciously, reinforces this connection for us. The early morning call of the prostitute in the opening scene invites us to link the white prostitute with the bride who is lying in Ben Loy's arms. The juxtaposition of the two women is meant to show the source of Ben Loy's guilt and its symptom, impotence. But the two women have even more in common than suggested by this opening image: both are dependent on the economically independent man as well as being objects of his sexual desire (though Ben Loy's is in temporary suspension). The prostitute sells her body just as Mei Oi marries a *gimsunhock* for his money and the chance to come to America. Even if this parallel is not intended by the author, Mei Oi has limited autonomy as a character and is manipulated by father, husband, father-in-law, seducer and, finally, the novelist—to achieve his narrative ends.

At best, Chu's Mei Oi calls up a sensual Suzy Wong, easily lured by attention and gifts. Vain and frivolous, the eighteen-year-old cannot handle the temptation of adultery: "Mei Oi's affair with Ah Song was the sort of thing that a country girl would never dream could happen to her. Once it happened it was not within the easy-going personality of Mei Oi to halt it" (103). Her beauty, as seen by Ben Loy and expressed in hackneyed Chinese terms, further casts her as a cardboard character: "Her eyebrows were like the crescent of the new moon. Her full lips, forming a small mouth, were cherry-red. Her nose . . . perfect as a distant star" (50). The telling scene of Mei Oi admiring herself in the mirror underscores her lack of an inner dimension: "Mei Oi turned to face the mirror again. She inspected the collar. She spun around and glanced at the curves reflected in the mirror. She tugged at the lower half of the dress and wiggled a little bit" (82). In this gesture she conforms with the male image of women: all exterior and no inner dimension. As the proverbial China doll and Suzy Wong combined, she displays no perceptible change or growth. She has no self-understanding and is solely propelled by vanity. For a fuller portrait of Asian American woman we have to wait for later writers—women writers—to reveal the struggle and confusion that crossing cultural boundaries could generate in the female psyche. *Eat a Bowl of Tea* adopts both the Western and the Chinese patriarchal caricatures of Asian women.

For all his ambiguous and stereotypical treatment of Mei Oi, however, Chu provides us with an alternative to the "rice cookers." Even Eng Shee, Mei Oi's rival and the 1950 facsimile of an old-time "rice cooker," does so little cooking that her husband brings home food from the restaurant. Such "new women" freely express their sexuality, as Mei Oi does by flirting with her husband's friend while carrying on an affair with another man. She does not tolerate a sexless marriage as a traditional wife would. But Chu's portrait of a liberated woman stops here. As a character, Mei Oi merely occupies the other side of the same coin as the shrewish "rice cooker," reinforcing the double-vision image of women in male eyes.

Female characters created by male writers that have come after Mei Oi are also subservient to their male counterparts; the female characters serve as foils for the flawed and ineffective husbands, sons, and fathers, who are casualties in a racist and stifling society. The authors are not interested in developing the women and granting them dimensions of their own. Rather than their sympathy for the plight of women, what is significant is these authors' criticism of a process that robs the men of their accustomed authority and manhood. In their eyes, women fare better in America. For all their criticism of patriarchy, the male writers perpetuate the patriarchy-centered world, in which the woman is a polemical tool to reinforce the emasculation of Asian males.

The lack of inner dimension in Chu's characters, male and female, is not necessarily a function of artistic failure but a result of the limited individual power such characters would have in Chinatown, and by extension in the larger American society. Several times, the plot teeters melodramatically on such flimsy devices as Wah Gay's knife or bowls of herbal tea. Chu cannot tell us much more about these characters who are limited by the limiting world that forms them. Moreover, Chu is himself a son of patriarchy, the source of his vision and understanding. The refurbishing of this tattered tradition was not within his capability.

Thus *Eat a Bowl of Tea* serves as a culmination of the early attempts to debunk patriarchy as a viable social structure in Asian America. On a scale and with a complexity not found in earlier works, Louis Chu uses patriarchy as the villain of his tragicomic story. That his story should survive as one of the influential texts in the post–civil rights decades indicates the lively interest Asian American writers still have in the patriarchal tradition. The same forces that stymied a marriage on the rocky soil of forced "bachelorhood" also hampered Chu from seeing a woman beyond her exterior and her mechanical role in the plot. Just as the community is not freed from the patriarchal vise, so Chu's handling of Mei Oi and other female characters is still dictated by male images of women. Whether a ghost or a living tyrant, the ubiquitous figure of the patriarch still stalks Asian American literature even as it concocts endless cures to ward off patriarchy's ill effects. But patriarchy remains incurable in *Eat a Bowl of Tea*.

WORKS CITED

Chu, Louis. *Eat a Bowl of Tea*. 1961. Seattle: University of Washington Press, 1979.

Hom, Marlon K. *Songs of Gold Mountain: Cantonese Rhymes from San Francisco Chinatown*. Berkeley: University of California Press, 1987.

Kwong, Peter. *Chinatown, New York: Labor and Politics, 1930–1950*. New York: Monthly Review Press, 1979.

Ling, Amy. "Writers with a Cause: Sui Sin Far and Han Suyin." *Women's Studies International Forum* 9.4 (1986): 411–419.

Lowe, Pardee. *Father and Glorious Descendant*. Boston: Little, Brown, 1943.

Wong, Jade Snow. *Fifth Chinese Daughter*. 1945. Seattle: University of Washington Press, 1989.

Wong, Sau-ling C. "Tales of Postwar Chinatown: Short Stories of The Bud, 1947–1948." *Amerasia* 14.2 (1988): 61–79.

9

"Don't Tell": Imposed Silences in The Color Purple *and* The Woman Warrior

King-Kok Cheung

BOTH Alice Walker's *The Color Purple* and Maxine Hong Kingston's *The Woman Warrior* open with parental warnings against speech. Celie's stepfather threatens, "*You better not never tell nobody but God. It'd kill your mammy*" (11). Maxine's mother admonishes her daughter, "You must not tell anyone . . . what I am about to tell you" (3). Despite these explicit prohibitions, both the black and the Chinese American protagonists proceed to tell all—on paper. Their needs for self-expression are obvious: they hang on to sanity by writing; they defend themselves with words; they discover their potential—sound themselves out—through articulation.

Less obvious are the ways in which Walker and Kingston convert their characters' sociocultural disabilities into felicities. Celie (an unschooled black) and Maxine (a Chinese American struggling to learn English) must overcome forbidding sexual, racial, and linguistic barriers. They work their way from speechlessness to eloquence not only by covering the historical stages women writers have traveled—from suffering patriarchy, to rebelling against its conventions, to creating their own ethos—but also by developing a style that emerges from their respective cultures. In the course of their odysseys, the destructive weapon of tradition is turned into a creative implement, and speech impediment becomes literary invention.

The heroines' inventiveness reflects the resourcefulness of their creators, who are politically and aesthetically concerned with conveying ethnic and feminist sensibilities. Like so many other American writers today, Walker and Kingston must grapple with a language and a literary tradition that have long excluded their kind. But the two minority writers must also choose to write either in the "dominant" mode or in a mode that reflects their own multicultural legacies. Though both authors have mastered standard English, neither claims it as her first tongue, and it is far removed from the speech of the people they write about. Their common quest, therefore, is to seek ways to transplant their native dialects to their texts, even if they risk being occasionally unintelligible to the reading majority (see Dasenrock's defense of "unintelligibility" in multicultural texts). The stakes are high, however. For both authors, reclaiming the mother tongue is much more than reproducing a dialect or marshaling a new vocabulary; it is also bringing to life a rich oral tradition in which women have actively participated. And if we agree with Werner Sollors that "ethnicity as a tenuous ancestry and the interplay of different ancestries may be the most crucial aspect of the American national character" ("Literature" 648),[2] these authors have instated themselves in the American tradition by hitting upon a syncretic idiom at once inherited and self-made. In *The Color Purple* and *The Woman Warrior* alike, breaking silence, acknowledging female influence, and preserving cultural and national characteristics are a coordinated art. These "speaking tests" expose the layers of silence that have threatened to choke the colored protagonists and raise the voices that have run the gamut (and gauntlet) of interethnic differences.

Since the particular agony and exceptional progress of the protagonists are inseparable from their gender and ethnic backgrounds —for Walker and Kingston equally—the knotty problems of distinguishing between authors and protagonists and of drawing cross-cultural comparisons must be addressed at the outset. For a critic interested in examining the linguistic struggles of the black and Chinese American heroines, it is particularly difficult to adhere to the texts without referring to the black and Chinese American authors. The danger lies in foreshortening the artistic distances in these works or, worse, in seeing the narratives as representative of the minority groups depicted. Because some white reviewers treat the two books as though they were definitive descriptions of minority experiences, several black and Chinese American critics not only lash out at these reviewers for their presumption but also blame the writers for distorting the facts about their respective ethnic groups.[3] Walker and Kingston do draw heavily on their cultures, but they are not cultural historians, nor are they committed to a purely realistic fictional form. On the contrary, they are feminist writers who seek to "re-vision" history (to borrow Adrienne Rich's word). If they are to be nurtured by their cultural inheritance rather than smothered by it, they must learn to reshape recalcitrant myths glorifying patriarchal values. Blinkering the authors by historical or ethnographic criteria denies their freedom as artists to mingle history and myth, fact and fiction.[4] To distinguish each fictive "I" from the writer, and to avoid confusing the representation of a particular experience with anthropology, I will focus my literary analysis primarily on the protagonists—Celie and Maxine—but refer to the authors when I wish to call attention to their artistry.

Similar considerations underlie my reluctance to extrapolate general cross-cultural comparisons based on the texts alone. Although informed by historical and social factors, the narratives do not necessarily illuminate the cultures at large. As women, both Celie and Maxine have been debased in their families. Celie is abused by her stepfather and her husband alike, and Maxine suffers the antifemale prejudice rooted in her parents' Chinese past. But to conclude from reading the two books that black men or Chinese people are misogynistic is to stereotype these groups invidiously.[5] I am also aware that sexism in the two cultures draws on different roots; that black silences, deepened by the history of slavery, are not the same as Chinese American silences, which were reinforced by anti-Asian immigration laws. The repression of Celie is much more violent and brutal than Maxine's, and her resources are at the beginning much more limited. Celie expresses herself tentatively at first because she lacks schooling; it is in school that Maxine becomes totally uncommunicative (because she has to learn a second language). But such differences are not my main concerns. Despite the heroines' disparate cultural experiences, their psychological imperative to expression is kindred. My intent is to trace the striking parallels in the protagonists' struggles and in the authors' narrative strategies. Gender and ethnicity—inhibitive forces when these texts open—eventually become the sources of personal and stylistic strengths.

Women authors and feminist critics have been unusually vocal on the theme of silence—as an artistic tool (Gubar, Sontag), as imposed invisibility (Griffin), and as the reticence enjoined upon women and felt most acutely by writers (see Gilbert and Gubar, Olsen, Rich, and Russ). Silence runs even deeper in the work of minority women. Paula Gunn Allen observes that persons caught between cultures are most likely to be "inarticulate, almost paralyzed in their inability to direct their energies toward resolving what seems to them insoluble conflict" (135). Carolyn Heilbrun describes minority women as "outsiders twice over" (37), excluded both from the mainstream and from the ethnic centers of power. Some of these women are, moreover, thrice muted on account of sexism, racism, and a "tonguelessness" that results from prohibitions or language barriers.

The three constraints are often interrelated. Both *The Color Purple* and *The Woman Warrior* begin with women who are punished by not being allowed to speak or to be spoken about. In both, it is not the male offender but the female victim who suffers the penalty for an illicit affair: he sentences her to hold her tongue. These tales are timeless variations on the Philomela myth, in which the tongue of the raped woman is cut off: victimization incurs voicelessness.[6] Celie and later her sister Nettie are violently coerced by their aggressors. Alphonso, who Celie thinks is her father but who is actually her stepfather, forbids her to speak about his repeated sexual assaults. Albert, Celie's husband, prevents the two sisters from corresponding after Nettie has rejected his lustful advances. Nettie writes to Celie, "He said because of what I'd done I'd never hear from you again, and you would never hear from me" (119). The threat proves real. By hiding Nettie's letters from Celie, Albert metes out the same punishment to Nettie that Alphonso does to Celie: the denial of communication.

Silence also entombs the no-name aunt in *The Woman Warrior*, who commits suicide after giving birth to an illegitimate child. Maxine speculates on what might have happened to her aunt: "Some man had commanded her to lie with him and be his secret evil. . . . His demand must have surprised, then terrified her. She obeyed him; she always did as she was told" (7). Maxine muses on her aunt's predicament: "The other man was not, after all, much different from her husband. They both gave orders: she followed. 'If you tell your family, I'll beat you. I'll kill you'" (8). The aunt obeys, submitting without protest. She can neither talk herself out of being raped nor declare her innocence afterwards. When she gets pregnant, she is harassed by villagers and repudiated by her own family, even after her death.

Maxine also has a living aunt, Moon Orchid, who has traveled from China to look for her husband in America, only to discover that he has taken a new wife. The husband snaps, "What are you doing here?" Moon Orchid can only "open and shut her mouth without any words coming out" (176). The unfaithful husband, not the wronged wife, flashes his anger: "He looked directly at Moon Orchid the way the savages looked. . . . She shrank from his stare; it silenced her crying" (177).

Both the "guilty" and the innocent aunt are hushed. Maxine's family tries to erase all knowledge of the dead woman, to carry on "as if she had never been born" (3). To expunge her name, to delete the memory of her life, is perhaps the cruelest repudiation her kin could devise.[7] No less cruel is the silencing of the living. Stared and scared into silence by her husband, Moon Orchid soon goes mad. Her niece later draws a connection between speechlessness and insanity: "I thought talking and not talking made the difference between sanity and insanity. Insane people were the ones who couldn't explain themselves" (216).

Associating voicelessness with victimization and with madness, young Maxine recognizes the exigencies of expression, but the brutal and domineering aspect of speech gives her pause. In a haunting travesty of the cases involving her aunts' stories, she tries to scold and pinch a quiet Chinese American girl into speech. "If you don't talk, you can't have a personality. . . . Talk, please talk," Maxine cries (210). Yet in the same breath she enforces silence: "Don't you dare tell anyone I've been bad to you" (210). Her frustration with the mute girl reflects her own anxiety: she is afraid of losing her identity, of being erased or unhinged—as her two aunts have been respectively erased and unhinged—through silence. At the same time, she cannot help linking utterance and coercion. Her protracted illness after the incident reflects her guilt and misgivings about verbal authority (and her psychosomatic attempt to evade the conflict). She views her aggressive act as "the worst thing I had yet done to another person" (210).

Not only sexist but racist repression can gag a person. Asked condescendingly by the mayor's wife to work as her maid, Sofia, the outspoken wife of Celie's stepson, answers: "Hell no" (86). The mayor then slaps Sofia, who counters his blow by knocking him down. She is consequently jailed and tortured. Celie relates: "They crack her skull, they crack her ribs. They tear her nose loose on one side. They blind her in one eye. She swole from head to foot. Her tongue the size of my arm, it stick out tween her teef like a piece of rubber. *She can't talk*" (87; my emphasis). The black woman who dares to return insult and exchange blows is imprisoned, brutalized, and muted. The impudent tongue is bludgeoned—to seal her mouth.

Discrimination also thickens the silence in Maxine's family, whose predisposition to secrecy is reinforced by anti-Asian immigration policies (Kim 200). Maxine writes, "There were secrets never to be said . . . immigration secrets whose telling could get us sent back to China." Even though she and her siblings are hardly privy to these secrets, they are cautioned against confiding in outsiders. "Don't tell," the parents repeatedly admonish (213–14); Maxine comments, "We couldn't tell if we wanted to because we didn't know" (213). The adults worry so much about deportation that they bid their offspring to withhold information withheld.

Silenced at home, Maxine also fails to raise her voice at work. Her boss at an art supply store takes pride in having coined the phrase "nigger yellow" to describe a paint color. When Maxine tries to gainsay him, she cannot make herself heard: "'I don't like that word' I had to say in my bad, small-person's voice that makes no impact. The boss never deigned to answer" (57). She is also disregarded by an employer at a land developers' association, who chooses to host a company banquet in a restaurant picketed by CORE (Congress of Racial Equality) and the NAACP. Maxine again makes a feeble pretext: "'I refuse to type these invitations,' I whispered, voice unreliable" (57–58). The minority protester is shown the door; her "small-person's voice," already "unreliable," is sent out of earshot and becomes wholly inaudible.

Notwithstanding Celie's quiet resignation and Maxine's impotent rage, the mayor's wife, the mayor, the police, and the bigoted bosses are all caught red-handed in the texts. The unspoken or unheard testimonies become powerful indictments on the page, and it is through the written word that Celie and Maxine give voice to their grievances and eventually find redress. At the beginning, however, composition is less a retaliatory tactic than a means of survival.

Constantly flustered, Celie and Maxine resort to writing as a way to escape mental contortions and assuage loneliness and pain. The more they are ordered to keep quiet, the more irrepressible their urge to cry out, if only on paper. Raped and impregnated by Alphonso, Celie writes to God, "Maybe you can give me a sign letting me know what is happening to me" (11). Nettie, much later, recalls, "I remember one time you said your life made you feel so ashamed you couldn't even talk about it to God, you had to write it, bad as you thought your writing was" (122). Without the unburdening that comes with expression, the traumatic experience Celie has undergone would drive her mad. She survives by unspoken prayer: she writes to God to share the burden of knowing that her father got her with child twice and sold her babies, that her husband chose her the way he chose her dowry cow, and that her stepson split her head open with a rock. She survives by thinking, "Long as I can *spell* G-o-d I got somebody along" (26; my emphasis). The word *spell* nicely connotes the almost magical healing effect of words. Nettie experiences this effect as well. She tells Celie, "When I don't write to you I feel as bad as I do when I don't pray, locked up in myself and choking on my own heart. I am so *lonely*" (122).

An older and wiser Celie, who has freed herself from domestic violence and the shame of incest, again expresses her unspeakable sorrow in writing. Shug, her friend and lover, has become infatuated with a boy of nineteen and, "dying to tell somebody," describes him at length to Celie, her usual confidante. Celie remains tight-lipped throughout this ordeal. "I pray to die," she writes, "just so I don't never have to speak." She finally scribbles Shug a note: "I said, Shut up" (220). This poignant exchange harks back to the period when Celie was too dumbfounded to talk to anyone and when writing was her last resort. Her note, to be sure, is also a clever way to go from mute acceptance to verbal command (as exemplified by her stepfather). But far from exerting despotic authority, the message conveys the heartbreak of one too distraught to speak.

Like Celie, Maxine must write her way out of tangles. As a daughter of Chinese immigrants, she is tossed between their antifemale prejudice and her personal ambition, between their Chinese past and her American present: "Those of using the first American generations have had to figure out how the invisible world the emigrants built around our childhoods fit in solid America." The emigrants confuse their offspring, who are "always trying to *get things straight*, always trying to *name the unspeakable*" (6; my emphasis). The greater the confusion, the stronger the need to name, and thereby to understand. Maxine tries to achieve some order in her life by writing down and sorting out her parents' jumble of totems and taboos. Even after she has left home, when life has become less of a muddle for her, she has to keep speaking her mind to soothe her "throat pain" (239).

Celie and Maxine feel the spell of verbal power already at an early age, but it takes time for them to learn to fight and create with words. In the process, they use words to describe wordlessness; writing is not the chosen but the desperate alternative to speech.

The difficulty of speaking is compounded for Celie by prohibition and for Maxine by a second language. Alphonso has used just about every means to silence Celie, short of cutting out her tongue: intimidation, deprivation, and false accusation. At her cry during his first rape he snaps, "You better shut up and git used to it" (11). He ensures her submission by depriving her of schooling: "You too dumb to keep going to school, Pa say" (19). Though the adjective accurately describes her reticence at the time, Celie is not "dumb" mentally, as Nettie reassures her. Not content with his dual attempt to stifle Celie, Alphonso (in his need to keep his sexual assault a secret) makes sure that even the little she speaks will be doubted. He tells Albert, who is about to marry her, "She tell lies" (18). Prevented both from speaking and from being believed, Celie accepts domestic violence without a whimper throughout the early part of her life. Told repeatedly that she is ugly and stupid, she hardly knows better. With little education or encouragement, she can express herself only haltingly.

Maxine's voice also falters initially. Just as Celie is judged "dumb" by her stepfather, so Maxine (who has to learn English among native speakers) is considered retarded by her American school teachers. Unable to express herself in class, in speech or on paper, she "flunked kindergarten and in the first grade had no IQ—a zero IQ" (212). She relates in haunting detail the curse that hangs over her:

> My silence was thickest—total—during the three years that I covered my school paintings with black paint. I painted layers of black over houses and

> flowers and suns, and when I drew on the blackboard, I put a layer of chalk on top. I was making a stage curtain, and it was the moment before the curtain parted or rose. . . . I spread [the pictures] out (so black and full of possibilities) and pretended the curtains were swinging open, flying up, one after another, sunlight underneath, mighty operas. (192)

Unlike Celie, young Maxine is acutely aware of the discrepancy between her external silence and her inner possibility. She does not simply paint layers of black; she paints them "over houses and flowers and suns." To call the layer of chalk "a stage curtain" implies that it will one day rise. But only Maxine herself knows what is behind the curtain. The poignancy of the passage lies not so much in the fact of silence as in the tension between the layers of black and the concealed sunlight, between the thick curtain and the resounding operas. The scene of imagination being buried alive—shrouded in black—is suffocating.

To facilitate the painful process of breaking silence, Celie and Maxine commune with imagined beings—Celie with God, Maxine with a legendary warrior. Yet these heuristic figures also manifest the very masculine attributes that have restricted the protagonists' self-expressions. The problem with this God is that he never answers Celie's letters. Worse still, trust in him leads her to accept the status quo: "This life soon be over," she reassures herself. "Heaven lasts all ways" (47). Worst of all, she identifies him with the oppressive father, as suggested by her response when her mother demands to know what happened to Celie's newborn baby (Alphonso's child): "I say God took it. He took it. He took it while I was sleeping. Kilt it out there in the woods" (12). In context "He" refers to Alphonso, but grammatically the pronoun refers to its antecedent—God. Male. In Celie's subconscious mind the almighty God merges with the all-powerful earthly father. Shug later argues that the traditional divine image does indeed epitomize male dominance: "Man corrupt everything. . . . He on your box of grits, in your head, and all over the radio. He try to make you think he everywhere. Soon as you think he everywhere, you think he God" (179). For Celie, who has been tyrannized by one man after another, God is a wrathful being: "He threaten lightening, floods and earthquakes" (179). Though writing to God is her only emotional outlet at the beginning, she writes to him with restraint. When she turns from a divine to a human audience—from God to Nettie—her letters become longer, more exuberant, and more dramatic.

Maxine has, right from the start, a much more congenial tutelary genius—Fa Mu Lan, the legendary woman warrior. For someone besieged by silence, self-expression is a heroic act, an offensive with verbal artillery. In her fantasy Maxine merges with the warrior, who must train rigorously and endure harsh discipline before wielding a sword in battle. In her real life Maxine has to take speech therapy and work through "layers of black" before she can control the voice and the pen that are her weapons. Her apprenticeship as a writer is strenuous, her achievement remarkable. (Her status progresses from retarded pupil to "straight A" student, and finally to writer.)

While the warrior legend opens Maxine to an unconventional way of asserting herself—both fighting and writing being traditionally male preoccupations—it still sanctions patriarchal values. As with the female writer who must assume a male pseudonym to be taken seriously, the woman warrior can exercise her power only when she is disguised as a man; after regaining her true identity, she must once more be subservient, kowtowing to her parents-in-law and resuming her *son*-bearing function. "Now my public duties are finished," she says to them; "I will stay with you, doing farmwork and housework, and giving you more sons" (53–54). Her military distinction itself attests to the sovereignty of patriarchal mores, which prize the ability to be ruthless and violent—to fight like a man. Trying to conform to both the feminine and the masculine ideals of her society, Maxine as warrior is caught in a double bind.

It is disturbing, though understandable, that the figures to whom Celie and Maxine first turn for help and inspiration hark back to those who subjugate them in real life. Celie's God, like Alphonso and Albert, demands submission and threatens punishment. Maxine's heroine desires only male progeny and distinguishes herself by excelling in manly exploits. Internalizing the communal denigration of women, the protagonists begin by assuming that only "manthropomorphic" beings can offer guidance, inspiration, and salvation.

But both Celie and Maxine overcome their initial dependence on imaginary beings. They come to command full articulation and attain positive identities as women through the influence of actual female figures: for Maxine these are the no-name aunt and Brave Orchid (Maxine's mother); for Celie they are Sofia, Shug, and Nettie. Subdued as women, Maxine and Celie gather strength through a female network.

Maxine speculates about the aunt she is forbidden to mention and attempts to conjure up the circumstances that could have resulted in an affair. In one imaginary version the aunt is not a rape victim but a seducer. As a rebel—a breaker of conventions—she is Maxine's "forerunner" (9). Maxine writes, "Unless I see her life branching into mine, she gives me no ancestral help" (10). The aunt is punished for producing an illegitimate child, for having "crossed boundaries not delineated by space" (8). In "naming the unspeakable"—presenting the prodigal aunt in the first chapter—Maxine at once sanctions the no-name woman's nonconformity and announces her own ambition. By inventing a seditious story, she too engages in forbidden creativity.

Maxine's mother, Brave Orchid, who at first seems an accomplice in enforcing female silence, is yet a "champion talker" (237). (Her behavior is consistently contradictory.) She enjoins Maxine not to mention the no-name aunt: "Your father does not want to hear her name" (18). Yet she herself disobeys the husband by telling her daughter the story. She predicts that Maxine will grow up to join the company of wives and slaves, yet she teaches her the song of the woman warrior, Fa Mu Lan, who excels in an arena traditionally closed to women.[8] Brave Orchid herself had defied tradition by working independently as a doctor in China—an unusual career for Chinese women at the time.

As a child Maxine resents her mother's inconsistency and conflation of fact and fancy, insufficiently aware how the eloquent and valiant Brave Orchid is inspiring her; as a writer Maxine herself resorts to this conflation as a narrative technique. She puts Chinese notions in American idioms, but she derives both the raw material and the strategy for her art from the matrilineal tradition of oral storytelling: "I saw that I too had been in the presence of great power, my mother talking story" (24).

Celie does not encounter any extraordinary women until well into her adulthood. Her first glimpse of a female existence beyond that of battered wife or slave is through Sofia, the big and outspoken wife of her stepson Harpo. Celie puts her hopes in an afterlife, but Sofia sees things differently: "You ought to bash Mr. ____ head open. . . . Think about heaven later" (47). So thoroughly has Celie internalized the tenets of female subordination and so envious is she of Sofia's strength against Harpo, however, that she counsels her stepson to beat his wife into compliance. Confronted by Sofia, Celie confesses her jealousy. Disarmed by the confession, Sofia tells Celie: "All my life I had to fight." "I love Harpo," she continues. "But I'll kill him dead before I let him beat me" (46). Sofia is a black woman warrior; her aggression is her means of preventing others from subjugating her. Her defiance in the face of brutal treatment provides Celie a model of resistance against sexual and racial oppression.

Celie's transformation is furthered by Shug Avery, a sexy and snappy blues singer. Just as Maxine speaks up for her adulterous aunt, so Celie defends Shug, another allegedly "loose" woman. Maxine rebels against her mother's teaching that a woman must subordinate herself to her society, must conform to its patriarchal code; Celie questions the values of her conservative community. The local preacher casts aspersions on Shug: "He talk bout a strumpet in short skirts . . . slut, hussy, heifer and streetcleaner" (48–49). In retelling the episode, Celie alters the moral perspective: "Streetcleaner. Somebody got to stand up for Shug, I think" (49). She does not accept the preacher's moral judgment—that God scourges the wicked—but presents the sermon as an unfair accusation.

Like Maxine, Celie gains strength from the woman she tries to vindicate. She learns a new language from her female idol. Shug, singer of sweet songs, also has a "mouth just pack with claws" (53); her vocal organ has built-in weapons. Celie relates how, when Albert tries to make advances to Shug, she snaps at him: "Turn loose my goddam hands. . . . I don't need no weak little boy" (51). Noting and recording Shug's brazen tongue, Celie eventually appropriates it; she will one day call her abusive husband "a lowdown dog" to his face (170).

But it is Nettie who, by disclosing the arbitrariness of social conventions and the bias of certain orthodox religious teaching, finally confirms what Celie has learned from Sofia and Shug. Describing the life of the Olinka peoples, Nettie writes to Celie that these peoples have a different version of the Adamic myth, that to them Adam was not the first man but the "first man that was white" (i.e., "naked" in the Olinka dialect), that Adam and Eve were driven out not by God but by blacks (239–40). The Olinka myth inverts the racial hegemony in America in the same way that the Chinese myth of the woman warrior partially subverts sexual hierarchy. To be sure, Nettie herself is "an object of pity and contempt" to the Olinka, whose women are "looked after" by men (149). But Nettie's account of another world with a different set of rules, along with her singular example, makes Celie all the more convinced that like Sofia and

Shug, she must hold her own: "Our own self is what us have to hand" (238).

Writing about Sofia, Shug, and Nettie allows Celie to relive and rehearse their speech or action, thereby composing a new self. They are to her what Fa Mu Lan, Brave Orchid, and the no-name aunt are to Maxine: feminist models daring to assert autonomy, challenge patriarchy, and shed feminine "decorum." These women (notably Shug and Brave Orchid) also teach Celie and Maxine how to speak and write. By stressing the formative influence of these figures, Walker and Kingston insist on giving women their due; their protagonists draw literary strengths less from the books of men than from the tongues of women.[9] (Nettie, who does adhere to conventional diction, is the exception that proves the rule; her prose pales beside Celie's.)

Inspirited by female figures, Celie and Maxine transform themselves from victims to victors by throwing angry words back at their voluble oppressors. But just as their earlier dependence on masculine idols kept them in thrall, their appropriation of patriarchal rhetoric and codes of behavior threatens to bind rather than liberate them. But the two women go beyond the violent behavior and abusive language of the tyrant to become truly themselves; their murderous impulses give way to artistic acts.

Bid to be quiet, Celie yet bears the brunt of brutish remarks. Both stepfather and husband shower indignities on her. Alphonso tells her that she is "evil an always up to no good" (13). Albert taunts, "You ugly. You skinny. You shape funny. You too scared to open your mouth to people. . . . You black, you pore . . . you a woman. Goddam . . . you nothing at all" (186–87). While in the past she would have absorbed such invectives, a transformed Celie now retorts, "I'm pore, I'm black, I may be ugly. . . . But I'm here" (187). She affirms her existence against her husband's alleged "nothing" by deflecting the man's abuse. She retaliates by turning his vicious word into a curse against him:

> Whoever heard of such a thing, say Mr. ____. I probably didn't whup your ass enough.
>
> Every lick you hit me you will suffer twice. . . .

> Shit, he say. I should have lock you up. Just let you out to work.
> The jail you plan for me is the one in which you will rot, I say. (187).

Earlier she had turned a preacher's sermon into an accusation. Now her husband's scathing words lend ammunition to her curse. Her curse is, moreover, so potent that Mr. ___ soon wilts in his own house. Celie herself now has a "mouth just pack with claws": speech and act are one.[10]

Celie speaks with a vengeance. She says to Albert, "You better stop talking because all I'm telling you ain't coming just from me. Look like when I open my mouth the air rush in and shape words" (187). The tables are turned: the woman now tells the man to pipe down. The sense of release is palpable in this secular parody of "speaking with tongues." Openly enjoying the freedom of back talk for the first time, Celie expresses herself with so much gusto that she feels inspired by forces outside herself. Her words, long dammed up by her domineering husband, now flow in torrents.

Maxine also grows up amid sexist gibes. She is told repeatedly by her parents and relatives: "There's no profit in raising girls. Better to raise geese than girls" (54). When her mother yells, "Bad girl!" (54), Maxine screams back, "I am not a bad girl," adding, "I might as well have said, 'I'm not a girl'" (55). Yet her protests fall on deaf ears, for her parents' culture disapproves of free speech, especially in women: "The Chinese say 'a ready tongue is an evil'" (190). Worse still, the Chinese language itself propagates sexism: "There is a Chinese word for the female *I*—which is 'slave.' Break the women with their own tongues!" (56)[11]

Yet from this very language Maxine finds the means to articulate and redress her grievances. She discovers that the Chinese idiom for revenge literally means to "report a crime" (63); to report—witness and record—the injustices done to her as a Chinese American woman eventually becomes her way of fighting back, of being a warrior. In her imaginary battle with the wicked baron—a war between the sexes—Maxine parries words with words:

> "Who are you?" [the baron asked.]
> "I am a female avenger."
> Then—heaven help him—he tried to be charming, to appeal to me man to man. "Oh, come now. Everyone takes the girls when he can. The families

> are glad to be rid of them. 'Girls are maggots in the rice.' 'It is more profitable to raise geese than daughters.'" He quoted to me the sayings I hated. . . .
>
> "You've done this," I said, and ripped off my shirt to show him my back. . . . I slashed him across the face and on the second stroke cut off his head. (51–52).

The warrior's back carries a text of scars, listing grievances that counter the baron's sexist language. The battle is as much a verbal match as a physical one.

Celie and Maxine speak and act aggressively to overcome domination and inhibition, but they also learn to channel anger into creativity. On discovering that Albert has for years intercepted Nettie's letters, Celie feels a compulsive urge to slit his throat—with his razor. Shug talks her into sewing instead, into holding a "needle and not a razor" (137). The violent behavior that Celie had thought necessary to get even with Albert gives way to artisanship. Sublimating righteous rage with a creative act, she develops a talent for designing unisex pants. Offering comfort to men and women alike, they emancipate the wearers from their gender-specific roles. By the end the blade has fully ceded to the needle—Celie is teaching a reformed Albert how to sew.

In Maxine's fantasy the blade used by the parents to carve words on the warrior's back is both injurious and empowering. Here Kingston adroitly melds two Chinese legends, grafting the story of Yueh Fei, a male general in the Sung Dynasty, into that of Fa Mu Lan. In the Chinese sources, it is the male warrior whose back is tattooed: before he left for battle his mother carved a motto on his back, enjoining him to be loyal to his country—China. If by transferring this ordeal to the woman warrior, Kingston is literalizing the painful truth of woman as text, as Gubar believes (251), she is also subversively claiming her right to recycle myths and transpose gender, her right to authorship. In reshaping her ancestral past to fit her American present, moreover, Kingston is asserting an identity that is neither Chinese nor white American, but distinctively Chinese American.[12] Above all, her departures from the Chinese legends shift the focus from physical prowess to verbal injuries and textural power. In the Yue Fei legend, only four ideographs are carved; other than being a patriotic reminder, they have no efficacy. In Maxine's fantasy, there are many words, arranged "in red and black files, like an army," to fortify the warrior (42).

Yet for all we know, this dorsal script mirrors the sexist remarks Maxine puts into the wicked baron's mouth; those remarks echo the demeaning sayings Maxine has grown up with—etched into her consciousness by her parents. The mementos of grievances are on her back because the Chinese American warrior is fighting against hurt she cannot see—prejudices against girls that her parents brought from old China, prejudices that make her American "straight A's" life "such a disappointment" (54). She writes, "When one of my parents . . . said, 'feeding girls is like feeding cowbirds,' I would thrash on the floor and scream so hard I couldn't talk" (54). By transferring the insults that used to leave her speechless into the enemy's mouth and by beheading the imaginary speaker, Maxine not only excises the lump in her throat but also forgives the parents who have afflicted her girlhood.

She goes beyond forgiveness to acknowledge the source of pain as the source of strength: the parents who disparaged her have also encouraged her. Yet it takes the magnanimous vision of the daughter—her identification with the warrior—to transform the aching words into amulets, scars into escutcheon, and humiliation into heroism:

> The swordswoman and I are not so dissimilar. . . . What we have in common are the words at our backs. . . . The reporting is the vengeance—not the beheading, not the gutting, but the words. And I have so many words—"chink" words and "gook" words too—that they do not fit on my skin. (62–63).

Maxine has nevertheless redefined heroism. Unlike the mythical Fa Mu Lan, Maxine as warrior avenges herself less by brandishing a sword than by spinning words. Instead of excelling in martial arts, Maxine has learned the art of storytelling from the mother who "funneled China" into her ears (89). Brave Orchid's endless tales, which could well have clogged the memory of young Maxine, have actually nourished her imagination. From this mother tongue—her Chinese heritage—she now invents tales that sustain and affirm her Chinese American identity.

Breaking the hold of a dominant tradition is a step toward self-deliverance for artists. Judged by strict academic criteria, Celie's prose is illiterate; and both hers and Maxine's smack of deviance. Kingston and Walker, however, transform liability into asset. Maxine's first tongue, which has impeded her communication in English, now invigorates her adopted language with new idioms, fresh metaphors, and novel images. The Chinese ideographs for revenge ("report a crime") are writ large in this self-vindicating autobiography, where Maxine not only breaks her own silence but gives voice to the other wronged women in her family—the ravished aunt, the jilted aunt, and even Brave Orchid (a renowned Chinese doctor who must resign herself to being a nameless American laundress). Maxine writes in an English that is inalienably and powerfully her own because it springs from a bicultural stream: "'chink' words and 'gook' words too." Even as she parrots the slurs others have directed at her—revealing the sting of racism by understatement—she exults in her intertextual self, in her felicity (and facility) as a minority writer.

Celie, though less sophisticated than Maxine, also makes defect into perfection. Unable to produce "proper" English, she writes colloquially, yet her Black English is what enables her to assert her selfhood forcefully: "It is uneducated but personal, difficult but precise" (Fifer 158). Along with her other breaches of norms—wearing trousers, leaving her husband, taking a female lover—it frees her from the demands and strictures of the dominant mores. The liberated Celie not only feels fine about her dialect but even resists her sewing companion's attempt to teach her to "talk proper," thinking to herself: "Look like to me only a fool would want you to talk in a way that feel peculiar to your mind" (194). Putting words down the way they sound and feel, Celie allows her self to shine through the pages and endows her prose with a disarming grace.

Her seemingly artless idiom certainly outshines Nettie's stilted diction. Where Celie learns from Shug—someone from her own language community—Nettie is taught by her guardians, missionaries who have been socialized into the dominant culture. In Nettie's increasingly long-winded letters, noticeably bland compared to Celie's, we are hearing what issues from the tongue of Nettie's mentors. Walker seems to imply that Celie's vernacular idiom, because it is hers alone, is all the more "proper."

Both Maxine and Celie have made a virtue out of necessity. Unable to speak at first, they have turned to writing for relief. Because their prose serves as a "mouthpiece"—taking cues from their mother tongues—it dissolves the boundary separating the spoken from the written word and percolates with a vigor often absent in formal writing. We can hear, not just read, Maxine's *talk* stories, which reverberate with the lore and rhythm of the Cantonese oral tradition. Similarly, Celie's telltale dialect talks us into her consciousness, spelling a personality.[13]

As they gain confidence in their female identities, Celie and Maxine find new voices and new models, supplanting martial with poetic ideals and switching allegiance from an imposing authority to a friendly muse. No longer blinkered by gender oppositions, they perceive differences among people of both sexes. Conventional dichotomies are dismissed in favor of personal variations.

Celie, gratified by her newfound rhetorical talent and her increasing mastery of language, evolves along with her writing—from a little girl baffled by what is happening to her to a self-aware and understanding woman, from a passive recorder of unstructured facts to a conscious artist. When she begins writing she merely jots down her immediate experience, noting the events around her with little introspection or analysis. Even in the face of outrage, such as Sofia's disfigurement by the police, she just swallows the unpalatable fact: "Scare me so bad I near bout drop my grip. But I don't . . . and I start to work on her" (87). Gradually, however, the facts she presents begin to generate questions and judgments. When she learns their shocking family history from Nettie, she begins to doubt the God who has hitherto made her accept everything silently. In her valedictory epistle to "Him," she writes:

> Dear God,
>
> . . .
>
> My daddy lynch. My mama crazy. All my little half-brothers and sisters no kin to me. My children not my sister and brother. Pa not pa.
>
> You must be sleep. (163)

Fed up with a god who does nothing to curb injustice, Celie replaces him with a winsome "It": the spirit that always tries to "please [people] back," smiling on all that people enjoy (178).

Neither male nor female, this spirit seems to relax the tension between the sexes and erase rigid gender categories. Celie learns to transcend her disgust with men and to love even Albert, the man she wanted so badly to kill and who now sews beside her. It is during her conversation with him that she explicitly challenges the putative notions of manliness and womanliness. The discussion begins when Albert tells Celie that he loves Shug because, like Sofia, she is more manly than most men:

> Mr. ___ think all this is stuff men do. But Harpo not like this, I tell him. You not like this. What Shug got is womanly it seem like to me. Specially since she and Sofia the ones got it.
>
> Sofia and Shug not like men, he say, but they not like women either.
>
> You mean they not like you or me.
>
> They *hold they own*, he say. And it's *different*. (236, my emphasis)

Celie and Albert, sewing amicably together, are not engaged in a "feminine" (and therefore "unmanly") activity.[14] Although they envy Shug's and Sofia's aggressiveness, they do not consider it unwomanly or specifically masculine—or intrinsically superior. Both sexes are allowed to craft their different lives, fashion their own destinies.

The dialogue also reveals Celie's increasing mental agility, incisiveness, and sophistication. Though quick to retort, Celie is learning that there is another side to the cutting edge of language. She has turned from writing to the God who is "big and old and tall and graybearded and white" (176) to writing Nettie, her devoted sister. Unlike her starkly descriptive letters to God registering her oppressors' voices, her letters to Nettie wax sweetly poetic. In one she writes: "Nettie, I am making some pants for you. . . . I plan to make them by hand. Every stitch I sew will be a kiss" (192). The intimate figure of speech threading together her three creative modes—writing, sewing, and loving—acquires freshness and distinctiveness by being so much a part of her self.

Celie's changing style reflects her growing self-awareness. Her letters progress from a simple registration to a sophisticated re-creation of dialogues and events, charged with suspense, humor, and irony (Fifer 160). She tells of her sorrow after Shug has deserted her:

> I talk to myself a lot, standing in front the mirror. Celie, I say, happiness was just a trick in your case. Just cause you never had any before Shug, you thought it was time to have some, and that it was gon last. Even thought you had the trees with you. The whole earth. The stars. But look at you. When Shug left, happiness desert. (229).

Although the passage expresses the pains of a lost love, the contemplative tone, the ironical perspective, and the metaphorical language show us how far Celie has traveled as a writer and how much more in control she has become than when she first wrote to God for help. Her dialect, once broken, has assumed a lyrical cadence. The woman who was "too dumb" to learn now creates poetry.

Similarly, Maxine evolves from a quiet listener to a talker of stories. Having transformed the military warrior into a verbal fighter, she recognizes that she herself is a powerful spinner of yarns and not just a receptacle for her mother's tales. Although many chapters of her autobiography are in a sense collaborations between mother and daughter, the daughter becomes increasingly aware of her own contribution, especially in the last section of the book: "Here is a story my mother told me, not when I was young, but recently, when I told her I also talk-story. The beginning is hers, the ending, mine" (240). It is toward the end of this story that the tone noticeably softens. Unlike Brave Orchid, the mother who would "funnel," "pry," "cram," "jam-pack" the daughter with unabated torrents of words, and unlike young Maxine, who has "splinters in [her] voice, bones jagged against one another" (196), adult Maxine modulates her notes to the music of her second tongue, in the manner of Ts'ai Yen, the heroine of her final tale.

Kingston reinterprets the legend of Ts'ai Yen—a poet amid barbarians—and, as she has done with the stories about the no-name aunt and the woman warrior, subverts its original moral. The Chinese version highlights the poet's eventual return to her own people, a return that reinforces certain traditional and ethnoecentric Chinese notions: "the superiority of Chinese civilization over the cultures beyond her borders, the irreconciliability of the different ways of life . . . and, above all, the Confucian concept of loyalty to one's ancestral family and state" (Rorex and Fong). Kingston's version, by contrast, dramatizes interethnic harmony through the integration of disparate art forms.

Ts'ai Yen, Maxine's last tutelary genius, resembles but transcends the various other influential female figures in her life. Like Fa Mu Lan, Ts'ai Yen has fought in battle, but as a captive soldier. She engages in another art hitherto dominated by men—writing—yet she does not disguise her sex, thus implicitly denying that authorship is a male prerogative. Like the No Name aunt, Ts'ai Yen is ravished and impregnated; both give birth on sand. But instead of being nameless and ostracized, Ts'ai Yen achieves immortal fame by singing about her exile. Like Brave Orchid, she talks in Chinese to her uncomprehending children, who speak a barbarian tongue, but she learns to appreciate the barbarian music. The refrain of this finale is reconciliation—between parents and children, between men and women, and between different cultures.

It is by analogy to Maxine—alienated alike from the Chinese world of her parents and the world of white Americans—that Ts'ai Yen's full significance emerges. The barbarians attach primitive pipes to their arrows, which thereby whistle in flight. Ts'ai Yen has thought that this terrifying noise is her nomadic captors' only music, until she hears, issuing night after night from those very flutes, "music tremble and rise like desert wind" (242):

> She hid in her tent but could not sleep through the sound. Then, out of Ts'ai Yen's tent, which was apart from the others, the barbarians heard a woman's voice singing, as if to her babies, a song so high and clear, it matched the flutes. Ts'ai Yen sang about China and her family there. Her words seemed to be Chinese, but the barbarians understood their sadness and anger. . . . She brought her songs back from the savage lands, and one of the three that has been passed down to us is "Eighteen Stanzas for a Barbarian Reed Pipe," a song that Chinese sing to their own instruments. It translated well. (243)

Recalling young Maxine's ambivalence toward language (because it is frequently associated with dominance), an ambivalence that is in a sense reinforced by the lethal text on the warrior's back, we can appreciate all the more the poet's alternative mode of expression. The American language, Maxine discovers, can send forth not just terrifying "death sounds"—threats, insults, slurs—but stirring tunes. Caught in a cross-cultural web of Eastern and Western chauvinism, Maxine too conveys sadness and anger through high-sounding words. She does not (and does not want to) return to China, but she reconnects with her ancestral culture through writing. Instead of struggling against her Asian past and her American present, she now seeks to emulate the poet who sings to foreign music. Not only have her Chinese materials and imaginings "translated well," in the course of such creative translation she has achieved an inner resolution. As the lyrical ending intimates, Maxine has worked the discords of her life into a song.

That the injunction to silence should provoke expression is not so paradoxical as it might seem, for the relief sought by those frustrated by silence—forbidden or unable to speak—can only come through articulation. Urgent and passionate, the testimonies of Celie and Maxine are in one sense a cathartic release. Their voices, moreover, have carried them further than they had expected: from surviving to protesting to recognizing themselves as special storytellers. Despite the excruciating process of change both women have endured, each text conveys a sense of triumph that is due, I believe, less to the happy ending itself than to the way the final stage is negotiated, to the means by which a voice truly each women's own is fostered.

To monitor the uplifting effect in these texts—texts that revolve around alienation and isolation—we must return to the connections between characters and authors. Walker and Kingston have allowed their protagonists to break through constraints to create opportunities. Although Celie and Maxine have suffered in their communities, they also tap communal resources: too human to be "nothing" in a white society, they turn to their ancestral cultures to emulate heroines of their own hue and to reclaim beliefs that subvert the existing hierarchy; hampered by dialects, they transform putative defects into stylistic effects. The credit for the transformation goes ultimately to the authors. Anticipating Mary Dearborn's insight that "American selfhood is based on a seemingly paradoxical sense of shared difference" (3), Walker and Kingston take in the differences of being female and colored to invent self-expressive styles that bestride literary and oral traditions and project ethnic and national heritages. As they write about the voicelessness endemic to minority women, they pay tribute to the female bearers of cultures. As they venture beyond linguistic norms, they perpetuate and revitalize the polyglot strains peculiar to America.

To emphasize these achievements is not to suggest that we forget Celie's and Maxine's nightmares, accept their afflictions, or discount their losses. Their ultimate success only reminds us of the many who, despite struggle, cannot achieve personal victories. I have called attention to the triumphant overtones to underscore the protagonists' resilience and the authors' determination. These writers dare to be themselves—to listen to their own pains, to report the ravages, and finally, to persist in finding strengths from sources that have caused inestimable anguish. Their way of breaking out of enforced silence is not by dissolving into the mainstream but by rendering their distinctive voices.

NOTES

Research for this essay was facilitated by an Academic Senate grant and a grant from the Institute of American Cultures and the Asian American Studies Center, University of California, Los Angeles. I want to thank Kenneth Lincoln for his incisive reading of an earlier version of the article; Martha Banta, Rosalind Melis, and Jeff Spielberg for their thoughtful suggestions; and Gerard Maré for his bountiful encouragement and criticism.

1. Showalter refers to these stages as *Feminine, Feminist,* and *Female* (13). The final stages perceived by Walker and Kingston however, seems closer to that advocated by Cixous (Conley 129) and Kristeva (33–34), which goes beyond the dichotomy of masculine and feminine.

2. Sollors takes his cue from Handlin, who writes, "Once I thought to write the history of American immigrants. Then I discovered that the immigrants *were* American history" (3). Sollors's theory, which he expounds further in *Beyond Ethnicity*, is endorsed by Dearborn (4).

3. Kramer, Johnson, Lewis, and Steinem are among the reviewers or journalists attacked; the attackers include Chan, Chin, Harris, and Reed (Chapple 17).

4. Walker admittedly "liberated" Celie (based on the author's great-grandmother) from the character's own history (Anello and Abramson). Kingston disclaims that her writing is representative of China or of Chinese America (Islas 12). When asked whether she considered *The Woman Warrior* fiction or nonfiction, she answered that "it's closer to fiction" (Brownmiller 210). She may have contributed to the generic confusion in allowing Knopf to classify her book as autobiography, though autobiography itself is often an "art of self-invention" (Eakin).

5. Sollors points out rightly that minority literature "is often read and evaluated against an elusive concept of authenticity" (*Beyond Ethnicity* 11). While this concept has its value, it does not do justice to artists uninterested in objective representation. Kingston's book, in particular, reveals highly subjective truth, filtered at times through the lens of a girl both endowed and plagued with an unbridled imagination. The elusiveness of objective reality is an insistent motif. For instance, Maxine suspects that her frenum had been cut to stunt her speech, but her mother insists that she performed the operation so that Maxine "would not be tongue-tied," so that her tongue "would be able to move in any language" (190). I do not know of

any Chinese or Chinese American whose frenum has been cut. Maxine either grows up in an untypical Chinese American family—if there is ever a typical one—or she has made up the incident. (She explicitly writes at one point that her stories are hardly factual but are "twisted into designs" [189].) In any case, the episode is remarkably effective in attributing verbal difficulty and facility to the same origins.

6. After being raped and silenced by Tereus, Philomela weaves her story "with *purple* / On a white background" (Ovid 148; my emphasis). Walker might have had this myth in mind in choosing her title and in telling the story of Louvinie (a slave woman in *Meridian* whose tongue was cut off). See also Rowe (53–58) for the connection between enforced silences and tale-spinning in the Philomela story.

7. Name is also crucial to personal identity in *The Color Purple*. Celie advises Squeak to insist on being called Mary Agnes, her real name; and Celie herself, though she appears completely submissive, subversively leave out Albert's name in her letters, thereby suggesting that her husband has no personality, that he is personified machismo: "Mr. ___."

8. Juhasz observes, "In telling her daughter stories of female heroism that directly contradict many of her other messages about the position of women, the mother shows her daughter another possibility for women that is not revealed in her equally strong desire for her daughter's conformity and thus safety in a patriarchal system" (180).

9. Where literacy has been traditionally a male or white privilege, it is women who have been the bearers of influential oral traditions. Kingston notes in an interview that even the stories about her male ancestors are told to her by female members of the family: "Many of the men's stories were ones I originally heard from women" (Kim 208). See also Rabine, 487–92.

10. Brienza explicitly compares Celie's curse to "speech acts" —words that do what they say.

11. The word is 奴 (*nu*), used by women in ancient times in a self-reference, thereby "breaking themselves with their own tongues." That usage is now obsolete. For the Chinese usage of this word, see *Cihai* 2: 2510.

12. Chin et al. argue that "Asian American sensibilities and cultures . . . might be related to but are distinct from Asia and white America" (viii).

13. Walker says that "writing *The Color Purple* was writing in [her] first language" (Steinem 90). But actually both Walker and Kingston interweave native idiom and standard English: Walker uses the two alternately through the letters of Celie and Nettie; Kingston combines the two by translating and transliterating Cantonese idioms into English.

14. Hence I disagree with Stade, who accuses Walker of emasculating Albert and Harpo (who likes to cook) "by giving them the courage to be women, by releasing the woman already in them" (266). Quite the contrary, Albert and Harpo are now free to be their own men.

WORKS CITED

Allen, Paula Gunn. *The Sacred Hoop: Recovering the Feminine in American Indian Traditions*. Boston: Beacon, 1986.

Anello, Ray, and Pamela Abramson. "Characters in Search of a Book." *Newsweek*, 21 June 1982, 67.

Brienza, Susan. "Telling Old Stories New Ways: Narrative Strategies in the Novels of Contemporary American Women." Paper delivered at symposium, Creating Women, University of California, Los Angeles, 8 March 1986

Brownmiller, Susan. "Susan Brownmiller Talks with Maxine Hong Kingston, Author of *The Woman Warrior*." *Mademoiselle*, March 1977.

Chan, Jeffery Paul. "Letters: The Mysterious West." *New York Review of Books*, 28 April 1977, 41.

Chapple, Steve. "Writing and Fighting: Ishmael Reed." *Image*, 14 June 1987.

Chin, Frank. "The Most Popular Book in China." *Quilt* 4 (1970): 6–12.

Chin, Frank, et al. *Aiiieeeee! An Anthology of Asian-American Writers*. 1974, Washington, D.C.: Howard University Press, 1983.

Cihai: The Encyclopaedic Chinese Dictionary. 3 vols. Shanghai: Ci Shu; Hong Kong: Joint, 1979.

Conley, Verena Andermatt. "An Exchange with Helene Cixous." In *Helene Cixous: Writing the Feminine*. Lincoln: University of Nebraska Press, 1984, 120–61.

Dasenbrock, Reed Way. "Intelligibility and Meaningfulness in Multicultural Literature in English." *PMLA* 102 (1987): 10–19.

Dearborn, Mary V. *Pocahontas's Daughters: Gender and Ethnicity in American Culture*. New York: Oxford University Press, 1986.

Eakin, Paul John. *Fictions in Autobiography: Studies in the Art of Self-Invention*. Princeton: Princeton University Press, 1985.

Fifer, Elizabeth. "Alice Walker: The Dialect and Letters of *The Color Purple*." In *Contemporary American Women Writers: Narrative Strategies*, ed. Catherine Rainwater and William Scheick. Lexington: University Press at Kentucky, 1985, 155–65.

Gilbert, Sandra M, and Susan Gubar. *The Madwoman in the Attic: The Woman Writer and the Nineteenth-Century Literary Imagination*. New Haven: Yale University Press, 1979.

Griffin, Susan. *Pornography and Silence: Culture's Revenge Against Nature*. New York: Colophon-Harper, 1981.

Gubar, Susan. "'The Blank Page' and the Issues of Female Creativity." *Critical Inquiry* 8 (1981): 243–63.

Handlin, Oscar. *The Uprooted: The Epic Story of the Great Migrations That Made the American People*. Boston: Little, Brown, 1951.

Harris, Trudier. "On *The Color Purple*, Stereotypes, and Silence." *Black American Literature Forum* 18.4 (1984): 155–61.

Heilbrun, Carolyn G. *Reinventing Womanhood*. New York: Norton, 1979.

Islas, Arturo. "Interview with Maxine Hong Kingston." In *Women Writers of the West Coast Speaking of Their Lives and Careers*, ed. Marilyn Yalom. Santa Barbara: Capra, 1983. 11–19.

Johnson, Diane. "Ghosts." Review of *The Woman Warrior*, by Maxine Hong Kingston. *New York Review of Books*, 3 February 1977.

Juhasz, Suzanne. "Maxine Hong Kingston: Narrative Technique and Female Identity." In *Contemporary American Women Writers: Narrative Strategies*, ed. Catherine Rainwater and William Scheick. Lexington: University Press of Kentucky, 1985. 173–89.

Kim, Elaine H. *Asian American Literature: An Introduction to the Writings and Their Social Context*. Philadelphia: Temple University Press, 1982.

Kingston, Maxine Hong. *China Men*. New York: Ballantine, 1981.

———. *The Woman Warrior: Memoirs of a Girlhood among Ghosts*. 1976. New York: Random House, 1977.

Kramer, Jane. "On Being Chinese in China and America." Review of *The Woman Warrior*, by Maxine Hong Kingston. *New York Times Book Review*, 7 November 1976.

Kristeva, Julia. "Women's Time." Trans. Alice Jardine and Harry Blake. *Signs: Journal of Women in Culture and Society* 7.1 (1981): 13–35.

Lewis, Richard Gregory. "Depicting Struggle: Survival Is the Task for Alice Walker." Review of *The Color Purple*, by Alice Walker. *National Leader*, 7 October 1982.

Olsen, Tillie. *Silences*. 1965. New York: Dell, 1972.

Ovid. *Metamorphoses*. Trans. Rolfe Humphries. 1955. Bloomington: Indiana University Press, 1974.

Rabine, Leslie W. "No Lost Paradise: Social Gender and Symbolic Gender in the Writings of Maxine Hong Kingston." *Signs: Journal of Women in Culture and Society* 12 (1987): 471–92.

Rainwater, Catherine, and William J. Scheick, eds. *Contemporary American Women Writers: Narrative Strategies*. Lexington: University Press of Kentucky, 1985.

Rich, Adrienne. *On Lies, Secrets, and Silence: Selected Prose 1966–1978*. New York: Norton, 1979.

Rorex, Robert A., and Wen Fong. Introduction to *Eighteen Songs of a Nomad Flute: The Story of Lady Wen-Chi*. New York: Metropolitan Museum of Art, 1974.

Rowe, Karen E. "To Spin a Yarn: The Female Voice in Folklore and Fairy Tale." In *Fairy Tales and Society: Illusion, Allusion, and Paradigm*, ed. Ruth B. Bottigheimer. Philadelphia: University of Pennsylvania Press, 1986. 53–74.

Russ, Joanna. *How to Suppress Women's Writing*. Austin: University of Texas Press, 1983.

Showalter, Elaine. *A Literature of Their Own: British Women Novelists from Brontë to Lessing*. Princeton: Princeton University Press, 1977.

Sollors, Werner. *Beyond Ethnicity: Consent and Descent in American Culture*. New York: Oxford University Press, 1986.

———. "Literature and Ethnicity." In *Harvard Encyclopedia of American Ethnic Groups*, ed. Stephan Thernstrom, Ann Orlov, and Oscar Handlin. Cambridge, Mass.: Harvard University Press, 1980. 647–65.

Sontag, Susan. *Styles of Radical Will*. New York: Farrar, 1966.

Stade, George. "Womanist Fiction and Male Characters." *Partisan Review* 52 (1985): 264–70.

Steinem, Gloria. "She Knows You: A Profile of Alice Walker." *Ms.*, June 1982.

Walker, Alice. *The Color Purple*. 1982. New York: Washington Square, 1983.

10

Tang Ao in America: Male Subject Positions in China Men

Donald C. Goellnicht

MAXINE HONG KINGSTON'S second (auto)biographical fiction, *China Men*, opens with a brief section entitled "On Discovery," the initial sentence of which runs as follows: "Open upon a time, a man, named Tang Ao, looking for the Gold Mountain, crossed an ocean, and came upon the Land of Women" (3).[1] Tang Ao, emblematic of Chinese male sojourners in America (the Gold Mountain), finds instead the Land of Women, where he is caught and feminized—his feet bound, his ears pierced, his facial hair plucked, his face painted. The closing sentence of this introductory tale states: "Some scholars say that that country was discovered during the reign of Empress Wu (A.D. 694–705), and some say earlier than that, AD 441, and it was in North America" (5). With characteristic interrogation of all her sources, Hong Kingston gives us two possible dates for this mythic event, but the narrator seems certain that the location of the Land of Women "was in North America." Yet, when asked in an interview with Paula Rabinowitz to compare *The Woman Warrior* with *China Men*, Hong Kingston responds: "Historically, of course, the men [of her family in particular, and Chinese male sojourners in and immigrants to America in general] went to a different country without their families, and so they had their adventures by themselves. It was as if they went to a men's country and they had men's stories" (179).[2]

How do we reconcile these apparently contradictory statements? To begin with, contradictory statements, or statements that contest one another, are not antithetical to Hong Kingston's art; they are integral to it.[3] But there is a sense in which no contradiction exists here: historically, only *men* from China were allowed into America for work—usually manual labor on plantations, in mines, on railroad construction, or in fishing; only the wives of a few treaty merchants, of students, and of teachers could enter America freely until 1952, when a provision of the Immigration and Nationality Act enabled "for the first time Chinese women . . . to immigrate under the same conditions as men" (*China Men* 158). By then, the restrictive and exclusionary laws instituted by the dominant white culture against the Chinese had emasculated these immigrant men, forcing them into "feminine" subject positions of powerlessness and silence, into "bachelor" Chinatowns devoid of women, and into "feminized" jobs that could not be filled by women.[4] It is no accident, then, that Tang Ao remains helpless to change his fate of becoming a courtesan and that, as they prepare to pierce his ears, the women joke that they are "sewing your lips together" (4), silence being presented as part of the female condition. Thus the "men's country" of the Gold Mountain, the place men went to find fame and fortune, the "country with no women" (54), becomes the Land of Women, a site where a legalized racism turns "men" into "women."[5] In this brief introduction, Hong Kingston has adapted a story from the early-nineteenth-century Chinese novel *Flowers in the Mirror* in order to mythologize the historical and political situation faced by China Men in America during the latter half of the nineteenth century and the first half of the twentieth.[6] (This situation is given a historical, rather than mythic, treatment at the center of the book—a prominent location—in the section entitled "The Laws," to which I will return.)

The significance of the privileged position that the Tang Ao legend occupies at the start of the text cannot, I believe, be underestimated. Like the Fa Mu Lan legend in *The Woman Warrior*, it acts as a kind of controlling myth—treated neither entirely reverentially nor entirely critically—for the rest of the text. Fa Mu Lan, the woman warrior, represents the attempts by women to break out of gendered positions, to cross over into "male" territory. Tang Ao is also involved in a gender crossover, but one representing a "demotion" in gender hierarchies and one forced on him rather than one willingly adopted: no one, it seems, wants to fill the "feminine" gender role.

But I should also observe that "White Tigers" (the story that presents the Fa Mu Lan myth) does not introduce *The Woman Warrior*; "No Name Woman," the story of Maxine's aunt—pregnant by a man not her husband, ostracized, and suicidal—does. The Tang Ao story also has affinities with this opening story of the earlier text. The no-name aunt had been affected by "the rare urge [to go] west [which] had fixed upon our [Maxine's] family, and so [she] crossed boundaries not deliniated in space" (*Woman Warrior* 9) by disobeying patriarchy, while Tang Ao "crossed an ocean" to the West and had his gender changed. Just as the no-name aunt is forced into a position of powerlessness and silence, both physically and linguistically (for her indiscretions, she is driven to suicide and denied a name) by the traditions of Chinese patriarchy that deny her existence once she has transgressed its laws, so too Tang Ao the sojourner finds himself forced into a position of powerlessness and silence by the Laws of the Ruling Fathers (the white majority). In this second introductory story ("On Discovery"), the gender inequity of the first ("No Name Woman") becomes intensified through its links to a general situation of racial inequity, as the rest of *China Men* makes clear. The feminization of Tang Ao acts metonymically for the emasculation of China Men in white America.[7]

To say that Hong Kingston discloses—for her feminist and mainstream white audience—the legalized humiliation and degradation suffered by China Men at the hands of the dominant race is not to say, however, that she wishes simply to recuperate and valorize the traditional Chinese culture, with its base in patriarchal Confucianism, that was undermined by America's exclusionary immigration laws. This is a point that two critics writing on this topic seem to have missed. Linda Ching Sledge, in a valuable early article, points out: "The inversion of sexual roles [in *China Men*] . . . illuminates the internal tensions accumulating in [sojourner] families as a result of the erosion of sex differentiation in the household. The strain on husband, wife, and children as a result of the father's 'emasculation' or failure as provider is clear" (10). She goes on to conclude, however, that Hong Kingston, in the final analysis, gives

> an overwhelmingly heroic account of sojourner family life. . . . Through-out *China Men*, the continuing hold of certain fundamental aspects of the primordial Confucian ideal of family unity, economic interdependence, and mutual help is maintained. . . . Rather than undermining the ancient notion

> of family accord, the scenes show that faith in the patriarchal family system . . . remains the ideal against which the daughter's [Maxine's] more modern definitions are measured. (13–14)

Alfred Wang also discusses the triumph of Hong Kingston's male protagonists over legalized discrimination and implicitly praises the survival of traditional Chinese culture by linking her "*Men Warriors par excellence*" to "Guan Goong, Liu Pei, and Chang Fei" (27), the military heroes of patriarchal Chinese literature and legend.[8]

The impulse to champion the survival of Chinese American family life in the face of repeated, conscious attempts to destroy it is both understandable and admirable; but Sledge and Wang have fallen victim, I believe, to thinking in binary oppositions: if Hong Kingston lambasts—as she does—the white racists for their behavior and attitudes, then, in her sympathy for the hero-victims, she must be supportive of the traditional family structures that have come under fire. This kind of thinking is anathema to Hong Kingston's feminist argument, which critiques all systems that establish social relationships as hierarchies of power and which is perfectly capable of a both/and approach instead of an either/or one. Hong Kingston can both deplore the emasculation of China Men by mainstream America *and* critique the Confucian patriarchy of traditional family life, as King-Kok Cheung has recognized. Of the Tang Ao story, Cheung writes: "I cannot but see this legend as double-edged, pointing not only to the mortification of Chinese men in the new world but also to the subjugation of women both in old China and in America. . . . The opening myth suggests that the author objects as strenuously to the patriarchal practices of her ancestral culture as to the racist treatment of her forefathers in their adopted country" (240). It is this double-edged antiracist, antisexist sword wielded by the narrator that I wish to examine here.[9]

As mentioned above, one of the most debilitating aspects of the exclusionary acts for Chinese and Chinese American men was the banning of female immigrants: "1924: An Immigration Act passed by Congress specifically excluded 'Chinese women, wives, and prostitutes.' Any American who married a Chinese woman lost his citizenship; any Chinese man who married an American woman caused her to lose her citizenship" (*China Men* 156). The deliberate agenda of using sexual deprivation to prevent any increase in the Chinese American population and to undermine the virility of Chinese and

Chinese American men is obvious. Through such discrimination, the "Oriental threat" could be contained by mainstream culture.

The narrator's attacks on the dominant culture's laws against female immigration, and her profoundly sympathetic grasp of the effects of such emasculation on male immigrants and sojourners, emerge clearly in almost every "talk-story." With Bak Goong, the great-grandfather, for example, it manifests itself in his imagined—all these ancestral stories are imagined by the female narrator—biting sarcasm. His comment upon being forbidden to talk while working on the Hawaiian sugar plantation is revealing: "If I knew I had to take a vow of silence, . . . I would have shaved off my hair and become a monk. Apparently we've taken a vow of chastity too. Nothing but roosters in this flock" (100). In contrast, Ah Goong, the railway grandfather, expresses his sense of loss of women through nocturnal fantasies on the myth of Altair and Vega, the Spinning Girl and the Cowboy transformed into stars and allowed to meet only once a year across the bridge of the Milky Way. The pathos of these meditations becomes heartrending: "He felt his heart breaking of loneliness at so much blue-black space between star and star. The railroad he was building would not lead him to his family" (129).

The wielding of such pathos and sarcasm in defense of China Men without women does not, however, prevent the female narrator from injecting her stories with more subtle barbs aimed at the very Confucian life these men long for. For example, in "On Mortality," a story of how a man named Tu Tzu-chun was offered immortality by a Taoist monk if he could pass the test of remaining silent when faced with various "illusions," one of those testing illusions is the threat of becoming a woman: "He heard gods and goddesses talking about him, 'This man is too wicked to be reborn a man. Let him be born a woman'" (120). Thus, in a more extreme form of the Tang Ao myth, Tu changes not only gender position but also his biological sex: "He discovered that he had been reborn a deaf-mute female named Tu." Again, as with Tang Ao, here muteness/silence is held up by patriarchy as an ideal of womanhood: "When she became a woman, her parents married her to a man named Lu, who at first did not mind [her muteness]. 'Why does she need to talk,' said Lu, 'to be a good wife? Let her set an example for women'" (121). This female silence is broken, however, by Tu-as-woman when Lu deliberately injures her child. In a play on the Western myth of the Fall caused by woman, here humanity loses the opportunity to gain immortality because maternal love (Tu-transformed-into-mother) disobeys a patriarchal (in this case monastic Taoist) injunction to silence. But while the Edenic myth presents Eve's disobedience as the cause of human suffering, here Hong Kingston displays maternal love as a superior attribute to immortality; it is an emotion even men (Tu-as-woman) must learn, for this love makes us intensely human, mortal, superior to the gods of patriarchy. Once more, the narrative subverts our expectations about gender roles.

Throughout the text, religion reveals itself as one of the powerful institutions of the masculine symbolic order that entrenches male privilege. Another pillar of this patriarchal structure is the law, in which sexism becomes allied with racism.[10]

"The Laws" section has been rightly praised for its "purely factual" account of the discrimination leveled against the Chinese who came to America, for its accurate record of legal history presented through "substantial documentary material" (Sledge 5–6) that nevertheless stands out as anomalous in Hong Kingston's variegated/multivalent/polyphonous narrative.[11] Yet there is also a sense in which "The Laws" is ironic. Sometimes the irony surfaces bitterly from the facts themselves, as in this juxtaposition: "Though the Chinese were filling and leveeing the San Joaquin Delta for thirteen cents a square yard, building the richest agricultural land in the world, they were prohibited from owning land or real estate" (153). More subtly, though, the section carries an ironic undertone: by imitating the monological voice of authorizing History—the history imposed by the dominant culture that made the laws—this section uncovers both the dullness of this voice and its deafness to other, competing voices, those of the minorities suffering legalized discrimination. This undertone of irony becomes most resonant when Hong Kingston quotes from the exclusionary laws enacted by federal, state, and municipal legislatures against Chinese workers and immigrants, especially when we measure these "laws" against the "invented" biographies of China Men that make up the rest of the text. Paradoxically, the imagined/fictional history proves more truthful than the official version.

There is also irony in the position of "The Laws." It occupies the middle of the book, a centric position that would appear to be one of (legalized) authority; yet this centric authority of American law is subverted and contested by the "eccentric" or marginal, but richly imaginative, stories of China Men that surround it. China Men lament the loss of their centric place when they come to America; but this "eccentric" text itself, in auto-representational fashion, illustrates the power of the margins, despite all the attempts to limit/eliminate that power.

As Alfred Wang observes: "No other racial group have been subjected to worse *legalized* personal, collective, and sexual deprivation than the Chinese male immigrants between 1868 . . . and 1952" (18). Wang is right to stress the legalized nature of this discrimination, for the law constitutes in many ways the center of the masculine symbolic order, the institution that inscribes and entrenches masculine privilege. The evidence presented here, however, indicates that, Lacanian theories of gender acquisition aside, the law does not encode the same subject position—traditionally a position of power, as in Confucian law as well—for all men. Instead, positions of power are reserved for the Ruling Fathers (men of the dominant group, white men), while men of other racial groups are forced into "feminine" subject positions of "inferiority."

The social and psychological repercussions of the exclusion laws on Chinese and Chinese American men were tremendous, and they have been documented by a number of historians and sociologists.[12] Elaine Kim has pointed out that with job opportunities scarce and women absent in the "bachelor" Chinatowns— ghettoes where Chinese and Chinese American men were forced to live—some of these men ended up, against their will, in traditionally "women's" jobs, as waiters, launderers, servants, and cooks. In "The Father from China" Hong Kingston presents her father and his partners as engaged in their laundry business for long periods each day—a business considered so low and debased that, in their songs, they associate it with the washing of menstrual blood, which links their occupation back to Tang Ao, whose foot-binding bandages smelled like menstrual rags when he was forced to wash them (4). The laundry partners sing as they iron:

> The laundry business is low, you say,
> Washing out blood that stinks like brass—
> Only a Chinaman can debase himself so. (63)[13]

At night, these "bachelors" engage in more "woman's work": they cook their own meals and hold eating races, with the loser washing the dishes. The absence of wives is stressed, but this has to do as much with the difficulty of taking on the menial tasks women would usually perform as with a sense of emotional deprivation. Once Brave Orchid—Ed/BaBa's wife from China—arrives in New York, the traditional roles resume: she cooks, cleans, and washes for the men. Once again, the female narrator sympathizes with these fathers but also critiques traditional gender roles.

Most criticism is leveled, however, at the dominant racist society. In what appears a deliberate attempt to trap China Men in the stereotypical "feminine" positions it had assigned them, American society perpetuated the myth of the effeminate or androgynous "chinaman," while erasing the figure of the "masculine" plantation worker or railroad construction worker.[14] We are all familiar with the stereotype of the Chinese laundryman or waiter, but few know that the railroads so essential to development in North America were built with large numbers of Chinese laborers, who endured tremendous hardship and isolation in the process, or that Hawaiian sugar plantations were carved out of tropical forests with Chinese labor. Hong Kingston presents a vivid example of one of these racist stereotypes in the figure of Chop Chop, who appears in the military comic book *Blackhawk*:

> Chop Chop was the only Blackhawk who did not wear a blue-black pilot's uniform with yellow and black insignia. He wore slippers instead of boots, pajamas with his undershirt showing at the tails, white socks, an apron; he carried a cleaver and wore a pigtail. . . . Fat and half as tall as the other Blackhawks, who were drawn like regular human beings, Chop Chop looked like a cartoon. It was unclear whether he was a boy or a little man. (274)

"Tall dragon ladies" are not attracted to Chop Chop as they are to the other Blackhawks.

Hong Kingston seeks to redress this wrong of stereotyping and historical erasure, not by a simple reversal the figure of laundryman/cook and that of railroad laborer/plantation worker, "feminine" and "masculine," respectively, but by a disruption of this gendered binary opposition—as we find in the Tang Ao and Tu Tzu-chun myths—which shows both roles and both job types to entail hardships and rewards. To this end she presents us with a variety of China Men from her family: Bak Goong, her "Great Grandfather of the Sandalwood Mountains," who endured the physical hardships of being a sugar plantation worker in Hawaii but who was also "a fanciful, fabulous man" (110); Ah Goong, her "Grandfather of the Sierra Nevada Mountains," a railway construction worker who risked his life from a suspended basket to set gunpowder charges in the mountains but whose intense loneliness at being a married "bachelor" finds expression in his nocturnal reveries on the myth of the Spinning Girl and her Cowboy (129); and BaBa, her father, the Chinese scholar who becomes an American laundryman. These generations of men are presented in all their pain and dignity.

The trajectories Maxine imagines for Baba's journey to the West in "The Father from China," be it the legal journey to San Francisco or the illegal one to New York, bear striking resemblances to the life journeys women had to go through in Old China. First, because of the discriminatory American laws, prospective sojourners to the Gold Mountain had to "change" their parentage, had to be "willing to be adopted by Gold Mountain Sojourners who were legal citizens of the United States" (46), just as a girl had to give up her own family and become part of her husband's when she married.[15] This family change for the purpose of illegal immigration also necessitated a change of name for the sojourner—Maxine's father had "unusual luck" in that his "bought papers had a surname which was the same as our own last name" (47)—a situation faced by women upon marriage. And like a Chinese bride who travels to her in-laws' house in a closed palanquin, unable to see where she is going, the father in one version of the immigration story travels by ship in a sealed crate from which his view is almost entirely restricted.[16] As he crosses over to a new world that he cannot control, he suffers the same sense of entrapment, fear, isolation, and apprehension for the future that a bride might experience as she travels to her new life with a man and a family unfamiliar to her.

The experience of powerlessness and humiliation that these "emasculated" China Men must endure becomes emphasized even further by their physical location on a floor below the Chinese women on Angel Island: "Diabolical, inauspicious beginning—to be trodden over by women. 'Living under women's legs' said the superstitious old-fashioned men from the backward villages. . . . No doubt the demons had deliberately planned this humiliation" (55). Once more, the narrator sympathizes with the immigrant men in their humiliation, which they presume to be a plot by the dominant white society, but she also mocks their feelings of superiority over Chinese women.

Once in America, the treatment China Men received at the hands of the dominant culture was remarkably similar to that suffered by women of all races for centuries: they were disenfranchised (142, 155), denied the right to become U.S. citizens; "they were prohibited from owning land or real estate" (153); they had no voice to "talk in court" (142); and they were forced to attend separate schools (156). As the white male order lost some of its legal power over one subordinate group—women—in the late nineteenth and early twentieth centuries, it turned to racial minorities to reassert such privilege. Hong Kingston exposes the injustice of privilege based on either race or gender.

The psychological effects of the dominant society's forcing minority men into "feminine" subject positions are perhaps even more profound, and it is here that Hong Kingston's explorations are especially cogent and incisive. We might expect that, having experienced a form of entrenched legal and personal discrimination based entirely on race, Chinese American men would be sympathetic to, and supportive of, the plight of Chinese American women, who have suffered doubly: as a racial minority and as women crossing between two patriarchal cultures, the traditional Chinese and the modern American. Linda Ching Sledge suggests such rapprochement between the sexes when she claims that "the myth [of Tang Ao] also speaks of the growing equality of the sexes as a result of the male's adventuring into unknown territories" (9). But, while Chinese women do assert their independence in the absence of sojourning men, Hong Kingston shows no acceptance of gender equality by the men. Quite the opposite is indicated: having been ground down themselves by white men, having been forced into "feminine" subject positions, Chinese American men often seek to reassert their lost patriarchal power by denigrating a group they perceive as weaker than themselves: Chinese American women.

Ironically, the strongest male sympathy for, and understanding of, women arises not in modern America but in traditional China, where Maxine's paternal grandfather so desired a daughter after producing three sons that he traded his fourth son, the valuable scholar, for a neighbor's daughter. Within the norms of Confucian society, this act is considered insane, not only by men but even more so by women (15–21).[17] It is the grandfather in China who blames his penis for failing to give him a daughter, thus attacking the symbol of the phallus that constitutes the very center of patriarchal law. The maternal grandfather from China also "was an unusual man in that he valued girls; he taught all his daughters how to read and write" (30). Hong Kingston thus subverts our expectations that life in China would have been more rigidly patriarchal than life in America, perhaps suggesting in the process that Chinese traditions were more rigorously observed by the immigrant community in America out of a sense of nostalgia for the lost homeland.

The father in America, having been forced into "feminine" subject positions as outlined above, lapses into silence—itself a state associated with the "feminine"—breaking that silence only to utter curses against women as a means of releasing his sense of frustration and powerlessness in racist America. The narrator Maxine addresses her father with one of the few facts based on her personal experience in the first half of the narrative: "You were angry. You scared us. Every day we listened to you swear, 'Dog vomit. Your mother's cunt. Your mother's smelly cunt.' . . . Obscenities. I made a wish that you only meant gypsies and not women in general" (12). Maxine then narrates a story of BaBa being tricked by gypsies and harassed by the police, an incident that results in his venting his rage on the women of the family. She traces her father's abuse of Chinese women back to his feelings of emasculation in America: "We knew that it was to feed us you had to endure demons and physical labor. You screamed wordless male screams that jolted the house upright and staring in the middle of the night" (13).

Baba's simmering rage, as mentioned above, takes two forms: one, the verbal and physical abuse of women (later Maxine relates a memory of her or her sister being beaten by her father); the other, silence. This is not a positive silence but the silence of resignation that signals withdrawal and humiliation, the inability to articulate his own subject position so that he is doomed to the one—that of inscrutable, passive "chinaman"—created for him by the dominant society. It is also a form of silence as abusive power over Chinese American women. As the daughter-narrator observes: "Worse than the swearing and the nightly screams were your silences when you punished us by not talking." Rather than empathize with Chinese women, who have been silenced by the symbolic order of patriarchy for centuries, unable or forbidden to inscribe their own identities, China Men like Baba seek to punish Chinese women with a silence that denies them a linguistically constituted identity: "You rendered us invisible, gone. . . . You kept up a silence for weeks and months. . . . You say with the few words and the silences: No stories. No past. No China" (14).

In her interview with Paula Rabinowitz, Hong Kingston expresses these same sentiments, but in a light and positive tone, when she says: "In fact, I wrote the characters so that the women have memories and the men don't have memories. They don't remember anything. The character of my father, for example, has no memory. He has no stories of the past. . . . He is so busy making up the present, which he has to build, that he has no time for continuity from the past. It did seem that the men were people of action" (180). Perhaps because this interview was conducted long after the writing of the book, which seems to have had a cathartic effect on Hong Kingston, here we find none of the feminist anger of *China Men*, where the daughter pleads with the silent father: "What I want from you is for you to tell me that those curses are only common Chinese sayings. That you did not mean to make me sicken at being female" (14). Of course, the personal intention of the father in these utterances is not important; the fact remains that the symbolic order of Confucian patriarchy inscribes for women these positions of inferiority, degradation, nonbeing, and BaBa's self-hatred stems from seeing his position in racist America mirrored in the subjection of women in traditional Chinese culture.

To be fair, Hong Kingston does not always present the father as morose and abusive in America. In a temporal reversal that may constitute a deliberate attempt to ameliorate the reader's and narrator's opinion of him, she presents earlier, more attractive memories of the father in the second half of the text, in "The American Father." Here he appears, not as a slave, but as a kind, gentle man who takes time to explain dark, mysterious places (the attic, the cellar with its well) to his daughter. In these early memories, the father emerges, along with the mother, as a hero of endurance, until he loses his gambling house job and deteriorates from the man in "power suits" to the ninety-pound weakling. Sympathy accrues to the father under this new form of "emasculation"—he is no longer the breadwinner—but this sympathy becomes severely compromised when the incident that galvanizes him out of his depression turns out to be a misogynous one: the beating of one of his daughters, either Maxine or her sister, as a means of venting his rage (253). This assertion of male power arouses him from his torpor, and he opens a new laundry; but such a positive result neither justifies his violence against women nor diminishes the fact that women have suffered for centuries what he now suffers.

That BaBa's self-hatred originates in his feelings of identity with Chinese women becomes apparent in Maxine's description of her father as the man "who inked each piece of our own laundry with the word *Center*" (15). In the face of silence, this inscription of the Chinese character *zhong*, center or middle, signifies BaBa's desire to return physically to China, the Middle Kingdom, *Zhong Guo*, but also his desire to reestablish his centric position of masculine authority, to break out of the "eccentric" (15) position of marginality into which China Men have been forced in America but which Chinese women have always occupied in a patriarchal culture.[18]

Ironically, BaBa, in his longing to recuperate his centric position of Confucian scholar—signaled by his calligraphy on the family laundry—fails to recognize the destabilizing power of an eccentric point of view as a place from which to critique the mainstream through subversive tactics, a kind of guerrilla periphery. This is a lesson that his daughter, the narrator, has learned extremely well—as this autorepresentational fiction, written from her double margin with amazing power, attests.[19] With a double irony, though, she uses her marginal vantage point, not only to critique the racist mainstream for its treatment of her forefathers but also to avenge herself on those very forefathers, the malestream, for their sexist treatment of Chinese women.[20] This text emerges, then, as both an act of compassion by the female narrator toward the father and a kind of subversive triumph over him. While he attempts, and fails, to deny her an identity with his imposition of silence, *she* imagines his-story, granting him a linguistically constituted identity in this text. It is, by and large, a positive identity, and she does request that he correct any mistakes she makes in the narrative (15); but his voice never intrudes to correct hers, so that the text, his-story, remains her creation. Thus, feminist subversive strategies prove more effective than the father's worn-out desire to return to male privilege and centric heroism. The father himself, along with other immigrants, seems to have recognized this situation when, on Angel Island, he and the other poets who covered the walls of this institution concluded that they "had come to a part of the world not made for honor, where 'a hero cannot use his bravery'" (55). The desire to employ masculine heroic tactics is there (56–57), but means and opportunities remain nonexistent for these imprisoned men.[21]

Not surprisingly, then, "feminine" strategies of subversion from the periphery, from positions of apparent powerlessness—"the skill of . . . deceits" (60)—are the very ones that brought success to the forefathers in their times of oppression.[22] Bak Goong, for example, finds himself in a "feminine" subject position when the "demon" owners of the Hawaiian sugar plantation impose silence on the laborers: "How was he to marvel adequately, voiceless? He needed to cast his voice out to catch ideas" (100). He rebels first in a direct fashion, singing instead of talking, but this leads to punishment. He then finds success through a form of triumphant deceit in which he speaks indirectly, disguising his words in his cough: "The deep, long, loud coughs, barking and wheezing, were almost as satisfying as shouting. He let out scolds disguised as coughs. . . . He did not even mind the despair, which dispelled upon his speaking it" (104).

Even the coughs cannot dispel the despair completely, however; Bak Goong must eventually join the other China Men in a group therapy session of shouting their desires, concerns, fears into a hole in the earth: "They had dug an ear into the world, and were telling the earth their secrets" (117). Their most intense desire is for "Home. Home. Home. Home." The attempt to fill an orifice with words, to find comfort in mother earth, and the desire for home, the domestic, love, the mother country/culture—"'Hello down there in China!' they shouted. 'Hello, Mother'"—reveal their psychological and sexual frustration caused by the exclusion laws against Chinese women.

The great-grandfather's shouting incident harks back in the narrative, and forward temporally, to the father's debilitating silence; it also anticipates Ah Goong's even more ingenious solution to the loss and frustration caused by emasculation: he fulfills his sexual desire by "fucking the world" from his suspended basket, setting off seminal explosions (133). Again, the desire to return to the mother is clear.

It is a desire shared by Ed/BaBa, who identifies with the wily mother, "the kind parent" (71) in the movie *Young Tom Edison.* In fact, Ed explains to Brave Orchid that "this cunning, resourceful, successful inventor, Edison, was who he had named himself after."

Ed may wish for the cunning of an Edison, but what his forefathers seem to have had in common that he lacks is a strong element of fantasy or the fabulous to mix with their cunning and deceit: "[Ah Goong] did not buy [a lottery ticket for a visiting prostitute]. He took out his penis under his blanket or bared it in the woods and thought about nurses and princesses" (144). The objects remain those of male fantasies, but from the start Maxine associates the ability to fantasize or fabulate with women and with Cantonese: "BaBa became susceptible to the stories men told, which were not fabulations like the fairy tales and ghost stories told by women" (41); "I want to talk to Cantonese, who have always been revolutionaries, nonconformists, people with fabulous imaginations, people who invented the Gold Mountain" (87). The reality of "emasculation" and discrimination on the Gold Mountain has destroyed her father's ability to fabulate, however; he has "no stories" to tell, and he dismisses dreams as fermentation, rot: "'Fermenting dreams' said BaBa. 'Dreams fermenting.' I heard in his scorn and words how dreams ferment the way yeast and mold do, how dreams are like fungus" (193).

I have said that *China Men* is to some extent an act of revenge on the father; but it is also an act of attempted reconciliation between daughter and father, just as *The Woman Warrior* was an act of reconciliation between daughter and mother. Unfortunately, it cannot match the competing dialogue between mother and daughter that the earlier fiction attained, for the father has no voice; therefore, it must be a pure gift, an act of restoring something he lacks. It is the restoration, though, not of the phallus he feels he lacks in white America but of the imagination America has robbed him of by "defeating" his dreams and by excluding him from its history. In a sense, he does not need a restoration of phallic power: the filial attendance of his children and the attentions of Brave Orchid demonstrate his "masculinity." Furthermore, he has the traditional Confucian solution to securing a place in history: procreation, family endurance, "the making of more Americans." What he needs to be a complete being is his-story, the very gift Maxine tries to give him in this text of her fantasies, her imaginings, her fabulations.

Ironically, there is another sense in which America is the Land of Women for Chinese immigrants: with the absence of men—through sojourning and immigration—from their villages in Guangdong, China, women became independent, controlling their own fate and giving voice to their own stories.[23] Thus, when they are permitted to immigrate to America to join their husbands, it is Chinese and Chinese American women who become the sources of "talk-story" in this new land, the Land of Women. "Talk-stories" have been a source of empowerment for Chinese women; the gift Hong Kingston attempts to give her father is polyphonous fabulation as a powerful form of shared rebuttal to the monological voice of dominant white history, which has attempted to erase Asian American experience. She challenges and disrupts the symbolic order with the semiotic.[24] She thus (re)claims for her forefathers the father land, America, the Gold Mountain they came to conquer, (re)claims this sublime goal not in any masculinist military sense—"The Brother in Vietnam" makes her pacifist ideology clear—but as a word warrior, a Fa Mu Lan of the pen instead of the sword. Unlike Fa Mu Lan, however, she can never return to being the filial daughter. She cannot even afford a return to Chinese legend to discover a figure like the poet Tsai Yen, who acted as the vehicle for tortured reconciliation with her mother and mother culture in *The Woman Warrior*. Instead, reclaiming the Gold Mountain involves putting her faith in the next generation of Chinese American men, "the young men who listen" to the stories of China Men, and whom she watches (308) to see if they have benefited from fabulation as she herself gives up trying to establish the facts of any particular version of how China Men discovered the Gold Mountain. She has given the gift of various fabulous versions of his-story in her text; one suspects that she now listens for the next generation of young men to respond with their own dialogical voices, to lay claim to their America.

NOTES

1. All quotations are from Maxine Hong Kingston, *China Men* (New York: Knopf, 1980); page numbers appear in the text.

2. Rabinowitz summarizes: "One might roughly say that China is a landscape inhabited, at least in the narratives, by the women and their myths, and the Gold Mountain, America, is really where the men are and that's where history is" (180).

3. Hong Kingston's description of Bak Goong, her great-grandfather, on opium could apply equally to her art: "Everything was true. He was Lao Tse's great thinker, who can embrace opposing thoughts at the same moment" (*China Men* 95). The experience of crossing between cultures—Bak Goong was sailing from China to Hawaii when he smoked opium—seems to enhance this ability to appreciate multivalent truth.

4. For a succinct summary of social conditions in "bachelor" Chinatowns and the literary depictions of these Chinatowns, see Kim, *Asian American Literature*, 91–121. Elsewhere, Kim writes: "Prevented from establishing families in the United States by exclusion and anti-miscegenation laws the Chinese American community was largely a community of aging men with wives in China, to whom they usually sent regular remittances from their laundry and restaurant labor. It was not until 1970 that the balance between the sexes among Chinese Americans approached the American norm" ("Asian American Writers" 53).

5. I employ the terms "men" and "women" in this context, not to denote biological sex, but in Kristeva's sense of a subject position in culture and language that can be occupied, at times, by men as well as women. Quotation marks indicate such usage. See Kristeva, "Women Can Never Be Defined."

6. I am grateful to Amy Ling for pointing out in a letter to me the origin of the Tang Ao story in "an early 19th century novel by Li Ju-chen, translated by Lin Tai-yi as *Flowers in the Mirror* (Berkeley: University of California Press, 1965). But as Hong Kingston modified the legend of Fa (Hua) Mu Lan, conflating it with the story of the general Yueh Fei, so she changed this story slightly. It was Tang Ao's brother-in-law, Master Lin, who landed in the Country of Women and had all those tortures inflicted on him." The shift in characters does not affect Hong Kingston's major concern, which is that a man experienced this situation.

7. Before going further, I should stress that, although Asian American men have been forced into feminine subject positions in work and social situations, there remains a significant area of distinction between their lives and those of minority women in general: men do not usually experience the threat of sexual victimization, of bodily assault, faced in minority women. As Houston Baker points out, such genuine fear of "the [white] patriarch-as-rapist" is a "dramatically foregrounded *topos* of the [black] woman's account" of the "economics of slavery" (54), and similar motifs abound in the narratives of other minority women.

8. Hong Kingston does link Ah Goong, her grandfather, and herself as writer-avenger, to Guan Goong: "Guan Goong, the God of War, also God of War and Literature, had come to America—Guan Goong, Grandfather Guan, our own ancestor of writers and fighters, of actors and gamblers, and avenging executioners who mete out justice" (149–50). Ah

Goong's triumph, however, is decidedly antimilitary and unheroic: he becomes "a homeless wanderer, a shiftless, dirty, jobless man with matted hair, ragged clothes, and fleas all over his body"; but he also manages to have an American "child of his own" despite the antimiscegenation laws (150–51). His triumph is not military but pro-creative, just as Hong Kingston's vengeance on behalf of her forefathers is literary rather than physical. Once more Hong Kingston disrupts the expectations aroused by our traditional hierarchized binary oppositions.

9. A more psychological reading might stress that two allegories of desire collide in this text: the desire for the recuperation of a lost and idealized family structure (a traditional family romance) and the desire for revision of the traditional family structure to enable the daughter's liberation from patriarchy.

10. Frank Chin and Jeffrey Paul Chan observe: "For the Chinese, [the white majority] invented an instrument of racist policy that was a work of pure genius, in that it was not an overtly hostile expression of anti-Chinese sentiment, yet still reinforced the stereotype and generated self-contempt and humiliation among generations of Chinese and Chinese-Americans, who after having been conditioned into internalizing the white supremacist Gospel of Christian missionaries, looked on themselves as failures, instead of victims of racism. This wondrous instrument was *the law*" ("Racist Love" 71). Chin and Chan make no reference, however, to the misogynous aspects of such legislation; in fact, their own discourse brims with misogynous rage.

11. Hong Kingston herself has explained "The Laws" in this way: "The mainstream culture doesn't know the history of Chinese-Americans, which has been written and written well. The ignorance makes a tension for me, and in the new book [*China Men*] I just couldn't take it anymore. So all of a sudden, right in the middle of the stories, plunk—there is an eight-page section of pure history. It starts with the Gold Rush and goes right through the various exclusion acts, year by year. There are no characters in it. It really affects the shape of the book and it might look quite clumsy" (Pfaff 26).

12. See the studies in "Part Two: Assimilation and Sex Roles" of *Asian Americans: Psychological Perspectives*, ed. Sue and Wagner, as well as Reed Ueda, "The Americanization and Education of Japanese-Americans."

13. The sense of debasement here stems not only from the perception that laundry work is "women's work" but also from the knowledge that white society considers this work humiliatingly menial. Paul C. P. Siu, in *The Chinese Laundryman: A Study of Social Isolation*, quotes the attitudes of whites: "My opinion of him [the Chinese American] is quite natural so long as he remains only a laundryman. . . . He is all right as long as he stays in his place and does not try to do too much"; "The Chinks are all right

if they remain in their place. I don't mind their working in the laundry business, but they should not go higher than that" (quoted in Kim, *Asian American Literature* 99).

14. Frank Chin and Jeffrey Paul Chan point out: The white stereotype of the Asian is unique in that it is the only racial stereotype completely devoid of manhood. Our nobility is that of an efficient housewife. At our worst we are contemptible because we are womanly, effeminate, devoid of all the traditionally masculine qualities of originality, daring, physical courage, creativity" ("Racist Love" 68). See also Wang 19–20, and Cheung 236–37; Cheung both employs and deconstructs Chin and Chan's argument, drawing out its sexist and homophobic tendencies.

15. In *The Woman Warrior* Hong Kingston quotes traditional Chinese sayings about girls which indicate that their parents consider them to be the potential daughters of their future husbands' families: "'There's no profit in raising girls. Better to raise geese than girls.' . . . 'When you raise girls, you're raising children for strangers'" (54).

16. A superb recent example of the literal and figurative limitations placed on the view of a traditional Chinese bride is found in the film *Red Sorghum* (China 1987; directed by Zhang Yimou). As the bride travels to her new husband, the camera forces us to see largely from her restricted perspective *inside* the sedan.

17. A classic example of women who have imbibed the values of the Confucian patriarchal system comes in the figure of Mad Sao's mother, who writes from China to her American son: "Why don't you do your duty? I order you to come back. It's all those daughters, isn't it? . . . Leave them. Come back alone. You don't need to save enough money to bring a litter of females. What a waste to bring girls all the way back here to sell anyway" (*China Men* 172).

18. A more clearly sympathetic portrait of a good man's failure to reestablish his centric position appears in Hong Kingston's narration of "The Li Sao: An Elegy," in which Ch'u Yuan the poet "had to leave the Center; he roamed in the outer world for the rest of his life, twenty years. He mourned that he had once been a prince, and now he was nothing. And the people were so blind, they thought he was a wrongdoer instead of the only righteous man left in the world" (*China Men* 256–57). This elegy becomes another parable of what China Men experience when they "go out on the road." Unlike her father, however, Ch'u Yuan managed to retain "his imagination and dreams" (257) in exile.

19. Chin and Chan do not agree with the idea that a minority position of "doubleness" can be a source of empowerment as well as of victimization. They claim that "the concept of the dual personality successfully deprives the Chinese-American of all authority over language and thus a means of

codifying, communicating, and legitimizing his experience" ("Racist Love" 76). My own position is expanded in "Father Land and/or Mother Tongue: The Divided Female Subject in *The Woman Warrior* and *Obasan.*"

20. In *The Woman Warrior*, Hong Kingston defines "revenge" as "not the beheading, not the gutting, but the words" (63). The words in *China Men* are all hers. The term "malestream" I have borrowed from Amy Ling, "I'm Here: An Asian American Woman's Response," 152.

21. On the conflicts in Asian American studies created by some male critics' attempts to recuperate a lost "heroic tradition"—conflicts that focus on Hong Kingston's feminist impulses—see Cheung, 241–45.

22. I do not employ "deceit" and "subversion" here with negative connotations; rather, I mean to suggest that such surreptitious avenues to power are usually the only ones open to women in patriarchal societies, and they can be just as effective as direct confrontation. As Emily Ahern observes of gender politics in Chinese culture: "According to the male ideal, power should be exercised by male heads of households, managers of lineages, and community leaders. No wonder the ability of women to exercise power of a very different kind, power wielded behind the scenes, unsupported by recognized social position, is seen as a threat to the male order. No matter how well-ensconced men are in the established positions of power, the surreptitious influence of women remains beyond their capacity to control" (201).

23. Sledge notes: "As historians have remarked, Cantonese women were forced to assume total family governance after the emigration of male villagers to foreign lands. Thus, there arose a strong tradition of womanly self-sufficiency and aggressiveness among Cantonese. Kingston shows the persistence of that tradition among those few Chinese women, like her mother, who were allowed to enter the U.S. during the lengthy period of exclusion" (9–10).

24. I use the term "semiotic" here in Kristeva's sense of preoedipal *jouissance*, strong traces of which can be found in "female" language. See Kristeva, *Revolution in Poetic Language*, sec. 1.

WORKS CITED

Ahern, Emily M. "The Power and Pollution of Chinese Women." In *Women in Chinese Society*, ed. Margery Wolf and Roxane Witke. Stanford: Stanford University Press, 1975. 193–214.

Baker, Houston A., Jr. *Blues, Ideology, and Afro-American Literature: A Vernacular Theory*. Chicago and London: University of Chicago Press, 1984.

Chen, Jack. *The Chinese of America*. San Francisco: Harper and Row, 1980.

Cheung, King-Kok. "The Woman Warrior vs. The Chinaman Pacific: Emasculation, Feminism, and Heroism." In *Conflicts in Feminism*, ed. Marianne Hirsch and Evelyn Fox Keller. New York: Routledge, 1990. 234–51.

Chin, Frank, and Jeffery Paul Chan. "Racist Love." In *Seeing Through Shuck*, ed. Richard Kostelanetz. New York: Ballantine Books, 1972. 65–79.

Chua, Cheng Lok. "Golden Mountain: Chinese Versions of the American Dream in Lin Yutang, Louis Chu, and Maxine Hong Kingston." *Ethnic Groups* 4.1–2 (1982): 33–59.

Goellnicht, Donald C. "Father Land and/or Mother Tongue: The Divided Female Subject in *The Woman Warrior* and *Obasan*." In *Redefining Autobiography in Twentieth Century Women's Fiction*, ed. Colette Hall and Janice Morgan. Garland: New York, 1991. 119–34.

Islas, Arturo. "Maxine Hong Kingston." In *Women Writers of the West Coast: Speaking of Their Lives and Careers*, ed. Marilyn Yalom. Santa Barbara: Capra, 1983. 11–19.

Juhasz, Suzanne. "Maxine Hong Kingston: Narrative Technique and Female Identity." In *Contemporary American Women Writers: Narrative Strategies*, ed. Catherine Rainwater and William J. Scheick. Lexington: University Press of Kentucky, 1985. 173–89.

Kim, Elaine H. *Asian American Literature: An Introduction to the Writings and Their Social Context*. Philadelphia: Temple University Press, 1982.

———. "Asian American Writers: A Bibliographical Review." *American Studies International* 22.2 (October 1984): 41–78.

Kingston, Maxine Hong. *China Men*. New York: Knopf, 1980.

———. "Cultural Mis-readings by American Reviewers." *Asian and Western Writers in Dialogue: New Cultural Identities*, ed. Guy Amirthanayagam. London: Macmillan, 1982. 55–65.

———. *The Woman Warrior: Memoirs of a Girlhood among Ghosts*. 1976. New York: Vintage, 1977.

Kristeva, Julia. *Desire in Language*. Ed. Leon S. Roudiez. New York: Columbia University Press, 1980.

———. "On the Women of China." Trans. Ellen Conroy Kennedy. *Signs* 1 (Autumn 1975): 57–81.

———. *Revolution in Poetic Language*. Trans. Margaret Waller. New York: Columbia University Press, 1984.

———. "Women Can Never Be Defined." In *New French Feminisms: An Anthology*, ed. Elaine Marks and Isabelle de Courtivron. New York: Schocken Books, 1981. 137–41.

Ling, Amy. "I'm Here: An Asian American Woman's Response." *New Literary History* 19 (1987): 151–60.

Lyman, Stanford M. *Chinese Americans*. New York: Random House, 1971.

Neubauer, Carol E. "Developing Ties to the Past: Photography and Other Sources of Information in Maxine Hong Kingston's *China Men*." *MELUS* 10.4 (Winter 1983): 17–36.

Pfaff, Timothy. "Talk with Mrs. Kingston." *New York Times Book Review*, 15 June 1980.

Rabine, Leslie W. "No Lost Paradise: Social Gender and Symbolic Gender in the Writings of Maxine Hong Kingston." *Signs* 12.3 (1987): 471–92.

Rabinowitz, Paula. "Eccentric Memories: A Conversation with Maxine Hong Kingston." *Michigan Quarterly Review* 26.1 (Winter 1987): 177–87.

Siu, Paul C. P. *The Chinese Laundryman: A Study of Social Isolation*. New York: New York University Press, 1987.

Sledge, Linda Ching. "Maxine Kingston's *China Men*: The Family Historian as Epic Poet." *MELUS* 7.4 (Winter 1980): 3–22.

Sue, Stanley, and Nathaniel N. Wagner, eds. *Asian Americans: Psychological Perspectives*. Ben Lomond, Calif.: Science and Behavior Books, 1973.

Tsai, Shih-Shan Henry. *The Chinese Experience in American*. Bloomington and Indianapolis: Indiana University Press, 1986.

Ueda, Reed. "The Americanization and Education of Japanese-Americans." In *Cultural Pluralism*, ed. Edgar G. Epps. Berkeley, Calif.: McCutchan, 1974. 71–90.

Wang, Alfred S. "Maxine Hong Kingston's Reclaiming of America: The Birthright of the Chinese American Male." *South Dakota Review* 26.1 (Spring 1988): 18–29.

Wolf, Margery. "Chinese Women: Old Skills in a New Context." In *Woman, Culture, and Society*, ed. Michelle Zimbalist Rosaldo and Louise Lamphere. Stanford: Stanford University Press, 1974. 157–72.

PART III

Borders and Boundaries

11

Sense of Place, History, and the Concept of the "Local" in Hawaii's Asian/Pacific Literatures

Stephen H. Sumida

COMMON GROUND

HAVING A longer history, the literatures of Hawai'i may in some ways foretell the course being run by their mainland Asian American counterparts. Not only a "minority" American but a colonial phenomenon, for a century Hawaii's Asian/Pacific American literature has welled up from cultural (but not hegemonic) pluralism in a setting where there is no majority ethnic group. Further, as has been occurring to Asian American literature nationally thus far in its history, for more than a century the most well-known traditions of Hawaii's literature have been read and predominantly defined through the eyes and in the interests of tourists.

Few places represented in American literature present so singular and simplistic an image to the rest of the world as Hawai'i. That Hawai'i since the 1970s has been undergoing a literary renaissance of concentrated and controversial vigor pushes against that image.[1] That this renaissance includes not only the native Hawaiian but also the "local" (as opposed to "universal") polyethnic, contemporary literatures of Hawai'i further controverts Hawaii's wide, blank appeal to a tourist world.[2] The metaphor of "renaissance" implies a rebirth of cultural *histories*, while the idyllic image of Hawai'i as paradise of the Pacific denies history. "Native Hawaiian" in the idyll usually conjures the reductive as well as Eurocentric notions of a Noble Savage and of Otherness against which the idea and reality of a "native Hawaiian renaissance" must necessarily act. Certainly even more than regionalism, the term "local" used by writers of Hawai'i to describe their works and traditions and by the general populace to label a racially mixed and charged, class-conscious polyethnicity championed by some, hated by others, glides with aplomb right against some of the most empowered literary studies in America. Among authors of Hawaii's native Hawaiian and "local" literatures are those who resist the imposition of critical theories upon their works not because they deny a need for criticism but because they suspect views other than "local" ones of being Eurocentric.[3]

Deeply undercurrent in Hawaii's Asian/Pacific American literatures are influences of local history and place, both of these concepts particularized in such an assertive way that these literatures inherently exercise resistance against presumed national, even mainland Asian American generalities. However easy it may be to see native Hawaiian and Hawaii's Asian American literary works as commodified evocations of a facile image of Hawai'i as paradise, this resistance and, further, the agency of self-definition are all the more vital in these literatures; for unless readers too are freed from tourist, colonial views of the subject, then the subject is bound still to be mistaken. Making matters better or worse for Hawaii's own literary power or its limitations (depending on one's point of view), history and place are not simply two separate elements of a worldview or of a sensibility in Hawai'i, but in Hawaii's island culture *place* is conceived *as history*—that is, as the story enacted on any given site.

In Hawai'i today it is a truism—sometimes severely tested—that any local concept of multiculturalism would be meaningless without a recognition of native Hawaiian culture. No true "renaissance" and observance of two hundred years of diverse European, Asian, Latino/Latina, African, and mainland American histories and cultures in Hawai'i would hold meaning for Hawaii's general populace if what is called the Hawaiian renaissance had not already been underway since the 1870s, with a renewal of vigor since the mid-1960s. To residents of Hawai'i, native Hawaiian culture ought to be recognized as a common ground, just as *ke one hānau*, the Hawaiian sand of individuals' births, represents the common ground upon which Hawaii's people of different races live. But this means neither that the grounds are there for the taking, to be appropriated and claimed at whim, nor that in practice native Hawaiian culture and history have the understanding and the power that the truism about the primacy of Hawaiian culture would imply.

Native Hawaiian oral literatures had for so long been thought to be receding that as early as the 1830s Davida Malo was compiling his record of Hawaiian cultural practices, *Ka Mo'olelo Hawai'i*. He and his colleagues themselves were converted Christians, native Hawaiian youths educated at Lahainaluna Seminary on Maui. The fact that the title of his compilation means "Hawaiian antiquities" says much: in it Malo records customs, lore, religion, and concepts of an ebbing and changing culture. This change, however, is told neither to glorify a native Hawaiian paradise now lost with the coming of foreigners nor to condemn that past and the people who lived it for being pagan. Likewise, one of Malo's colleagues in the Hawaiian Historical Society at Lahainaluna in the 1830s, Samuel Manaiakalani Kamakau, undertook the more recent history of change through the time of Kamehameha, during the late eighteenth and early nineteenth centuries. Kamakau's history includes but is not dominated by an account of the 1778 to 1779 arrivals of Captain James Cook. Like Malo, Kamakau draws powerfully from Hawaiian oral sources (his *kūpuna*, men and women elders) and sometimes appears biased by his kinship with historic individuals and families locked in Hawaiian political rivalries: thus both explicitly and implicitly Kamakau narrates, describes, critiques, and dramatizes *differing* politics and interpretations of history among his subjects. This narrative history, first compiled in 1866 from Kamakau's essays and known today as *Ruling Chiefs of Hawaii*, is dynamic; it is about changes underway from long before Cook's arrival, changes occurring through acts backed by political motives and decisions of the Hawaiian rulers. While it may appear that, unlike Kamakau, Malo aimed simply to preserve antiquities already lost, his assignment to record them was part of the larger project of these native Hawaiian historians to connect an antique past with the present in an unbroken flow. The relatedness of the assignments undertaken by Malo and Kamakau implies that they set out to express the life, and not the death, of Hawaiian culture in their generation. And in their views *haole* (foreigners, nowadays meaning Caucasians) are neither Christ nor Satan, not the only ones with power to effect change for the better or for the worse.

But the decades of Christian teaching following the deployment of Congregational missionaries beginning in 1820 of course came to influence how concepts of Hawaiian historical change were to be interpreted. By the 1870s King David Kalākaua (elected king in 1874, died in 1891) perceived the decline of his population and culture to be so pronounced—due to an influx of Christian Europeans, in effect a colonization of the Hawaiian monarchy, and to venereal diseases, measles, leprosy, and other plagues newly introduced from abroad—that he instituted a native cultural and scientific renaissance. His mission was not only to record and interpret, as Malo and Kamakau had done, but also to recover and, further, to revive. Succeeding Kalākaua was Hawaii's last monarch, Queen Lili'uokalani, one of Hawaii's most talented composers of *mele* (poems) set to her music. She was deposed in 1893 by a band of American businessmen led by Sanford Dole, who sought by the illegal takeover to resolve the perennial problem of securing favorable American taxation of Hawaiian sugar. The solution Dole and his cohorts implemented was to make Hawai'i part of America so that their product would no longer be liable to a United States tariff on foreign sugar. Thus the native Hawaiian monarchy was overthrown in the name of the American domestication of Hawai'i, in 1893, some two years short of the monarchy's centennial. It was not until 1898, however, a year of strategic, military, territorial gain for the American empire with the victory in the Spanish-American War, that President William McKinley saw it politically possible to accept Hawai'i as a territory despite the dubious way that the monarchy had been snatched from the Hawaiians.

The other major colonial enterprise in Hawai'i besides sugar, pineapple, and the military defense industries, masks this history and the seriousness of the Hawaiian renaissance. I refer again to the tourist industry.

The common, touristic notion of Hawai'i as an "earthly paradise" is a peculiarly Christian dream with deep sources and expressions in Western myths and histories. Clearly it ought not be expected—but is often simplistically assumed—that in native Hawaiian literature expressions of *aloha 'āina*, a value meaning "love of the land" and predating the arrival of Christians, are evocations of a Christian earthly paradise. Some of the most overt statements about *aloha 'āina* in *mele* are not idyllic at all. Composed in protest shortly after the overthrow of Lili'uokalani, her queen, Ellen Wright Prendergast's "Kaulana nā Pua" ("Famous Are the Flowers," i.e., the people) has sometimes been called "Mele Aloha 'Āina" and "Mele 'Ai Pohaku" ("Stone Eating Song") because of its central expression:

'A'ole makou a'e minamina	We do not value
I ka pu'ukālā a ke aupuni.	The government's sums of money.
Ua lawa mākou i ka pōhaku,	We are satisfied with the stones,
I ka 'ai kamaha'o o ka 'āina.	Astonishing food of the land.

Not overtly patriotic, more usual poetic expressions of aloha 'āina sometimes resemble Western evocations of earthly paradises and pastoral retreats; but such mele about special places typically honor a home, the family residing there, and the history of the place—all symbolized by its natural setting, the qualities of which are not anthropomorphic but are assumed to parallel and be unified or congruent with the human and the spiritual. In "Nā Hala o Naue" ("The Pandanus of Naue") J. Kahinu pays respect to Queen Emma. Upon the death of her husband Kamehameha IV in 1863, the queen assumed the name Ka-lele-o-nā-lani (the flight of the royal ones), which she changed from a nearly identical name her husband had given her but which differed in that it was in the singular—referring to the flight of the royal one, their infant son who died a year before the king. The *haku mele* (weaver of words) Kahinu honors her with this history by singing of Naue, on the island of Kaua'i, which the poet associates with Ka-lele-o-nā-lani:

Nani wale nā hala, 'eā, 'eā	So beautiful are the pandanus
O Naue i ke kai, 'eā, 'eā.	Of Naue by the sea.
Ke 'oni a'ela, 'eā, 'eā	Moving there
Pili mai Hā'ena, 'eā, 'eā.	At Ha'ena.
'Ena aku nā maka, 'eā, 'eā	Fiery eyes,
'O nā manu i ka pua, 'eā, 'eā.	Birds upon the flowers.

The *mele* is graced by the Hawaiian poetic technique of "linked terminals," where between the second and third stanzas (and others not quoted) the sounds, in this case of "Hā'ena" and "'Ena," are repeated. In the *kaona* (underlying meaning) of the *mele* runs a sexuality, in the sensuous descriptions of nature, again in keeping with native Hawaiian poetics. The *mele* concludes with the identification of Ka-lele-o- nā-lani with the place and her story of double bereavement:

ʻO koʻu lei ia, ʻeā, ʻeā	She is my lei
O ua laʻi lani, ʻeā, ʻeā.	And regal peace.
Haʻina ʻia mai, ʻeā, ʻeā:	Tell the refrain:
ʻO Ka-lele-o-nā-lani, ʻea, ʻea.	The-flight-of-the-royal-ones.

Coursing over and through the momentous event of the end of the monarchy, an ahistoric, touristic conception of native Hawaiian culture has been constructed. This image—or duality of images—has little to do with a Hawaiian renaissance except that the works of the renaissance can easily be snatched out of historical context to serve exoticist interests of tourism, whether in popular culture, the arts, or in scholarship. I say that this is a "duality of images" because on the other side of the simple pastoral of Hawaiʻi and the South Pacific promoted in tourism is the spectacular, melodramatic violence in television series such as *Magnum P.I.* and the grossness in the novel *Hawaii* by James A. Michener. These versions of the islands draw heavily upon contrasts between an exceptionally hospitable natural setting, on the one hand, and on the other hand a simple goodness or simple savagery of the peoples in it. The conflict-driven narrative and dramatic face of this tourist "literary" tradition of Hawaiʻi, then, exploits an assumed potential for contrast between nature and people, an implicit alienation of one from the other. It is a view of natural and human relationships foreign to the usual assumptions in Hawaiian traditions.

A touristic view is of course foreign, though well known to other residents of Hawaiʻi along with the native Hawaiians. Most of Hawaii's Asian Americans arrived, settled, and grew up not with vacation dreams; but they immigrated to labor. The sugar industry in particular was a mainstay of the European, transatlantic colonial enterprise since the seventeenth century; and islands like Jamaica, worked by slaves when the withering native people proved inadequate to the labor needs of sugar, were direct models for sugar industries in the Hawaiian islands in the mid- and later nineteenth century when, however, slavery was no longer feasible. The sugar planters of Hawaiʻi implemented "contract labor": masses were recruited from abroad and held to their agreements to work on plantations for a specified number of years, during which time accumulated debts made some unable to do anything but renew their terms of indenture. Yet some among them still managed to begin an Asian American literature of Hawai'i.

Contemporary "local" literature of Hawai'i inherits and often interprets this history of labor. It also inherits cultures and languages of many immigrant and indigenous origins, none of them presumed to be in any "pure" form since "local" culture is itself conceived in terms of continual change, indeed of whatever the current fads may be. This conception tends again to work against or to complicate the idyllic and simply nostalgic, in this case the notion of a simple past populated by simple folk. For instance, while I myself am by no means adept or informed enough in native Hawaiian language and cultural studies to do more than sample Hawaiian arts and scholarship, in their way my immigrant grandparents from Japan knew colloquial Hawaiian much better than I, and their linguistic milieu was more complex. Their daily life included the varieties of pidgin, Portuguese, Spanish, English, and other European languages, especially in the Hawai'i of the 1880s to 1920s. My generation receives this daunting multilingualism and pidgin not as a multiply fractured polyglot but as a language of our own, Hawaii's creole, that is our native tongue, born from the self-conscious efforts of our forebears to devise means from communicating across cultures. The past was no simpler than our present, and for the Hawaiian and local renaissance to continue, it is crucial that history be researched, questioned, learned, and infused within Hawaii's arts and society. Unseen, unheard influences within contemporary culture in Hawai'i are rising to the surface of understanding and making room for other myths and subtexts underground.

PLACE AS HISTORY

How can *history*, which assumes concepts of ever-changing time, define *place*, usually thought to be a tangible, fixed topography (though boundaries change for political reasons and other volcanoes) upon which history is played but which itself seems to exist independently from history's acts and beyond the run of any one show in the theater?[4] Far more than we might like to admit, we of a postcolonial world are habituated to the notion that Hawaii's history began in 1778 with Captain Cook's arrival and the report of his expedition back to Great Britain. This colonial version of Hawaii's history literally begins with Europeans writing and reading it. Even for most people residing in Hawai'i the times before Cook's arrival seem characterized not by "ancient Hawaiian" *history* but by images of a self-sufficient, static, timeless way of life about which we—except for the true experts among us—really know almost nothing. That time to us is mythical, oral, and uninscribed—not historical—in our imaginations and lives today. It seems that Hawai'i the *place* has existed since the Creation, whereas Hawaii's *history* is only two hundred and fifteen years old. So how can history define place?

James Cook had no choice but to see Hawai'i in an ahistorical way, though he had to try immediately to learn the indigenous history. When he first caught sight of Hawai'i in January of 1778, he noted in his journal that once more his expedition had come to "a land of plenty" (264). He and his shipmates soon began bartering for fresh food with the Hawaiians who came to them in canoes from the shores of Waimea, Kaua'i. The British currency in this barter was iron, which Cook surmised was to be used for the making of domestic implements, while the natives called it *pahoa*, stonelike material for making daggers—weapons. Despite the scientific purposes of the expedition, the initial "transactions" with the island's natives were perceived by Cook in ways tinted by his own native myths. Cook at first assumed the natives to be at peace in their land of plenty. Thus early editors of his journals exaggerated the impression that Cook thought he had discovered a fabled Blessed Isle floating beyond history's reach, a long-established place in European mythology.

Though historical contexts for Cook's third expedition into the Pacific are well known in American history, we Americans seldom associate that context with his voyage and his arrival in Hawai'i. Cook set sail from Great Britain in 1776. Who was the king of Britain at the time of Cook's stays in Hawai'i? It was George III, ruling in the time of the American Revolution. These facts fit a certain yet somehow unexpected pattern of understanding, unexpected because of how ahistorically Hawai'i is usually imagined, how "unreal" a place it therefore is in tropical idylls. With simple historical contextualizing, then, it makes sense that in O. A. Bushnell's novel *The Return of Lono* and Aldyth Morris's monodrama *Captain Cook*, the plots turn on such facts as the "scamping" or shortchanging of equipment to Cook's expedition in 1776, when the British Admiralty averted funds from Cook's mission for finding the Northwest Passage to quelling the uprising in the American colonies. Cook was given two converted colliers and sails that rotted in "Pacific" storms. How deeply such facts contributed to the tragedy of that expedition—that is, to the manner of Cook's death and its meanings—I believe may be felt mainly through the two works of literature of Hawai'i I have just now cited, provided, however, we readers take the trouble to learn Cook's history in Hawai'i as well as that of Great Britain and the American Revolution.

Consider then the contemporaneous, native Hawaiian observation and experience of the event of Cook's arrival in Hawai'i. There is no talk of "a land of plenty," no suggestion of an idyllic view of Hawai'i. But there is this, from Kamakau, who evidently took his account from the eyewitness—indeed, participant—account of an elder in his family: "It was eighty-eight years ago, in January, 1778, that Captain Cook first came to Hawaii. Ka-'eo was ruling chief of Kauai, Ka-hahana of Oahu and Molokai, and Ka-hekili of Maui, Lanai, and Kahoolawe" (*Ruling Chiefs* 92). Kamakau thus begins his account of Cook's arrival by *placing* it within a *historical* setting that clearly expresses a native Hawaiian point of view most of us do not know until we read and are struck by Kamakau's naming of chiefs and their respective realms, their places emblems of their histories predating Cook's arrival. Kamakau assumes that these histories are known by his readers because the histories are the running topic of his extensive work. George III does not appear at all in the naming of chiefs. Kamakau goes on to narrate how the *kahuna* named Ku-'ohu, a priest of the god Lono, in effect positioned himself to mediate among Cook, the people, and his chief by declaring that Cook was Lono, so that Ku-'ohu thereby negotiated and gained some political power through access to the visitors' iron for making weapons for himself and his party in a time of warfare among great chiefs. Cook's arrival is not the dominant occurrence in Hawaiian history of the era which Kamakau and his colleagues generally called "ka wā o Kamehameha," the time of Kamehameha (not "of Cook"). Indeed, because Cook and his company had been at sea since 1776, it was they who in 1778 and 1779 knew very little of the momentous events that were currently making history in their own lands of origin.

Place identifies the chiefs that Kamakau names—the chiefs represent ruling families. Both in heroic forms of expression and in lyric poetry, place and history are linked, though in different ways. In "Nā

Hala o Naue" and other lyrical, rather than narrative, *mele*, the identification of places by their associations with natural features and with honored persons is static and evidently meant to be so.[5] Though history underlies it, the poem seems not to be tied to the *movements* of history. In the promotion of the image of Hawai'i as a vactionland, at best it is such lyrical, seemingly secular and apolitical *mele* that have held sway and have thus been mistaken for the whole of Hawaiian music and poetry. Much less heard by tourists—until recently in the current renaissance—have been the *oli* or chants such as dirges, historical narratives, or epics, sacred chants, genealogical chants, genital and prŏcreative chants, and other Hawaiian literary genres expressing struggle, conflict, spiritual power, heroism, and unpuritanical passions.

An interesting historicism sometimes does occur in startling ways in mele. A profound historical, modern (i.e., twentieth-century, in this case perhaps 1920s) identification of a place in Hawai'i occurs in Helen Lindsey Parker's "Maunaloa." Its historical dimension is entirely undercurrent, in the underlying meaning, or kaona, of the poem:

'Auhea wale 'oe Maunaloa lā	This I say to you Maunaloa
Kīkala nui	Ship with a broad stern
Ho'iho'i mai'oe ku'u aloha la	Bring my love back
Ē, ē, ē,	E, e, e,
Ka'awaloa nei	Here to Ka'awaloa.

The setting of this mele is Ka'awaloa, explicitly at the era, into the early part of the twentieth century, when the interisland ship *Maunaloa* called at Hawaii's ports. Billowing smoke and steam from its vents, the ship was aptly (as if "naturally") named after the actively volcanic mountain. The *mele's* speaker, a woman of Ka'awaloa, goes on to allude to her romance with an "illicit lover" (*ka ipo manuahi*) who works aboard the ship and who evidently calls on different women along his route. The third stanza is biting, for in it the woman addresses her lover and describes the state of their affair in sharp and concrete images:

Ko hinakā popopo lā	Your tattered handkerchief
'Ai 'ia e ka 'eluelū	No longer as beautiful as it was
A na'u nō ia kāwele nei lā	So let me wipe

Ē, ē, ē,	E, e, e
Ko kāma'a miomio	Your pointed-toe shoes

Their love is "tattered"; the worn token of their love is worthy now of being a rag for wiping the man's shoes; and those shoes are a metonymic symbol for the urban, "civilized" life that the man comes from aboard his machine, the *Maunaloa*. This *mele* is a wry song of farewell, a taunting request for "that one kiss" (*honi ho'okahi lā*) in parting. In Parker's *mele* we are presented with a woman's point of view from the shore, rather than the male sailor's point of view from the deck of his ship as he bids farewell—or deserts—the native woman with whom he has enjoyed a fling. The sailor's is a tourist's view as old as Tommo's in Herman Melville's *Typee* (1846, where Melville questions that point of view) and Odysseus's in Homer's epic—and, a close male counterpart to the view in Parker's *mele*, the view of the narrator John Forrest (which again the novelist questions) in O. A. Bushnell's *The Return of Lono*, set at Kealakekua Bay, in 1779.

The setting of "Maunaloa," Ka'awaloa today is the site of the memorial to Captain Cook: it is the village on Kealakekua Bay where the Hawaiians killed him on 14 February 1779. In being about a local woman's affair with a lover wearing "pointed-toe shoes" from a faraway place and coming and going by ship, "Maunaloa" is in a deep and playful sense about the comings and goings of Cook's crews and other touring outsiders thereafter. The lovely *mele* is also an intimation of shoe-wearing visitors' historic fate in Parker's view.

In his edition and translation of *I ka Wā o Kamehameha, In the Time of Kamehameha: Selected Essays by Samuel M. Kamakau*, Malcolm Naea Chun observes that Kamakau, Malo, S. N. Haleole, and other students at Lahainaluna Seminary in the 1830s "under the tutelage of teachers such as Reverend Sheldon Dibble, began the first intensive, ethnographic and historical field work conducted in Hawai'i. Dibble and the other teachers probably first introduced Hawaiians to chronology as it is known by dates rather than the typical Hawaiian means of remembering by event or person" (13). Remembering chronology "by event or person," in a "typical Hawaiian" way, is consonant with the ways of identifying place by history in the native Hawaiian works discussed above.

An ahistorical tourist tradition of literature of Hawai'i and the South Pacific did not begin with uncritical depictions of the islands.

Melville not only shows in *Typee* that its narrator is ethnocentric in thinking that the native people of a South Pacific island are "noble savages" and their valley an "Eden," but he also uses Hawai'i as his main point of contrast to that Eden: in the narrative, Hawai'i represents a land utterly corrupted by "civilization." Furthermore, the horror is that the narrator Tommo proves unable to understand the Typee of supposedly Edenic Nukuhiva at all, contrary to his tale's plot of seemingly growing understanding and sympathy. His understanding is nothing but preconceptions of earthly paradises, until Tommo's sight of a dried head, evidently a European's, kept by the Typee, breaks open his illusions. Mark Twain also criticized the Paradise of the Pacific cliché already in evidence when he visited Hawai'i in 1866. He dealt with it sometimes satirically, sometimes bluntly, and, in a never-published novel he wrote about Hawai'i, he saw the supposed paradise tragically.

But something more fundamental is a definitive characteristic of a "colonial" view of Hawai'i, and it is this assumption that Melville and Twain attacked in their different ways from inside the colonialism they too were part of. It is the concept of Hawai'i as an undeveloped site, Michener's Hawai'i as an empty, uninscribed stage or tablet. Upon this site a minority group of colonizers who exercise power over the majority, in part by assuming a superiority based on race and culture, in part by a show of military force, is destined to build a civilization. In 1820 the missionaries from Connecticut scarcely dreamt of their destination as a "paradise." They arrived to work—to convert and to educate the natives in Christian ways. The land seemed hospitable, though perhaps not comfortably so to men and women dressed in heavy wool in a humid clime where the temperature almost never drops below sixty degrees Fahrenheit. For the missionaries in their attempts at "civilizing," it was the native people who needed to be worked upon and tamed, a somewhat different prospect from what John Winthrop envisioned in 1630 upon approaching Massachusetts, when he concerned himself not with the native peoples already there but with the wilderness amidst which to build "a city upon a hill." The Hawaiians' pagan history was the forest the missionaries had to clear away in order to make room for new developments both religious and secular; and this mission was one side of a tension, the other being the ethnographic interest—the secular historiography—of teachers such as Dibble in the history and antiquities of Hawai'i before the arrivals of Europeans and Americans. The colonial vision of Hawai'i is in part characterized by discontinuities.

But to the contrary, the histories underlying other traditions of Hawaii's literatures and the identities of places are continuous ones—history, that is, as a continuous record of change. Today we find much evidence of newer, immigrant histories in literature and in people's senses of place. Certain works of Hawaii's local poets come to mind: "Manoa Cemetery" by Eric Chock, references to that same cemetery in Wing Tek Lum's "Grateful Here," and Cathy Song's "A Pale Arrangement of Hands" are among the very numerous works rooted in some local writers' sensibilities of place. In fiction, Susan Nunes and Juliet Kono make their own histories and sensibilities inseparable from their places of origin in their *A Small Obligation and Other Stories of Hilo* and *Hilo Rains*, respectively, while Darrell Lum's pidgin and creole stories and dramas are unmistakably of Honolulu settings and therefore of urban Hawaiian activities, characters, and hangouts.[6] These writers within Hawaii's Asian American tradition have a sensibility related to the native Hawaiian sense of place yet learned as well from their Asian American forebears, who themselves generally emigrated from villages, provinces, and families of highly localized identities.

"The Unwilling Bride" by Patsy Saiki, a Nisei of Hawai'i, exemplifies a congruence of visions and values between her immigrant characters and the culture of the Hawaiians on whose land they have come to settle. It rests upon a set of values which we make into a cliché today but which Saiki somehow vivified back in 1951 when she wrote it. These values are *aloha 'āina* (love of the land) and *'ohana* (family). In other words, the story is about a place and the people who live there. Told by a Japanese immigrant woman—a picture-bride—whose story is itself retold by her daughter, "The Unwilling Bride" is a reminiscence of how Namiko and her husband Shuji moved from a sugar plantation to a plot of their own on the Hāmākua coast, where to remind themselves and their children of a Japan the couple wished vainly to see again, Shuji cultivated a garden in a Japanese style. In Hāmākua, however, the garden is quite different from a Japanese memory; Shuji and Namiko's garden includes three tall pine trees rather than gnarled, severely trained ones. Years after Shuji's death, Namiko's own death by cancer imminent, she says to her children that she has always wanted a formal kimono bearing her family crest, the "three-pine-trees design." The kimono arrives too late from Japan. The children, now grown, regret that they were unable to fulfill their mother's last request.

But clearly in Saiki's story the request has already been fulfilled. The three pine trees growing in the garden identify the land with Namiko as eloquently as a kimono would; and the three pine trees that compose her family crest in Hāmākua, Hawai'i, are an emblem for her and Shuji's histories, their lives, and their children's futures in Hawai'i, U.S.A. In this case, the emblem is literally rooted in the land, the place cultivated by the family: thus *aloha 'āina*, the reciprocal love of the land and of the people who cultivate it, and *'ohana*, family, come together in Saiki's understated story.

This is to suggest again that in the case of Hawaii's local, polyethnic, multiracial literature, one generation of which Saiki's story may exemplify, there are strong and numerous instances where history and culture are assumed to reach back into the Hawai'i of the native Hawaiians before the arrival of everyone else and are not broken and reinvented by the series of arrivals. Indeed the first novel of Hawai'i in English, James Jackson Jarves's *Kiana* (1857), is an interesting attempt by a newcomer resident and historian of Hawai'i to imagine an event long before Cook to establish a continuity (a history which he calls a "tradition") that has since fallen out of sight. Jarves bases his novel on what his research suggested was a colony of Spaniards who were perhaps shipwrecked on the island of Hawai'i in the mid-sixteenth century. Among them is a conquistador standing as a prefigurement of "Lono," a type which Cook would fulfill two centuries later. So the impulse not to divorce ourselves from history but to place ourselves in history, through arts and the imagination, is strong and old in Hawai'i among peoples of various races. This is not to say, however, that everyone in Hawai'i believes, understands, or appreciates this point of view. For most "locals," a sense of place as history is intuitive and inchoate at best, for colonialism discourages the contemplation of such empowering knowledge as local history.

When envisioned as being empowered, history in Hawai'i is a flow of changes, very much like the fire goddess Pele when she takes the form of a volcanic flow, "fiery blanket without corners" (an image in Kimura, "Kapalaoa"). At the conclusion of John Dominis Holt's contemporary native Hawaiian novel, *Waimea Summer*, the first-person narrator, while sitting at noon on the stones of Pu'u Koholā, Kamehameha's temple to his "island snatching" war god

Kūkā'ilimoku, experiences a dizzying vision of the warriors, chiefs, and priests of Kamehameha (whose name means "the lonely one") preparing for war. The vision is stone-black and blood-red, a powerful warning to the boy that history is not to be romanticized and relived but must be studied and interpreted so that it need not be relived. Often credited with being one who has reinvigorated the Hawaiian renaissance since the 1960s, Holt titles his novel, his fictive embodiment of his sense of history, by naming a place (Waimea) and a season or time (summer) where and when the protagonist also travels far within himself to understand his own identity, itself inseparable from his sense of the places in his story.

ABSTRACTING THEORY

At the annual conference of the Association for Asian American Studies in 1989, Wing Tek Lum asserted that in Hawai'i today poetry is generally characterized by a "concreteness" of description imagery, and allusion. Local poets, he suggested, eschew self-consciously crafted postmodernist constructions and deconstructions of thoughts, emotions, perceptions, and associational designs. I would concur that, for instance, Cathy Song's poem "The Youngest Daughter" supports Lum's incipient theory. Perhaps the poem's only troublesome lines and image occur at its very end, where the speaker tells of how "a thousand cranes curtain the window, / fly up in a sudden breeze" (6). Richard Hugo introduces Song's *Picture Bride* and this poem in it by interpreting the lines as showing "that freedom is momentarily known in the sudden dramatics available to the visual imagination" (xiii). Without knowing Song's allusion, Hugo seemed to have little choice but to attempt a shaky postmodernist reading, which takes the lines out of a larger context than the themes that the poem otherwise lucidly and quite directly describes. Within the poem, the themes include the need of the youngest daughter, herself in weak health, and the aged, diabetic mother to care for each other, the daughter no longer young but confined to an endless filial role from which she says "even now [I am] planning my escape." But pointing outside the poem, Song's description of the thousand cranes pictured in the fabric of the curtains alludes to a local custom, in Hawai'i, of decorating a wedding hall with a thousand origami cranes folded by their friends and relatives to wish the couple a thousand years of marital happiness. In Japanese custom the cranes also signify a wish for a thousand years of good health. The youngest daughter in Song's poem has had neither of these wishes granted and evidently no hope for their ever coming true; the tone of the concluding lines involves regret, a dull depression, wistfulness, and indeed a sense of humor (and much more) about the speaker's condition in life. Through the symbol of the cranes, the tone is thus expressive of the feelings that precede these lines in the poem; the lines follow in an emotional and psychological continuity and are not a momentary escape from those feelings through "the visual imagination." Here, it is not that his comment contradicts Song's allusion but that without his knowing it, Hugo in 1982 was being simplistic and reductive in his interpretation and judgment of the lines which he considered to rise free from the poem's contexts.

To say that readings of Hawaii's literatures ought to be "culturally specific" like the works themselves is an understatement. To say that the mode of analysis best applicable to the task is "close reading" is not enough, for Hugo closely read Song with his sensitivity for poetic techniques and qualities but fell somewhere short of comprehending or truly appreciating her poems and poetics because of his lack of contextual knowledge and failure to recognize not images but symbols. Similarly, literary theories based heavily on linguistics, when these theories are ahistorical, are insufficient and often misleading when applied to Hawaii's literatures.[7] One must also closely read, interpret, and question Hawaii's past and contemporary histories and historiographies in order simply to make a start at interpreting and judging. The task of reading would seem to be further burdened by the insistence of some writers of Hawai'i in calling themselves "local"; and it must seem also worsened by the conjunction of the Hawaiian values of *aloha 'āina* and *'ohana*, underlying what I call "place as history." When divorced from their Hawaiian historical, cultural, and even geological contexts, these values of "love of the land" and "family" may too easily seem vaguely fatuous, just another Hawaiian tourist trap or else too esoterically of the Other to fathom. But why is *learning* Hawaii's localism a problem?

In Asian American studies, some historians such as Gary Okihiro, Sucheng Chan, Gail Nomura, and Ronald Takaki localize their research on a variety of settings, in part to counterbalance the predominance of generalizations drawn from urban experiences, mainly of California. In the interests of literary studies, recognition of local

Asian American histories is needed because a presumed lack has indirectly discouraged readers from contextualizing Asian American literature in anything but the most general, common, and very possibly mistaken ways.

Yet Hawai'i does not lack general histories written about it; so the anxiety that a reader is at sea entirely without a rudder when facing a work of Hawaii's literature is needless.[8] A relative lack of explicit, developing theoretics abstracted from the literature is, however, a serious problem, particularly when among the first barriers a potential reader faces is a question of aesthetics: is the pleasure of an informed reading of Hawaii's literature worth any additional effort of becoming informed? Is the writing worth it? This is one of many dilemmas of a "minority" literature: being unempowered and "minor" means being generally perceived as adrift somewhere at the "margins" of a nation's centrist history. I cannot simply in literary, stylistic terms answer the aesthetic question of how much reading pleasure might make extraliterary studies worthwhile and why; aesthetic judgments are not, I believe, usually motivated by features within literary works but by standards reflecting conditions (political and otherwise) that readers—and authors—bring from their lives to the works. In this regard, it is not as if a need for cultural, social, and political studies of Hawai'i has gone unrecognized. For at least as far back as Jarves's novel *Kiana*, Hawai'i has been a test tube for social scientists and cultural critics in the study of multiraciality and of hybrid cultures, thus foretelling America's demographically pluralistic future. If cultural studies and theories did not arise from Hawaii's literatures, then the understanding of this pluralism—which I believe is a humanistic, literary concept that at the same time is an actual demographic phenomenon—would remain stunted. There *seems* to be strong extraliterary need for taking Hawaii's polyethnic literatures seriously.

As for the further development of literary theories of Hawai'i, two lines diverge from the experience and study of works of the native Hawaiian and local traditions: (1) the placement of literature within analytical frameworks (for instance, of oral traditional and folkloric theories, gender studies, and theories of ethnic cultural criticism) in ways which may be presumed to derive "power" by the "universalizing" of the subject through the identification or relation of the subject with European and mainland American systems of analytical discourse recognized in the academy, the "university"; and (2) the culturally, historically, locally specific criticism and interpretation of literature and its contexts, where "power" is thought to be derived from the placement of the subject within a historical community and its culture, a local community from whose interpretation in literature culturally specific theories may be abstracted and then compared and related to theories from other locales and traditions of literature. By "power" I mean the ability to control the means, in this case literary criticism, by which literary works and their traditions are judged, valued, denied, commodified, empowered, ignored, recognized, or validated by being read and discussed—or to choose not to deal in such judgments but to approach literature with some entirely different purpose or attitude.

For historical and cultural reasons underscored by the natural setting of Hawai'i, authors of the local, polyethnic, contemporary literature of Hawai'i tend to espouse the latter view, of which Wing Tek Lum's comment about the concreteness of local poetry is but a part, with its implication that the prime intended audience is one sensitive to the contexts within and by which a detail (such as Song's thousand cranes) has meaning and not, say, an academic audience nationwide. By definition, local literature cannot be assumed to have great numbers of "local" readers (but then again, the community audience assumed by local writers outnumbers literary scholars in America). The numbers are not to be found just among the roughly one million inhabitants today, a figure that seems about the limit the islands can support and the people can stand. The numbers of people who symbolically back Hawaii's local and indigenous literatures include generations of forebears and of descendants yet to come: this is what is envisioned as "the community" that empowers local writers. While conceivably comparisons might be made with other small communities such as New England of the seventeenth century where solidarity meant survival, native Hawaiian and local literatures more closely resemble those of other American ethnic and racial minorities in certain respects—if not yet in explicitly shared theory then at least in themes. For example, the principle of power is derived from a community and from tradition, without denying individualism but affirming the individual's strength in history and in myth, may recall for us the assembling of the community at the ending of Toni Morrison's *Beloved* or the way in which N. Scott Momaday, Leslie Silko, and Joy Harjo draw upon their American Indian myths and forebears, going on to "augment" them in their novels, stories, and poems for the sake of present and future generations by the act of keeping myth current, alive.[9] With these and with Latino/Latina literatures, too, the native Hawaiian and the local in general owe much to oral traditions and vernaculars, which again imply the existence of dynamic, vocal communities.

Out of the observations and literary examples above, three points emerge; these points are part of what may be called a conceptual and theoretical base of a polyethnic literary renaissance of Hawai'i: (1) literatures of Hawai'i today are sustained by communal, historical, and cultural sources and their continuing revival; (2) this revival involves issues of innovation and tradition, "ancients" or "purists" versus the "moderns," and a strong interest in mutability, or change; and (3) in native Hawaiian and local polyethnic, largely Asian American literatures there is overt, spirited use of vernaculars and of other cultural features that are or have become native and local. These and other features coincide with what is commonly meant by the term "renaissance," including its use to refer to the great European and American ones, in Western literary studies.

With the currency of the term "Hawaiian renaissance," many of Hawaii's writers are well aware of how ambitious their literary visions may be. They are also aware of how ironic the reminder of the European Renaissance is, when like the Harlem Renaissance, the Hawaiian one still mainly flows against the prow of imperial powers which have been denying it while literally enjoying the service and fruits of the place, tended by peoples mostly unseen, unheard—and unread, or "read" in uninformed ways. Hawaii's Asian/Pacific American literatures are no different from their mainland "minority" counterparts when subjected to touristic readings which neither growth of audience nor time abates. It is safe to say that elements of Hawaii's literatures—particularly lyric mele played like Muzak in the air breathed by tourists and locals alike—have had a larger audience through the past two centuries than any other works or traditions in Asian/Pacific American literature. But even discounting this fact (since few of the hearers of mele have understood the Hawaiian language and allusions of the poems), Hawaii's literatures and contexts can still be said to have received longer scholarly attention than any other Asian/Pacific American literature and history, as my citations of Cook, Malo, Kamakau, and so forth only faintly indicate here.

NOTES

I spell Hawaiian words and names either as found in the texts from which I quote or by including the *'okina* (glottal stop) and *kahakō* (macron indicating vowel elongation) required in Hawaiian spelling, except when I am writing Anglicized adaptations of individual words as in "Hawaiian" or "Hawaii's." After a "foreign language" term is introduced, I drop the italicization since the term is no longer "foreign" to the discussion.

1. For an overview of this literary renaissance, see my *And the View from the Shore*; for a brief literary history, see my "Waiting for the Big Fish." I have adapted parts of the present essay from my works just cited and also from my essay "Place as History in Hawaii's Literatures."

2. Following Hawaii's vernacular, by "Hawaiian" I specifically mean "native Hawaiian" (i.e., Polynesian of Hawai'i, not anyone of any race associated with the place). I try to define the Hawai'i creole term "local" in context; I comment explicitly on the concept in *And the View from the Shore*, xiv–xviii and passim.

3. It is not my purpose in this essay to discuss at greater length how various literary theories are adaptable to the reading and judging of Hawaii's literatures. My own criticism here is mainly concerned with introducing and interpreting particulars of texts and contexts, whether my readers be in or outside Hawai'i. Aside from my attempts to abstract theory from Hawaii's literatures, theorizing these literatures is an eclectic affair of scavenging parts from culturally specific ethnic literary criticisms of American peoples from places outside Hawai'i, studies of postcolonialism worldwide, new historicism, Marxist and related theories of historical processes and critiques of the commercialization of cultures and multiculturalism, certain principles of deconstruction, the so-called New Western history, and gender criticism (see Trask, who is inspired by what she calls her "fighting spirit and Hawaiian soul").

4. Michener thus uses a conceit of an empty stage to characterize the place, in his novel *Hawaii*.

5. On the typology of mele centered on "place," see Elbert and Mahoe, 11–12, 17–18, 23–24.

6. Selections from these poets and fiction writers occur in Chock and Lum. Also among the many writers in the volume is Watanabe, who won an O. Henry Award for 1991 with "Talking to the Dead," a story first published in *Bamboo Ridge*. She, like Song (winner of the 1982 Yale Series of Younger Poets Award), assuredly has a nationwide audience. The nature of various audiences' interests and understandings of works assertively of Hawai'i, however, is a much-discussed topic among the writers.

7. For a simple example, there is the still often-cited account of Hawaii's pidgins and creoles by Carr, where a linguistic history is shaped by a sociological theory of cultural and racial assimilation in America. History and people, however, have not cooperated with the theory throughout the twentieth century, nearing the end of which the creole spoken by Hawaii's youngsters is not melting away into the standard English of schools and mass media, as Carr postulates; if anything, the vernacluar has been enjoying a rejuvenation, resurgence, and continuation as creole rather than as broken English being mended. Insightful historical studies by linguists such as Derek Bickerton at the University of Hawaii, meanwhile, have contributed directly to cultural criticism with views of a living creole language, interculturalism, and their roots in the native Hawaiian language and in the development of pidgins.

8. Standard histories written in the later twentieth century include the ones by Fuchs, Daws, and Joesting. Ethnic histories of Hawai'i are too abundant for me to list here. The point is that whether in quantity, generality, specificity, or variety, studies of historical contexts for Hawaii's literatures are abundant and accessible.

9. I thank TuSmith for passing on to me from her sources an explanation of how in European American literary traditions "author" has come to mean "originator," while in American Indian storytelling "author" means "augmenter."

WORKS CITED

Bushnell, O. A. *The Return of Lono*. 1956. Reprint. Honolulu: University of Hawaii Press, 1979.

Carr, Elizabeth Ball. *Da Kine Talk: From Pidgin to Standard English in Hawaii*. Honolulu: University of Hawaii Press, 1972.

Chock, Eric, and Darrell H. Y. Lum, eds. *The Best of Bamboo Ridge: The Hawaii Writers' Quarterly*. Honolulu: Bamboo Ridge Press, 1986.

———. "Manoa Cemetery, for Moi Lum Chock." In *Talk Story: An Anthology of Hawaii's Local Writer*, ed. Eric Chock et al. Honolulu: Talk Story, Inc. and Petronium Press, 1978. 92–94.

Chun, Malcolm Naea. "He Mo'olelo no S. M. Kamakau, He Mo'oku'auhau: A Biographical Essay of S. M. Kamakau, Historian." In, *I ka Wa o Kamehameha*, by S. M. Kamakau. Honolulu: Folk Press, Kapiolani Community College, 1988. 11–22.

Cook, James. *The Journals of Captain James Cook on His Voyage of Discovery*. Vol. 3, "The Voyage of the *Resolution* and *Discovery*, 1776–1780," part one. Ed. J. C. Beaglehole. Cambridge: Cambridge University Press for the Hakluyt Society, 1967.

Daws, Gavan. *Shoal of Time: A History of the Hawaiian Islands*. 1968. Reprint. Honolulu: University of Hawaii Press, 1974.

Elbert, Samuel H., and Noelani Mahoe, eds. *Nā Mele o Hawai'i Nei: 101 Hawaiian Songs*. Honolulu: University of Hawaii Press, 1970.

Fuchs, Lawrence H. *Hawaii Pono: A Social History*. New York: Harcourt, Brace, 1961.

Holt, John Dominis. *Waimea Summer*. Honolulu: Topgallant Publishing [now Ku Pa'a, Inc.], 1976.

Hugo, Richard. Foreword to *Picture Bride*, by Cathy Song. New Haven: Yale University Press, 1983.

Jarves, James Jackson. *Kiana: A Tradition of Hawaii*. Boston: James Munroe, 1857.

Joesting, Edward. *Hawaii: An Uncommon History*. New York: Norton, 1972.

Kahinu, J. "Nā Hala o Naue." In Elbert and Mahoe, 80–81.

Kamakau, Samuel Manaiakalani. *I ka Wa o Kamehameha, In the Time of Kamehameha: Selected Essays by Samuel M. Kamakau*. Ed. Malcolm Naea Chun. Honolulu: Folk Press, Kapiolani Community College, 1988.

———. *Ruling Chiefs of Hawaii*. 1866. Honolulu: Kamehameha Schools Press, 1961.

Kimura, Larry Lindsey. "Kapalaoa." In *Forgotten Pages of American Literature*, ed. Gerald W. Haslam. Boston: Houghton Mifflin, 1970. 139–41.

Kono, Juliet S. *Hilo Rains*. Honolulu: Bamboo Ridge Press, 1988.

Lum, Darrell H. Y. *Sun: Short Stories and Drama*. Honolulu: Bamboo Ridge Press, 1979.

Lum, Wing Tek. "Grateful Here." In *Expounding the Doubtful Points*. Honolulu: Bamboo Ridge Press, 1987. 89–90.

Malo, David[a]. *Hawaiian Antiquities (Mooleleo Hawaii)*. Trans. Nathaniel B. Emerson. 1838. Reprint. Honolulu: Bernice P. Bishop Museum, 1951.

———. *Ka Mo'olelo Hawai'i*. Ed. Malcolm Naea Chun. Honolulu: Folk Press, Kapiolani Community College, 1987.

Melville, Herman. *Typee: A Peep at Polynesian Life During a Four Month's Residence in a Valley of the Marquesas*. 1846. Evanston: Northwestern University Press and the Newberry Library, 1968.

Michener, James A. *Hawaii*. New York: Random House, 1959.

Morris, Aldyth. *Captain Cook*. Typescript. 1977.

Nunes, Susan. *A Small Obligation and Other Stories of Hilo*. Honolulu: Bamboo Ridge Press, 1982.

Parker, Helen Lindsey. "Maunaloa." Record liner of the Peter Moon Band, *Cane Fire!*, Panini Records, PS1012. 1982.

Prendergast, Ellen Wright. "Kaulana nā Pua." In Elbert and Mahoe, 62–64.

Saiki, Patsy. "The Unwilling Bride." In *Talk Story Big Island Anthology*, ed. Arnold Hiura, Stephen Sumida, and Martha Webb. Honolulu: Talk Story, Inc. and Bamboo Ridge Press, 1979.

Song, Cathy. "A Pale Arrangement of Hands." In *Picture Bride*, 75–77.

———. *Picture Bride*. New Haven: Yale University Press, 1983.

———. "The Youngest Daughter." In *Picture Bride*, 5–6.

Sumida, Stephen H. *And the View from the Shore: Literary Traditions of Hawai'i*. Seattle: University of Washington Press, 1991.

———. "Place as History in Hawaii's Literatures." In *Defining a Sense of Place: A Humanities Guide*. Honolulu: Hawaii Committee for the Humanities, 1990. 12–15.

———. "Waiting for the Big Fish: Recent Research in the Asian American Literature of Hawaii." In Chock and Lum *The Best of Bamboo Ridge*, 302–21.

Takaki, Ronald. *Strangers from a Different Shore: A History of Asian Americans*. New York: Penguin, 1989.

Trask, Haunani-Kay. *Eros and Power: The Promise of Feminist Theory*. Philadelphia: University of Pennsylvania Press, 1986.

TuSmith, Bonnie. "Alternative Visions: Perspectives on Community and Individualism in Multiethnic American Literatures." Ph.D. diss., Washington State University, 1989.

Watanabe, Sylvia A. "Talking to the Dead." In *Prize Stories 1991: The O. Henry Award*, ed. William Abrahams. New York: Doubleday, 1991. 376–88.

12

Momotaro's Exile: John Okada's No-No Boy

Gayle K. Fujita Sato

JOHN OKADA'S *No-No Boy* was reclaimed from oblivion in the 1970s and has since become a classic of Japanese American literature, but its construction of "Japanese American" remains problematic. Critics and writers have observed in different ways that *No-No Boy* reflects the negative legacy of "dual identity," a conceptualization of "Asian American" which divides "Asian" and "American" into separate spheres of existence (Chin, Chin et al., Inada, Kim, McDonald). Although the self-destructive potential of "dual identity" is fully elaborated in Ichiro Yamada's struggle, the same binary opposition ultimately defines his "redemptive" journey. *No-No Boy* attempts to affirm "Japanese American" through a character who rejects everything "Japanese."

The novel's binary opposition of Japan and America can be analyzed through two subtexts—the loyalty oath and "Momotaro." The former, technically known as "War Relocation Authority Form 126 Rev." (Weglyn 136), was created during World War II for the purpose of dismantling internment camps and recruiting Japanese American soldiers for a racially segregated combat unit. Men who answered negatively to two key questions came to be called "no-no boys." "Momotaro," a Japanese folk tale, is mentioned twice by Ichiro and furnishes a broader basis than the loyalty oath for examining his exile from Japanese America. Whereas the loyalty oath contextualizes the novel in postwar America, revealing how the concept of dual identity limited the terms of Okada's narrative, "Momotaro" both specifies this circumscription and suggests a different construction of Japanese American subjectivity. If the loyalty oath as subtext expresses a desire to expel "Japanese" from "American," "Momotaro" as subtext reformulates "loyalty" in terms of mutual alliances.

No-No Boy is set during the period immediately after World War II when Japanese Americans are resettling their old communities on the west coast. Among those returning to Seattle is twenty-five-year-old Ichiro Yamada, who has just finished a two-year prison term for answering "no" on the loyalty oath to the following key questions that were supposed to distinguish "loyal" from "disloyal":

> *Question No. 27*: Are you willing to serve in the armed forces of the United States on combat duty wherever ordered? *Question No. 28*: Will you swear unqualified allegiance to the United States of America and faithfully defend the United States from any or all attack by foreign or domestic forces, and foreswear any form of allegiance or obedience to the Japanese emperor, to any other foreign government, power or organization? (Weglyn 136)

Retrospection has clarified the bitter ironies summarized in these questions—that since citizenship was legally denied to Asian immigrants, Issei cut themselves adrift politically and psychologically by forswearing allegiance to the Japanese emperor; that these potentially "disloyal" Issei had lived in the States an average of twenty to forty years; that included among them were veterans of the First World War; that their children, American citizens by birth, were being asked to defend political freedoms blatantly violated by the internment policy; that the method determining "loyalty" through self-declaration had not been raised as an alternative to internment; and that distinctions between "yes-yes" and "no-no" Japanese Americans were irrelevant in the context of continued racial discrimination after the war. As far as a large sector of "loyal" America was concerned, Japanese Americans were still "Japs."

Since the definitions of racial and national identity which produced the loyalty oath have not disappeared with the dismantling of internment camps, "no-no boy" remains a significant figure in Japanese American culture. Examined for its construction of "Japanese

American," *No-No Boy* reflects an internalization of the loyalty oath. The novel begins from the premise that saying "no" was a mistake, and it affirms Ichiro's quest to return to a perceived prelapsarian condition of "undivided," "unquestioned" loyalty. It does not exploit the ironies and thus critical potential of the rhetoric of "loyalty"—that "undivided" could mean a refusal to split "Japanese" from "American," that "unquestioned" could mean a failure to examine definitions of "loyalty." However, the actual contradictory nature of Ichiro's "backward progress," backward because it reproduces the old terms of imprisonment, is reflected in the novel's parallel but antithetical plots. The seeming "progressive" component of Ichiro's journey is rendered through a plot of perpetual motion—a rapid succession of meetings with various friends, neighbors, acquaintances, and strangers. These encounters generate another kind of plot—a succession of conversations and internal monologues that comprise Ichiro's numerous acts of confession, self-chastisement, and reaffirmation. The regressive component of Ichiro's "backward progress" is revealed in this verbal drama, which is repetitive rather than creative, aimed not at reformulating but reiterating a declaration of "loyalty" against a conviction that the right to do so has already been forfeited. Thus despite the appearance of perpetual motion, the novel's essential drama is static rather than dynamic—reifying rather than deconstructing the terms of ethnic self-destruction. Despite an apparent multiplicity of viewpoints implied in the diversity of Ichiro's encounters and in the duration, frequency, and intensity of his internal monologues, the plot of *No-No Boy* boils down to a single rhetorical gesture—Ichiro's reaffirmation that he is "American." He has thus reconfirmed himself to a mode of redemption that rehearses the loyalty oath.

No-No Boy appears one-dimensional compared to other novels that inscribe constructions of ethnicity—such as Ralph Ellison's *Invisible Man* and Joy Kogawa's *Obasan*—in which the protagonist's self-expression is based on a multitiered process of revelation, backtracking and revaluation. Conceived as an act of faith, the "yes" Ichiro seeks to recover can only be declared, not analyzed, into being. A further contrast is that strategies of self-articulation in *Invisible Man* and *Obasan* come from the protagonist's home culture. In each case, "home" is critically reformulated but not eliminated as a source of redemption or transformation. The declarative act of *No-No Boy* cannot contain such doubleness. Ichiro's struggle toward "yes" cannot escape being a profoundly negative act of ethnic self-denial, since "yes" belongs to the binary opposition "Japan" or "America." Ichiro's torment arises from this externally imposed division, but his struggle is not focused on destroying it. Rather, recovery of "American" identity is enacted through a rejection of "Japanese," as becomes clear through an examination of the "Momotaro" subtext.

Generations of Japanese have grown up with the story of "Momotaro." All Japanese schoolchildren know the song about his heroism, and there is even a city, Okayama, which claims to be Momotaro's birthplace. The tale has been handed down in Japanese American culture through storytelling and Japanese language schools. The English version I refer to is the one in *Japanese Children's Favorite Stories* edited by Florence Sakade. The story begins with a childless couple, an old man who goes to chop wood in the mountains every day and an old woman who goes every day to the river to wash clothes. One day the woman finds a huge peach floating down the river and carries it home for supper. When they are about to cut the fruit, a beautiful baby boy jumps out and becomes their son. The three live happily together and Momotaro, as he is called ("momo" is Japanese for "peach," and "Taro" is a boy's name that can also be used as a suffix, as in "Kentaro" or "Takutaro"), grows up into a splendid young man. When he reaches adulthood, he undertakes a dangerous journey. The village has been constantly subject to attacks and looting by a band of ogres ("oni" in Japanese), and Momotaro will try to recover the villagers' money and valuables. The old man and woman part with him willingly, for it is a courageous act confirming what a fine son he has become. On the day of departure, Momotaro's father gives him a sword and armor, and his mother prepares a lunch of "kibidango," or millet dumplings, and he sets off. On the way he meets a dog, monkey, and pheasant, to each of whom he gives a dumpling in return for their promise to help him. Together they succeed in storming the ogres' fortress, and they return triumphantly with the village's lost treasures.

By undertaking such a journey, Momotaro earns the respect and gratitude of his community, thereby discharging the debt children owe parents in the Japanese Confucian family tradition. Momotaro's homecoming means that he is a filial son, having repaid parents, country, and culture for his identity and existence. Clearly the story is relevant to Ichiro's situation, and he recalls it during his first hours at home in a powerful passage of nostalgia and yearning. Momotaro's surfacing at this point early in the novel suggests that "Japan" and "Japanese" are crucial terms in Ichiro's conflict. If he is to fight well, he must clarify his vision of "home" in order to locate his adversaries.

The first allusion to Momotaro occurs during Ichiro's incredulous homecoming. His mother finishes stacking bread on the shelves before turning to welcome him, whom she has not seen for two years, with a sparse "I am proud that you are back. I am proud to call you my son" (11). She then shows Ichiro a letter that speaks of Japan's victory in the war and the imminent arrival of ships to transport loyal Japanese patriots back to the motherland. When Ichiro repudiates the letter and asserts that he will no longer act by her ideas, she replies, "Think more deeply and your doubts will disappear. You are my son, Ichiro" (15). The key interlocked issues—filiality and loyalty—surface immediately, triggering the first of Ichiro's many monologues seething with incomprehension, anger, and despair:

> There was a time when I was your son. There was a time that I no longer remember when you used to smile a mother's smile and tell me stories about gallant and fierce warriors who protected their lords with blades of shining steel and about the old woman who found a peach in the stream and took it home and, when her husband split it in half, a husky little boy tumbled out to fill their hearts with boundless joy. I was that boy in the peach and you were the old woman and we were Japanese with Japanese feelings and Japanese pride and Japanese thoughts because it was all right then to be Japanese and feel and think all the things that Japanese do even if we lived in America. Then there came a time when I was only half Japanese because one is not born in America and raised in America and taught in America and one does not speak and swear and drink and smoke and play and fight and see and hear in America among Americans in American streets and houses without becoming American and loving it. But I did not love enough, for you were still half my mother and I was thereby still half Japanese and when the war came and they told me to fight for America, I was not strong enough to fight you and I was not strong enough to fight the bitterness which made the half of me which was you bigger than the half of me which was America and really the whole of me that I could not see or feel. (15–16)

Ichiro understands family and ethnic self in terms of a binary opposition whereby "Japanese" identity can properly belong only to childhood, to be gradually, inevitably, and affirmatively replaced by an "American" identity as the child becomes an adult. In this crucial first monologue, Momotaro and Mother are associated with the undersirable "Japanese" half self, and in the course of the novel, both will function as concrete embodiments of "Japan" through which Ichiro can reject the "Japanese" in him and therefore achieve his declaration of (loyal) "American" identity.

The eradication of Momotaro as a viable paradigm for adult identity is completed in the third chapter. In this second allusion to Momotaro, contrary to Ichiro's assertions of an irrecoverable childhood in the passage just quoted, the folk tale is linked to his university life:

> He vividly brought to mind, with a hunger that he would never lose, the weighty volumes which he had carried against his side so that the cloth of his pants became thin and frayed, and the sandwiches in a brown grocery bag and the slide rule with the leather case which hung from his belt like the sword of learning which it was. . . . Where was the slide rule, he asked himself, where was the shaft of exacting and thrilling discovery when I needed it most? If only I had pictured it in my hands, I might well have made the right decision, for the seeing and feeling of it would have pushed out the bitterness. . . . I would have gone into the army for that and I would have shot and killed, and shot and killed some more, because I was happy when I was a student with the finely calculated white sword at my side. (53)

Nisei had grown up with racism as a fact of American life, but internment could not be handled in the same manner as a passing remark or being refused service in a restaurant. If the "slide-rule" slipped, it is also true that internment camps were by nature finely calculated toward this end. Ichiro lost sight of his weapon when he lost sight of what needed defending.

Momotaro's ogres, in contrast, were always clearly visible, undisguised adversaries, but this does not invalidate an application of the folk tale to Ichiro's situation. Between birth and battle, where the "fairy tale" elements inhere, is the world of human time and space where Momotaro is prepared for battle through the experience of family, and even the tale's extraordinary elements are more relevant than they first appear. Birth in the human world is as much a matter of chance, as "illogical," as a peach bearing a human child. Ichiro was born a Japanese American who happened to come of age during the war. As Gary, another no-no boy, says: "Tough to have a name like Ohara and feel that maybe when they made up the batch of orders upstairs one of the Lord's workers neglected the apostrophe and so the guy turns up in the U.S.A. a Jap instead of an Irishman" (227). As for the matter of battles, ogres and the loyalty oath pose the same challenge in proportion to either warrior's skills. Momotaro is given some divine assistance against his nonhuman adversaries, but the loyalty oath, product of men like Ichiro, can by implication be successfully engaged despite its monstrous proportions. This is implied by the fact that Ichiro's first meditative act is to recall not just "Momotaro" but other stories of "gallant and fierce warriors . . . with blades of shining steel." This is a promising start, since "sword" represents both "American student" and "Japanese warrior"; but when binary oppositions substitute for lost "sword," the Momotaro paradigm dissolves before it even has a chance to operate.

Why does this happen? Even if the chaos surrounding internment prevented perception of the loyalty oath as "ogre," Momotaro's success is based less on proper identification of the adversary than on the family's cultivation of heroic character. The tale's enduring appeal in Japanese culture may lie precisely in the fact that it valorizes family—parents receive a miraculous child because they are worthy; a child becomes a hero because of wise parenting. But Mrs. Yamada, who might have played the role of Momotaro's mother, who according to Ichiro did play that role in the past, has somehow by the time of the novel's events become transformed into Momotaro's ogre. Comparing the folk tale family with the real one reveals that the Momotaro paradigm must be aborted because family does not exist for Ichiro.

Whereas Momotaro began his journey with a precious gift of homemade kibidango, used to win appropriate fighting companions, Ichiro is not similarly prepared for battle. In contrast to Momotaro's supportive mother, Mrs. Yamada is portrayed from the first chapter to the last as Ichiro's primary antagonist. Ichiro's father, meanwhile, is portrayed as an effeminate man, his "natural" role as head of the family having been usurped by a woman. Setting aside for the moment the issue of reconstructing the patriarchal family (the potential for "feminist families" exists in other works such as *Obasan* and *The Woman Warrior,* but not in *No-No Boy*), this family arrangement represents Ichiro as doubly deprived—not nourished by "mother's food" nor supplied with "father's weapons." The Momotaro paradigm is inverted: Ichiro's home becomes a battleground. There is an almost absurd imbalance between the lack of support available to Ichiro at home and the variety of help he receives from nearly every person outside his family. Kenji, Kenji's father, Emi, and Mr. Carrick are Ichiro's primary friends, but even those who turn against him, like Eto in the first chapter and Bull in the last, give Ichiro positive help in clarifying his point of view.

In short, Ichiro's failure to triumph like Momotaro owes more to the absence of family than confusion about the "enemy." More precisely, the absence of family generates and is constituted by such confusion. Although Mrs. Yamada transmits the folk tale to her son, she is not the mother who nurtures, sends off, and receives back her child, but an adversary to be extinguished, which is exactly what constitutes the plot's climax and resolution. Mrs. Yamada's characterization reflects the self-destructive power of dual identity—the manner in which it can undermine even a paradigm as central to the Japanese psyche as "Momotaro" and even in the context of a novel that struggles to affirm "Japanese American."

"Momotaro" is emphatically a story of life. A healthy child bursts forth from a peach. An old, childless couple become parents. The waters carrying the peach, and the peach itself, connote fertility, fruitfulness, eroticism; but in *No-No Boy*, Mrs. Yamada is consistently associated with imagery that questions or even mocks her role as a life-generating mother. She is introduced as "a small, flat-chested, shapeless woman who wore her hair pulled back into a tight bun. Hers was the awkward, skinny body of a thirteen-year-old which had dried and toughened through the many years following but which had developed no further. [Ichiro] wondered how [his parents] had ever gotten together long enough to have two sons (10–11)." Subsequent descriptions serve only to elaborate this initial image. She is "the rock that's always hammering, pounding, pounding, pounding" (12). Her expression on learning of Ichiro's friendship with a veteran, Kenji, is a "twisted mouth contorting the slender, austere face into a hard mass of dark hatred" (104). We remember her most clearly as a figure of repression and despair gone out of control: stacking and knocking down cans of evaporated milk, or hanging laundry in the rain, her hair "drenched and hanging straight down, reaching almost to the tiny hump of her buttocks against which the wet cotton dress had adhered so that [Mr. Yamada] could see the crease" (175). Even after death the picture admits no sympathy; we learn that Mrs. Yamada once smashed a phonograph to bits. Since she embodies "Japan," such a characterization is curious because it violates a stereotype of the Japanese mother whose make-up includes tenderness and an infinite capacity for self-sacrifice and self-effacement as well as an iron will and physical stamina. There is nothing soft about Mrs. Yamada, who is reduced to a parody of the Japanese mother's strength.

The characterization of Ichiro's father contributes to this parody. He is seen washing teacups and tending to the *tsukemono*, or pickled vegetables, like an Issei housewife. He accommodates his wife's demands no matter how unreasonable or oppressive to himself and the children. He is overweight, domestic, gentle, generous, passive, childlike, conciliatory. Some of this might be a welcome act of "refiguring the father" (Yaeger and Kowaleski-Wallace) except that Mr. Yamada's deviations are devalued. They emphasize Mrs. Yamada's monstrousness, and disgust Ichiro, whose point of view doubles as the novel's point of view.

If Momotaro's mother and father are conspicuously absent from Ichiro's family, the novel does provide a positive parental figure in the person of Mr. Kanno. Herein lies the heart of the novel's binary opposition between "Japan" and "America," for Mr. Kanno's fatherhood is embedded in a family rendered in self-consciously non-Japanese terms, contrasted in all respects to Mrs. Yamada's representation of "Japan." To begin with, there is a thorough contrast in physical size and atmosphere between the Kanno and Yamada homes. Ichiro's home is "a hole in the wall with groceries crammed in orderly confusion on not enough shelving, into not enough space" (6). In back of the store are "a kitchen, a bathroom, and one bedroom," and Ichiro "felt like puking" when he thought about the four of them sleeping in the same room (7). Kenji's house is not exactly luxurious but is clearly better situated and pleasantly roomy: "an old frame, two-story, seven-room house which the family rented for fifty dollars a month from a Japanese owner who had resettled in Chicago after the war" (117). Located on a hill that offers a view of Seattle's postwar expansion (new freeways, gas stations, stores), the Kanno house suggests the possibility of change. The Yamada family's "new" quarters at the small store formerly run by the Ozakis is clearly a step backward. Ichiro's suffocating surroundings are contrasted to the comparatively plush interior of Kenji's home—"polished mahogany table . . . new rugs and furniture and lamps and the big television set with the radio and phonograph all built into one impressive, blond console" (118). The last item is of course in pointed contrast to the borrowed phonograph that Mrs. Yamada destroyed.

The contrast in houses is further elaborated by antithetical father-son relationships. Mr. Kanno receives gifts of "good blended whisky" (117) whereas Ichiro's father buys his own "cheap blend" (35). Ken jokes about his father's capacity for liquor; Mr. Yamada is an alcoholic. The Kanno men are intimate and at ease with each other: "the father . . . loved his son, and the son . . . both loved and respected his father, who was a moderate and good man" (118). Ichiro's relationship with his father is a mixture of pity, disgust, abuse, and resignation. Kenji is "genuinely grieved" to hear Mr. Kanno call himself a "young fool" whose dreams of getting rich in America were paid for by Kenji's wound (119), a conversation counterpointed a few pages earlier when Ichiro calls his father a "Jap" and "a goddamn fool" (115) for telling him that Mrs. Yamada's psychological illness is more important than a no-no boy's problems. Immediately following this exchange, Mr. Yamada is described by the narrator as a "man who was neither husband nor father nor Japanese nor American but a diluted mixture of all" (116). Mr. Kanno embodies the very opposite—his authority and maleness emphatically undiluted though he performs all the functions of a traditional mother.

Like Ichiro's parents, Mr. Kanno originally planned to return to Japan after making enough money in America. At the beginning, then, long before the events narrated in the novel, both families certainly experienced the same generation gap between Japan-oriented immigrant parents and American-born children. The framework presented in the novel for resolving this gap is two kinds of families, one reproduces "Japanese" children and the other produces "Americans." Given Mrs. Yamada's violent resistance to American society and the rigid, humorless standard of "samurai" behavior she imposes on her sons, the novel judges this binary oversimplification in favor of "American." The fact that the binary opposition must be dissolved rather than rehearsed is everywhere apparent in Ichiro's rage and negative bonding with his mother. Yet, given the thorough contrast between Mrs. Yamada and Mr. Kanno, no reconstitution into something "Japanese American" is possible.

In inverse proportion to his mother's fanaticism, Ichiro's conception of "home" is empty of all "Japanese" signifiers: "I will buy a home and love my family and I will walk down the street holding my son's hand and people will stop and talk with us about the weather and the ball games and the elections," and "it will not matter about the past, for time will have erased it from our memories and there will be only joy and sorrow and sickness, which is the way things should be" (52). This ideal is reflected in the depiction of Kenji's farewell dinner, placed at the heart of the novel in the sixth chapter. Unlike comparable domestic scenes in fiction by Nisei writers such as Toshio Mori, Hisaye Yamamoto, and Joy Kogawa, none of the details in Okada's description of Kenji's home explicitly signifies "Japanese." Instead they suggest an opposite emphasis on mainstream white culture: mahogany table, Wm. & Rogers silverplate, roasting chicken from Safeway, lemon meringue pie, baseball game on television, "coffee and milk and pop and cookies and ice cream" (130). Such a conspicuous lack of ethnicity seems intended to express the "Americanness" of Kenji's family, especially in comparison to Ichiro's first meal at home consisting of "eggs, fried with soy sauce, sliced cold meat, boiled cabbage, and tea and rice" (12). Ichiro's clearly "Japanese" meal reflects his parents' rejection of and alienation from an "American" life. The same meal could be used toward different ends, but there are no occasions in *No-No Boy* of explicitly Japanese things or settings imbued with positive meaning.

Ichiro's "no-no" and Kenji's "yes-yes" decisions are consistent with their parents' stances toward Japan vis-à-vis America, but obviously the ideology alone did not influence Kenji, who had always brooded over the ironies of American democracy, nor Ichiro, who loved American culture. The difference has to do finally with parenting. Rejection of "Japan" counterpointed by valuation of "America" is given final expression in contrasting depictions of parent-child relationships, embodied in contrasting partings through death.

Kenji's death enacts the extinguishing of cynicism and doubt under the weight of parental love:

> "I want this other place to have only people because if I'm still a Jap there and this guy's still a German, I'll have to shoot him again and I don't want to have to do that. Then maybe there is no someplace else. . . . I'd like that too. Better an absolute nothing than half a meaning. The living have it tough. It's like a coat rack without pegs, only you think there are. Hang it

> up, drop, pick it up, hang it again, drop again. . . . Tell my dad I'll miss him like mad." (165–66)

Kenji has no answer to the coat rack analogy of life, but his father provides a stable point of reference. Earlier, Mr. Kanno had said goodbye to him in a similar fashion:

> [Kenji] started the motor and turned on the headlights and their brilliant glare caught fully the father standing ahead. Urged by an overwhelming desire to rush back to him and be with him for a few minutes longer, Kenji's hand fumbled for the door handle. At that moment, the father raised his arm once slowly in farewell. Quickly, he pulled back out of the driveway and was soon out of sight of father and home and family. (131–32)

The last three items in Kenji's vision are what Ichiro does not possess. Mrs. Yamada's death does not valorize "home and family" but because it releases Ichiro from a vacuum, he can now search for the real thing.

The day before Mrs. Yamada's suicide, Ichiro vows to return home, reasoning that "the past had been shared with a mother and father and, whatever they were, he too was a part of them;" "if he was to find his way back to that point of wholeness and belonging, he must do so in the place where he had begun to lose it" (154–55). Even when he finds his mother's body, it is not really "too late," for this is the point from which many stories of self-discovery and reconciliation begin. However, Ichiro's reactions—"only disgust and irritation," "a mild shiver," "momentarily unnerved," "an odd sense of numbness" (185)—deny the possibility of revaluating "home":

> Dead, he thought to himself, all dead. For me, you have been dead a long time, as long as I can remember. . . . So, now you are free. . . . Go to the Japan that you so long remembered and loved, and be happy. . . . If it is only after you've gone that I am able to feel these things, it is because that is the way things are. Had you lived another ten years or even twenty, it would still have been too late. If anything, my hatred for you would have grown. (186–87)

Since home for Ichiro has always been "anti-American," his behavior and thoughts surrounding Mrs. Yamada's death merely confirm the suicide's function of erasing "Japanese."

Although Mrs. Yamada's past haunts the novel through the fact of Ichiro's struggle to free himself from it, she is nowhere significantly fleshed out. Whereas her inverse, Mr. Kanno, takes all of chapter six to narrate his history and perspective, Mrs. Yamada never speaks in her own voice, providing no basis for analyzing Ichiro's hostility. Occasionally there is evidence of Mrs. Yamada's reasonable, gentler nature. She remembers how Ichiro likes his eggs done, she silently overlooks the cigarette butts and ashes he deliberately drops on the floor. She probably fixed the sandwiches that Ichiro recalls carrying to university every day together with his beloved books and slide rule. She once "smiled a mother's smile" and fired Ichiro's imagination with tales of Momotaro. These are the few concrete details that point toward the possibility of a more "natural" or at least more complexly drawn mother.

Two scenes in particular suggest the possibility of developing Mrs. Yamada's characterization. One is the reading of a letter from her sister that divulges a secret in a desperate attempt to penetrate Mrs. Yamada's silence. Hearing this reference to the long ago episode of almost drowning, Mrs. Yamada is swept back into childhood and her fragile hold on reality finally breaks. When we next see her, she is lining shelves with cans of evaporated milk and knocking them to the floor. Prior to the reading of the letter, Ichiro expressed a desire to know more about his mother's past, enough that would enable him to see her as more than a monster or "rock of hatred." The letter surely contains this potential, but when Mr. Yamada hastily denies its contents upon seeing their effect on his wife, Ichiro's only reaction is rage obliterating all possiblity of sympathy. Another scene that sheds light on Mrs. Yamada's past—Mr. Yamada's recollection of their engagement—becomes only another occasion for confirming her negative image. The squalid atmosphere created by Mr. Yamada's stupor, cheap liquor, and unpalatable characterization; the irony of narrating the consummation of the marriage at the moment Mrs. Yamada is drowning herself, and Mr. Yamada's evaluation of the consummation as a scene of "black shame" (178) undermine the potential for sympathy that such a revelation of the past might have contained, as well as its potential to counter Ichiro's demeaning remarks about his mother's sexuality.

Negative liquid imagery associated with Mrs. Yamada—a near drowning, laundry hung out in the rain, evaporated milk, excess alcohol, suicide by drowning—play a crucial part in portraying her as an insufficient mother, dissociated from "life-giving waters. Clearly she is not Momotaro's mother who washes laundry in the river and discovers in it a miraculous peach. Given that Mrs. Yamada is the novel's sole "developed" example of Japanese motherhood, it seems only "natural" for Ichiro to reject Japanese culture.

The novel's negation of "Japanese" seems bottomless, as Mrs. Yamada's "removal" continues even after her funeral. Moments after Ichiro recalls his mother's destruction of the phonograph while he was away at a church dance, and her disapproval of even the radio as too much interference with studying, Emi appears and he takes her dancing. Ichiro is transported from the memory of his mother's warped instincts into Emi's palpable, self-confident sensuousness: "Other women [men] undress. Me they undress and put in bed," she murmurs on the dance floor, leaving Ichiro "feeling immensely full and wanting that moment to last a lifetime" (211). He returns to find his father boxing supplies for Japanese relatives with "an insuppressible air of enthusiasm and bubbling glee" (212). After all, the text comments, "he was a reasonable man," "a man of natural feelings," not "manufactured feelings" like his wife (212). The final gesture in the scene puts Mrs. Yamada to rest as far as the novel's themes are concerned, as Mr. Yamada "work[s] the tie loose from his neck" (213).

Mrs. Yamada's death no doubt liberates both husband and son, but the events following her funeral do not address the genesis of "manufactured feelings." No sooner has Mrs. Yamada been formally buried than life for the Yamada men blossoms. Mr. Yamada finally expresses criticism of his wife's behavior. Ichiro nestles in the arms of the only Japanese woman depicted as attractive in the novel, who also happens to be a striking sensual contrast to stick-figured Mrs. Yamada: "Emi . . . was slender, with heavy breasts, had rich, black hair which fell on her shoulders and covered her neck, and her long legs were strong and shapely like a white woman's" (83). The scene is conspicuously ungenerous, like the gratuitous ugliness of the priest who presides over Mrs. Yamada's funeral. It is also a scene that enables revaluation of Okada's construction of "Japanese American" by evoking another writer's treatment of the same themes, including the Momotaro paradigm. The writer is Canadian Nisei Joy Kogawa, and the work is *Obasan*, a novel published in 1981.

In the post-funeral scene just discussed, there is an implicit contrast between Mr. Yamada's generosity and Ichiro's self-centeredness. Mr. Yamada is fundamentally other-directed even though it takes the questionable form of refusing to challenge his wife's delusions and so results in prolonging the suffering of their relatives. Ichiro's decision to go dancing is colored by self-gratification; he is absorbed, here as elsewhere in the novel, by his own perspective and emotional needs. Earlier, he was enraged by Mr. Yamada's greater concern for his wife's psychological illness than his son's no-no boy difficulties. While Okada does not take a critical stance on Ichiro's behavior, we can imagine such a critique through Kogawa's use of Momotaro in *Obasan*, particularly her association of the folk tale with reciprocal behaviors of self-gratification and solicitousness.

Naomi Nakane, thirty-six when the novel begins, is the central character and first-person narrator of *Obasan* Japanese for "aunt" or "woman"). She was about five years old at the time of the Japanese Canadian internment. She explains that there, men were segregated into labor camps while women, children, and the elderly of both sexes were left to manage relocation themselves. Naomi's father's health deteriorates under the harsh conditions of labor camp, and he dies before the war ends. Naomi's mother had gone to Nagasaki on family business in September of 1941. She is stranded there with the outbreak of war between Canada and Japan and never sees her family again, although she does not die from wounds sustained in the atomic bombing until several years later. Young Naomi and her brother are put in the care of Aunt Aya who raises them in the old country tradition—serving Japanese meals, speaking the Japanese language, and, as it turns out, teaching Japanese behaviors which will enable Naomi's self-redemption when she becomes an adult. Faithfully following Mrs. Nakane's instructions in a letter sent from Japan, traditional Aunt Aya, or Obasan as she is called, withholds from the children all information of their mother's fate. As the years pass, Naomi finally stops asking after her mother, but the psychological damage is deep. She internalizes her mother's disappearance as abandonment and a sense of personal failure. The death of her uncle, Obasan's husband, in 1972 finally pushes her to seek some kind of healing knowledge. She is aided in this difficult process by another aunt, her mother's younger sister, who has become a political activist for the Japanese Canadian community. Through the years, this Aunt Emily has tried unsuccessfully to arouse Naomi's interest in the history of Japanese Canadian internment and its aftermath; now her newspaper clippings and wartime diary are finally to have an impact on Naomi's consciousness.

Resembling Okada's juxtaposed characterizations of Mrs. Yamada and Mr. Kanno, Obasan and Aunt Emily represent "Japan" and

"Canada," respectively. Yet Naomi ultimately needs both women and the different things they teach in order to achieve homecoming. Kogawa's theme of mutual alliances is summed up when Aunt Emily asserts that "Momotaro is a Canadian story" and tells Naomi that she "was raised on milk and Momotaro" (57). Contrary to its function in *No-No Boy*, "Momotaro" in *Obasan* furnishes the basis for an enduring, positive bond between mother and child enabling them to transcend physical death and years of suffering. "Momotaro" still represents in *Obasan*, as it does in *No-No Boy*, Japanese culture and Japanese motherhood, but it is also "a Canadian story" of value in the Western world through adaptation to new situations. In *Obasan*, the meaning of "Japanese Canadian" lies in such adaptation.

At a point early in the novel, Naomi gives a detailed recollection of her favorite bedtime story from childhood, namely "Momotaro." Naomi does not tell the whole story, but rather ends midway at the point when Momotaro journeys forth to subdue the ogres. Momotaro's "return" is later enacted by the narrator in the form of her own inner change. When Naomi recovers historical knowledge of self-esteem by reentering painful memories of internment, she performs the equivalent of Momotaro's battle with the ogres. Only then can she "return home"—to Japanese Canadian subjectivity—as triumphantly as Momotaro marching back with the recovered treasures of his village.

Naomi's "substitution" for the folk tale's ending adapts the folk tale into the kind of "mother food" and "father's weapons" needed for doing battle in the real world:

> Alone in the misty mountains once more, the old folk wait. What matters in the end, what matters above all, more than their loneliness or fears, is that Momotaro behave with honour. At all times what matters is to act with a fine intent. To do otherwise is shameful and brings dishonour to all.
>
> To travel with confidence down this route the most reliable map I am given is my mother's and Grandma's alert and accurate knowing. When I am hungry, and before I can ask, there is food. If I am weary, every place is a bed. No food that is distasteful must be eaten and there is neither praise nor blame for the body's natural functions. A need to urinate is to be heeded whether in public or visiting friends. A sweater covers me before there is any chill and if there is pain there is care simultaneously. If Grandma shifts uncomfortably, I bring her a cushion.
>
> "Yoku ki ga tsuku ne," Grandma responds. It is a statement in appreciation of sensitivity and appropriate gestures. (56)

"Ki ga tsuku" translates variously as "notice," "pay attention," "be aware of." "Yoku" means "much," and "ne" is a particle with various functions of softening, emphasizing, or inviting/expressing agreement with the phrase it punctuates. The meaning of "Yoku ki ga tsuku ne" is thus something like "thank you for being so alert and thoughtful." As the narrator's examples indicate, the "map" which Grandma and others teach and reinforce by saying "ki ga tsuku" is a behavior based on attending to the needs of others. One tries to observe and respond before being asked, and in turn receives the comfort of knowing that one's needs are also being anticipated.

Naomi rediscovers the primacy of this "attendance," which is Kogawa's poetic one-word translation of "ki ga tsuku," when she makes the journey into the past. (I elaborate the meaning and structure of "attendance" in an earlier essay, "'To Attend the Sound of Stone'": The Sensibility of Silence in *Obasan*.") Naomi recognizes that "attendance" must be practiced especially in times of great stress. In her version of Momotaro's departure, his parents are careful "not to weight his pack with their sorrow" (56). From her own life, Naomi recalls the example of when she last saw her father's parents:

> Obasan held Grandma Nakane's hand tightly until the driver came to close the ambulance door. Grandpa Nakane strained to sit up and tried to smile as he waved good-bye to Stephen and me, the ends of his moustache rising and falling. None of us spoke.
>
> It is always so. We must always honour the wishes of others before our own. We will make the way smooth by restraining emotion. Though we might wish Grandma and Grandpa to stay, we must watch them go. To try to meet one's own needs in spite of the wishes of others is to be "wagamama"—selfish and inconsiderate. Obasan teaches me not to be wagamama by always heeding everyone's needs. . . . That is why, when I am offered gifts, I must first refuse politely. It is such a tangle trying to decipher the needs and intents of others. (127–28)

"Attendance" is a tangle because it must be learned; but having learned well, Naomi is reminded, through a dream, not to be wagamama about the one death that brought the deepest loss. The dream is a nightmare in which a Grand Inquisitor questions Mrs. Nakane, who refuses to speak. Identifying with the relentless questioner, Naomi realizes that she has comprehended neither her mother's suffering nor her love which tried to hide that suffering through silence. When self-centeredness is replaced by attendance, Naomi is able to recall her lost mother, and lost self.

Obasan depicts a situation remarkably similar to that in *No-No Boy*. Like Okada, Kogawa creates a nisei protagonist whose sense of national identification and psychic wholeness are threatened by, then resolved through, the experience of internment and its effect on family, in particular the loss or estrangement of mother and father. A major difference is that whereas Okada "resolves" his character's identity crisis through a binary opposition valuing "(white) American" over "Japanese," Kogawa seeks to differentiate and bind "(white) Canadian" and "Japanese." Although Obasan's silence about Mrs. Nakane has eroded Naomi's sense of self as much as any fanaticism of Mrs. Yamada brought grief to Ichiro, Kogawa creates Obasan as someone eliciting love and respect from the Canadian-born generation and at the same time rooted in Japanese traditions.

Kogawa's Momotaro paradigm provides a very different analysis of "natural feelings" from that in *No-No Boy*. In the framework of "ki ga tsuku," feelings can be gratified because reciprocity is assumed. One's own needs and pleasures are fulfilled because someone else sees to them. According to the code of behavior associated with "Momotaro" in *Obasan*, both Ichiro and Mrs. Yamada are selfish and self-centered. Perhaps this is why Mrs. Yamada finds her sister's letter intolerable. Perhaps proud Mrs. Yamada reads her sister's willingness to beg for the children's sake as an indictment of her own failure as a "Japanese mother," and if so, this is what probably broke her hold on life.

If Ichiro could not have learned "attendance" from such a mother, he might have learned it from his father. However, Mr. Yamada's attentiveness is portrayed in *No-No Boy* as weakness. Ichiro's allusion to "Momotaro" suggests that there was once a tender bond between mother and son; but her role as storyteller and teacher of Japanese culture is unconnected to Ichiro's later resistance and resentment. There is nothing shown or remembered of Mrs. Yamada as a loving mother except in the undeveloped allusion to Momotaro. The paradigm remains truncated, engulfed by Ichiro's seething emotions, with the result that "Japan" can never be part of Ichiro's reconstructed self-esteem.

In the novel's first chapter, before realizing his mother's intention of showing him off as a "true" Japanese son, Ichiro accompanies her to call on former neighbors and friends. After two disastrous visits, one with a woman like Mrs. Yamada who harbors delusions of a Japanese victory in the war, and the other with parents whose only son died in combat, Ichiro follows his mother home consumed by helpless rage. She, of course, had not prepared him for either visit, especially the latter one where he innocently asked after the whereabouts of the son, his friend from college days. By the novel's last chapter, Ichiro has walked and talked his way through a dozen characters and situations since those first painful encounters with the Ashidas and Kumasakas, and has achieved a measure of peace in his own terms: "He walked along, thinking, searching, thinking and probing, and, in the darkness of the alley of the community that was a tiny bit of America, he chased that faint and elusive insinuation of promise as it continued to take shape in mind and in heart" (251). Clearly Ichiro's pace and perspective have changed from frantic self-chastisement to calmer self-assurance. However, he is emphatically alone at the end of the novel. His mother is dead and his brother leaves home for the army. Ichiro's potential best friend and another no-no boy whom Ichiro tried to save have both died. Ichiro has rejected two job offers, one where he could have worked for good pay as an engineer. He resists falling in love with a desirable woman who invites his companionship.

As he walks off into the future, moving away from home and hometown, his solitary, vanishing figure diminishes the novel's initial implications of return. In retrospect, Ichiro seems to have been determined not so much to come home but to return in order to leave. He comes back for another chance to declare "yes-yes." A different treatment of the Momotaro paradigm might have conceived redemption in terms of cultural difference and multiple loyalties. As he is portrayed, Okada's no-no boy can only represent Momotaro in exile.

WORKS CITED

Chin, Frank. Afterword. In *No-No Boy*, by John Okada. Seattle: University of Washington Press, 1981. 253–60.

Chin, Frank, et al., eds. "An Introduction to Chinese- and Japanese-American Literature." In *Aiiieeeee! An Anthology of Asian-American Writers*. 1974. Washington, D. C.: Howard University Press, 1983. xxi–xlviii.

Ellison, Ralph. *Invisible Man*. New York: Vintage, 1972.

Fujita, Gayle K. "'To Attend the Sound of Stone': The Sensibility of Silence in *Obasan*." *MELUS* 12.3 (1986): 33–42.

Inada, Lawson Fusao. "Introduction." In *No-No Boy*, by John Okada. Seattle: University of Washington Press, 1981. iii–vi.

———. "Of Place and Displacement: The Range of Japanese-American Literature." In *Three American Literatures: Essays in Chicano, Native American, and Asian-American Literature for Teachers of American Literature*, ed. Houston A. Baker, Jr., Intro. Walter J. Ong. New York: Modern Language Association, 1982. 254–65.

Kim, Elaine H. *Asian American Literature: An Introduction to the Writings and Their Social Context*. Philadelphia: Temple University Press, 1982.

Kingston, Maxine Hong. *The Woman Warrior: Memoirs of a Girlhood among Ghosts*. 1976. New York: Vintage Books, 1977.

Kogawa, Joy. *Obasan*. 1981. Boston: David R. Godine, 1984.

McDonald, Dorothy Ritsuko. "After Imprisonment: Ichiro's Search for Redemption in *No-No Boy*." *MELUS* 6.3 (1979): 19–26.

Mori, Toshio. *"The Chauvinist" and Other Stories*. Intro. Hisaye Yamamoto. Los Angeles: Asian American Studies Center, University of California, 1979.

———. *Yokohama, California*. Intro. William Saroyan. Caldwell, Idaho: Caxton, 1949. Intro. Lawson Fusao Inada. Seattle: University of Washington Press, 1985.

Okada, John. *No-No Boy*. 1957. Seattle: University of Washington Press, 1981.

Sakade, Florence, ed. "Peach Boy." In *Japanese Children's Favorite Stories*, illus. Yoshisuke Kurosaki. 4th ed. Rutland, Vt.: Charles E. Tuttle, 1961. 9–16.

Weglyn, Michi. *Years of Infamy: The Untold Story of America's Concentration Camps*. New York: Morrow, 1976.

Yaeger, Patricia and Beth Kowaleski-Wallace. *Refiguring the Father: New Feminist Readings of Patriarchy*. Carbondale: Southern Illinois University Press, 1989.

Yamamoto, Hisaye. *"Seventeen Syllables" and Other Stories*. Intro. King-Kok Cheung. Latham, N.Y.: Kitchen Table Press, 1988.

13

Blue Dragon, White Tiger: *The Bicultural Stance of Vietnamese American Literature*

Renny Christopher

TRAN VAN DINH'S *Blue Dragon, White Tiger: A Tet Story* is a novel about biculturality and identity, about the penetration of Western culture into Viet Nam, about one Vietnamese man negotiating his own identity, and his country's, and coming to find that, ironically, he can only be "truly Vietnamese" in exile in the West. The struggle to remain bicultural, to bring Vietnamese culture to America, is a theme that runs through most of Vietnamese American literature; it is prominent in works such as Le Ly Hayslip's *When Heaven and Earth Changed Places* and Nguyen Thi Thu-Lam's *Fallen Leaves*, both of whom like Tran and most other Vietnamese American authors, tend to write more about life in Vietnam than about the assimilation process in America. In this way Vietnamese American literature seems better described as a refugee literature than an immigrant literature.

That the negotiating of two cultures is the subject matter of this book is clear from the very beginning. It takes as its epigraphs a traditional Vietnamese cosmology, a Vietnamese folk song, and a quote from General Westmoreland:

> The Thanh Long, Blue Dragon, designates the eastern quadrant of the Uranosphere, the Bach Ho, White Tiger, its western section. The Blue Dragon represents spring and tenderness, the White Tiger, winter and force. All

> beings and all things on earth are affected by the constant struggle between the Blue Dragon and the White Tiger.
>
> —traditional Vietnamese belief

> The first month of the year is for eating Tet at home. The second month is for gambling. And the third month is for going to the festivals.
>
> —Vietnamese folk song

> The minds of the Vietnamese in Saigon and the other cities were preoccupied with the approaching Tet holiday, and our efforts to change this state of mind were only partially effective.
>
> —General William Westmoreland, 1968

The novel uses the Vietnamese Tet (New Year celebration) as one of its symbols for Viet Nam and Vietnamese identity. Westmoreland's attempt to "change this state of mind" does become effective in the novel as American culture changes Viet Nam, much to the disgust of the novel's main character.

Professor Tran Van Minh is suspended between two cultures. As the novel opens in 1967, he is a Vietnamese living in the United States, teaching at a progressive college in Massachusetts. He has been away from Viet Nam for most of his adult life and is comfortable in the United States. He is a writer and has written antiwar articles for American magazines and newspapers. He has continued, as well, to write in Vietnamese and to publish novels and poetry in Viet Nam, under the pseudonym Co Tung, which means "lone pine tree." His choice of pseudonym emphasizes the isolation he feels as a result of being between cultures, of being unreconciled with either culture in its entirety.

By the end of the novel, Minh has participated in the National Liberation Front's struggle for liberation and in its triumph in 1975, but has become disillusioned and decided that "only with freedom can I be a Vietnamese, can I appreciate the Vietnamese culture, wherever I may be" (310). He turns the revolution against itself with his decision to leave, saying, "I shall remain independent and free, according to your advice, respected Uncle Ho" (305). He is using Ho's slogan to justify his own Western-style individualism.

His decision represents his biculturality—only by returning to the West can he continue to live by his own definition of what it means to be Vietnamese. He is an internationalist, appreciating bits of various cultures that he finds admirable, from the Swede Dag Hammarskjold's book *Markings* to the American Revolution to Vietnamese cuisine. But his internationalism makes him lonely, makes him isolated. He says to his friend Loc, a staunch Party member, "I need all the personal freedoms that make me creative as a writer and an individual. You're part of a country, a Party; I'm all by myself" (307). He has returned to the position he held at the beginning, that "even if poetry and politics blend, poetry and communism certainly cannot" (44).

Minh works with polar opposites throughout the novel—polarities are what drive both his character and the plot. In the end, he opts for biculturality by following the only course that will let him keep both cultures. In Viet Nam the Communist Party, which has grown rigid, demands that Minh adhere monoculturally only to its ideology. He rejects this demand, and moves toward greater freedom back in the United States, where he can be both an American and a Vietnamese. Minh has created himself as a "hyphenated" American, desiring to live out both identities. He does not wish to assimilate to American culture, but he also does not wish to assimilate to the Communist Party in Viet Nam. He remains an individualist, a concept he has adopted from America, but he intends to use that individualism to maintain his Vietnamese culture and identity, thus making of himself a permanent paradox.

The novel itself attempts to be bicultural in its structure, to bring the experience of biculturality to its American readers. It constantly juxtaposes elements of the two cultures. It uses as its chapter epigraphs quotations from traditional Vietnamese poetry and literature and incorporates into its narrative passages explaining Vietnamese culture to the American reader in an attempt to make both sides of Minh's character accessible. These passages, while part of the story, also perform a didactic function:

> On important festive days, especially Tet, Vietnamese homes, rich and poor, are decorated with two lines of poetry or prose written on red cloth or rice paper. When he was only six Minh was initiated into the complicated art of calligraphy. (63)

> As in all Vietnamese homes, the Ancestors' Altar occupied the central place, hidden from the living room by a silk curtain embroidered with figures of dragons and phoenixes. The beautifully prepared dinner lay spread about the altar. Brass candleholders in the shape of cranes on turtles' back were set on the altar on opposite sides of a porcelain incense burner. Behind a vase

> of lotus flowers, in an inlaid pearl frame, was a photograph of Minh's mother. (65)

Minh participates in Viet Nam's quest to fit Marxism into its culture. In one of the novel's most important passages, Minh's friend Loc, a Party member, explains how Viet Nam can appropriate Marxism, using the traditional concepts of

> *Tinh*, feeling, and *Ly*, reason. At the present time, our *Tinh* is grounded in our culture and our *Ly* is rooted in our just struggle for independence and freedom, and socialism. *Ly* helps us clarify our *Tinh*. . . . *Tinh*, in turn, humanizes our *Ly*. . . . *Tinh* and *Ly* form the unbroken circle in which our national communication operates.
>
> In Marxist terminology, *Tinh* represents the 'superstructure' and *Ly*, the 'economic base.' . . . Looking back at our history, we can see that from our original culture we've drawn the necessary strength to absorb and Vietnamize Confucianism, Taoism, and Buddhism. There's no reason to suppose that we can't Vietnamize Marxism as well. (96)

For Minh, however, Marxism fails to become Vietnamized. The Party never develops sufficient *Tinh* but is rather overwhelmed by *Ly*, and therefore it fails to form the "unbroken circle" that would Vietnamize the Western ideology of Marxism. *Tinh* and *Ly* form two poles that Minh travels between in the course of the novel. He can never reconcile the two in terms of Marxism. He has worked with the Party for years without being a member. When he is invited to join, he must, "accept reform or . . . undergo transformation. To reform was to give up one's reason; to transform was to deny one's feeling" (304). He decides that, ironically, the only way he can maintain *Tinh* and *Ly*, the only way he can remain Vietnamese, is to leave Viet Nam.

The novel sets up a structure of polar opposites and depicts the attempt to reconcile them into an unbroken circle. Viet Nam and America are two such opposites, and Minh does eventually succeed in reconciling them for himself, although his reconciliation represents only his own individual life and does not extend any further to a reconciliation of the two nations. Minh's biculturality is an individualist proposition.

Further, the novel combines the conventional narrative structure of an American novel—beginning, middle, end, a plot driven by cause and effect and character development—with a Vietnamese plot turning on fate. Three women in the novel represent aspects of culture for Minh, and their appearances in the story are governed by fate. The workings of fate might look like coincidence to an American reader, but they represent the influence of Vietnamese literature on Tran's writing. The novel's worldview makes Viet Nam and its war the center of the world, around which fate turns. Everything that happens to Minh happens for a reason controlled by fate. The women appear in the story whenever Minh needs them to teach him a lesson; thus they are not fully developed characters but plot devices that Dinh manipulates to engineer Minh's development.

The first woman, Jennifer, represents America for Minh. With Jennifer he has attempted to walk the path of bicultural understanding. When he speaks with her, he quotes both Vietnamese poetry and Dag Hammarskjöld. He blends, in his person, the intellectual traditions of Europe and Asia, and his life reflects his biculturality—he is a Vietnamese in love with an American, a professor of politics who teaches about Third World revolutions at a U.S. college and, later, about the American Revolution at the University of Hue in Viet Nam. Minh's survival depends on being able to span both cultures; when he is cut off from one or the other, he is not happy. He describes himself as an "internationalist," yet he finds he still has a "strong loyalty to his society" (47). He thinks of himself as "Americanized and Europeanized, what we call in Vietnamese *Mat Goc*, losing roots" (133).

Minh has left America with regret. Upon arrival in Viet Nam, he thinks of Jennifer constantly. Escorted by soldiers he believes are arresting him and taking him to his execution (in fact, they are not), he hopes he will have "several hours left to think of Jennifer, or perhaps, if he was allowed, to write her a poem" (21).

Working with the National Liberation Front (NLF), he eventually stops thinking about Jennifer. However, Jennifer comes to Viet Nam with the American Friends Service Committee. Taken prisoner during the uprising in Hue, she is brought to the tunnel complex where Minh works. They see each other briefly before she is released in a prisoner exchange. Minh is allowed to walk part way to the exchange point with her. American B-52s drop bombs and napalm. Minh is wounded; Jennifer and all the other prisoners, Vietnamese and American, are killed. Minh does not find out about her death until a year later in Paris, where he has been sent both as a reward for his wounds and as part of the NLF delegation to the peace talks.

Jennifer reminds Minh of America just when he is becoming disillusioned with his work for the NLF. Living in the tunnels, "he wasn't even sure he was in Vietnam at all" (214). Jennifer's death represents for Minh the necessity of stopping the war, which mirrors the war going on in his soul. When he decides to return to America at the end of the novel, he believes he is doing what Jennifer would have wanted. In his return to America he reasserts his love for Jennifer, his symbol of biculturality.

The second woman, Xuan, is one of Minh's students at Hue University. She is his younger brother Phong's girlfriend, and she is suspected by the police of being Viet Cong. Xuan disappears and then reappears at the end of the novel, when Minh is escaping from Viet Nam by boat. Fatefully, Xuan is on the same boat. She tells Minh that she is going to integrate into the U.S. Vietnamese community as a Party spy. She also tells him the story of her involvement with the Party.

> In 1964, when I was a young girl in Hue, I was raped right in my living room by two army officers, one American and one Vietnamese. . . . Yet I didn't fall, I recovered, thanks to the care of the Party. The Party was the only place where I could regain and maintain my self-esteem. It was the warm womb from which I was reborn. (327)

Xuan's story can be seen as the story of Viet Nam—raped both by the corrupt Saigon regime and the Americans, the Communist revolution was the only way for it to be reborn. Xuan's fate, like Viet Nam's, is tragic. Her service to the Party causes her death. Minh tells the captain that she is a spy. He betrays her without any soul-searching—he has burned his bridges, his ties to the Party. But fate saves Minh from the guilt of his betrayal. The captain plans to kill Xuan in the night, but that day Thai pirates board the boat, rape and kill her, and throw her body overboard.

In terms of Minh's fate, Xuan represents a path that he has not chosen—that of bicultural adherence to the Vietnamese Communist Party. Her death at the hands of Thai pirates, in an ironic repeat of the experience that originally drove her into the Party, serves as a message to Minh that his decision to embrace biculturality was the correct one—that the Communist Party cannot provide the home that Xuan and he have sought.

The third woman who comes to Minh as a messenger from fate is Thai, his high school love, working as an NLF cadre. While Minh is in the NLF tunnels preparing for the 1968 Tet uprising, he encounters Thai, who is now a political commissar. She is cold to him and shows no sign of recognizing him. Her attitude symbolizes the part of Vietnamese communism that ultimately causes Minh to leave Viet Nam—he sees her as all *Ly*, with no *Tinh*, no heart. Later, when Minh is asked to join the negotiating team in Paris, Thai becomes head of the delegation. He is attracted to her because she is the only link he has with the past that means so much to him and from which he is so cut off. When he writes her a letter asking for recognition of their old love and for friendship, she denounces him to the delegation for his "bourgeois nostalgia." He decides, then, that "in order to exist, he must resist" (258). He continues to work for the Party, but the *Tinh* has gone out of it for him. Thai's rejection of him symbolizes for Minh the cost of adhering to the Party—it will mean rejecting the Vietnamese culture of his youth, which he loves so much. Fate has sent Thai to him to teach him this lesson.

Throughout the novel Minh wavers, unable to find his way through the complexities of his situation. He constantly wants to take action but is unable to; he waits for fate to bring events to him. The only actions he takes of his own initiative are his decision at the beginning to leave the United States to return to Viet Nam and his decision at the end to leave Viet Nam to return to the United States. At the beginning and end of the novel, Minh takes action like a Western-style character; in the middle, he is controlled by his responses to fate, like a Vietnamese-style character. The novel thus blends the two traditions to create a form that is unique, as its main character is unique.

Unlike many American works entrenched in monoculturalism, *Blue Dragon, White Tiger* asserts that bicultural understanding is a real possibility. Minh is able to read both Vietnamese and Americans—he has no trouble understanding either people. Upon meeting the American vice-consul in Hue, Minh thinks, "There's something phony about the man" (58). American faces are not unreadable to him. Likewise, some of the American characters are able to read Vietnamese characters. Minh, mistakenly arrested by South Vietnamese soldiers, is rescued by an American lieutenant who recognizes Minh's innocence. The lieutenant says, "A black man in America learns to tell truth-tellers from liars. By the way you speak, your conduct, I know you're not a liar, professor" (84).

Minh's quest throughout the novel is a quest for identity. His identity is never singular but always multiple. This multiple identity is the essence of biculturality. He is Professor Tran Van Minh in both America and Viet Nam, but he is also the poet Co Tung who writes against the war from a noncommunist position. As Co Tung, he is anonymous; even his own cousin doesn't know his identity (3). In Saigon, he is serenaded by his own poem set to music at a dinner party. Even in "a city without secrets" (29), Minh can remain an enigma. When he first arrives in Viet Nam, his identity as Co Tung is mentioned frequently, showing him to be an outsider in his own culture, as the "lone pine tree" he has become because of his embracing of the West.

When he joins the NLF, his identity both as Tran Van Minh and as Co Tung are taken from him. When he takes the path to the liberated zones, his guide asks him to "leave everything behind" (204). He is given a new name, Phan Viet Dieu, which he keeps until he goes to Paris, where "he noted immediately that his name had been changed once more, this time to Tran Van Thong" (240). All his years in exile, first in the tunnels, then in Paris, he lives under false names.

He gets his old name, Tran Van Minh, back upon his return from Paris to Hanoi. But his other identity, Co Tung, haunts him. When he meets a famous novelist in Hanoi, she mentions Co Tung's works (269). But Minh is not ready to reclaim that part of his identity yet. He does not tell her that he is Co Tung. In effect, at this point in his story, he is not Co Tung; he has not been Co Tung since he left his identity behind to join the NLF. When he returns to Saigon, he is again known as Co Tung. His new superior says to him, "I've read your books and poems, so I feel as if I know you already" (281). Almost without Minh's will, Co Tung comes to reclaim Minh.

Minh takes on one last identity in his escape from Viet Nam. His code name with his contact is Chuong. "The code signal was taken from the name of Vu Hoang Chuong, a well-known Vietnamese poet rumored to have died in a re-education camp after the liberation" (305). Minh leaves Viet Nam so that Co Tung will be reborn. Co Tung represents Minh's bicultural personality. As Co Tung he is a Vietnamese poet, but one who writes his Vietnamese poetry from his position as an American university professor. The multiple naming represents the transitions that Minh goes through as he tries on various identities. In the end his identity remains multiple: Tran Van Minh/Co Tung. For a person who immigrates from one culture to another and insists on preserving his old culture while simultaneously adopting his new culture, only a multiple identity is possible.

Although Minh respects and admires his adopted American culture, he is not uncritical of it; Minh is anything but naive. The novel is critical of some aspects of America, of Viet Nam, and of communism, at the same time it embraces other aspects of each. In this way, it is much more sophisticated than the majority of books about the war.

While he is in Viet Nam, Minh begins to see how American culture, which he has been so at home in, has affected Viet Nam. He meets a woman at a party who has had her nose "corrected" and who complains that she does not have enough money to also have her eyes "broadened like Sophia Loren's" (28). American culture has colonized Vietnamese women's bodies, creating in them the internalized oppression that causes them to want to alter their looks to fit the standard of the dominant culture of America, which has been exported to Viet Nam. Minh is disgusted.

The American war is also literally and metaphorically poisoning Viet Nam. Minh's father tells him that they can no longer put lotus stamens in their tea because "the water in the moats and ponds has become so polluted with poisonous chemicals it's dangerous to use them" (61). Minh's two teenage cousins are rude and disrespectful, and spend their time watching "I Love Lucy" on Armed Forces TV. In Viet Nam, Minh sees the destructive aspects of American culture. Vietnamese culture is in danger of being erased, as his father says when Minh tells him that a radio report has not given the name of a Buddhist nun who has immolated herself in protest. "No name! The Vietnamese have no name any more. The whole of Vietnam ceases to have a name. We are a battlefield, pawns for the greedy and the powerful" (140).

Minh cannot, however, free himself from Western culture entirely; it is part of his being, part of his self. Visiting the Buddhist patriarch of the Thien Mu pagoda, "Minh listened attentively to the Patriarch's every word. A few rays of sunlight passed through the window and shone on his clean-shaven head. An aureole seemed to surround his body, like those Minh had seen in paintings of Christian saints" (78). Thus, even while in a Buddhist pagoda, part of his native culture, he brings to it the perceptions of his adopted culture: he sees both a Buddhist patriarch and a Christian saint.

One of the cultural elements Minh works to negotiate is that of family. He is tied to Viet Nam by his family, and it is at his father's request that he returns to Viet Nam from the United States. His father is a traditional Buddhist, a scholar, a descendent of an old and noble family of Hue. He preserves his serenity by isolating himself from visitors and the outside world. Minh's own mother is dead, but he is close to his father's minor wife, his "Auntie," the mother of his two half-brothers, both of whom are in the ARVN (Army of the Republic of [South] Viet Nam). Although An and Phong have taken their positions partially to protect their father, the old man disapproves of the Saigon government. Because An is a soldier of the corrupt Republic of Viet Nam, his father warns him not to disgrace the family. This passage shows the many double binds of the war—An has joined the ARVN to protect his family, but his father counts that protection as worth little since it jeopardizes the family's honor.

Minh's father's sympathies lie with the NLF. He tells Minh the true story of Minh's mother's death, which had been previously concealed from Minh: she was killed by the French while working with the Viet Minh. His father tells him the story in order to persuade Minh, the oldest son, to join the right side in the war. Minh's father demands of Minh that he reject America entirely: "Remember, it's the American wood that sets the Vietnamese house on fire" (66). Ultimately, however, Minh decides that he cannot live as his father has lived. When Minh returns to Viet Nam from Paris in 1973, he longs to return to "a normal Vietnam" (259), but he has not learned the lessons that have been given to him by fate—that there is no longer a "normal" Viet Nam. When he lands in Hanoi, he feels "colder at the Vietnamese airport than he had" in Paris (262). Minh has been changed by his experiences, and it is not possible for him to live the life his father has envisioned for him.

After liberation, Minh finds out that his family has been killed. His family ties, which had brought him home in the first place, are dead. Nonetheless, Minh stays on in Viet Nam for three years. When he does decide to leave, part of what he tries to recapture in his escape is a sense of family. The group he escapes with refer to themselves as family. The captain of the boat calls them "our boat family"

(323). Minh has never found this sense of family among the Party members he has worked with for the last several years. He must define himself, along with his boat family, against the Party in order to constitute himself as part of the boat family. The reason he betrays Xuan so easily is that she is not a member of the boat family; she is still a member of the rival Party family. Minh is taking his place among the "family" of refugees and, as such, will live as part of the Vietnamese exile community in the United States; he will reconstitute his Vietnamese family, and thus maintain his ties to the part of his native culture that he loves and respects, while living in America.

Minh returns to the United States via Thailand. In Bangkok he notices

> the noise, the dirt, the smell, the chaotic traffic on the crowded narrow streets didn't bother or annoy him as they had the last time he was here. He even liked them now. They were, he believed, part of the necessary, insignificant price one had to pay for individual liberty. (333)

Minh has learned in the course of the novel that in order to live by the Western definition of freedom that he has chosen, one must accept the destructive elements of Western culture as well, the choice that Bangkok symbolizes. In exile, Minh will preserve his heritage. "But it would be henceforward the spirit of the historic Vietnam that he held in his heart, not the political one—the mystic Vietnam, not the vulgar and brutal one" (334).

By the end of the novel Minh has come full circle, and in that circle he finds a reconciliation with himself.

> I've lost everything, but at the same time, I'm gaining everything back. I'm reclaiming myself. Thank you, Jennifer, and you too, Xuan and Loc. Thank you, Vietnam, thank you, Vietnam Communist Party. Thank you all. I've lost you all in different ways and in different circumstances, but I've gained everything. I've regained myself. (332)

Maxine Hong Kingston writes in *The Woman Warrior*, "I learned to make my mind large, as the universe is large, so that there is room for paradoxes" (35). The self that Minh has built by the end of the novel is one that is large and has room for paradoxes, so that losing all can also be gaining all.

WORKS CITED

Hayslip, Le Ly. *When Heaven and Earth Changed Places*. New York: Plume, 1989.

Kingston, Maxine Hong. *The Woman Warrior: Memoirs of a Girlhood Among Ghosts*. New York: Vintage, 1976.

Nguyen Thi Thu-Lam. *Fallen Leaves*. New Haven: Yale Southeast Asia Studies, 1989.

Tran Van Dinh. *Blue Dragon, White Tiger: A Tet Story*. Philadelphia: TriAm Press, 1983.

14

From Isolation to Integration: Vietnamese Americans in Tran Dieu Hang's Fiction

Qui-Phiet Tran

THE PARADOX of modern mass media is its quickness in keeping its audience abreast of the latest event in the world and simultaneously its disposition to misinform them about that event. Reporters tend to fashion their coverage from a theme that they think might be of interest to the public, overlooking the real nature and meaning of the event being covered; they will also drop a subject they believe is worn out or no longer interests the audience.

The picture of Vietnamese refugees has received this kind of media treatment in the United States. Generally, the resettlement of Vietnamese in the new land has been presented as a success story. They enjoy a better life, their children excel in American schools, and they are no longer plagued by anxieties about the future as they were when they first arrived in America. To dramatize the smooth transition from their former society to their present one, the mass media portray these newest Americans beaming with happiness and pride as they celebrate major American holidays such as Thanksgiving and the Fourth of July. For Vietnamese immigrants, reporters like to tell us, America is not only the land of freedom and peace but the land of opportunities for those who were denied a future in their former countries.

To the casual observer this representation of Vietnamese Americans is nearly perfect. Resourceful, law-abiding, tenacious, and, most importantly, capable of adjusting quickly to American society, Vietnamese Americans are blessed with all the necessary qualities which enable them to join the melting pot with great ease. Surprisingly, this delineation of Vietnamese Americans matches the picture portrayed by the Vietnamese media. Stories about these newest Americans' successes in various areas appear on the front pages of major Vietnamese newspapers and magazines (many of which are bilingual) and on Vietnamese television. Vietnamese communities relish news about the opening of Little Saigon shopping center, the appointment of student X as Rhodes scholar, and the admission of valedictorian Y to Harvard University. These successes give Vietnamese refugees a sense of great joy and pride and justify the cause of their voluntary exile in the new land.

This idyllic portrayal of Vietnamese immigrants ironically finds no echo in Vietnamese American literature. For less than two decades since the arrival of the first wave of refugees in 1975, Vietnamese readers have witnessed a spectacular phenomenon that I call the flowering of exile Vietnamese literature. Written primarily in Vietnamese, this literature is the preoccupation of a great number of authors, many of whom are "boat people" and had never tried their hand at literature before. While the horrors of the refugees' journey to freedom—piracy, rape, starvation, death—are dominant themes in this literature, its main focus is the ordeal of being the newest Americans. After the nightmare of their sea voyage is past, Vietnamese refugees find themselves in another crucible: facing the uncertainties and difficulties of their life in America.

The problems of adjustment that confront the refugees find their fullest expression in Vietnamese emigre literature. Viewing themselves as exiles, Vietnamese writers see their haven in America as a "penal colony" where "one's body and soul are wearing away" with "mountains of grief and agony".[1] They also react strongly to American civilization which they find too mechanical and hectic to allow one to enjoy "the quiet and leisure," the Tao of living of the East (Vo 67; Qui-Phiet Tran 104, 105). This view of the Vietnamese exile experience and American culture can be attributed to the refugees' frustrations about problems such as cultural differences, language barriers, and changes in their socioeconomic status as a result of their resettlement in the United States.

Because venting their bitterness about their American experience becomes a compelling need or perhaps a mode of salvation for many

Vietnamese immigrants, writers have little difficulty in getting published. Though an official count of authors, their publications, and publishers is not available for lack of an adequate archival system, a quick survey of literary materials on display at a typical Vietnamese bookstore in an area with a large concentration of Vietnamese immigrants such as Orange County, California, will leave the researcher convinced about the boom in exile Vietnamese literature and publishing during these last sixteen years. Vietnamese experiences are richly documented in books, magazines, music, and art work. Authors are apprentices in creative writing or veterans in their fields. Publishers range from major firms to authors who print their own work expressly in order to alleviate their pain of exile.

The flowering of this literature is enhanced by a wide readership. Vietnamese immigrants turn to their literature for reasons similar to those for which their authors write: to recognize (and face) their problems, to understand how the stories of their ordeal are told and how their voices are rendered. They also turn to this literature for another important reason. Written in Vietnamese, it responds to the emotional needs of many Vietnamese who wish to relieve their nostalgia by seeking familiar images of their past in the process of reading.

These preliminary remarks suggest that to see the true picture of Vietnamese immigrants, we should, as Jacques Lacan might advise, turn away from the idea that the conscious "autonomous" ego is the center of the human psyche. The mass media's view of the Vietnamese American as an objective, strong, and healthy ego capable of synthesis, integration, and adaptability to realistic norms is, according to Lacan's theory, an illusion because the human subject is neither unified nor unifiable (Ragland-Sullivan 120). To understand the complexity of Vietnamese Americans' psyches, we should therefore turn to their literature. Again Lacan's teaching about the role for literature in unraveling the repressed unconscious, the reservoir of signifiers and language of the real, is useful.[2] When studying Vietnamese Americans we take up their literature because literature, in Lacan's view, is not only "unthinkable without repression" but equated with the language of the unconscious—the language of indestructible desire, dreams, and madness. "But one has only to listen to poetry . . . for a polyphony to be heard, for it to become clear that all discourse is aligned along the several staves of a score," Lacan explains (Bowie 203). Vietnamese American literature, in depicting the refugees' aspirations as well as their outrage, anguish, and insanity, is what we should concern ourselves with in our study of the Vietnamese experience in the United States.

This representation of the Vietnamese American psyche is bound up with the identity of the speaking subject. A quick glance at the bulk of publications by Vietnamese American writers reveals this interesting fact: women write more extensively and offer a different rendering of the Vietnamese American experience than men. Men concentrate on their past ordeal at home and in refugee camps; women present problems of adjustment to the new society. Men speak about their exile and missed opportunities with anger; women speak about their destiny with anguished resignation. Men see their quest for happiness as a dead end, women see the quest as a meaningful and rewarding experience. Men, probably because they are still bitter about the United States "betrayal" of South Vietnam in 1975, are angry with America and refuse to draw any significance from their American experience, whereas women view the whole story at worst as a karmic debt and at best as a dear price the refugees have to pay for their freedom.

An important representative of contemporary Vietnamese women writers who have explored the above problems is Tran Dieu Hang.[3] Her two major collections of short stories, *Vu dieu cua loai cong (The Peacock Dance*) and *Mua dat la (The Rain Falls on the Strange Land)* deal with the complexity of the refugee consciousness and unconscious, the adverse circumstances Vietnamese Americans face and the death instinct they try to repress, their hopes and expectations as well as their despair and fear. The following essay examines these issues in Tran Dieu Hang's writing.[4]

The Vietnamese exodus to the United States in 1975 had no parallel in Vietnam's history. It happened so suddenly that most evacuees had little or no time to prepare themselves for their permanent departure. Not only did many leave Vietnam empty-handed, but also they had no knowledge of the language, customs, and culture of the country to which they were fleeing. No sooner did they get over the panic of their escape than they found themselves wrestling with a new life for which they were totally unprepared. In their moments of greatest depression many Vietnamese had second thoughts about their American experience. They questioned the purpose of their expatriation (which they came to regard as a brutal uprooting from their native land); they lost interest in their struggle to integrate into American society; they gave themselves up to despair or escaped to their idyllic past. America, which they had thought was a haven, turned out to be a penal colony in the minds of these exiles.

The problems that confront Vietnamese immigrants assume a special meaning and perhaps more tragic dimensions in Tran Dieu Hang's fiction because most of her protagonists are women. Victims of circumstances harsher than male refugees', they are both objects of men's desire and targets for cultural, sexist, and racist discrimination. Unlike male refugees who are able to channel their outrage against injustices into violent acts, women are condemned to bear their indignities in secrecy, silenced many times over by deeply rooted cultural inhibitions, male oppression, language barriers, and menaces of damnation from the dominant host culture.[5]

The protagonist of "Bong toi, que nguoi" ("Darkness, Strange Land") epitomizes the educated Vietnamese female immigrant's condition. Chan, a former student from the University of Saigon now toiling in a sweatshop to support herself and her family, finds herself in "an anguished state of self-defense" because of the repeated advances made to her by her Vietnamese and American coworkers and the hostile attitude of her female colleagues (*Vu dieu* 75). Chan's condition as a young female refugee—an object of male seduction and female hatred compounded by her overweening pride in her Asian heritage, her indignation over her tribulations, and her educational background—plunges her into a stubborn silence and causes her to turn down her American friend's marriage proposal. Chan's utter estrangement and loneliness mark the gloomy aspects of her, and other Vietnamese women's, integration into American society and are suggested by her bidding farewell to Tim as darkness pervades the landscape.

One of the reasons Chan cites to decline Tim's offer is her concern about the oppression of her native culture by her suitor's. Clearly, her conditions preclude a future with Tim and what he represents. She wants her future husband to be able to appreciate things Vietnamese that are endearing to her; she wants her future children to be able to "sing Vietnamese songs that her mother had taught her" (90). Unlike her American friend who thinks that "language is just a means of communicating immediate ideas and feeling" and is not connected at all with memories, Chan argues in defense of her native tongue that language is a vital link between the past and future of a people and to suppress language is to sever that link, their mode of survival. Chan's dilemma as a transplanted Vietnamese American is unresolved, nonetheless. While apparently succeeding in preserving her identity by escaping into her past and cutting off her contact with the host culture, she imposes silence on herself, deprives herself of the power of language as well as of the opportunity for self-expression, and exacerbates her condition of exile.

Chan's condition results from her choice not to participate in the mainstream of American life. By contrast, most of Tran Dieu Hang's other characters are caught up in their dilemma of integration. Representing mostly the larger group of refugees known as the "boat people" who came to America to seek freedom and a better future, these characters express for the refugees a fervent desire to integrate into American society. Their dream of becoming Americans, however, is thwarted by practical realities such as language problems and racism. This drama of Vietnamese acculturation is aggravated by the subversion or even destruction of Vietnamese traditional values, which have morally sustained many Vietnamese immigrants in their exile, by the formidable force of American culture. The family, the foundation of Vietnamese culture and society, disintegrates under the onslaughts of American material civilization. Ideal values such as loyal friendship and matrimony, filial piety, and reverence for old age are rejected by many Vietnamese Americans in favor of individualism and materialism. As always, women, rather than men, fall victims to these cruel circumstances.

Two stories, "Mua dat la" ("The Rain Falls on the Strange Land") and "Roi ngay van moi" ("There Will Come New Days"), dramatize the difficulties of integrating into American society. The narrator of the former story, a young refugee reunited with a mother who married an American, feels rejected by her new American family because of her language problems. Muted by her repressed outrage over her handicap, her siblings' hostility, cultural dissimilarities, and particularly her mother's remarriage while her father languishes in a reeducation camp in Vietnam (a grave violation of the Confucian ethical code for Asian women), she stays out of the mainstream like "a dumb, insignificant shadow," viewing her being in "Mr. John's" family as superfluous, "a scion grafted on to an alien stock" (*Mua* 43). Her alienation increases when she finds American life threatening. Seeing the vortex of a freeway interchange packed with traffic, the menace of American life, she is led to think of "a colossal monster whose lightest breath can crush me to death" (40).

While in "The Rain Falls on the Strange Land" America is seen as an imminent threat, in "There Will Come New Days" it turns into a destructive power. Wishing to dissolve quickly into American culture by choosing to live with an American family, Thoi, a peasant from the Mekong Delta, is horrified to find her dream smashed. Taking advantage of her vulnerability, her sponsor rapes her despite her tearful pleas in broken English and then he attempts to buy her silence. Her successful escape from her offender's home and her determination to learn English suggest her realization that speech is a weapon to resist male oppression and to fight for recognition in American society.

While articulateness is thought by some of Tran Dieu Hang's characters as a possible way to fight sexist and racist oppression, it proves useless when coping with their tragic condition as refugees and women. Victimization is not merely associated with male brutality and female muteness but also stems from the tension between Asian and Western cultures, and particularly from the encroachment of American materialism on Vietnamese moral and spiritual values. Jealousy alone, therefore, cannot be blamed for the death of a young beautiful woman gunned down by her husband in "Can chung cu so 7" ("Apartment 7"). Trapped in the clash between the traditional culture to which he clings and the new culture to which she is drawn, both characters fall victims to, and are silenced by, the force of circumstances, one behind bars and the other in the grave. Similarly, the victimization of the woman does not merely result from male brutality in "Cho tam" ("Temporary Asylum"). Not only is the protagonist jilted by her husband and sexually abused by her lover, but also she is alienated by the new society which condemns her and her little child to a quest for a temporary asylum which they can never find. The final scene of the story suggests a Kafkaesque quest in a wasteland completely despoiled of humanity: "The road in front of us is vast and endless, and our footsteps are the solitary sounds in the cold winter morning when the town is half-awake" (*Mua* 89). In their utter despondency Vietnamese women blame American mechanical life for their condition. "Have you wondered," the protagonist of "Ngay thang qua doi" ("The Onrush of Time") ponders, "why there are so many vehicles rushing on the highway and yet you can't find a companion for yourself? And why does twilight often make you feel that you never come to the end of your journey?" (*Vu dieu* 155).

The quest for an ideal, however illusory, as a way to cope with victimization is behavior common to many of Tran Dieu Hang's characters. Their search for happiness, however, is doomed to failure. In "Mot chut bien chieu" ("The Seas of Evening") a thirty-year-old woman and a middle-aged man, despite their attempt to converge with each other, are "destined to return to their loneliness . . . like the two trains heading off in opposite directions" (*Mua* 105). Missed opportunities, lost time, and advanced age are some of the main causes of Vietnamese adults' estrangement not only from American society but also from their native community. Though at times these solitary souls manage to come together, they end up torturing each other because of their incompatibilities. "There is something wrong, something disjointed," comments the narrator of "Bua tiec" ("The Feast") on the union of a young couple with nothing in common (*Mua* 19). The union is "wrong" because in their eagerness to come together to help each other wrestle with the difficulties of life the two characters do not see love as most essential to matrimonial happiness.

The trauma of family discord caused by "mismatching" is depicted at length in "Ben ngoai khung cua" ("Outside the Window"). Nga's incompatibility with her husband, a materialist, flippant, and hypocritical man, plunges her into a series of fantasies (or flashbacks?) about an idyllic love. Her last fantasy becomes a death-wish at the story's end when her husband shows no sign of caring for her after her labor. The story illustrates a dilemma faced by many adult refugees. While loneliness brings them together, their union estranges and victimizes them. Still, their incompatible characters compel them to search again for an illusory, impractical mode of salvation, alienating them even more from reality.

The victimization of Vietnamese adults by adverse circumstances, is, though brutal, not entirely tragic. Dreaming away sorrowful reality or searching for an unattainable ideal, they are not completely deprived of hope for a better future. The condition of elderly refugees, in contrast, is desperate. Threatened by prospects of damnation in the new land because they are ill-equipped to deal with reality and rejected by the Americanized young generation, old Vietnamese escape into their past, go insane, or resort to self-destruction. Though

Tran Dieu Hang's fiction does not exclusively dramatize this last recourse, it does portray the sad consequences of the elders' uprooting from their native land and their maladaptation to American life. In "The Feast" a group of old artists seeks to voice through music the repressed sorrow of exile—their only means of survival—and succeeds somewhat in evoking momentarily a happy past. Yet, the elderly characters' brief joy is tainted with anguish over their present condition. Instead of hymns, they choose to sing doleful dirges. For these old people, seeking salvation in the past is futile because songs from their past can give them only a brief respite from reality. After the concert, the parents of the protagonist have to make the painful decision, because of their daughter-in-law's disrespect, to move out of the house of the son with whom they were just reunited. Very soon they will have to lead a solitary life and face a reality that quells their creative voice, their only way of holding on to their past and identity.

The themes of the shock of reality and, particularly, the tragic consequences of the old Vietnamese refugees' quest for the past are treated at length in "Chuyen xe ve lang Dai Tu" ("The Trip to Dai Tu Village"). Instead of sustaining them like a life force, the past victimizes and destroys them. The grandmother in the story suffers a schizophrenic split. Completely losing hold of the real world (she is no longer aware of her body's biological functions), she paradoxically recalls the most minute details of her distant past, which in her mind is transformed into a permanent present. Her continual conversation with her absent son (who is pining in a reeducation camp in Vietnam) and with her fictional friends during her imaginary trip back to her native village in North Vietnam are reminiscent of Proust's observation of people who can talk to physical objects as if they possessed an animate life. Freud attributes the power of this sort of memory to the unconscious, whose process he sees as timeless because it is not altered by the passage of time.[6] Bergson speaks of pure memory which, because it hovers far above the plane of experience out of touch with reality, is able to keep our entire past life intact.[7] The narrator of Tran Dieu Hang's story provides yet another interesting interpretation of this perception phenomenon. The grandmother has little recollection of the recent past and is completely cut off from the present because her memory, like a roll of film nearing its last exposure, can no longer store current information. The last time she saw her son, her last memory-trace (to use a Freudian trope), remains nevertheless indelible in her damaged memory because it is associated with her fear for his safety, which in time becomes a permanent delirious obsession and plunges her into schizophrenia.

The general picture of Vietnamese Americans depicted thus far in Tran Dieu Hang is that of outcasts, misfits, and recluses—unfit for American society. This picture also applies to a group of Vietnamese often neglected by other writers: the adolescents. For many Vietnamese and Americans these youngsters are adjusting too well to American society to pose any problem detrimental to their future in this country. By contrast, Tran Dieu Hang portrays a gloomy picture of these young Vietnamese Americans. Electrified by the new macho culture and at the same time suffering from his inferiority complex, Binh in "Cuoc choi" ("The Game") joins a gang to test out his newly learned "Godfather theory": survival of the fittest. The meaning of the story, according to the narrator, is crystal clear: in his quest for salvation, Binh "chose a violent, tragic end destined for wild plants that seek to grow too fast, not caring about the consequences of their reckless course of action" (*Mua* 63). The story's hero typifies a predicament faced by many Vietnamese American adolescents. Too young and too rebellious to be held back by their roots, they dissolve too fast into America's destructive subculture. Binh's final cry, as well as that of many Vietnamese adolescent refugees who suffer from a destiny like his, a destiny that forces them into early maturity, also confirms the emptiness of life. "His cry," says the narrator, "disappeared into silence, nothingness. It was the cry of the kids who already lost their innocence, though not yet fully grown" (63). It is the cry that disturbs the narrator, the young hero's mentor, who wonders who should be held responsible for his young friend's folly—fate or his lack of care for the teenager's education.

An analysis of a selection of Tran Dieu Hang's stories suggests that Vietnamese immigrants have traveled many roads in search of different meanings. Some have cut short their journeys or dropped out, but others stay on to fulfill their arduous destinies. Who remains in this second group and what enables them to endure? This question is answered in many of Tran Dieu Hang's stories and particularly in her trilogy, "Nguoi em vuon ngoai" ("The Young Cousin"), "Giac mo cua co" ("The Dream of Grass") and "Roi ngay van moi" ("There

Will Come New Days"). In general, characters in these stories are able to withstand their catastrophic times and avoid the despair of suicide because they are equipped with a rural background, rooted in their native soil, armed with a strong belief in their traditional values, or capable of dreaming harsh reality away.

Conceived in the same vein as "The Game" but obviously purported to counteract the baneful effects of American culture, "The Young Cousin" advocates returning to the Vietnamese past. Interestingly, the past, no longer viewed as an abstract ideal representing unfulfilled dreams, is now equated with a concrete life force, "a property so simple and yet so solid like the earth" to which the protagonist "usually return[s] in imagination when I feel I have lost my identity, when I am alienated, weak, and cowardly in this strange world" (129–30). Empowered with the past, the fountainhead of protection, security, and love, the protagonist feels undaunted, like "a traveler who has eaten a hearty meal before making a long trip" (130). He feels sorry for his cousin who is deprived of such an important heritage because she left home at a very tender age. Lured by a culture too permissive, this young cousin commits the most vicious acts imaginable, short of destroying herself. Having no weapon with which to fight harsh circumstances, she is a lost soul in the new country.

The association of the past with the earth suggests that the past is bound up in *place* and derives its redemptive power from it. According to Eudora Welty, place transcends the human world, because, instead of being hostile to the latter, it "heals the hurt, soothes the outrage, fills the terrible vacuum" (131). More important, both art and feelings, as Welty puts it, are tied to the native soil from which they spring (118). Welty's remarks about the role of place in fiction explains Tran Dieu Hang's preoccupation with her native land as a mode of salvation in her trilogy. It abounds with homely and simple images such as "our garden-grown fruits," "our farm-raised shrimps," "ricefield mud," "reflections of coconut trees on a tranquil rivulet." The exception to Welty's theory of place is that Tran Dieu Hang's characters, lacking a physical locality due to their exile in a strange land, are not able, as Welty might observe, to "put out roots, wherever birth, chance, fate or our traveling selves set us down" (Welty 132–33). Unlike American and European writers whose nomadic destiny Welty seems to have in mind, Vietnamese authors, because of their reluctance to accept their "second homes," have to compensate for their loss by dreaming about their native soil. "The Dream of Grass" illustrates this quest for salvation. Though becoming full-fledged Americans, the protagonist and his narrator do not give up their search for an idealistic vision—"rowing on a moonlit night when the country is at peace and listening to the vast river echo our voice reciting poetry" (*Vu dieu* 133). Though place is an illusory ideal for Vietnamese immigrants, it is inseparably bound up with their destiny. Pursuing this quest—dreaming of going home—is not only their mode of behavior but, as the narrator exclaims at the end of the story, a means for keeping them sound and safe "till our last breath" (136).

The glorification of the native soil finds its fullest and perhaps clearest expression in "There Will Come New Days." Native locality provides moral and spiritual values and principles that have contributed to the victory of the Vietnamese people over countless adversities in their nation's tormented history: endurance, fortitude, and faith. Thoi, the most unfortunate victim of the force of circumstances and yet the most heroic protagonist in Tran Dieu Hang's fiction, embodies such principles and values. Brutally violated by pirates in her sea voyage, ravished and gagged by her sponsor in America, handicapped by the language barrier, she nevertheless turns her outrage and death instinct into her determination to fight for a better future. Her resolve to study English and to enroll in a vocational training program indicates her realization that speech and action are the only way for a refugee woman to transcend her condition. Her moral strength comes from her faith in the redemptive power of suffering and endurance and from her conviction about the dear price she has to pay for her freedom. This strong belief, the source of her fortitude, has been nurtured, as her narrrator puts it, by her family's and her native country's traditional values and particularly her rural upbringing (*Vu dieu* 195). Her cultural values explain both her formidable will power and, paradoxically, her "innocent, care-free manners as if she never bothered to know that she had in hand that mighty weapon" (195). By creating this unique character in whom is crystallized the best of Vietnam's cultural heritage and by significantly titling her story to point optimistically to the future, Tran Dieu Hang demonstrates that the truest Vietnamese, to borrow Welty's apt metaphor, "put out roots whenever . . . fate set[s] down" (Welty 132–33) and achieve their dreams by apotheosizing their native values.

"The Dream of Grass," "The Cousin," and "There Will Come New Days" suggest that Vietnamese immigrants have come full circle in their American experience. No longer isolating themselves in their enclaves, these stories demonstrate their desire and ability to integrate into the mainstream, as their ultimate goal. Yet, for these people integration does not spell cooptation or monologic dominance by the host culture. Rather, by merging with the mainstream without repressing their nostalgic dreams, native heritage, and distinctive voices, they can assert their identity and participate as Americans in the enrichment of their new country's pluralistic culture. Tran Dieu Hang's vision recalls Ihab Hassan's "critical pluralism" which calls for "pragmatic constituencies of knowledge that would share values, traditions, expectancies, goals" to "bring back the reign of wonder into our lives" (Hassan 182). In this apocalyptic age, as the world is giving up its "totalizing principle" (169) and opening to dissenting views and consciousnesses, one can only hope, as Hassan might say, that the Vietnamese voice will be heeded in the polyphonic postmodern discourse.[8]

NOTES

1. Qui-Phiet Tran 101–10, esp. 104.
2. For discussion of the role of repressed psychology in literature see, for example, Davis 983–84; Bowie 135–63.
3. Born in Hanoi, Tran Dieu Hang moved to Saigon at age two with her family after the partitioning of Vietnam in 1954. In 1975 she came to the United States as a refugee and attended Santa Ana College and California State University, Fullerton, majoring in information systems. She makes her home in the Los Angeles area with her two small children and is currently a programmer analyst for an oil company in Southern California. *Chom Chom yeu dau (Chom Chom, My Darling)*, her third book of short fiction, was published in 1989.
4. All translations from the Vietnamese are my own.
5. For this discussion of women's victimization, I am indebted to King-Kok Cheung 162–74. It is interesting to note that minority women writers share similar concerns about ethnic women's condition.
6. For detailed discussion of memory and old age in Freud, see Blau 13–36.
7. Bergson's concept of memory is embedded in most of his writings and treated in great detail in *Time and Free Will* and *Matter and Memory*. For a discussion and application of Bergson's theory, see Douglas 142–65.

8. I would like to thank Shirley Geok-lin Lim and Amy Ling for their encouragement, suggestions, and criticisms in an earlier version of this essay.

WORKS CITED

Bergson, Henri. *Matter and Memory*. Trans. Nancy Margaret Paul and W. Scott Palmer. New York: Macmillan, 1911.

———. *Time and Free Will. An Essay on the Immediate Data of Consciousness*. Trans. F.L. Pogson. New York: Macmillan, 1910.

Blau, Herbert. "The Makeup of Memory in the Winter of Our Discontent." *Memory and Desire: Aging, Literature, Psychoanalysis*. Ed. Kathleen Woodward and Murray M. Schwartz. Bloomington: Indiana United Press, 1986. 13–36.

Bowie, Malcolm. *Freud, Proust and Lacan: Theory as Fiction*. Cambridge: Cambridge United Press, 1987.

Cheung, King-Kok. "'Don't Tell': Imposed Silences in *The Color Purple* and *The Woman Warrior*." *PMLA* 103 (1988): 162–74.

Davis, Robert Con. "Lacan, Poe, and Narrative Repression." *Lacan and Narration: The Psychoanalytic Difference in Narrative Theory*. Ed. Robert Con Davis. Baltimore and London: Johns Hopkins United Press, 1983. 983–1105.

Douglas, Paul. *Bergson, Eliot, American Literature*. Lexington: United Press of Kentucky, 1986.

Hassan, Ihab. *The Postmodern Turn: Essays in Postmodern Theory and Culture*. Columbus: Ohio State United Press, 1987.

Proust, Marcel. *Time Regained*. Trans. Andrea Mayor. New York: Random House, 1981.

Ragland-Sullivan, Ellie. *Jacques Lacan and the Philosophy of Psychoanalysis*. Urbana: University of Illinois Press, 1986.

Tran, Dieu Hang. *Mua dat la*. Ontario: Viet Publications, 1986.

———. *Vu dieu cua loai cong*. Westminster, Calif.: Ngoc Lu, 1984.

Tran, Qui-Phiet. "Vietnamese Artists and Writers in America: 1975 to the Present." *Journal of the American Studies Association of Texas* 20 (1989): 101–10.

Vo, Phien. *Lai thu gui ban*. Westminster, Calif.: Nguoi Viet, 1979.

Welty, Eudora. *The Eye of the Story: Selected Essays and Reviews*. New York: Vintage Books, 1979.

15

South Asia Writes North America: Prose Fictions and Autobiographies from the Indian Diaspora

Craig Tapping

We are like "chiffon saris"—a sort of cross-breed attempting to adjust to the pressures of a new world, while actually being from another older one.

—Feroza Jussawalla

A man who sets out to make himself up is taking on the Creator's role, according to one way of seeing things; he's unnatural, a blasphemer, an abomination of abominations. From another angle, you could see pathos in him, heroism in his struggle, in his willingness to risk: not all mutants survive. Or, consider him sociopolitically: most migrants learn, and can become disguises. Our own false descriptions to counter the falsehoods invented about us, concealing for reasons of security our secret selves. A man who invents himself needs someone to believe in him, to prove he's managed it.

—Salman Rushdie

LIKE OTHER ethnic literatures in North America, writing by immigrants from the Indian subcontinent is concerned with personal and communal identity, recollection of the homeland, and the active response to this "new" world. Its forms are multiple and in many traditional and some newly created genres; but an autobiographical impulse—the desire to name experience and to create identity, to emerge from the dominant language and gaze of "nonethnic" America—impels even the shortest fictions, despite frequent disclaimers by the writers. Bharati Mukherjee, for example, argues that "I am not at all an autobiographical writer, but my obsessions reveal themselves in metaphor and language" (Hancock, "Interview" 36).

Indo-American and Indo-Canadian writing are also postcolonial literatures. That they write in English—a linguistic choice that influences patterns of migration and affiliation among writers as disparate as Ved Mehta, Rohinton Mistry, Bharati Mukherjee, Suniti Namjoshi, Michael Ondaatje, Vikram Seth and Sara Suleri—is a direct consequence of British imperialism. This historical situation unites all of these writers who variously emplot their relation to the partition of the Indian subcontinent in 1947, to the consequent political histories of newly created nations and the nationalities which the writers have variously left, and to the construction once again of even newer identities in the countries to which they have immigrated.

In its postcolonial forms, writing from the Indian diaspora is frequently described in terms of the literary careers of V. S. Naipaul and Salman Rushdie. A writer like Sara Suleri, for example, is scrupulous in her critical analysis of Naipaul's place and influence as a writer of decolonized literature ("Naipaul's Arrival"). Bharati Mukherjee, in contrast, negotiates a transformative distance in her critical writings, between these two models of an international school of Indian writing ("Prophet and Loss"). As neither Rushdie nor Naipaul write from an American or Canadian perspective, however, North America's Indian writers must now create their own traditions.

These traditions are still young, and are often found in journals which collect and anthologize disparate writings from otherwise unpublished new writers of Indian background. In such collections, the reader is guided through the developing voice of community and individual creative artist. In her recent introduction to an edition of *The Literary Review* dedicated to writing from the Indian diaspora, Bharati Mukherjee explains that Indo-American literature is a new phenomenon and as yet only in the process of becoming a tradition:

> The literary commonwealth of Indian-origin authors is a comparatively recent phenomenon, still largely unremarked in this country. . . . In Canada, where the East Indian population is proportionally greater than in the U.S.,

> more names leap readily to mind. . . . Since I'm a frequent visitor to writing classes in both the U.S. and Canada, I can't help noticing the number of young Americans and Canadians of my own general background who seem to be writing seriously and semi-professionally. . . . I'm moved and a little daunted; I know the immigrant world well enough to know that each young writer is a doctor, accountant, or engineer lost; a bright hope, a bitter disappointment. I left India for the freedom to write and make my own life; I can imagine people somewhat like myself, but . . . it will take another ten years for the Indo-American writers to start making their mark. ("Writers" 400)

The list of her writers, and the explanations of their homeland and newly formed communities elsewhere, confirm this argument. In compiling her anthology of Indo-American writing, Mukherjee conflates the term to include a range of writers from across the Indian diaspora. The problematic result is only partially solved by an editorial disclaimer that "choices for this volume may appear whimsically eccentric" ("Writers" 400). Most of her North American writers have immigrated into Canada or the United States from already established Indian communities in Africa or the Caribbean. Some, she admits, are Indian only by marriage.

Such a dispersive flavor to the literary samplings thus anthologized can be puzzling. Many of the writers are more accessibly read in the contexts of Indo-Caribbean or other so-called Third World literary traditions. Ketu Katrak and R. Radhakrishnan, editors of the *Desh/Videsh* special edition of *Massachusetts Review*, expand already vague horizons by including visual art, critical essays, poetry, and pieces from outside the North American locus.

What becomes clear from such a quick, and of necessity reductive, survey is paradigmatic, however. Domicile and ethnicity do not alone determine Indo-American or Indo-Canadian identities: geographical, lexical, political, and cultural differences are the signifying tropes of Indo-American ethnic literatures. Sam Selvon, Cyril Dabydeen, and Neil Bissoondath of Canada are perhaps racially classifiable as "East Indian," to use Mukherjee's editorial naming—which she elsewhere rejects when it is applied to her own status ("Invisible Woman" 38). They have little in common with Mukherjee beyond this and are better read in the context of Caribbean and Third World literatures. Mukherjee and other explicitly Indo-American writers belong to the "Fifth World": that of the economically and politically displaced immigrants of the twentieth century, transposed into alien contexts from where they redefine and newly construct alternative identities and communities (Arthur).

For this essay, then, I have chosen to inflate the prefix "Indo" to mean the subcontinent, and have therefore included writers born in what are now Pakistan and Sri Lanka with those from what is now politically defined as India. I read these writers with an eye and ear alert for their notations of difference between Canada and America.

Ved Mehta's autobiographical enquiry—which now extends through several volumes—locates what may be the foundations of an Indo-American writing tradition. In form and breadth of vision, *Daddyji, Mamaji*, and *Vedi* are almost conventional, however, and contravene none of the readerly expectations that the genre, autobiography, arouses. They locate the Mehta family in the Punjab in the nineteenth century, suggest the transformations that placed the family there, and detail in a surprisingly sensual form the geographical and climactic terms of that landscape. The attention to specifics of contour, shape, density, and color are more than exotica in these reconstructions of the past. Mehta has been blind since preschool age, and these rich depictions are his transcribed records of conversations, research, and communal inquiry. The Mehta family becomes a representative gathering of clan and individuals: this is a history of India read through one family's tree.

The Ledge between the Streams shifts ground, somewhat. Having explained his parents' independent and then mutual lives and family lines, and having chronicled his own childhood and schooling, Mehta departs from idyllic representation halfway through this volume in the chapter titled "The Two Lahores." This and subsequent chapters move the writing from the merely personal and awkwardly old-fashioned kind of universalizing memoir into the postcolonial, and nonrepresentative autobiography. Suddenly, the world of religious fanaticism, ethnic separatism, politics, and communal violence erupts, disrupting an otherwise quiet and—despite its intimacies—reticent chronicle. Now, Mehta explains his consternation, the family's unpreparedness for social and public confrontations with dogmatism and bigotry, and the intrusion of such assaults into the sitting rooms and kitchens of a formerly becalmed middle-class household.

In a configuration repeated by subsequent writers, Mehta links the bloodletting and trauma of partition to the emigration of a generation of trained professionals. Partition and its adherents—those who fought for separate ethnically and religiously defined states—introduce a dogmatic sense of purity and authenticity, both of which deny and exclude the plurality of India before independence. This, too, is a repeated figure and informs, for example, Salman Rushdie's three novels about postcolonial India and Pakistan.

Departure and exile during the riots that accompanied the creation of two and later three new countries are made synonymous with liberal tolerance of difference, and bourgeois social aims and aspirations. For Mehta, however, the new place of settlement and career is not the subject. India—what it was, what it became, and what it might have become—remains the subject of his autobiographical explorations to date. The United States enters his writing only through acknowledgment pages and the unacknowledged presence of a calm study in an entirely other world from which he remembers and recreates a more turbulent epoch of personal, would-be universal history.

The reader is left with an image of the author akin to that of Borges. Mehta, the blind archivist of an order destroyed by politically charged events which he literally failed to see and which socially his class was unprepared to admit or transform, continually recatalogues his library from memory, thumbing through various otherwise forgotten pages from the ever-receding past.

Feroza Jussawalla, in her article "Chiffon Saris: The Plight of Asian Immigrants in the New World," addresses a critical issue often read as problematic in much Indo-American writing. Admitting that the writers and critics of Indo-American literature are usually privileged by caste and economic class, she nonetheless avers that the literature must reflect the conflicts and social violence that are mundanities for the entire ethnic community.

Such criticism, despite its noble aspirations and humane motivations, is problematic. First, the call for a social realist mode of literary production is anachronistic. Such an approach damages both reading and writing. Second, grouping writers ethnically inscribes them as insignificant, except sociologically. No one condemns or calls to task the "non-ethnic" writer for his or her avoidances and transgressions. Third, to read this literature for its universalizing representation of an already disparate ethnic community patronizes that community, denies individual differences, and ignores those textual features which readers use to privilege other, non-ethnic writings as "literature." In short, it is what Henry Louis Gates, Jr. calls "the ruinous desire to be representative, to collectivize the first person" (38).

The literature now being published by Indo-American writers is very significant, literate, informed, and worldly wise. Writers foreground and articulate their personal, familial identities and sociopolitical contexts, explaining how and why they came to be where they are and to write what they do. This conscientious explication of the construction of their own identities is tied to the recognition that being a universal exemplar for an entire subclass is a logical and political impossibility, except if one should deal in stereotype and blinkered vision.

For example, Sara Suleri, Michael Ondaatje, and Bharati Mukherjee all extend the autobiographical tradition of Mehta in quite different ways. Suleri describes *Meatless Days*, an impressionistic mediation on history, family, politics, gender, and race, as a collection of "quirky little tales" (156). Ondaatje's *Running in the Family* transgresses several generic boundaries. Ondaatje uses writing itself to disrupt previously cherished notions of truth, voice, and history. By the end of this memoir of Sri Lanka and his family during the 1930s and 1940s, the reader is both elated at the sheer exuberance of the many kinds of narratives in which Ondaatje revels (including the photographic) and confused by the denied outcomes and deferred truths that each genre promises and then withholds. Mukherjee's most explicitly autobiographical piece, the second part of *Days and Nights in Calcutta*, also confronts the veracity promised by personal witness as she cuts across the narrative truths delivered in the first part which is written by her non-Indian husband. Each of these writers, then, uses autobiography to explore not only the self and the larger community but also to explore and subvert readerly expectations which adhere to this most personal mode of writing. Truth, presence, and verifiably witnessed history are all called into question variously by these would-be confessionalists.

In *Meatless Days*, Sara Suleri probes language and the names we give—in English and in Urdu, in America and in Pakistan—to foodstuffs, loved ones and family members, rituals and social customs, political events and personal memories. The chapters weave through this labyrinth of languages and their usage, opening by turns into rooms of objective catalogue, historical account, subjective memoir, dream work, and oblique parable. Suleri uses analogies from Islamic and British Imperial architectural styles and habits of self-presentation, as well as recipes and folklore concerning various foodstuffs, to imply her own methodologies.

There are meditations on the Third World which she aptly describes as "locatable only as a discourse of convenience" (20), and accounts of life in Pakistan during and after independence. With her father editing and the family proofreading and helping to assemble the galleys of various daily newspapers throughout Pakistan's recent history, Suleri is well-placed to record her own observations on this postcolonial history. Her descriptions of the partitioning in 1947 as the "perpetual rewriting" of boundaries (87) lead to an ironic questioning of contemporary nationalisms as she considers

> those bewildered streams of people pouring over one brand-new border into another, hurting as they ran. It was extravagant, history's wrenching price: farmers, villagers, living in some other world, one day awoke to find they no longer inhabitied familiar homes but that most modern thing, a Muslim or a Hindu nation. There was death and panic in the cities when they rose up to flee, the Muslims traveling in one direction, the Hindus in the other. (116)

In an aside about the architectural splendors and confusion of Lahore, Suleri names herself and fellow residents from this part of the subcontinent "we Indians" (152): more nationally-defined labels are the result of European imperial history. The proximity to this history entangles Suleri in a debate with her father about Pakistan, humanity, and writing. This last concern explicitly enmeshes her consideration of women in the chronicles of nationhood and independence.

Meatless Days begins, in one of its many paths through the maze of language and history, as answer to an American student's question about equal representation on the syllabus of a literature course devoted to the "third world" and ends in fulfilling that question while undermining our perhaps ethnocentric hopes for a more satisfactorily definite answer. Suleri answers "there are no women in the third world" (20), after explaining:

> the concept of woman was not really part of an available vocabulary: we were too busy for that, just living, and conducting precise negotiations with what it meant to be a sister or a child or a wife or a mother or a servant. By this point admittedly I am damned by my own discourse, and doubly

> damned when I add yes, once in a while, we naturally thought of ourselves as women, but only in some perfunctory biological way that we happened on perchance. Or else it was a hugely practical joke, we thought, hidden somewhere among our clothes. (1)

From this perspective, Suleri's ruminations on her sisters and their mother, a woman who migrated from Wales via London into Pakistan after independence, is the extended answer to that question. So, too, her own departure for America is presented, in part, as the end of an argument with her father and a history made by generals and other men who engineered "Islam's departure from the land of Pakistan. The men would take it to the streets and make it vociferate, but the great romance between religion and the populace, the embrace that engendered Pakistan, was done. . . . God could now leave the home and soon would join the government." (15)

The leave-taking is never final, however. Suleri's book continues the dialogue long after the severance, and it carries her sense of being "an otherness machine" (115) from these arguments with her brother and father into the heartland of New England. In America, she considers how to assemble the chronicle she now writes—"I have washed my hands of sequence" (76)—and how to convey the almost impossible, "to explain the lambent quality of the periphery, its curious sense of space" (106).

The curious sense of space and its lambent qualities at the margins of empire can be said to concern Michael Ondaatje's *Running in the Family* as well. Ondaatje interweaves photographs, musical notations and the lyrics of imported American dancehall recordings, historical accounts, a wide reading through European and American portrayals of Ceylon, his own diary's examination of a return with his children to Sri Lanka after twenty years in Canada (often in the form of poetry), family legends, gossip and local rumors—in his memoir of his parents and their halcyon days in pre-independence Ceylon.

The pervasive comedy of his text is never far, however, from the recognition of imperial history and Western literary erasure of cultures beyond the edges of canonical event, like his family's. For example, a seemingly insignificant epithet from Paul Bowles inspires an outpouring of inventive versifying that is both an ars poetica in its exploration and almost definitive exhaustion of the metaphor as device and, not incidentally, the reinvention of a non-Western culture's bardic invectives. The poem, "Sweet Like a Crow," is one of Ondaatje's more celebrated improvisations on a theme—Bowles's contention that "Sinhalese are beyond a doubt one of the least musical people in the world." Ondaatje demonstrates a pitch, line, and rhythm quite other than what Bowles would obviously hear or appreciate, and thus decenters the ethnocentric notion that there is but one standard for judging poetry (*Running* 76). Similarly, the photographs that are interleaved with the writing offer an ironic commentary on the linearity and verisimilitude of Ondaatje's narrative.

Perhaps the most revealing moment of self-reflexivity in Ondaatje's chronicle, however, is also one of the more concealed. After the close of his book, and having brought his narrative to a tentative conclusion, Ondaatje—as is frequently customary with other writers—offers acknowledgments and explanations of his funding, times and places of writing, and gratitude for the help he received in reconstructing the "history" of his family. At this point, long after we have finished reading and in the small print as it were, we encounter a refusal of the genre's label and consequent readerly promises that is benignly non-Western in its broad sweep across all claims to "truth": "While all these names may give an air of authenticity, I must confess that the book is not a history but a portrait or 'gesture.' And if those listed above disapprove of the fictional air I apologize and can only say that in Sri Lanka a well-told lie is worth a thousand facts" (206).

More recently, Ondaatje has again written "ethnic" fiction in his novel, *In the Skin of a Lion*. His characteristically cinematic cutting between images that hang in the consciousness as if they were feathers to imagination's airstream and his concerns to write between the official pages of history are here used to evoke what it meant to be "ethnic" and "immigrant" in Toronto at the beginning of this century. That city emerges as this novel's protagonist and is built by the snatches of conversation and sometimes intimate voices of several different communities (all of them "immigrant" and all engaged in constructing a new world) that the novel embodies.

In a like manner, Bharati Mukherjee is exuberantly polyphonic in her drive to assimilate and refashion the American dream—at least since leaving Canada both residentially and imaginatively. Mukherjee is not so widely known for her examinations of Canadian racism in different genres—investigative journalism, personal essay, literary review, autobiographical memoir, novel, and short story. Her many attempts to represent the Canadian establishment's oblique responses to its communities of ethnic Indians enmesh autobiography and fiction, attesting to the depth and range of what has not always been read as a constructive and ameliorative vision clearly *because* the life does enter the work at several points. Thus, Spivak dismisses Mukherjee's cultural criticism as almost worthless because it represents the privileged perspective of "liberal third worldist feminism" (256). Similarly, Jussawalla contemptuously dismisses Vikram Seth as "the totally assimilated yuppie of the Silicon valley: no qualms, no hint of Indianness except the name and the baggage of Anglo-Indian education . . . superficially acquired, possibly in an Indian mission school" (585). In both arguments, there is an appeal to some kind of essential "Indianness" which, rather too obviously, privilege and education deny: it reads in either disguise as a confused condescension toward those who might be more "real" than author or critic and whose agendas therefore determine both writer's and analyst's political correctness. Seth's own work might be profitably considered in terms of his returning the gaze that has so often found India exotic on that most exotic hothouse of late twentieth-century capitalist culture, California.

Similar autobiographical fictions by American writers of color suggest that the interference of life-facts and other particularities of individual experience should instead be read as interreference as such writers attempt to translate two disparate cultural spaces—theirs and ours—into a third, intercultural or postcultural space. Euro-American conventions of reading frequently, however, overlook this new territory from where new literary genres, mostly ethnic, emerge (Fischer).

A major theme in Mukherjee's nonfiction is that Indians in Canada have been subjected to racist assaults, physically and psychologically. The government has failed its citizens. She writes that she identifies with these victims, and she has explained her own traumatic sense of entrapment and claustrophobia while living in Canada ("Invisible Woman"). The claims of identification are frequently couched in terms of class expectation, without apology: "Great privilege had been conferred upon me; my struggle was to work hard enough to deserve it. And I did. This bred confidence, but not conceit. . . . Calcutta equipped me to survive theft or even assault; it did not equip me to accept proof of my unworthiness" ("Invisible Woman"

36, 38). Even in the recent essay on Rushdie, Mukherjee does not demur from such contextualizing. This is the generation who "traded top-dog status in the homeland for the loss-of-face meltdown of immigration" ("Prophet and Loss" 12). Unfortunately, this knowledge of the life, foregrounded by the essayist in her readers' consciousnesses, limits the ability of some North American critics—with their almost endemic but often vicarious interest in politically correct and socially austere lives—to read the fictions sensibly.

If she is right that she wants to embrace the new, the dilemma is that she also carries a lot of the old with her—which we then read as élitism and class-exclusive aspirations. Rejection on these grounds, however, suggests that only those who have suffered or continue to suffer explicit economic violence should testify against a bourgeois culture's insensitivities. These "others" have no voice or access to that discourse in the first place. Thus, in both instances, we use such rules to silence a community.

Read differently, this very privilege, this sense of having "traded top-dog status," is an inscribed Canadianism of Mukherjee's writing. Another immigrant, the nineteenth century writer Susanna Moodie, suffers the same disillusion of class expectations when confronted with the great leveling effects of community in Canada. Moodie, character in and author of *Roughing It in the Bush* (first published in 1852, now a "classic" founding text of Canadian literature), complains throughout that immigrants to Canada and the United States have abandoned their European sense of class and a concomitant respect for their "betters." In the historic moment of the 1960s and early 1970s described at some length in both Blaise's and Mukherjee's sections of *Days and Nights in Calcutta*, Toronto is again "bush" in comparison to the metropolitan cultures of London and the intellectual sophistication of Calcutta.

In Mukherjee's "Canadian" stories—"The World According to Hsü," "Isolated Incidents," and "Tamurlane" from *Darkness* and "The Management of Grief" from *The Middleman and Other Stories*—racist violence is not fictionalized. The attacks on Indians are not digested narratively, but emerge as factual news headlines, eruptions in the text not to be achieved or constructed as fiction but rather to confront the reader. The inclusion of these violent facts makes extra-textual appeal to the lived experiences of her non-Indo-Canadian readers. It reminds the reader of the daily newscasts on radio and television. It is a narrative strategy of confrontation that does not allow complacent reading. It does not allow the domestication and comfort of metaphor.

Why this does not happen in Mukherjee's American stories is another question, suggested by analyses of similar moves in other writings of immigration and violence. Perhaps a "yearning for sincere interlocutory speech"—the reforming anger directed at the Canadian body politic and her outrage at the betrayal of her silenced community—"gives way to a play on written substitutes"—the exuberance and polyvocality of the American stories, celebrating a newly found sense of inclusion (Clifford 111).

For the protagonists of *The Tiger's Daughter* and for many of the immigrant protagonists in Mukherjee's short stories, America is the way out of the cul-de-sac of upper-class existence in Calcutta. In *Wife* and *Jasmine* America is a place of random and excessive violence, and her American characters are subject to the uncertainties of life in such a state. For Dimple Dasgupta, ill-fated heroine of *Wife* who cannot adjust to her new rootlessness and the breakdown in community support and behavioral systems which immigration has meant, this violence breeds anomie and then further violence. Mukherjee argues that her target—despite the American geography in this novel—is Canada ("Invisible Woman" 39). In her other fictions—especially *Jasmine*—America is celebrated as the mythic center of an emergent world characterized by its "romance . . . its infinitely possible geography, its licence, sexiness and violence" (McKay 46).

Mukherjee's nonfiction is central to the range of expression in her short fiction. For example, we cannot read "The World According to Hsü" without recognizing that it resonates with, and extends the documentary evidence of, both "An Invisible Woman" and *Days and Nights in Calcutta*. The disjunction of Canada's two metropolises is somewhat bizarre and the heroine's dread at the prospect of Toronto is inexplicable until we read the nonfictions. The Montréal experience of the memoirs explains how the protagonist of the short story can recall her strangely comfortable existence there, a nostalgia produced by the irrelevance of her own position, cultures, and languages to the warring factions in either strife-torn city. In contrast, Toronto occasions only anxieties that are relentlessly critiqued in the essay. Fear of personally directed racist violence builds in the story as she recalls the incidents and newspaper headlines that the essay cites for its authority.

So, too, "The Management of Grief," recognizably something quite other than her graphs of American life in *The Middleman*, is a fictional extension of Mukherjee's nonfiction analysis of Canadian experience. This story must be read in conjunction with *The Sorrow and the Terror*, a nonfiction collaboration described as a quite different variation on the opening of Rushdie's *Satanic Verses* ("Prophet and Loss" 10).

The destruction of Air India Flight 182 is explicitly the violent and repressed other of Canada's fumbling and misdirected multiculturalism, a series of blind negations of new immigrants most of whom revealed "a determined responsiveness to Canada" (*The Sorrow* 124) but all of whom were classified as non-Anglo-Saxon or "visible minorities." Mukherjee deconstructs this last term to condemn its inscription of a racist metaphysics, a never-to-be overcome difference. Canada's loss—a generation of immigrants—is the vitality and idealistic future that she now fictionally locates in America, most clearly in *Jasmine*.

This relation between the fiction and the nonfictional analyses of power and transformation is both autobiographical and tribal. Mukherjee's prolonged examination of Canada and her embrace of America are ethnographic in that both reveal how the misrepresented "other" responds, individually and communally, to the shame and defilement of an exclusion that is always more clearly understood and more fully recognized on the margins that it is by the practitioners of casual disregard at the centers of our national hegemonies. By the time she emerges from this harrowing exploration of Canada's institutionalized racism, India is no longer a geographical place that connotes "home" for Mukherjee, but rather a way of perceiving reality and adapting to the empirical world. As she explains in the introduction to *Darkness*, "Indianness is now a metaphor, a particular way of partially comprehending the world. Though the characters in these stories are, or were, 'Indian,' I see most of these as stories of broken identities and discarded languages, and the will to bond oneself to a new community against the ever-present fear of failure and betrayal" (3).

The immediate characteristic of Rohinton Mistry's approach to the issues of ethnicity in Canada is that he is much less vehement than Mukherjee, and even gently ironic. *Tales from Firozsha Baag* is an exemplary postmodern postcolonial literary collection. It stages the translation of oral cultures into literature with a commentary on the traditional society from which such practices derive, it reflects on its textuality and on the growing consciousness and literary abilities of its protagonist-author, it mocks well-meaning Anglo-Saxon liberalism through satire, and it appropriates the inherited narratives of the imperial canon in parody that opens our understanding of such figural systems. Not insignificantly, Mistry's own voice as author, as citizen, as fellow Parsi and Indian, is only obliquely present in this collection of stories.

Mistry further distances himself from the engaged passion of Mukherjee's work by explaining that his autobiographical situation creates a different set of circumstances and contexts for his fictional encounters with Canada: "My characters are outside Hindu India. And because of the history of the Zoroastrian religion, it does not provide a solid anchor like Hinduism or Judaism or Islam" (Hancock, "Interview with Bharati Mukherjee" 149). Mistry's "low" culture pursuits as a former folksinger—one reviewer refers to his otherwise unremarked upon previous career as "Bombay's Bob Dylan" (Sullivan)—suggest further variant cultural and political expectations, as does his adoption of a suburban retreat in Brampton, Ontario, for writing base in contrast to Mukherjee's choice of metropolitan New York for its "gradual Calcuttaization" (Hancock, "Interview with Bharati Mukherjee" 31).

"Squatter," one of the *Tales from Firozsha Baag*, is an almost archetypal contemporary postcolonial literary artifact. Exemplary of the collection, it mixes the sacred with the profane, the high with the low. Its author is self-effacing in the manner of other postmoderns: commenting on another's literary performance, he obliquely alerts us as to how we should be reading his own.

The story begins by asserting the humor and self-assurance of the immigrant who gives himself ten years to become a Canadian or return to Bombay. Compared to the hackneyed truism that Canadians do not know who they are, it is revelatory to read an "other's" confident summation of our national characteristic. The public display and reception of such a hero's encounter with life in Toronto, and his ensuing moral responsibilities to his community, constitute the tale and its performance by the guardian of the word, the uncle who stayed behind in India.

The tale, a communal Indian rehearsal of Canadian multiculturalism, conflates high and low art forms, deflates liberalism abroad, and celebrates outsider status in its travesty of immigrant desperation. To convey the bathos of not learning how to use toilets in Canada within his protagonist's self-imposed ten year time limit, Mistry plunders eighteenth-century English satiric modes—the scatological visions of Swift were never such unabashed fun—and that Renaissance classic of "otherness," *Othello*. In Mistry's tale, the canon of English literature is appropriated and revised: an empire of literature displaced by a text hilariously performing an oral event in a subject-culture's contemporary repertoire.

In this and other Mistry tales, his characters are most eager to join others in the latest wave of immigration, the newest tide of those who will reinvent Canada. His protagonists purchase shameless Western bathing suits and, quite literally, jump into the deep end. Imagery of bathing suits with their sudden exposures of otherwise hidden body parts, deep ends of swimming pools, the public humiliations of swimming classes and changing rooms, overwhelming tides (of migration) or waves (of immigrants) are all drawn, of course, from the concluding story of *Tales from Firozsha Baag*, "Swimming Lessons." Here, the immigrant is no longer the paranoid solitaire, but just one more citizen in this experiment in social construction called by some a "New World."

WORKS CONSULTED

I would like to thank Emmanuel Nelson for his help in compiling this bibliography.

Arthur, Kateryna. "Fifth World." Unpublished paper delivered at conference on "The History of Ukrainian Settlement in Australia." Melbourne, 1990.

Carb, Alison. "An Interview with Bharati Mukherjee." *Massachusetts Review* 29.4 (1988): 645–54.

Clifford, James. *The Predicament of Culture: Twentieth Century, Ethnography, Literature, and Art*. Cambridge and London: Harvard University Press, 1988.

Fischer, Michael M. J. "Ethnicity and the Post-Modern Arts of Memory." In *Writing Culture: The Poetics and Politics of Ethnography*, ed. James Clifford and George E. Marcus. Berkeley, Los Angeles and London: University of California Press, 1986. 194–233.

Gates, Henry Louis, Jr. "Remembrance of Things Pakistani: Sara Suleri Makes History." *Village Voice Literary Supplement* 81 (December 1989): 37–38.

Hancock, Geoffrey. "Interview with Bharati Mukherjee." *Canadian Fiction Magazine* 59 (1987): 30–44.

———. "Interview with Rohinton Mistry." *Canadian Fiction Magazine* 65 (1989): 143–50.

Jussawalla, Feroza. "Chiffon Saris: The Plight of Asian Immigrants in the New World." *Massachusetts Review* 29.4 (1988): 583–95.

Katrak, Ketu H. and R. Radhakrishnan, eds. *Desh-Videsh: South Asian Expatriate Writers and Artists. Massachusetts Review* 29.4 (1988).

McKay, Gillian. "Bharati Mukherjee." *Domino* (May 1989): 46.

Mehta, Ved. *Daddyji/Mamaji* (1972/1979). London: Picador/Pan Books, 1984.

———. *The Ledge between the Streams* (1984). London: Picador/Pan Books, 1985.

———. *Vedi* (1982). London: Picador/Pan Books, 1985.

Mistry, Rohinton. *Tales from Firozsha Baag*. Markham, Harmondsworth, and New York: Penguin, 1987.

Mukherjee, Bharati. *Darkness*. Markham and Harmondsworth: Penguin, 1985.

———. "An Invisible Woman." *Saturday Night* (March 1981): 36–40.

———. *Jasmine*. New York and Markham: Viking Penguin, 1989.

———. *The Middleman and Other Stories*. New York and Markham: Viking Penguin, 1988.

———. "Prophet and Loss: Salman Rushdie's Migration of Souls." *Village Voice Literary Supplement* 72 (March 1989): 9–12.

———. *The Tiger's Daughter* (1971). Markham, Harmondsworth, and New York: Penguin, 1987.

———. *Wife* (1975). Markham, Harmondsworth, and New York: Penguin, 1987.

———. "Writers of the Indian Commonwealth." In *Writers of the Indian Commonwealth*, ed. Bharati Mukherjee and Ranu Vanikar. *Literary Review* 29.4 (1986): 400–401.

Mukherjee, Bharati and Clark Blaise. *Days and Nights in Calcutta* (1977). Markham, Harmondsworth, and New York: Penguin, 1986.

———. *The Sorrow and the Terror: The Haunting Legacy of the Air India Tragedy*. Markham, London, and New York: Penguin, 1987.

Namjoshi, Suniti. *The Blue Donkey Fables*. London: Women's Press, 1988.

———. *The Conversations of Cow*. London: Women's Press, 1985.

———. *Feminist Fables*. London: Sheba Feminist Publishers, 1981.

———. *From the Bedside Book of Nightmares*. Fredericton, Canada: Fiddlehead Poetry Books and Goose Lane Editions, 1984.

———. "Poetry or Propaganda?" *Canadian Woman Studies/Les Cahiers de la Femme* 5.1 (1983): 5–6.

Ondaatje, Michael. *In the Skin of a Lion*. Toronto: McClelland and Stewart, 1987.

———. *Running in the Family*. Toronto: McClelland and Stewart, 1982.

Rushdie, Salman. "Minority Literatures in a Multi-Cultural Society." In *Displaced Persons*, ed. Kirsten Holst Petersen and Anna Rutherford. Sydney, Australia and Mundelstrup, Denmark: Dangaroo Press, 1988. 33–42.

———. *The Satanic Verses*. London and New York: Penguin, 1988.

Rustomji, Roshni. "Rhodabeh." *Literary Review* 29.4 (1986): 527–37.

Rustomji-Kerns, Roshni. "Expatriates, Immigrants, and Literature: Three South Asian Women Writers." *Massachusetts Review* 29.4 (1988): 655–65.

Seth, Vikram. *The Golden Gate*. New York: Random House, 1986.

Spivak, Gayatri Chakravorty. *In Other Worlds: Essays in Cultural Politics*. New York and London: Methuen, 1987.

Suleri, Sara. *Meatless Days*. Chicago and London: University of Chicago Press, 1989.

———. "Naipaul's Arrival." *Yale Journal of Criticism* 2.1 (1988): 25–50.

Sullivan, Rosemary. "Who Are the Immigrant Writers and What Have They Done?" *Globe and Mail*, 17 October 1987, E1.

PART IV

Representations and Self-Representations

16

Creating One's Self: The Eaton Sisters

Amy Ling

The story is no longer about the things that have happened to men and women and how they have reacted to them; instead it is about how the subjective and collective meanings of women and men as categories of identity have been constructed. If identities change over time and are relative to different contexts, then we cannot use simple models of socialization that see gender as the more or less stable product of early childhood education in the family and the school.

—Joan Wallace Scott

Consciousness is never fixed, never attained once and for all because discursive boundaries change with historical conditions.

—Teresa de Laurentis

Selves which are coherent, seamless, bounded, and whole are indeed illusions. . . . You are not an 'I' untouched by context, rather you are defined by context. One could argue that identity and context are inseparable.

—Dorinne Kondo

THESE THREE feminist scholars—a historian, a film theoretician, and an anthropologist—all iterate what has by now become almost a truism: that the self is not a fixed entity but a fluid, changing construct or creation determined by context or historical conditions and particularly by power relationships.

Nowhere do we find this phenomenon more clearly, even literally, demonstrated than in the choice of identity made by persons of mixed race. Unhampered by physical features which may declare a particular exterior identity at odds with interior realities, mixed-race people, particularly those combining Caucasian and Asian races, are free to choose the identity or identities that suit a particular historical moment. Not only are more choices open to them than to people of monoracial ancestry, but these choices are fluid and may change during one lifetime. The story of the Eaton sisters provides a striking illustration of identity as a conscious creation of the self.

As far as our research has uncovered to date, Asian American fiction may be said to have had its beginning with the publication of Sui Sin Far's first short story, "The Gamblers," in the February 1896 issue of *Fly Leaf* and with Onoto Watanna's first novel *Miss Nume of Japan* in 1899.[1] If we use an author's ethnic origin as an identifying criterion to classify her writing, then we may say, without qualms, that Chinese American fiction began with Sui Sin Far, but we may not say that Japanese American literature began with Onoto Watanna. In fact, we would have to say that *Miss Nume of Japan* was the first Chinese American novel and that the twelve other "Japanese" novels of Onoto Watanna should be classified, despite their themes and settings, as Chinese American fiction (Cheung and Yogi ix), for Sui Sin Far and Onoto Watanna were two of the fourteen children of a Chinese woman, Grace Trefusis, and her English husband, Edward Eaton. Sui Sin Far was the pseudonym of Edith Maude Eaton, and Onoto Watanna was her younger sister (Lillie) Winnifred Eaton (Babcock) (Reeve).[2] Thus, it is a fact that the two texts named above were published in the years cited and that Asian American fiction, as far as we know, had its start with those texts, but it is also a fact that the ethnicity of one of the authors was very much a fiction.

The lesson of the Eaton sisters is a lesson in the permeability of the boundaries of the self. In *Between Worlds: Women Writers of Chinese Ancestry*, I have traced the context and historical conditions of the turn of the century as background to a discussion of the Eaton sisters' autobiographical and fictional writing. A brief review may be necessary and useful, but this paper will focus on the creation of the sisters' separate identities through their individual choices of pseudonyms and persona. Setting Winnifred Eaton into the context of contemporareous pseudonymous writers will shed new light on her choice of a persona and enable us to read this choice as a biographical enactment of the literary trickster.

The choice of a pseudonym is an act of self-creation, a choice of identity. Pseudonyms are chosen for a variety of reasons, as Joseph Clarke has pointed out in the brief introduction to his reference book on the subject. In theater and film, a stage name is chosen because it conveys more glamour, a more attractive image than the name one was born with, such as Marilyn Monroe for Norma Jean Mortenson and Cary Grant instead of Archibald Leach. In politics, one may be motivated by fear of persecution or discovery, as was Dzhugashvili when he took the name Stalin. Among writers, particularly prevalent in the nineteenth century, one could change one's sex and be more readily published. More women took men's names, of course, than vice versa; however, Clarke mentions one William Sharp who published romantic novels as Fiona Macleoud. Sharp fabricated a biographical entry for Macleoud that was published in *Who's Who* at the turn of the century, as Winnifred Eaton would later do for Onoto Watanna. Literary historian Karl Miller has described the 1880s and 1890s as "an age tormented by genders and pronouns, by pen-names, by the identity of authors" (209).

For both of the Eaton sisters, the choice of a pseudonym was a cloak to mask their patronymic and to emphasize their matronymic and for both, even Edith, though to a lesser extent than her sister, the pen-name was a contextual construct. Though biologically half Chinese through their mother, the Eaton sisters were culturally English and Canadian. In her 1909 autobiographical essay "Leaves from the Mental Portfolio of an Eurasian," Edith relates that their mother as a child was adopted by an English couple, educated in English schools and always dressed in Western clothes. Edith and five siblings were born in England before the family immigrated to America, arriving in Hudson City, New York in the early 1870s and finally settling in Montreal, Quebec, where Winnifred was born. Edith writes that at age six when she saw her first Chinese workmen, "uncouth specimens of their race, dressed in working blouses and pantaloons with queues hanging down their backs, I recoil with a sense of shock" (126). In their childhood home in Montreal, their mother read them Tennyson's *Idylls of the King*; the children took parts and performed minidramas. Several children wrote poetry, but all communication within the family was in English. Edith notes that when she began her work in the Chinese community, one drawback was that "save for a few phrases, I am unacquainted with my mother tongue." Furthermore, "the Americanized Chinamen actually laugh in my face when I tell them that I am of their race" (131).

Nonetheless, since only three Chinese women resided in Montreal in the 1870s, Grace Eaton's ethnicity colored all, and the perception of outsiders was that this was a Chinese family. To be Chinese at this period and for several preceding decades was to be considered subhuman by the dominant society. After the Civil War had abolished black slave labor, workers by the thousands were imported from China to complete the transcontinental railroad and to supply agricultural labor. However, in the 1870s, when an economic depression ensued, Chinese laborers became the scapegoat. The ambivalence of North America's attitude toward the Chinese is clear in the words of a Montana journalist, published in *The Mountanian*, March 27, 1873: "We don't mind hearing of a Chinaman being killed now and then, but it has been coming too thick of late. . . . Soon there will be a scarcity of Chinese cheap labor in the country. . . . Don't kill them unless they deserve it, but when they do—why kill 'em lots" (Lyman 165). On the one hand, the Chinese were desirable as cheap labor; on the other hand, they were like vermin, deserving of extermination.

In this hostile climate, prevalent throughout Canada and the United States, the Eaton sisters grew to maturity. Perceived as Chinese, they were subject to all the abuse heaped on that group. One sister, Grace, reported that a girl at school refused to sit next to her because she was Chinese. A young man in their dancing class said he'd "rather marry a pig than a girl with Chinese blood in her veins" (Far 130). Years later, a dinner conversation recorded in Edith's autobiographical essay demonstrates the continued persistence of sinophobia. Edith, then in the United States, had just obtained a position "in a little [midwest] town away off on the north shore of a big lake." Among those at the dinner table were her new employer, her new landlady, the town clerk, and a young girl. A trainload of Chinese workers passing through the town sparked the ensuing conversation:

> My employer shakes his rugged head. "Somehow or other," says he, "I cannot reconcile myself to the thought that the Chinese are humans like ourselves. They may have immortal souls, but their faces seem so utterly devoid of expression that I cannot help but doubt."
>
> "Souls," echoes the town clerk. "Their bodies are enough for me. A Chinaman is, in my eyes, more repulsive than a nigger."
>
> "They always give me such a creepy feeling," puts in the young girl with a laugh.
>
> "Now I wouldn't have one in my house," declares my landlady.
>
> "Now the Japanese are different altogether. There is something bright and likeable about those men," continues Mr. K. (Far 129)

Edith, though tempted to keep silent after this conversation, spoke out, identified herself as Chinese and left that town—an act of courage and defiance. She made it her life's work to defend her mother's much maligned race, and a Chinese pen-name served her purpose well. Winnifred, however, chose to be the admired "oriental."

To understand why the Japanese were admired, we have only to look at a few facts of history. First, there were few Japanese in the United States in the late nineteenth century and therefore they were not an alternate labor source posing an economic threat to white workers. Second, Japan, an island empire, had fought and defeated two large continental nations—China in 1895 and Russia in 1905. Japanese militarism was seen as the noble embodiment of the samurai tradition until it was directed against the United States decades later, at Pearl Harbor.

Since the Chinese and Japanese were indistinguishable to Western eyes and since Edith was already mining the Chinese vein, Winnifred Eaton chose to be Japanese. Her choice paid off, in the form of astonishing success. She published hundreds of short stories in national magazines and two dozen novels that were nearly all bestsellers, most published by Harpers. Several novels were translated into many European languages. Her second novel, *A Japanese Nightingale* (1901), was adapted as a play and performed on Broadway in 1903 to compete with David Belasco's long-running *Madame Butterfly*.[3] From 1924 to 1931 Onoto Watanna wrote scripts for Hollywood and for a period was chief scenarist for Universal Studios. She had a play produced in Paris, "The Road to Honor," and worked on such early films as "Show Boat," "Phantom of the Opera," and "Shanghai Lady" before retiring with her second husband, Francis Reeve, to Calgary, Alberta.

Winnifred Eaton was the author of her own life story in supplying *Who's Who* with the following "facts": born in 1879 in Nagasaki, Japan to a Japanese noblewoman. Her actual birth year was 1875, her birthplace Montreal and her mother, of course, Chinese. In a very literal way, Winnifred created herself, drawing no distinctions between her books and her life, and in fact, extending her fiction-making skills into her life. Her keen marketing instinct and sense of timing were precisely accurate, for orientalism was in full flower at the turn of the century. Her sense of the importance of ethnic validity as manifested in a name, however, was so strong that it overshadowed her belief in her imagination and her storytelling powers, both of which were considerable. In midcareer, for example, Winnifred submitted a novel in Irish American dialect, *The Diary of Delia*, under the name Winnifred Mooney. The publisher, Doubleday, chose to publish this book under her well-known pseudonym, Onoto Watanna. Thus, for the first, and undoubtedly only, time in literary history, we have a novel written in Irish American dialect by a Chinese Eurasian Canadian published under a Japanese name. (In so blatantly disregarding boundaries and facts, she has given literary scholars a major headache: how do we classify this anomaly?)

In her excellent study, *Dark Twins: Imposture and Identity in Mark Twain's America*, Susan Gillman differentiates between British writers whose pen-names were neutral and innocuous, such as George Eliot or Acton, Currer and Ellis Bell, and Americans who chose names that dramatized and fostered a personality cult, such as Artemus Ward, Petroleum V. Nasby, Josh Billings, and Mark Twain. She quotes Walter Benjamin, who criticized this tendency still manifested in our present-day film industry: "The cult of the movie star . . . preserves not the unique aura of the person but 'the spell of the personality,' the phony spell of a commodity" (29). Clearly Onoto Watanna's name had become a commodity too valuable to ignore.

Sui Sin Far is Cantonese for narcissus, also known as "Chinese Lily." Onoto Watanna sounds Japanese but is not a legitimate Japanese name.[4] Each sister selected a pseudonym to authenticate the subject matter she had chosen to make her own. It was a choice not all of their siblings made. With English names and racially indeterminate facial features, the racial identification of the Eaton offspring, on reaching adulthood, varied. The eldest son, Edward, denied his Chinese heritage, marrying an aristocratic white woman who had little to do with her parents-in-law and joining a Montreal rifle club whose members were exclusively Anglo-Canadian. One sister, May, is believed to be the Eurasian described in "Leaves" in this fashion:[5]

> Her face is plastered with a thick white coat of paint and her eyelids and eyebrows are blackened so that the shape of her eyes and the whole expression of her face is changed. . . . Living for many years among the working class, she had heard little but abuse of the Chinese. It is not difficult in a land like California, for a half Chinese, half white girl to pass as one of Spanish or Mexican origin. This the poor child does, tho she lives in nervous dread of being "discovered." (131)

Though their specific choices differed, all of the Eaton children were responding to the same hostile environment. Despite the differences in their specific choices—passing as Mexican, as English, as Japanese, as Chinese—there were essentially only two responses to their embattled position: resistance or accommodation. Edith was the only one among fourteen children to choose resistance, the more difficult and more noble path.

Conventional wisdom decrees that "honesty is the best policy," that integrity and truthfulness are noble while lying and accommodation are cowardly and condemnable. And yet, should accommodation always be condemned? If we look more closely at the situation, can we not deconstruct this hierachy?

We can begin by noting that in nature and in warfare, for example, the fittest survive, and survival depends on adaptation to one's environment. Camouflage is not only a legitimate strategy but a clever and critical one. Was it not the British soldiers' red coats and straight military lines that made them easy targets during the Revolutionary War? Is not the broad-leaved, thick-trunked oak that stands firm against the wind more easily blown over and uprooted than the thin, pliant, hollow-centered bamboo? Ironically, Edith in asserting her Chinese ancestry was like the English oak, while Winnifred, in assuming a Japanese persona, was more like the bamboo, regarded by the Chinese as a symbol of nobility. What Rosenblatt noted as true of Afro-Americans like Malcolm X also held true for Asian Americans like Winnifred Eaton: "Recognizing an elusive and unpredictable situation, they adapt to it for survival, becoming masters of both physical and psychological disguise, in part to avoid their hunters" (175).

In *Dark Twins*, Gillman represents "that process of continual self-construction and destruction by someone who is both critic and child of his culture" (13). Though Gillman is writing of Samuel Clemens, this was equally true of Winnifred Eaton. In assuming a Japanese persona, and making liberal use of orientalist materials in her novels, she was a child of her culture and yet, since all was a conscious fantasy and in time a disillusionment, she was a critic of it as well.[6] The dark twin is a trope for the Other within the Self, and the pseudonym is a manifestation of that inner split. Though Gillman recognizes the moral dimensions of imposture, she sees it primarily as a useful strategy for the writer:

> Since "posture" already implies posing or faking, "imposture" is the pose of a pose, the fake of a fake. The word implies no possible return to any point of origin. Synonyms for imposture complicate this ambiguity by distinguishing degrees of intentionality on the part of the impostor. "Deceit" is strongly condemnatory because it refers to "purposeful" deceiving or misleading, whereas "counterfeit" and "fake" may or may not condemn "depending on culpable intent to deceive." Thus imposture raises but does not resolve complex connections between morality and intentionality. Its multiple confusions leave room for lawyers, confidence men, and, ultimately, the writer himself to erase boundaries and circumvent the law, making suspect the premise that knowledge is possible—by legal or any other means. (6)

Further, Gillman writes: "The confidence man presides over the comic tale as hero, not villain. Simon Suggs, a character created by Johnson J. Hooper, another humorist, proclaims in his favorite motto, 'It is good to be shifty in a new country'" (22).

It is crucial to remember that the trickster figure from the perspective of the disempowered is a hero, not a villain. In situations when power is unequal and legally obtained justice is impossible, outsmarting the system is the only means of resistance available. In folk tales of Native Americans and African Americans, the trickster figure—despite what would normally be considered faults—chicanery, cheating, and lying—has the sympathy of the audience because it is through this clever deviousness and deception that unjust situations too large and too difficult for the small person to handle are overcome and victory or a balance of the scales is achieved. In this inversion of established power, the powerless person may take vicarious delight. Furthermore, in contrast to the flexibility and variousness of the trickster, the morally sanctioned stance of his/her opponent at the top of the established hierarchy appears foolishly rigid.

Thus, we may read the novels of Onoto Watanna as the brain children of Asian America's first trickster hero.

Undoubtedly Suggs was not the only person who realized that a new country provides a fresh start, releasing one from the constraints of the past, from the restraints of family and of history. One has the freedom to create oneself anew, and the West, both in Canada and the United States, in the late nineteenth and early twentieth centuries was still a relatively "new" country. Under the big tolerant skies of the prairies, and in valleys protected by tall mountains, anything seemed possible; one had only to assert it. Winnifred Eaton had at least two well-known contemporaries in Western Canada who, like her, assumed personaes unsubstantiated or not wholly substantiated by facts.

The first of these was Grey Owl (1888–1938). He claimed to be the son of an Apache Indian and a Scot and achieved an international reputation as a writer/naturalist, whom the London *Times* called a Canadian Thoreau. Unlike Thoreau, who spent only two years at Walden Pond and was always within walking distance of Concord, Grey Owl lived much of his adult life far from civilization and in close harmony with the animals of the woods, particularly beavers. His love of beavers and their regard for him were captured, incredibly, on film that showed the beavers swimming back and forth bringing sticks to repair his cabin. Initially a trapper, he was convinced by his Iroquois wife, Anahareo, of the need for conservation, the central theme of his writing and of their work. The couple's success in creating a sanctuary for beavers in northern Quebec, described in Grey Owl's book, *Pilgrims of the Wild* (1930), attracted the attention of the Canadian government, which then appointed him Honorary Park Warden and built a home for Anahareo, Grey Owl, and their beavers at Lake Ajawaan in Prince Albert National Park, Saskatchewan. His many articles and four books were so popular that he made two highly successful lecture tours of England and the United States in 1935–36 and 1937–38, concluding with a lecture before the royal family at Buckingham Palace. After his death in 1938, a great public furor followed the discovery that Grey Owl had had no Indian blood at all and was born Archibald Stansfeld Belany in Hastings, England.

Reared by two maiden aunts and his grandmother, Belany had an unhappy childhood and a passion for North American Indians. In his late teens, he immigrated to Canada, became a guide and packer in Northern Ontario, and lived six years with a band of Ojibwa Indians on Bear Island in Lake Temagami. By his own account, he was adopted into this tribe and given the name Grey Owl. In 1910 he married an Ojibwa woman, Angela Eguana, but left the tribe in 1912 to serve in World War I and was wounded in service. While recuperating in England in 1917, he married his childhood sweetheart, Constance Holmes. This marriage was brief, for he soon returned to Canada where, in 1926 he married Anahareo. This marriage was the turning point of his life. After his death, Anahareo wrote two books about him, *My Life with Grey Owl* (1940) and the more revealingly titled *Devil in Deerskins* (1972). His grave is beside his cabin on Lake Ajawaan in Prince Albert National Park. The original cross with his English name was replaced with a stone bearing the name Grey Owl, as if to assert that the identity he had chosen and created was of greater lasting significance than the one thrust upon him at birth.

The other notable persona of this period was Long Lance, another celebrated Indian, whose years (1919–27) in Calgary overlapped with Winnifred's. He like Sui Sin Far, began as a journalist. In Calgary, he discovered his calling when he began to visit Indian reserves in the outskirts of Calgary and then published articles about the plight of the various Indian tribes of western Canada. In 1922 he was adopted into the Blackfoot tribe and given the name Buffalo Child, a warrior known for his bravery. In 1923, Long Lance staged a kidnapping of the mayor of Calgary as a publicity stunt for the Calgary Stampede. His biographer, Donald Smith, describes the event in this way:

> Long Lance with seven chiefs and a healthy assortment of Blackfoot, Stoney and Sarcee warriors all painted and feathered and mounted on war ponies charged down 7th Avenue to City Hall. Led by Long Lance, they entered the mayor's office, ordered him to vacate his chair and installed Running Rabbit (who spoke no English) as mayor. Photographers recorded the "event." Mayor Webster was tied to a horse and ridden to the center of the city (8th Avenue and 1st Street West). The Indian mayor officially adopted the captive white mayor as Blackfoot, naming him Chief Crowfoot, and then returned the charge of the city to the white chief who was now one of them. (110)

Though one cannot help thinking of this as an elaborate charade invented and relished by boys who have refused to grow up, Long Lance carried off the stunt with such aplomb that the story "made a great splash in Eastern Canada" and in the United States (Smith,

106). He had himself photographed astride an Indian pinto attired in white buckskins, mocassins, and full feather war headdress. When an Indian was sought to play the starring role in "The Silent Enemy," a silent film about Indians, Long Lance was called to Hollywood. Despite his public high jinks and celebrity, his private life was unfulfilled; he never married, cut himself off from his family, had no close friends, and shot himself on March 20, 1932 at the estate of Anita Baldwin, a rich philanthropist, outside Los Angeles. He was forty-two years old.

Long Lance was born Sylvester Long in Winston-Salem, North Carolina on December 1, 1890 to parents who claimed exclusively white and Indian blood. His mother was three-quarters white and one-quarter Croatan. Despite the family's denial, however, photographs of his father and brother show them to have strongly African features, though Long Lance himself, in the photographs, seemed to have straight hair. Smith explains that discrimination against black people in the American south was so oppressive that Sylvester Long "got out and asserted his Indian heritage." Claiming Cherokee blood, Sylvester Long gained admission to Carlyle Indian School, though when Carlyle School investigated further, the Cherokee nation disclaimed any knowledge of him. After graduation, he applied to West Point but decided instead to join the Royal Canadian Air Force. Here, again, he ran into difficulties concerning his claim of an Indian identity and finally decided to go west in search of his fortune.

What all four—Mark Twain, Onoto Watanna, Grey Owl, and Long Lance—had in common, in addition to the use of pseudonyms, of course, was the means by which all made their living. To be a good writer, one must be good storyteller. Where does one draw the boundary between fiction and lying? And, to play the devil's advocate, why must storytelling cease when one's own life is concerned? Who among us does not enjoy the pleasures of "hamming it up" and role-playing?

Furthermore, according to William James humbugging may be a universal trait. In "Final Impressions of a Psychic Researcher," James asserts that the medium's "will to personate" raises "questions about our subconscious constitution and its curious tendency to humbug." He tentatively concludes that far from being uncommon, "every sort of person is liable to it [humbugging], or to something equivalent to it" (Gilman 163–64). Is this statement an indictment of the human race or a description of one of our imaginative and unique pleasures?

Is the assumption of a persona merely telling a useless lie or is it pointing out a useful truth about the values of the society in which we live?

I would argue that, in cases where no harm to others is done by the deception, assuming a persona is a form of defiance to free one's self from the fetters applied by a society concerned with the insignificancies of skin color and eye shape. To exploit, consciously and cynically, the prejudices and stereotypes of the dominent society in its misperceptions of the racial minority in its midst is one step toward exploding the prejudices. As the grandfather in Ellison's *Invisible Man* advised his grandson, "Agree 'em to death and destruction" (497). Clearly, though her own personal stance differed from her younger sister's, Edith Eaton wrote in her defense in "Leaves":

> The Americans, having for many years manifested a much higher regard for the Japanese than for the Chinese, several half Chinese young men and women, thinking to advance themselves, both in a social and business sense, pass as Japanese. They continue to be known as Eurasians; but a Japanese Eurasian does not appear in the same light as a Chinese Eurasian. The unfortunate Chinese Eurasians! Are not those who compel them to thus cringe more to be blamed than they? (Far 131)

Edith Eaton makes a strong and irrefutable point. The creation of a more acceptable identity, particularly in the cases of Winnifred Eaton/Onoto Watanna and Sylvester Long/Long Lance, is indeed a defensive reaction to an unacceptable embattled situation: the rejection and devaluation of the biological self. For this provocation, the society that made such harsh judgments in the first place should be called to account.

NOTES

I wish to acknowledge my indebtedness to the Asian/American Center at Queen's College, CUNY for the 1989–90 Rockefeller Fellowship that enabled me to do the research for this chapter; to Jack Tchen for his encouragement and insightful suggestions; and to Jean Tener and Apollonia Steele, archivists at the University of Calgary Library, for introducing me to Long Lance and Grey Owl and for general assistance beyond the call of duty.

1. I am indebted to Annette-White Parks for this correction. In an earlier article, "Revelation and Mask: Autobiographies of the Eaton Sisters" I mistakenly cited "A Chinese Ishmael" (*Overland Monthly*, July 1899) as Sui Sin Far's first story.

2. Lillie appears on her birth certificate as her first name with Winnifred as a middle name; however, she apparently never used Lillie. Her grandson, Paul Rooney, who lived with her, was surprised to learn of this first name when Winnifred's birth certificate was retrieved in the spring of 1990. Bertrand Whitcomb Babcock was Winnifred Eaton's first husband, from 1901–17; the marriage ended in divorce. Her marriage to Francis Fournier Reeve lasted from 1917 until her death in 1954.

3. It is not generally known that Puccini's popular opera began as a short story by John Luther Long that appeared in *Century* magazine in 1898. From Long's story, David Belasco created a one-act curtain raiser, "Madame Butterfly," so popular that it remained in production at different theaters in New York City from 1900 until 1905. Enchanted by the play, Puccini bought the rights and created his world famous opera.

4. Onoto was the name of a pen made in London or the United States (the archival materials contain contradictory information) and imported to Japan from 1907 until 1955, except during World War II (says one source) and sold in the Maruzen Book Store 1923–27 (says another). According to Yoshiro Ando, a scholar from Fujisawa City, Japan who wrote a thesis on Onoto Watanna and began a correspondence with Doris Rooney, Winnifred Eaton's daughter, the Onoto pen was used by "almost all novelists and poets in the Meiji era. . . . A professor of English wrote me that 'Onoto pens produced the westernized culture in our country'" (letter from Yoshiro Ando to Doris Rooney, dated June 17, 1971). In his thesis, Ando wrote that Onoto was the name of a character in "From the Eastern Country," a work by another Eurasian writer, Lafcadio Hearn. Ando goes on the say, presumably receiving his information from Doris Rooney, that Winnifred Eaton was asked by the manufacturer of the pen, Thomas de la Rue Company, for permission to use her name; she gave them permission and disclaimed any credit or royalties.

5. This is the hypothesis of L. Charles Laferriere, grandson of Edith and Winnifred's sister Agnes. A photograph of May in his possession, shows a young woman with heavily darkened eyelids, which would seem to corroborate M. Laferriere's theory.

6. I use the term "orientalist" in the sense defined and discussed by Edward Said in his classic study of cultural imperialism, *Orientalism* (New York, 1978). See also Zhang Longxi, "The Myth of the Other: China in the Eyes of the West" in *Critical Inquiry* 15 (1988) 108–131. Zhang takes Foucault and Borges, among others, to task for perpetuating the myth of the strangeness and illogicality of the Chinese.

WORKS CITED

Cheung, King-Kok and Stan Yogi. *Asian American Literature: An Annotated Bibliography*. New York: Modern Language Association, 1988.

Clarke, Joseph F. *Pseudonyms*. Nashville: T. Nelson, 1977.
De Laurentis, Teresa. *Feminist Studies/Critical Studies*. Bloomington: Indiana University Press, 1988.
Ellison, Ralph. *Invisible Man*. New York: Signet, 1952.
Far, Sui Sin. "Leaves from the Mental Portfolio of an Eurasian." *Independent*, January 21, 1909. 125–32.
Gillman, Susan. *Dark Twins: Imposture and Identity in Mark Twain's America*. Chicago: University of Chicago Press, 1989.
Kondo, Dorinne. *Crafting Selves: Power, Gender, and Discourses of Identity in a Japanese Workplace*. Chicago: University of Chicago Press, 1990.
Ling, Amy. *Between Worlds: Women Writers of Chinese Ancestry*. New York: Pergamon Press, 1990.
Lyman, Stanford. "Strangers in the City: The Chinese in the Urban Frontier." In *Roots: An Asian American Reader*, ed. Amy Tachiki, Eddie Wong, Franklin Odo, Buck Wong. Los Angeles: University of California, Los Angeles Asian American Studies Center, 1971. 159–87.
Miller, Karl. *Doubles: Studies in Literary History*. New York: Oxford University Press, 1985.
Oxford Companion to Canadian Literature, ed. William Toye. Toronto/New York/Oxford: Oxford University Press, 1983.
Rosenblatt, Roger. "Black Autobiography: Life as the Death Weapon." In *Autobiography: Essays Theoretical and Critical*, ed. James Olney. Princeton, N.J.: Princeton University Press, 1980.
Said, Edward. *Orientalism*. New York: Vintage, 1979.
Scott, Joan Wallach. *Gender and the Politics of History*. New York: Columbia University Press, 1988.
Smith, Donald. *Long Lance: The True Story of an Imposter*. Lincoln: University of Nebraska Press, 1983.
Watanna, Onoto. *The Diary of Delia*. New York: Page, 1907.
———. *A Japanese Nightingale*. New York: Harper, 1901.
———. *Marion: A Story of an Artist's Model by Herself and the Author of Me*. New York: Watt, 1916.
———. *Me, A Book of Remembrance*. New York: Century, 1915.
———. *Miss Nume of Japan*. Chicago: Rand, McNally, 1899.
White-Parks, Annette. "Sui Sin Far: Writer on the Chinese-Anglo Borders of North America, 1885–1914." Ph.D. dissertation, Washington State University, Program in American Studies, 1991.

17

The Production of Chinese American Tradition: Displacing American Orientalist Discourse

David Leiwei Li

CONTEMPORARY Chinese American literary production arises as a consensual but not necessarily consciously collective endeavor to claim legitimacy in the masterpiece theater of American literature. I use "contemporary" to bracket the last three decades, when a new generation of writers emerged. I choose "Chinese American" over "Asian American" because the latter umbrella term, coined in the 1960s to promote political solidarity, may diminish the specificity of various Asian American cultural groups. I adopt "literary production" to emphasize the material circumstances that are part and parcel of artistic activity instead of "creation," with its conventional connotation of the sovereignty of individual talent. By "consensual but not necessarily consciously collective endeavor," I mean that, in spite of the common desire to insert themselves into an American literary canon, contemporary Chinese American authors disagree on what should constitute the form and theme of their works. For example, the now-famous controversy over *The Woman Warrior* is just an indication of this persistent authorial as well as critical difference. Though a discussion of the specific dispute is not within the scope of this paper, the type of investigation I have in mind is a related enterprise. To be truly meaningful, any interpretation of Chinese American texts, I contend, ought to deal with the specificities of Chinese American history. Without knowledge of the political and cultural nexus in operation, the concept of a Chinese American literary tradition makes little sense. With this purpose in mind, I undertake a dual task: first, outlining a history of two contemporaneous discourses, and second, theorizing the making of a Chinese American tradition in light of that history. While I feel obliged to contextualize, this essay does not (and should not lead the reader to) view literary production as a pale and passive reflection of history, but rather as an active engagement with it. Since historicization of the political unconscious and elaboration of cultural erasure are the bases upon which contemporary Chinese American writers start their work, so will they be for this critical project.

The history of American writing on/about the Chinese was significantly marked by the nature of the Sino-American exchange around the mid-nineteenth century. First, the signing of the 1844 Wanghsia treaty granted the United States all the advantages the British had gained over China after the Opium War. Second, large-scale Chinese immigration to America began partly as a result of foreign invasions that subsequently dislocated the Chinese domestic economy. American entry into China, with its "trader bugs, diplomat bugs and missionary bugs," to borrow Twain's "Fable of the Yellow Terror," gave birth to a powerful and hegemonic American discourse (Twain 369).[1] It provided a conceptual framework for viewing the Chinese and, by both extension and confusion, the Chinese American, a framework I call American Orientalist discourse. Meantime, Chinese entry into the United States gave rise to a powerless, private discourse practiced by members of the immigrant community. It was a product of Chinese interaction with American reality and an indispensable part of their creative life. I will call this Chinese American discourse. For almost a century and a half, these two streams of cultural crosscurrents have existed simultaneously. However, because the two discourses evolved at the historical juncture when America emerged as a power in an imperialist global system while China's self-authorized centrality no longer held, their relationship is characteristically asymmetrical. Therefore, there is no true dialogue between the two; they coexist in a predetermined mode of domination and resistance.

American Orientalist discourse originates from a Eurocentric desire to appropriate the Asiatic Other for the consolidation of Self. Thus, depending on its needs, it swings like a pendulum between the extremely good and the extremely bad renditions of the Chinese/Chinese American. For certain founding fathers of the United States, such as Benjamin Franklin and Thomas Jefferson, China was at once a source of technical innovation and a model of political and commercial isolation (Hunt 32–35). In nineteenth-century New England minds, the Confucian social order strangely inspired transcendental manifestos. Ralph Waldo Emerson, for instance, hailed Confucius as the "sage of the Absolute East," "the Washington of philosophy, the Moderator" (Christy 129). But the pendulum shifted when Emersonian euphoria was displaced by an American missionary rhetoric that deplored, in the words of Bridgman and Parker, "the gross darkness of the [Chinese] people" and its land of "moral wilderness" (Hunt 35). The celebrated superiority of Chinese civilization vanished overnight, and the use value of the Chinese remained in their provision of skilled labor to help fulfill America's manifest destiny. As Herman Melville's Ishmael comments: "in the construction of the American Canals and Railroads . . . the native American liberally provides the brains, the rest of the world as generously supplying the muscles" (127). "The Heathen Chinee" soon emerged to serve as a scapegoat for the economic crisis of the times. When Bill Nye's con game was spoiled by the inscrutable "childish" Ah Sin, he burst out in anger, "we are ruined by Chinese labor." Regardless of Bret Harte's self-proclaimed good intentions, the Sinophobic lynch mob marched toward the Chinese in San Francisco, chanting his infamous lines (Harte 85–89). Here, representation becomes reality in what seems to be a convergence of popular sentiment and poetic license. In a single stroke, American Orientalist discourse prompted antagonism toward the Chinese *and* furthered its own legitimation. What seemed to be a harmless literary discourse ultimately was institutionalized in legal discourse: the 1882 Chinese Exclusion Law validated white racism by severely restricting Chinese immigration.

The omnipresence of American Orientalist discourse was such that Chinese American discourse was reduced to a near absence. Chinese theaters, Chinese "talk stories," and the plethora of Chinese newspapers that developed in Chinese America as the community's willful opposition to white suppression of their culture were conveniently wiped out of public consciousness. Not one Chinese newspaper was mentioned in a twenty-page survey of nineteenth-century immigrant journalism in a recent reconstruction of American literary history though such documentation is readily available (Sollors; Lo and Lai). The nineteenth-century Chinese American *Muk Yu* (Wooden Fish) lyrics that created a crucible of folk sensibility, the English-Chinese phrase books that become an internal manual of strategy for Chinese American survival, and the short stories by Chinese American writer Sui Sin Far offering images of self in prestigious mainstream journals, the Cantonese rhymes of early San Francisco, and the prison poetry of Angel Island, all these and more, did not become part of American intellectual property until recent Chinese American writers and critics unearthed them and fought for their niches in the discursive domain (Chan; Solberg; Lai, Lim, and Yung; Hom).

While such Chinese American writings located their experience upon American soil, American Orientalist discourse perpetuated its fanciful views of China, regardless of the Chinese American presence in this country. If Ezra Pound's projection of China claims an American poetic filiation, Pearl Buck's penetration of China opens a new province of American paternal humanism, which, while emphasizing the common humanity of an alien race, points to the need to improve their lot with American missionary tutelage. The pendulum of the discourse took another swing when it became "important to see behind the mask and realize," in Albert W. Palmer's words, "how genuinely likable, how overwhelmingly human the Oriental is" (Kim 59). This shift of American Orientalist discourse led to a wave of Chinese American works that take the glorification of Chinese civilization to be the main agenda.[2] The assimilationist effort was largely a trapped and cornered reaction—the life of Chinese Americans without political rights is subhuman and a living death—and the wish to affirm Chinese humanity by resorting to an unpracticed ancestral high culture is an understandable but still pathetic gesture. The identification with China seemed more to reinforce the popular conception of Chinese Americans as foreigners in the United States than to intervene effectively against the hegemonic marginalization of the political and cultural lives of Chinese Americans. Nevertheless, a survival instinct persisted for the next few decades. When the exclusion law of 1882 was finally rescinded in 1943 because political exigency required that American and China become allies in the war against Japan, Chinese American writing was boosted to confirm the discursive claim of the American Dream. Though the autobiographical writings of Jade Snow Wong and Pardee Lowe's generation attempted to depict a Chinese American humanity different from stereotypical renditions, in turning their works into texts of racial uplift they could barely overcome the power of hegemonic appropriation.

When contemporary Chinese American writings emerged in the late 1960s and the early 1970s, its authors had to confront the dual burden of at once subverting an American Orientalist discourse based on their cultural oppression and reconstructing a Chinese American tradition that would mark their cultural liberation. A dramatization of the Chinese American writer's condition appears in Frank Chin's *The Chickencoop Chinaman*. In an extended metaphysical conceit Chin's protagonist, Tam, voices his superimposed ontological alienation:

> My dear in the beginning there was the Word! And there was me. And the Word was CHINAMAN. And there was me. . . . I lived the Word! The Word is my heritage. . . . I am the natural born ragmouth speaking the motherless bloody tongue. No real language of my own to make sense with, so out comes everybody else's trash that don't conceive. . . . Born? No! Crashed! Not born. Stamped! Not born! Created! . . . No more born than nylon or acrylic. For I am a Chinaman! A miracle synthetic! Drip dry and machine washable. (6–8)

The parody of Biblical authority and the polemic against the arbitrary and artificial construction of the Chinese American by American Orientalist discourse can hardly be mistaken. What underlies these lines of agony and wrath, however, is the desire to claim a Chinese American language that is self-referential and that will relate to others. The play in many ways textualizes this hidden impulse in Tam's repeated and often-times failed quests. Though Tam is able to reject the story of Helen Keller because he finds its analogy in the model minority thesis about his ethnic community, he is susceptible to the seductive "Lone Ranger," who is "the CHINESE AMERICAN BOY of the radio [he's] looked for" (Chin, 1981, 32). Not until the Ranger shoots him in the hand does Tam awaken from his lifelong idolatry. Disillusioned with this white hero of his childhood, Tam nonetheless continues his search for the father of a black light-heavyweight champ, an aggressive antithesis of white authority, if you will, only to find himself immersed in yet another unreliable legend. One solution to such misidentifications of role models, the play suggests, is to look into the stories of Chinese America. "Turn off them radios and listen in the kitchen! My grandmaw told me," Tam recalls fondly towards the end of the play, "in the Old West when Chinamans was the only electricity and all the thunder in the mountains . . . sometimes she heard a train. A Chinaman borne, high stepping Iron Moonhunter, liftin eagles with its breath!" (65). What Tam had rejected earlier as the Chinaman "not born" but "created" and "crashed" has now interestingly been resurrected as "a Chinaman borne," an auspicious birth that can only be understood in terms of Tam's self definition. Once he breaks from the discursive imprisonment of American Orientalism and finds nourishment in the indigenous stories of his grandma, he transforms himself from an artificial object to an autonomous subject, a moment of self creation that effectively reverses what Chin calls the "pen[ned] up" position of being the ineffective other (Chin, 1972, 1, 5).

I wish now to use two works of Frank Chin and Maxine Hong Kingston to illustrate the power of producing tradition—the power of the textual working out of their contextual difficulties and the power of reauthorizing self and community for contemporary Chinese Americans. Though radically different in their idiosyncratic procedures, both authors engage themselves in the textual displacement of American Orientalist discourse, in the process creating a Chinese American tradition that is distinct both formally and thematically.

Frank Chin's "Confessions of the Chinatown Cowboy" (1972) enacts a narrative strategy for his particular discursive condition. In other words, his is a process of making identifiable selves in the denial of non-slaves.The piece opens with Ben Fee, "a bare knuckled unmasked man, a Chinaman loner out of the old West, a character out of Chinese sword-slingers, a fighter (58). The description not only displaces the stereotypical submissive Chinese American male but also questions the heroic contour of the Ranger, whose masquerade obviously lacks the candor and valor of the "Chinaman loner." With one bold, contrastive stroke, Chin immediately erects his ideal not as someone who apes the Western hero but as an alternative hero, a hero from the fighting tradition of ancient China but who belongs to the frontier of America. This image of a native hero is fascinatingly reflected in the projection of the narrative self: "My hair was long, parted in the middle," the narrator tells us, "but it was me then . . . [with] a silver vest a toothpick in my mouth and a Chinese wiseass beard making me solid affectation" (58). The conscious stylization of self is not to be assumed but to be affirmed. The narrative captures this anxious anticipation in a moment when "me" meets Ben Fee: "Everything about him shifted into a 'Who the hell are you?' when, suspecting this was Ben Fee, I said, 'Ben Fee?'" (58).

The occasion of interview has now taken a peculiar turn—it is no more an occasion in which the narrator/reporter seeks information from his subject than an occasion of reciprocal seeking. When the young man and the old man come into view of each other, it is a face to face matching. The answers to their mutual questioning are, however, not ready made—there is no assurance that being members of the same race means a natural sharing of their essence. The answers can only come through narrative structuring. Chin resolves the problem by sounding out the "code of Chinatown," both verbal and nonverbal, before applying a series of associative devices to make "Ben" and "me" connect:

> *Ben Fee and me* both from home, a generation between us, out of the town, working in white businesses that have done Chinese America bad in the past. . . . *Between us* was our awareness of our history, white racism's success with our people, and the new wave of writing about us calling white racism's success our success. . . . *Between Ben and me* it was all a matter of language, whether or not we talked, because we were Chinamen in America . . . and the most suspicious kind of Chinamen. (Italics mine, xxx. 59)

Rhetorical pairings help construct the links of "Ben and me" to make it clear that their similarity is not a matter of biological affinity but of shared social and cultural circumstances. It comes as no surprise that only after inter-viewing each other and each other's history that Chin is able to offer the following scene:

> He [Ben] stepped forward, up close to me, grinned and said, "Welcome, Chinatown Cowboy," and I was finally glad to see him. Thanks, Ben. Ride with this Chinatown Cowboy a bit, while I run off to rustle strange words and maverick up a language to write this mess in (59).

Ben's movement toward intimacy is accompanied by his act of naming while the named narrator reckons his designation by inviting his namer for a ride of language. What starts as "suspicious" seeing eventuates in a mutual recognition when the historical "Chinatown Cowboy" and "this Chinatown Cowboy" reflect each other not only in face but also in name. "*The* Chinatown Cowboy" (my italics) of the title refers therefore not to a single self but rather to a group whose collective identity can only be recognized by its members. The narrative answer to both parties' initial queries—"Who the hell are you?" and "[Are you] Ben Fee?"—is not available until this embracing affirmation of each other's name and place in their respective history. Chin has indeed "maverick[ed] up a language" that has "[made] Chinese-America APPEAR!" in the inter-viewing of a Chinese American tradition (69). The interactive authorization of "Ben Fee" and "me" is a discursive act of re-viewing a Chinese American tradition and a re-membering of a semiotic chain, once broken by the clamor of American Orientalist discourse.

It is on the basis of this re-viewed tradition that the narrator is able to deconstruct the American Orientalist discourse, Charlie Chan's sissy distortion, Tom Wolfe's "Aramco psychology," and even writings of "loyal Chinese-American citizens" that have historically made "Ben and me" disappear (63). The irony of Chin's seeming "confessions" is betrayed in the very contentious nature of his discourse. The narrator shows no reservation in his negation of prevalent Western myths of the self; neither does he hesitate to replace them with his own: "The individual rides alone, fights alone and duels man-to-man, is exercised only by fools and the badguy in Chinese movies." The narrator weighs the Western code of heroism against the Chinese, "the individual combat will go down in gang action . . . the individual needs friends. The balls of Chinese movie celebrated in Chinatown was [*sic*] gang balls and didn't really clash with John Wayne" (66). Chin's understanding of the minority's vulnerable social condition seems to lead him to an affirmation of group identity and solidarity, a conviction realized in his narrative positioning of self and community. In the inter-viewing of "Ben and me," the killing instinct of Oedipal revolt and the poetic anxiety of influence become extraneous. Instead, we see "Ben and me" as complete and complimentary selves in the trajectory of history, empowering one another in a "collective assemblage of enunciation" (Deleuze and Guattari 18).

If Frank Chin's "Confessions of the Chinatown Cowboy" is a successful narrative example of producing a Chinese American tradition, Maxine Hong Kingston's *The Woman Warrior* (1976) is a *tour de force*. While Chin challenges the discursive and institutional obliteration of Chinese America by drawing a line between what is "me" and "not me," Kingston confronts the same discursive situation by her interrogative narrative. For her, the self is foregrounded by resolving the contradiction in the subject, not only the conscious self who speaks but also the one who is spoken to: "Chinese Americans, when you try to understand what things in you are Chinese, how do you separate what is peculiar to childhood, to poverty, insanities, one family, your mother who marked your growing with stories, from what is Chinese? What is Chinese tradition and what is the movies?" (Kingston 6).[3]

The interrogative persistency of Kingston's narrator is directed at the "movies" of Orientalist America and the stories of her mother's Chinese America, two contradictory versions of reality, two competitive discourses that simultaneously summon her being. "The call would come from a bird that flew over our roof," the narrator tells us. "In the brush drawings it looks like the ideograph for 'human,' two black wings. The bird would cross the sun and lift into the mountains (which look like the ideograph 'mountain'), there parting the mist briefly that swirled opaque again" (24). The imaging of self in a bird's flight, symbolic of one's freedom and transcendence, is probably as old as literary romanticism, both Western and Eastern. What makes it new, in this instance, is the narrator's conscious merging of the image of the bird, the Chinese ideograph for human, and the humanity of the girl that "follow[s] the bird." The self is thus declaratively conceived in the Chinese language, her mother's tongue. However, the Chinese language spoken in the narrator's immigrant household would probably not be reintroduced in the text were it not for Ezra Pound, whose celebrated modernist experimentation with poetic and ideographic Chinese might have given Kingston's image of self an aesthetic legitimacy that her mother's tongue does not automatically provide. That the bird "part[s] the mist briefly that swirled opaque again" seems to exemplify metafictionally the narrator's test flight in the blurring of two discourses, American Orientalist and Chinese American.

Moreover, it seems that the "lift" off itself is a sharing of power—Chinese American discourse can emerge from a Calibanic appropriation of the dominant discourse. "Part[ing]" is a moment of differentiation while "opaque[ness]" is the given discursive condition. As the narrator continues, "everything so murky. There would be just two black strokes—the bird," she is questioning and questing a self from murky grounds, on extended wings (Kingston 24, 25).

Unlike Frank Chin, who clears murky grounds by looking into "hard" history, excavating the remains of Chinese American written documents and interviewing living heroes, Maxine Hong Kingston solicits "ancestral help" by tapping into the resources of familial oral stories (10). Such ancestral help comes to the narrator, however, neither custom-made nor well-tailored; it demands that the narrator figure out herself before figurating herself. The mode of interrogation therefore sustains the entire narrative of *The Woman Warrior*. "How can Chinese keep any tradition at all? They don't even make you pay attention." The narrator resumes her interrogation even toward the end of the book: "I don't see how they kept up a continuous culture for five thousand years. Maybe they didn't; maybe everyone makes it up as they go along. If we had to depend on being told, we'd have no religion, no babies, no menstruation . . . no death" (216).

This internal dialogue is so pervasive that it reveals the devastating effects of American Orientalist discourse on the narrator's young consciousness: that the Chinese ballad of Fa Mu Lan is woven with the scenario of Gung Fu and Western films and that the metaphor of footbinding is occasionally intertwined with personal stories about Chinese America show the narrator's confusion about her ethnic history and tradition. When the narrator asks, "How can Chinese keep any tradition at all?" she might as well have asked, "What is Chinese American tradition?" The narrator's inquiries exhibit her suspension of belief in the received categories of information mediated by American Orientalist discourse. At the same time, however, she is also probing an alternative existence in a native tradition that neither rationalizes nor publicizes itself. "Traditions," the narrator suggests, could mean "manners" in Chinese (199)—manners being unspoken codes of behavior that sustain human community. Social and cultural practices, in other words, do not explain themselves—"If we had to depend on being told, we'd have no religion, no babies, no menstruation . . . no death." But tradition continues when "everyone makes it up as they go along." It is in the making-up and maintenance of its praxis that a Chinese American tradition becomes an effective counterdiscourse.

Latent in *The Woman Warrior* is precisely an ideology of form both manifesting the narrator's application of a Chinese American tradition and undermining a totalizing American Orientalist discourse. Kingston, the narrator/protagonist, writes herself into life through a particular Chinese Box form of narrative acts. The emphasis upon an interpellational, dialogical, collective (yet not anonymous) narrative mode as the box-opening analogy shows and is unique for Kingston's subject constitution. Furthermore, this subjective formation is also intricately couched in terms of a birth metaphor, when the unfolding of the various female stories in the book is construed as a process of birthing. The mother Brave Orchid is both a literal and literary midwife: she was an obstetrician back in China and she transmits stories to her daughter until the girl claims that she can also "talk story" (240). Together, the multiple stories unfold a message that the ethnic woman cannot authorize herself without a full recognition of the shared stories of her gender and her race. The multiple narration also encourages the reader to participate in the narrative acts creating a talk-story community in which both the speaker and listener are involved in a powerful creation of themselves. Kingston's absorption of the Chinese tradition of familial binding and interrelatedness as reflected in the narrative structure constitutes her formal critique of the monolithic narrative of the sovereign self in Western autobiographical writings.

Chinese American tradition stands not as a singular literary phenomenon but as a social practice in relation to dominant writings; its formation is as much a self-suggestion as a counter hegemonic reaction. Chin and Kingston demonstrate that the deprivation of an identifiable ethnic history of writing due to the prevalence of American Orientalist discourse did not become for them a condition of their being but rather an occasion of their becoming. Both writers address their historical distortion and obscurity by inventing particular strategies and producing a tradition to meet the specific needs of our time. The diversity of their specific discursive mediations reflects the changing diaspora of Chinese America, and the multiplicity of their form speaks for variant formations of a tradition. Such a tradition is evolving to enable a change of current status and to constitute a new field of knowledge about Chinese America.

NOTES

1. Infinitesimal in number (0.02% of the total U.S. population in 1880), the Chinese nevertheless bore the brunt of the U.S. economic crisis

and became a convenient racial scapegoat. See Ronald Takaki, *Strangers from a Different Shore: A History of Asian Americans* (Boston: Little, Brown, 1989), 110. Whitman's song of laborers (I have in mind titles like "A Passage to India" and "Salut au Monde!"), with its affirmation of a multiracial American working class and his vision of cosmic democracy with its all-equal and all-inclusive American cultures, was an exceptionally lonely and anachronistic voice.

2. Lin Yu Tang, whose *My Country and My People* (1935) is a sample of this movement, attempts to redeem Chinese American humanity by playing the role of a messenger from a superior civilization and a mediator of Chinese and American cultures.

3. The questions Kingston's narrator raises are not unlike those of Frank Chin's dramatic persona, Tam, as we have noted earlier.

WORKS CITED

Chan, Jeffery Paul et al. "Resources for Chinese and Japanese American Literary Traditions." *Amerasia* 8:1 (1981). 19–31.

Chin, Frank. "Don't Pen Us Up in Chinatown." *New York Times* (October 8, 1972), 1.

———. "Confessions of the Chinatown Cowboy." *Bulletin of Concerned Asian Scholars* 4:3 (1972). 58–70.

———. *The Chickencoop Chinaman and the Year of the Dragon*. Seattle: University of Washington Press, 1981.

Christy, Arthur. *The Orient in American Transcendentalism: A Study of Emerson, Thoreau, and Alcott*. New York: Octogon, 1972.

Deleuze, Giles and Felix Guattari. *Kafka: Toward a Minor Literature*, trans. Dana Polan. Minneapolis: University of Minnesota Press, 1986.

Harte, Bret. "Plain Language from Truthful James." In *The Poetical Works of Bret Harte*. Boston: James R. Osgood, 1872.

Hom, Marlon K. *Songs of Gold Mountain: Cantonese Rhymes from San Francisco*. Berkeley: University of California Press, 1987.

Hunt, Michael H. *The Making of a Special Relationship: The United States and China to 1914*. New York: Columbia University Press, 1983.

Kim, Elaine. *Asian American Literature: An Introduction to the Writings and Their Social Context*. Philadelphia: Temple University Press, 1982.

Kingson, Maxine Hong. *The Woman Warrior: Memoirs of a Girlhood among Ghosts*. New York: Vintage, 1976.

Lai, Him Mark, Genny Lim, and Judy Yung, eds. *Island: Poetry and History of Chinese Immigrants on Angel Island 1910–1940*. San Francisco: HOC DOI (History of Chinese Detained on Island), 1980.

Lin Yu Tang. *My Country and My People*. New York: John Day, 1935.

Ling, Amy. "Edith Eaton: Pioneer Chinamerican Writer and Feminist." In *American Literary Realism, 1870–1910*. 16:2 (1983). 287–98.

Lo, Karl and H.M. Lai. *Chinese Newspapers Published in North America, 1845–1976*. Washington, D.C.: Center for Chinese Research Materials, 1976.

Melville, Herman. *Moby Dick or The White Whale*. New York: New American Library, 1961.

Solberg, S.E. "Sui Sin Far/Edith Eaton: First Chinese-American Fictionalist." *MELUS* 8:1 (1981). 27–40.

Sollors, Werner. "Immigrants and Other Americans." In *Columbia Literary History of the United States*, eds. Emory Elliott et al. New York: Columbia University Press, 1988.

Takaki, Ronald. *Strangers from a Different Shore: A History of Asian Americans*. Boston: Little, Brown, 1989.

Twain, Mark. *The Devil's Race-Track: Mark Twain's Great Dark Writings*, ed. John S. Tucky. Berkeley: University of California Press, 1980.

18

Clashing Constructs of Reality: Reading Maxine Hong Kingston's Tripmaster Monkey: His Fake Book *as Indigenous Ethnography*

Patricia Lin

> A postmodern artist or writer is in the position of a philosopher: the text [s/]he writes, the work [s/]he produces are not in principle governed by preestablished rule, and they cannot be judged according to a determining judgment, by applying familiar categories to the text or to the work. Those rules and categories are what the work of art itself is looking for.
>
> —Jean-Francois Lyotard

IT HAS BEEN close to fifteen years since Maxine Hong Kingston first published *The Woman Warrior: Memoirs of a Girlhood among Ghosts*. In the ensuing years, the work has been both praised and censured. In one of the first critical essays on the work I had suggested that the form within which Kingston chose to frame her story was very much in keeping with the vision and agenda of the postmodern writer (Lin-Blinde 1979). Then, as it is today with her most recent work, *Tripmaster Monkey: His Fake Book*, any attempts at reading Kingston require a revision on the part of the reader's assumptions about literary genres, authorial voice, and the question of veracity—particularly as her works pertain to "truthful" or "accurate" representations of Chinese Americans (Wong 1988). Attention to form as a structure of knowledge as well as a principle for organizing experience, in other words, is a requisite activity in any attempt at understanding a cultural projection of postmodernism such as Kingston's new work (Connor 5; Fischer 208–13.

The Woman Warrior was and still is categorized (and hence read) as an "autobiography" even by otherwise sophisticated readers and critics. This generic label continues to lend itself to readings that are locked into the expectations associated with autobiographies, including the demand that Kingston's accounts of her family's history and Chinese American reality adhere to some determinable measure of truth. Interviews of Kingston's mother have been undertaken to "prove" that the writer had in fact misrepresented events in the family's history, as well as distorting Chinese American culture. Kingston's detractors who claim that she has distorted the Chinese American experience (Chan 1977) have similarly responded to the ideological precepts inherent in the autobiographical form. Their contentions are that there are uncontestable truths about Chinese Americans. Any experience that deviates from a set of given parameters about the Chinese American experience does not conform to the truth-telling mandate of the autobiography and is thus fictive, that is, an untruth. There is of course a circularity to this logic: if autobiography (as a mechanism for organizing and retelling the life of an individual) delimits what can be regarded as "truth," it does so by setting up the sort of "truth" that necessitates excluding what cannot be accommodated. The "truth" which emerges is hence the kind of truth that Nietzsche saw as possible only through the "lies" of exclusion.

On the cover jacket of *Tripmaster Monkey* we are discreetly told in small print that the work is a "novel" and on the inside flap the publishers announce that "this is Maxine Hong Kingston's first work of fiction." As with *The Woman Warrior* the rush to delineate Kingston's new work within recognizable formal boundaries threatens to minimize some critically important aspects of *Tripmaster Monkey.* More significantly, the failure to recognize *Tripmaster Monkey* as something both more and less than a novel deprives the work of a place among the representative voices of the postmodern era. Furthermore, the narrow definition assigned to Kingston's most recent work detracts attention from the crucial recognition that ethnic Americans, by virtue of their hybridized experiences as identified by critics of postmodernism such as Baudrillard, Jameson, and Lyotard, in a sense have always carried the essential germ of the postmodern

(Baudrillard; Connor; Giroux; Gitlin; Jameson 1983, 1984a, 1984b; Lyotard; Newman). Specifically, their experiences identify them as persons at the intersections of contested cultural codes and discourses who are uniquely positioned and enpowered to undertake what new anthropology terms the task of the "indigeneous ethnographer (Clifford 9).

Within the last decade anthropologists have grappled with the privileged status of the Western world's most characteristic discursive modes including the discourses of science, philosophy, and literature. Rejecting the authority and rhetorical stance to represent those deemed "primitive," "without culture/history," or "pre-literate," new ethnography mirrors the postmodern condition in its efforts to represent the multiplicity of human existence using a much wider range of discourses than the approved scientific, textual, and empirical approaches of "the classic norms of social analysis [that] have eroded since the late 1960's" (Rosaldo 28). "Writing reduced to method: keeping good field notes, making accurate maps, 'writing up results'" (Clifford 2) have given way to a postmodern ethnography that is

> a cooperatively evolved text consisting of fragments of discourses intended to evoke in the minds of both reader and writer an emergent fantasy of a possible world of commonsense reality, and thus to provoke an aesthetic integration that will have a therapeutic effect. It is, in a word, poetry—not in its textual form, but in its return to the original context and function of poetry, which, by means of its performative break with everyday speech, [evokes] memories of the ethos of the community. (Tyler 125–26)

The argument for reading *Tripmaster Monkey* as an ethnographic enterprise of the postmodern era rather than as a novel is based on the premise that it "anthropologizes" rather than novelizes the United States. In other words, ethnography exposes the constitution of everyday or taken for granted realities—unlike the novel, whose representations of reality are meant to simulate the actual. The lenses through which both Kingston and the book's protagonist Wittman Ah Sing view the world around them, and to which the reader in turn is subjected, are in effect those which defamiliarize the familiar. "Letting it all come in"—as Wittman puts it (4), uncensored and uneditorialized by some internalized authorial voice—becomes one of the work's central tropes for the multilayered postmodern condition: a condition that challenges us with its contradictions., discontinuities, repetitions, and complexities. Correspondingly, the ethnographic enterprise is the reflexive attempt to talk about the inconsistencies of life in the latter third of the twentieth century.

The complexities are particularly evident in the person of Wittman Ah Sing. A fifth-generation native Californian of Chinese American ancestry, he is a descendant of a great-great-grandfather who arrived in the New World on the Nootka, a boat "as ancestral as the Mayflower" (41). (Nootka Sound off British Columbia was the first settlement of Chinese in North America.) With this, his claim to American nativism is established, even though as a Chinese he and his family are part of a community historically disenfranchised in American society. The contradictions are further heightened by the fact that, unlike many native Chinese Americans who are descended from laborers who arrived in the United States in the nineteenth century, Wittman is able to trace his lineage to a long line of actors and entertainers. Instead of coming in search of gold during the Gold Rush, Wittman's folks came to California "to play . . . [staging] plays that went on for five hours a night, continuing the next night, the same long play going on for a week with no repeats" (250). He himself was "born backstage in vaudeville" and kept in a theatrical trunk with "wall paper lining, grease paint, and mothball smells, paste smell" (13). His mother, a Chinese American showgirl, was a "Flora Dora girl" named Ruby Long Legs. She was part of a roadshow known as Dr. Woo and the Chinese Flora Dora Girls that traversed the United States "boogie-woogying and saluting right through World War II" raising money for war bonds. His father, who has the unlikely name of Zeppelin Ah Sing, was a "Stagedoor Johnny" who was later incorporated into the roadshow, first as a backstage electrician then an onstage emcee.

The personal history is an overly familiar one in American lore. It resonates comfortably with stories about the early lives of others in American entertainment history—"The Seven Little Foys," a fifties movie starring Bob Hope, for instance, depicted the itinerent life of vaudevillian Eddie Foy and seven of his children who were part of his family act. Likewise, the popular song "Born in a trunk at the Princess Theatre/in Pocatello, Idaho" clearly reaffirms the American tradition that there is an innateness to being an entertainer. In Wittman Ah Sing's case, a note of dissonance is struck by the fact that the players in his story are Chinese. The comfortably familiar and well-entrenched "born in a trunk" story is thus "defamiliarized," if we are to use Shklovsky's term (Lemon and Reis 4), giving us a decentered, double vision of the story: from this perspective we see the historical exclusion of the fact that Chinese Americans too have been part of America's theatrical and vaudeville lore.

The disjunctured, decentralized perspective is an important characteristic of postmodernism. In an era where material artifacts and information proliferate and bombard the senses it becomes humanly impossible to trace things to single causes and "truths," much less to be able to reach back to points of origins. The dictum of the era is the impossibility of the new, namely that there are no new stories, ideas, or constructs left to be made since all things that can be said or done have so been done. Jameson in his critique of postmodernism thus identifies *pastiche* as the only interpretive mode that remains possible. As a mode, it capitalizes on the "already made" by borrowing, even plagiarizing, and repeating bits and pieces of other works wholesale with little or no commentary. Through this "metareferencing," that is, the placement side by side of two fragments of a work, each work is flattened and emptied of its specific contents, thus blurring the distinctions between past, present, and future (Jameson 1983, 117). In the postmodern era, what is finally left for the artist is the task of re-presenting representations. No "realism" or "realistic" representations are possible, Jameson adds, once we become conscious that "we seem condemned to seek the historical past through our own pop images and stereotypes about the past, which remains forever out of reach (Jameson 1983, 118).

What is actually going on in postmodernism and informing Kingston's *Tripmaster Monkey* is the recognition that we, like Wittman Ah Sing, all arrive in an "already made" world. This is a world (as we have increasingly been made aware of since the sixties) that is preinhabited and defined by mythologies, stereotypes, and cultural constructs, all of which have equal though arbitrary claims on our lives. For Wittman Ah Sing, who graduates during the Vietnam era from the University of California, Berkeley with a major in English literature, his own life becomes a converging point of pre-scripted texts and clashing cultural constructs. These textual and cultural constructs occupy a "polyphonic space," where they offer an interplay of voices from a range of different sources that shape and actualize Wittman's existence.

From the opening pages of *Tripmaster Monkey* the reader is moved along with Wittman from one pre-written text to another. Rilke's *Malte Laurids Brigge* is tightly interwoven into the contextual ground of Wittman's life to the point where it forms a prescription or template for Wittman's existence. Like Malte Laurids, Wittman is an aspiring writer. They are about the same age (Rilke/Malte Laurids was twenty-eight when he arrived in Paris in 1902; Wittman is a year out of college), both adrift in busy metropolitan cities. The extensive excerpts of *Malte Laurids Brigge* that appear in *Tripmaster Monkey*, as well as the obvious parallels between Malte Laurids and Wittman, underscore the point that lives are dictated by preexisting textual scripts, thus undermining the question of either the uniqueness or privileged status of identity. In contrast to the novelistic determinants vis à vis character and its development, we find that Wittman is less a signifier of human typology than a locus for the recovery of prior texts, codes, and representations. As a Chinese American, however, Wittman's scenario is also the unique rendezvous point of numerous classical Chinese texts such as Shih Nai-An/ Lo Kuan Chung's *Shui Hu Chuan* (variously translated as *The Water Margin*, *The Water Verge* and *All Men Are Brothers*); Wu Cheng-en's *Hsi Yu Chi* (translated as *Monkey*, *Tripitaka*, and *Journey to the West*); and various other works from the Chinese classical canon including *The Three Kingdoms* and *The Dream of the Red Chamber*.

Significantly, Kingston uses Monkey (Sun Wu Kong) as Wittman's choice of an alter ego: "I am really," he says, "the present-day U.S.A. incarnation of the King of the Monkeys" (33). In the Chinese classic, Monkey springs *sui generis* from a stone egg. On a dare from other monkeys in the forest he penetrates a water fall and discovers an edenic world. For his bravado he is made king of the monkeys and leads the other simians into the new kingdom. Monkey later seeks immortality by entering a monastry and acquires the Taoist/Zen-like name, "Aware of Emptiness." He masters the art of seventy-two transformations, which allows him to change his size and appearance, perform diverse magical acts, as well as cover great distances at a single leap. In the best known part of *Hsi Yu Chi*, Monkey accompanies the somewhat befuddled monk Tripitaka on a journey west to India to find the Buddhist scriptures. The details of *Hsi Yu Chi*, and particularly the figure of Monkey, are used contextually with Rilke's *Malte Laurids Brigge*, to elucidate both the meaning of Wittman's artistic pursuit and characteristic postmodern awareness, namely the "awareness of emptiness" where all things deemed "true" or "real" are fundamentally human-made constructs. As such, nothing really new can be invented and the work of the artist lies simply in the rearrangement of prefabrications in such a manner as to simply suggest the new. As would-be writer and playwright in the post-modern sixties, Wittman's fate is not to invent but to retell stories and stage an epic based on ancient established Chinese stories. He is, like Monkey, a trickster since his tale-spinning and dramatic renditions of something old are enterprises requiring manipulations and "magical" transformations of reality to produce a sense of novelty. "[In] all magic acts," Wittman muses, "you have to cheat, the missing step is cheating" (17).

Like Monkey, the postmodern man Wittman has no origins to which he can make absolute claims. His parents both defy traditional definitions of parenthood, and he has a mysterious grandmother he is not sure is in fact his grandmother. As a fifth generation Chinese American, he feels no connections to the large numbers of recent Chinese immigrants: "What did he [Wittman] have to do with these foreigners? With F.O.B. emigres?" he wonders (41). Deracinated from those with whom he shares nothing except national origins, he is ostensibly free through the trickery of disguise, change of costume, hair length, and beard to take on whatever appearances or forms he chooses from the range of prototypes that he, as a Chinese American, is able to avail himself from both the Euro-American and Chinese reservoirs of culture and history. As a product of Berkeley in the sixties, however, Wittman opts for the appearance of "a Chinese hippy." His wardrobe consists of a grab bag of used mismatched clothes: a blue pinstriped suit ("of some dead businessman," 44) bought for five dollars from the Salvation Army, a green shirt and tie, and Wellingtons. Neither the suit nor the shirt and tie match and the outfit clashes incongruously with his long hair. The effect, he hoped, would be "an affront to anybody who looked at him" (44). Defiance of cultural norms is obvious at one level, but the deliberate combination of mismatched articles of clothing suggests a transformational magic at work—namely, the creation of a new if bizarre look salvaged from oddments and discards. Self-creation through costume changes as well as cosmetics and surgery is clearly linked to the fictive and fluid status of identity in postmodern society. As a late twentieth century "trip master" (i.e., one skilled at manipulating halluncinations, if we are to use the sixties coinage for "trip"), Wittman stands for the constituted self that is eclectic, ephemeral, and an empty signifier moving from one theater of action to another without serious engagement in the actualities. Disengagement through disguise becomes a means of both challenging and transcending social and cultural boundaries and norms: one can be anyone one wants through a change of outfits, yet costumes which hold their own signified meanings can also be made to signify something other than what they were originally intended to signify. Specifically, the banker's suit that Wittman wears with his hippy hair-do and Wellingtons no longer signifies the wearer's profession or social standing, placing its wearer instead in another realm or "theater" of society.

However, because he is racially Chinese and clothed irrevocably in "this-color wongsky skin," Wittman still wears the "uniform" that marks him as marginal in white America. In this society that essentially has not or will not catch on to the arbitrariness of externals as a basis for hierarchical ordering, Wittman (alias the individual "Aware of Emptiness," particularly of empty signifiers) is nevertheless helpless despite his insights.

The Monkey parallelism is brought home in this instance as Wittman's Chineseness resonates with the fact that Monkey, despite his considerable magical prowess, was often at the mercy of both humans and the gods who could not transcend their experience of him as a simian. Tripitaka, Monkey's Buddhist master, for instance, tricks him into putting on a gold band around his head. This band becomes a device to control Monkey, for in the event Monkey does not act in accordance to Tripitaka's wishes, the Buddhist monk mutters a prayer and the band squeezes around the monkey's head causing him to writhe in agony until he promises to conform. Kingston uses instances from the *Hsi Yu Chi* to suggest Wittman's vulnerability, in an episode where his "showbiz" parents actually treat him as a monkey when he is a child. In one episode, while his father Zeppelin plays a hurdy-gurdy, little Wittman, dressed in an outfit actually meant for a monkey complete with opening for a tail, collects donations from the audience. But it is this reduction to animal status that enables Wittman to function as the subversive factor in terms of whatever undesirable circumstances he finds himself. Thus, in both *Tripmaster Monkey* and *Hsi Yu Chi* the interplay of vulnerability versus obvious empowerment suggests the paradox where it is the very appearance of powerlessness that ultimately enables Wittman and Monkey to master both their environments and those around them, to be a "trip master."

The American pop-culture counterpart to this paradox is "Superman" and in one scene Wittman actually merges the two myths. "Listen Lois [Lane]," Wittman tells an astonished date, "'underneath these glasses'—ripping the glasses off, wiping them on his sleeve . . . I am really" and here he interjects the Chinese myth that he is the Monkey King rather than the expected Superman (33). The side-by-side placement of Superman and Monkey serves to demonstrate the arbitrariness in cultural choices about the constitution of heroism as well as to present the potential that this offers to Wittman Ah Sing and Everyman to reconstitute their own personae after whatever images of heroism they choose. In America, which has a culture that de Toqueville saw as resembling the marketplace jamboree, a powerful alien from Krypton can thus hide out in a busy metropolis as mild-mannered, bespectacled Clark Kent until the demands arise for him "to leap tall buildings in a single bound," as well as display supranormal abilities in the service of good over evil. Likewise Wittman Ah Sing, the incarnation of Monkey, is capable of pole-vaulting into the skies and leading his band of heroes into battle against the "havoc monster" and so represents another entry into the postmodern cultural marketplace of unlikely heroes.

Wittman's dream, however, is to stage an already-written text—the Chinese classic *The Water Verge*. To Wittman the ultimate "trip" or constituted scenario is one where the boundaries between what is conventionally agreed upon as "real" merge with fictional reality. The dualistic enterprise at work in Wittman's project is to write both within the dramatic constructs as well as against them; by doing so he exposes the fictive, that is, the man-made and self-enclosed staginess of traditional drama. The spike of its contrived nature, Wittman thus tells his Caucasian lady love, his play nevertheless "continues like life" (169).

The play eventually includes his friends, various sundry denizens of his neighborhood, and his mother's band of now-retired, elderly, former showgirls who perform a reprise of their World War II showgirl routine. *The Water Verge* or *Shui Hu Chuan*, upon which Wittman's play is loosely based, is an epic with a hundred and eight characters; thirty-six of them are major characters and seventy-two of them are minor ones. The characters are all victims of a corrupt system and are forced to live their lives as fugitives and outlaws. Wherever possible, these outlaws take on evil government officials, and a la Robin Hood and his band, plunder the rich to help the poor and the oppressed. Although the *Shui Hu Chuan* is set in thirteenth century China, it resonates thematically with the social protests and counterculture movement of the time during which Kingston's work is based. For Wittman, restaging the *Shui Hu Chuan* is a means of protesting the war in Southeast Asia: "Our monkey, master of change staged a fake war, which might very well be displacing some real war" (306). Wittman, however, cannot claim this protest as his own "voice"—that protest is already embedded in the authorial voice of the writer of the *Shui Hu Chuan* and the only way that Wittman the postmodern playwright can claim preeminence is by repeating an existing text.

In one of Jorge Luis Borges' short stories, "Pierre Menard the Author of Don Quixote," Pierre Menard, the principle character, actually wants to write the work *Don Quixote*, that is, to commit an act of textual repetition. To this end, Pierre Menard initially considers actually becoming Cervantes but eventually rejects this scheme as being less interesting than writing *Don Quixote* by being Pierre Menard himself. The point of Borges' fable, Alicia Borinsky explains, is to suggest the idea of authorship/authority as "the production of voice" and to raise questions about how this voice is extended in its discourse (Borinsky 92). In rewriting *Don Quixote*, Pierre Menard used the archaic Spanish version of Cervantes and, according to Borinsky, "re-enacted Cervantes"—in other words, he used Cervantes' discursive mode since he, Mennard, cannot be Cervantes and hence cannot create an original work.

A similar situation presents itself to Wittman Ah Sing, who as an American of Chinese descent must "re-enact" writers from both the Euro-American and Chinese canon since he receives the discursive voices from both traditions. In both *Tripmaster Monkey: His Fake Book* and "Pierre Menard, Author of Don Quixote," the underlying message is that since claiming authorial authority over one's own life is an impossibility, the only artistic and hence independent claim that either Wittman or Menard can achieve is through their visibly proclaimed presences in the reenactment of prior discursive voices. Thus, while Cervantes and Lo Kuan Chung, the writer of the *Shui Hu Chuan*, are rendered invisible by virtue of their authorial positions, Wittman and Menard are visibly evident because of their repetitive activities as artisans or makers of artificial texts (hence in Wittman's case his "fake" book).

In Pierre Menard's case, Borinsky even notes that "Menard's work [his rewritten *Don Quixote*] is considered to be superior to the original *Don Quixote* because it is a higher level of artifice" (Borinsky 92). Its patent artificialness stands in contrast to the original *Don*

Quixote which Menard describes as a "spontaneous work" written "à la diable, swept along by inertias of language and invention" (Borinsky 92).

In the case of Wittman Ah Sing, the additional level of artifice through repetition functions as a device for the evocation and attempt to locate something quintessentially identifiable as "Chinese Americaness," or as Michael M. J. Fischer puts it, the attempt to claim "a voice or style that does not violate one's several components of identity." This is an identity that is "an insistence on a pluralistic, multidimensional, or multi-faceted concept of self . . . a crucible for a wider social ethos of pluralism" (Fischer 196). As such, both Kingston and, by extension, Wittman engage in repetitions of other literary texts, as well as extensive excavations and inventorying of received cultural lore. The "fakeness" of *Tripmaster Monkey* lies in the trickery with which the word "book" is used. It is a literal book in its material sense, but a nonbook in terms of the received understanding that Western civilization has come to understand the meaning of the word. It is a "fake" book in that it is not a source of original thought, but rather itself a repetition and catalogue of other textual, experiential and cultural constructs.

In his essay "The Fantasia of the Library," Foucault identifies the same activity on the part of Flaubert, particularly in his final book *Bouvard et Pecuchet*. Foucault identifies this work as "a book produced from other books" (Foucault 105), an encyclopedia of human attempts at achieving permanence through textual means. Bouvard and Pecuchet, after ten years of living by everything they have read, commit themselves instead to the task of simply copying every book in existence including their own. By previously believing and acting on what they had read or heard about. Bouvard and Pecuchet, according to Foucault, believed "immediately and unquestioningly in the persistent flow of discourse" (Foucault 107). In contrast, their repetition and inventorying of books, objects, and experiences allowed them to *become* the things they copied "because to copy," according to Foucault, "is to do nothing; it is to be the books being copied" (Foucault 107). Furthermore, in the repetition of inventories, Bouvard and Pecuchet are incorporated into the continuous movement of textual repetition that stretches on for as long as humans exist.

As a twentieth-century Californian, Wittman (notwithstanding his Chinese racial origin) is a cultural by-product of scenarios from books as well as movies. These movies represent another discursive source that is projected not only onto the rear screen of Wittman's own life but also at times provides the actual formulae by which he goes about pursuing a course of action. The reflexive interaction between Hollywood's creations and human life is characteristically evident. "The movie marquees," Wittman notes, "seemed to give titles to what was going on—*Mondo Cane*, *The Trial*, *Lord of the Flies*, *Dr. No*, *Manchurian Candidate*, *How the West Was Won* . . . not educational films but big-bucks full production-values American glitz movies" (70).

Movies also provide Wittman with ontological reference points or parallel narratives to his own life. The Steinhart aquarium, for instance, exists through its referential reality in *The Lady from Shanghai* starring Orson Welles and Rita Hayworth. While making love with his Caucasian wife, Taña, Wittman's thoughts and conversation are fragmentary evocations from movies such as *Far from the Madding Crowd* and *Hiroshima Mon Amour* (155). When they go on an excursion to Reno at the Washoe County Courthouse, Wittman and Taña sit "on the steps that Marilyn Monroe had walked down after her divorce in *The Misfits*" (209). Later they eat at a restaurant "famous for boarding the cast and crew of the *Gold Rush*." (212).

The search for ethnic authenticity is also referenced against an inventory of Hollywood's representations and misrepresentations.

> Films of the '50s did not use Blacks "so Russ Tamblyn . . . the gangleader with kinky hair indicates Blackness . . . like Leslie Caron with her wide mouth as Mardou Fox in *The Subterraneans* is supposed to be Black. George Peppard as Jack Kerouac, also as Holly Golightly's boyfriend in *Breakfast at Tiffany's*. Mickey Rooney with an eye job and glasses as Holly's jap landlord, speaking snuffling bucktoof [sic] patois. The leader of the Sharks [in *West Side Story*] is . . . George Chakiris. Greek Danish Puerto Ricans of the East Coast. (71)

Asian Americans, particularly those in the acting professions, are themselves manipulated by Hollywood to conform to the movie industry's perceptions about what they ought to look like or how they are supposed to behave. Nanci Lee, the object of Wittman's true love, is told at auditions that she does not look "oriental" and that she "doesn't sound right" in regard to Hollywood's expectations of how Chinese women are supposed to look or sound. Her Chinese physical characteristics are deemed aberrent in terms of white American standards, while working as an extra in both a movie and a television show, a makeup artist attempts to give her "an Irish nose," and another remarks that "there's just so much we can do about those eyes" (24). "History" Wittman notes, "is embodied in physical characteristics" (213); many characteristics identified as being Chinese (at least in American history) are constructs manufactured by Hollywood and perpetuated in society as signifiers of inferiority. For Wittman, the reclamation of Chineseness necessitates abandonment of the trappings affected by Chinese women in order to look more "desirable" in American terms. In his monologue to his audience after the performance of his play, Wittman exhorts the actresses to "take off their false eyelashes, to go bare faced and show what we look like" (312). Even worse than cosmetic attempts at defacing Chineseness, he adds, are plastic surgery and orthodontics. New beauty, he promises, can be discovered only by voiding white America's definitions of beauty, and his pronouncement, "I declare my looks—teeth, eyes, nose, profile—perfect" (314), represents both self-affirmation and the reclamation of what he terms the "lost I" (91). Specifically, the "lost I" refers to Hollywood movies where historically Chinese people are repeatedly presented as being unable to use the pronoun "I" to represent self as subject. Instead, Chinese characters over several decades of movies are made to say "me no likee," or "me name-um Li'l Beaver," reducing them to the level of passive objects rather than active subjects (318). Hollywood's linguistic incapacitation, however, can be rectified through remembrance of the historical roots of the word for "I" in the Chinese language—an ideograph that depicts the "I" as "I-warrior . . . the same whether subject or object, 'I-warrior' whether actor or the receiver of action" (31). Thus self-retrieval, and particularly the retrieval of a self-as-subject, emerges as a central thread in *Tripmaster Monkey.* It is a project that is even more significant for ethnic populations such as Chinese Americans, who live under the the encumbering weight of representations that others have fashioned about them.

Ultimately, the act of self-retrieval from amidst a morass of prefabricated representations is accompanied by rejection of the idea that there is finality or permanence of any text, truth, or representation. The transformational "monkey power" that informs *Tripmaster Monkey* suggests that "there is no 'complete' corpus of First Time knowledge, that no one . . . can know this lore except through an open ended series of contingent, power-laden encounters" (Clifford 8). To this end, *Tripmaster Monkey* transcends the protocols and demands of the novel in that it challenges the ideology of textual authority as well as textual finality. Within the work, Wittman's task is to effect the "power-laden encounters" between various cultural and literary constructs, and to orchestrate the juxtapositions between imaginative and lived experience so as to discover relevant meanings. As the "writer" of *Tripmaster Monkey*, Maxine Hong Kingston extends the continuum of making meaning not through use of the totalizing strategies of the novel but through deliberated disjunctions of language and texts. Less novelist than ethnographer, she performs the postmodern ethnographic role of producing a "cooperatively evolved text consisting of fragments of discourse" (Tyler 125).

Unlike traditional fiction the fantasy evoked by the ethnographic enterprise, according to Tyler, does not entail a locus of authorial judgement outside the text, but rather, as in *Tripmaster Monkey*, allows an interjection of judgements and perspectives derived from several authorial voices and discourses which by turns compete and harmonize with one another (Tyler 125–26). Within a space that permits a "dispersed authorship" both writer and text share a tentative status. Hence, gleaning the authenticity of *Tripmaster Monkey* lies in comprehending its re-presentation, rather than representation, of reality. Its irresolutions signify a mediative abatement that needs to be understood as representative of the tentative status of artists and their creations. This abatement is different from "the willing suspension of disbelief" that has heretofore been required of the reader of the traditional novel. Within the novelistic pact between writer and reader, the reader is promised "truths" only for as much as s/he is willing to countenence the boundaries established by the single authoritative author. Within the space of "dispersed authorship," however, the irresolutions set up by the divergent voices offer a proliferation of possible scenarios that enable reality to ultimately be "transformed, renewed, and sacralized" (Tyler 125–26).

WORKS CITED

Baudrillard, Jean. *Simulations*. New York: Semiotext(e), 1983.

Borinsky, Alicia. "Repetition, Museums, Libraries: Jorge Borges." *Glyph* 2 (1977): 88–101.

Chan, Jeffrey Paul. "Jeff Chan, Chair of San Francisco State Asian American Studies, Attacks Review." *San Francisco Journal*, 4 May 1977.

Clifford, James. "Introduction: Partial Truths." In *Writing Culture: The Poetics and Politics of Ethnography*, ed. James Clifford and George E. Marcus. Berkeley, Calif.: University of California Press, 1986. 1–26.

Connor, Steven. *Postmodern Culture: An Introduction to Theories of the Contemporary*. Cambridge, Mass.: Basil Blackwell, 1989.

Fischer, Michael M. J. "Ethnicity and the Post-Modern Arts." In *Writing Culture: The Poetics and Politics of Ethnography*, ed. James Clifford and George E. Marcus. Berkeley, Calif.: University of California Press, 1986. 194–233.

Foucault, Michel. *Language, Counter-Memory, Practise: Selected Essays*, ed. Donalf F. Bouchard. Ithaca, N.Y.: Cornell University Press, 1980.

Giroux, Henry A. "Modernism, Postmodernism and Feminism." *Postmodernism, Feminism and Cultural Politics*, ed. Henry A. Giroux. New York: State University of New York Press, 1991. 1–59.

Gitlin, Todd. "Postmodernism Defined at Last." *Utne Reader* July/August (1989): 52–61.

Jameson, Fredric. "Postmodernism and Consumer Society." *Anti-Aesthetic: Essays on Postmodern Culture*, ed. Hal Foster. Port Townsend, Washington: Bay Press, 1983. 111–18.

———. "Postmodernism or the Cultural Logic of Late Capitalism." *New Left Review* 146 (1984a): 53–92.

———. "Periodizing the Sixties" *The Sixties without Apology*, ed. Stanley Aronowitz et al. Minneapolis: University of Minnesota Press, 1984b. 178–215.

Kingston, Maxine Hong. *Tripmaster Monkey: His Fake Book*. New York: Alfred Knopf, 1989.

Lemon, Lee and Marion J. Reis. *Russian Formalist Criticism: Four Essays*. Lincoln: University of Nebraska Press, 1965.

Lin-Blinde, Patricia. "The Icicle in the Desert: Perspective and Form in the Works of Two Chinese American Women Writers." *MELUS* 6:3 (1979). 51–71.

Lyotard, Jean-Francois. *The Postmodern Condition: A Report on Knowledge*, trans. Geof Bennington and Brian Masumi. Minneapolis: University of Minnesota Press, 1980.

Newman, Charles. *The Postmodern Aura: The Act of Fiction in an Age of Inflation*. Evanston, Ill.: Northwestern University Press, 1985.

Rosaldo, Renato. *Culture and Truth: The Remaking of Social Analysis*. Boston: Beacon Press, 1989.

Tong, Benjamin R. "Critic of Admirer Sees Dumb Racist." *San Francisco Journal*, 11 May 1977.

Tyler, Stephen A. "Post-Modern Ethnography: From Document of the Occult to Occult Document." In *Writing Culture: The Politics and Politics of Ethnography*, ed. James Clifford and George E. Marcus. Berkeley, Calif.: University of California Press, 1986. 122–40.

Wong, Cynthia Sau-ling. "Necessity and Extravagance in Maxine Kingston's *Woman Warrior*." *MELUS* 15:1 (1988). 3–26.

19

The Death of Asia on the American Field of Representation

James S. Moy

> The Spectacle presents itself as something enormously positive, indisputable and inaccessible. It says nothing more than "that which appears is good, that which is good appears." The attitude which it demands in principle is passive acceptance which in fact it already obtained by its manner of appearing without reply, by its monopoly of appearance.
>
> —Guy Debord

IN HER recent treatment of the "undoing of women," Catherine Clement asserts that only through her death does the character Cho-Cho san in *Madama Butterfly* emerge as a true Asian character: "Butterfly, whose Japanese name is masked in Italian by the English signifier for an insect, regains her country at the same time she dies a Japanese death" (Clement 58). While this is merely a passing comment in Clement's impressionistic feminist reading of opera, it provides the outline for a larger trajectory which I intend to trace in this essay, as I look at the rather troubling tendency for Asians (both female and male) to find death on the American field of representation.

Generally speaking, despite the realities of Asian life on America's western frontier, theatrical events displaying Asianness prior to the end of the nineteenth century were part of a benign colonialist institution of representation. While the images were relatively unflattering, they at least did not constitute a real threat to Asian American life.

The earliest advertised representations of Asians on the American stage seemed to be limited to the popular entertainment mode. For example, in 1808, a circus troupe in New York featured "THE YOUNG CHINESE" who would "display a variety of comic attitudes and Vaulting, over his Horse in full speed." In 1834, the *Commercial Advertiser* announced the presence of a "Chinese Lady" at the American Museum in New York City. Later that same year, Afong Moy, presumably the aforementioned "Chinese Lady" was again displayed at 8 Park Place, "in native costume." A contemporary print dated 1835 seems to suggest that the display included an appropriate chinoiserie setting (Fessler 6). From the illustration it seems the simple foreigness of Afong Moy was deemed sufficient novelty to warrant her display. Likewise, beginning in the 1830s, P.T. Barnum's displays of the "Siamese Twins," Chang and Eng, the most famous stage display of Asianness in the nineteenth century, further contributed to the institutionalization of this pattern (Bogdan 202–4). Clearly, the context for this type of display is the anthropological gaze associated with modern museums in which the power and authority of an audience member's privileged look is affirmed, usually at the expense of the novel "primitive" objectified dead Other. Thus, the audience members could become "masters of all they survey."

Beyond the pure anthropological display of Anglo-American constituted Otherness, Asian stage representations are found inserted into literary theatrical texts beginning in the second half of the nineteenth century. These generally offered a neutralized Asian—usually Chinese male—character in some comic form. The methods employed in the disfigurement of this type of Asian character are significant, and were doubtless wildly entertaining to Anglo-American audiences of the late nineteenth century. A moment in James J. McCloskey's *Across the Continent; Or, Scenes From New York Life and the Pacific Railroad* (1870) provides some insight into how such a "Chinese" character might have amused:

> CHI: [*Runs up to her*] You like some ricee—[*Aunt Susannah turns back on him. . . . Sits down and takes drink out of bottle*]
> CHI: Ah ha—Melican woman like jig water. Me likee, too. [*Takes bottle of water out of her hand and drinks. Offers it back several times, but fools her and*

drinks himself, talking Chinese all the time, and keeps this up till the bottle is empty] Me makee mashee. [*Sits beside her*] Ah, there my sizee—me stealee you. [*Tries to put his arm around her. She jumps quickly—he falls, then chases her*]

JOE: Here—what is the matter tart?

CHI: [*Joe comes forward with Tom*] Melican woman fightee.

JOE: Come here, Tart. [*To others*] Watch me telephone to China. [*Takes Tart's cue*] Hello, Tart!

CHI: Hello!

JOE: You're crazy.

CHI: Me, too. [*joe Turns away laughing*] Now me talkee. [*Takes end of cue*] Hello—hello—hello—[*Jerks his cue disgusted—jumps on box*]. (McCloskey 107)

While the McCloskey piece can be dismissed as mere popular entertainment or touristic travelogue, attempts by writers who were revered as serious in their desire for greater literary realism did little better.[1]

In *Ah Sin* (1877), Mark Twain and Bret Harte attempt to provide a realistic treatment of a growing and increasingly problematic California Chinese population, "sympathetically" referring to the title character as a "slant eyed son of the yellow jaunders, . . . you jabbering idiot, . . . you moral cancer, you unsolvable political problem."[2] The audience is instructed, "Don't mind him—don't be afraid. . . . Poor Ah Sin is harmless—only a little ignorant and awkward." Another character complains that "when he shakes his head it makes me nervous to hear his dried faculties rattle" (*Ah Sin* 52–53).

Visually, Mark Twain and Bret Harte constituted the Chinese as a "poor dumb animal, with his tail on top of his head instead of where it ought to be" (*Ah Sin* 52–53). In this regard some of Bret Harte's earlier "John Chinaman" writings are revealing. "The expression of the Chinese face in the aggregate is neither cheerful nor happy. . . . There is an abiding consciousness of degradation, a secret pain or self-humiliation, visible in the lines of the mouth and eye. . . . They seldom smile, and their laughter is of such an extraordinary and sardonic nature—so purely a mechanical spasm, quite independent of any mirthful attribute—that to this day I am doubtful whether I ever saw a Chinaman laugh" (Harte, "John Chinaman" 14:220). Harte described the typical Chinese face: "His complexion, which extended all over his head except where his long pig tail grew, was like a very nice piece of glazed brown paper-muslin. His eyes were black and bright, and his eyelids set at an angle of 15 [degrees]; his nose straight and delicately formed, his mouth small, and his teeth white and clean" (Harte, "Wan Lee, the Pagan" 2:264). Later, Harte claims that despite the surface cleanliness, the Chinese "always exhaled that singular medicated odor—half opium, half ginger—which we recognized as the common 'Chinese smell'" (Harte, "See Yup" 16:144). A figure composed of the most obvious aspects of difference, Ah Sin exists on the margins and is intended to disrupt the orderly progress of narrative. Here, then, Ah Sin serves as little more than comic relief despite his title character status.

This tendency to show the Asian as witless, sexless, and therefore harmless beings emerged as the Western colonialist powers were consolidating their economic subjugation of East Asia. This forced "opening" of Asia required that the victors return with trophies of their greatness. As the ancient Romans articulated their imperial power through the display of foreign slaves and curious animals, so the nineteenth-century apparatus of representation produced harmless human entities for display and amusement. Asians, of course, were just one of many stereotypical immigrant ethnic creations of the nineteenth century. Unlike the Irish, the Germans, or the Italians, whose initial stereotypical representations would ultimately be replaced by dominant title role characters in realistic dramas, Asians in America were never allowed to emerge into the realm of the real.

Beyond this, however, a new troubling tendency emerges by the end of the nineteenth century. For it seems that at this point in American representational history, what had previously been simply nonthreatening stereotypical-comic portrayals of Asianness developed into displays which increasingly included dead Asian representations. It may be significant to note that at about this time one of these newly "opened" and supposedly subjugated East Asian powers was beginning to behave in a fashion not unlike its European mentors. Japan early on understood the need to confront the West on its own terms. In colonizing pieces of Korea, China, and other parts of East Asia, its agenda began to resemble that of the European powers. To the extent that it defeated Russia in the Russo-Japan War of 1904–5, it clearly constituted a threat to the Eurocentric perception of the world order. As is all too often the case, the Western response was to simply have the threat eliminated, killed. In representational terms this meant the previously nonthreatening laughable portrayals of Asianness had to be transformed into figures of death, or preferably mystified figures worthy of death.

Inspired by the success of John Luther Long's short story, "Madame Butterfly" (1898), New York director David Belasco in 1900 collaborated with Long to produce the mythic stage representation of *Madame Butterfly*. While these early projects enjoyed some success, it was not until Puccini's operatic rendering of *Madama Butterfly* (1904) that the killing of Asia on stage achieved truly international dimensions.

The story of *Madama Butterfly* is well known. Pinkerton, a bored U.S. Naval captain stationed in Nagasaki, fakes a wedding to develop a liason with a local Japanese woman. After he departs, she gives birth to his child and then anxiously awaits his return. Pinkerton returns, of course, with his elegant American wife, but only to claim his child. As "death with honor is better than life with dishonor," the only action left open to Cho-Cho san is suicide.

In the story of Madame Butterfly, then, the Asian ceased to be a novelty from which the West could learn. Asia ceased to exist as a place whose ancient wisdom might provide secrets to help America. Rather, Asianness was reconstituted as an object to be looked at as before, but now pinned to a board with a precisely placed needle through its heart; now, framed like a butterfly arranged for survey in a museum diorama display. Despite the potential for real understanding and exchange resulting from the increased contact between Asia and America, there developed a tendency to kill off Asians. As if to articulate an unwillingness, an impatience, or simply a lack of desire to understand, to learn from. This tendency finally articulates a Eurocentric colonialist way of looking at the world, a kind of tunnel vision, a provincialism. As these collocated aspects of difference hardened into stereotypes on the stage of America's east coast, the representational apparatus of the newly emerging cinema fixed it permanently, enshrined it, inscribed, and inserted it into the popular text of American consciousness.

One of the first feature-length films to exploit the neutralized suicidal Asian male was D. W. Griffith's *Broken Blossoms* (originally titled *The Chink and the Girl*, 1919). The piece features Lillian Gish as Lucy, the daughter of a murderously brutal prize fighter. After a vicious beating administered by her father, Lucy collapses before the "Chink" storekeeper whose subsequent developing love for the girl can only end in tragedy. Characterized as dreamy, frail, and sensitive, the "Yellow Man" here can offer only a love devoid of sexuality. A love so pure, so exquisitely sacred, and ultimately so tediously maudlin, that only suicide seems to provide a proper closure for the piece. Indeed, the elements of the film fit so well together that any other ending would be unacceptable. Death, it would seem, is this "yellow man's" destiny. Still, intended as a sympathetic treatment of the Asian character, the piece displays the latent anti-Asian racism inherent even in such "liberal" representational projects of the time.

The subsequent popular cinematic text is full of such representational figures. The list of suicidal Asians as Emperors, princesses, soldiers, now turned evil seems endless, while whole careers (like Anna May Wong's) in the industry centered on death by one's own hand.

The pervasiveness of this strategy of representation and the hopelessness of transcending this deadly stereotype can be seen in ("Father of American Drama") Eugene O'Neill's feeble attempt to contrast the decadent Babbit-like commercialism of the West with the "Oriental" wisdom of the East in *Marco Millions* (1927). Here, again, while O'Neill clearly hoped to offer a "liberal's" positive view of Asia, he finally could provide little more than a reinscription of the suicidal "Oriental" in an exotic setting. As Kucuchin dies for the love of Marco Polo who in turn loves only money and commerce, the viewer comes away with little more than a touristic view of an imaginary China while apprehending only the failure of the supposed wisdom of the Orient.

Not until the cultural awareness of the 1960s do plays by Asian Americans emerge to counter the institutionalized dead or dying Asian representational figure. David Henry Hwang in his Tony Award–winning *M.Butterfly* (1988) summarizes the attack:

> It's one of your favorite fantasies, isn't it? The submissive Oriental woman and the cruel white man. . . . Consider it this way: what would you say if a blond homecoming queen fell in love with a short Japanese businessman? He treats her cruelly, then goes home for three years, during which time she prays to his picture and turns down marriage from a young Kennedy. Then, when she learns he has remarried, she kills herself. Now, I believe you would consider this girl to be a deranged idiot, correct? But because it's an Oriental who kills herself for a Westerner—ah!—you find it beautiful. (Hwang 17)

In addition, an angry Philip Kan Gotanda assails the results of such displacements as one of his characters in *Yankee Dawg You Die* (1988) complains that the only roles open to Asians are "waiters, viet cong killers, chimpanzees, drug dealers, hookers, sexless houseboys. . . . They fucking cut off our balls and made us all houseboys on the evening soaps. 'Get your very own neutered, oriental houseboy!'" (Gotanda 36). Unfortunately such overt, powerful attacks have been for nought as many recent Asian American playwrights have chosen to attack the stereotype while reinscribing it in newly disfigured characters to gain popular Anglo-American audience acceptance.[3] The failure of this self-subverting attack on the dead stereotype can be seen in the fact that even before *M.Butterfly* had completed its run, *Miss Saigon* (1989), a new variant on the *Madama Butterfly* theme, opened in London with a much anticipated New York production scheduled for 1991.

This failure suggests the need for a reassessment of the very possibility of identifying a representation of Asianness which can succeed with Anglo-American audiences. For it seems that only representations which reinscribe the stereotype in some form can find success on the popular stage.

Few playwrights have tried to circumvent this imperative to reinscribe the stereotype while attacking the representational apparatus of Anglo-America. In the 1970s, Frank Chin provided some of Asian America's earliest overt attacks on Anglo-American representational practice. Both his *The Chickencoop Chinaman* (1972) and *The Year of the Dragon* (1974) largely avoided the reinscription of the stereotype by providing Asian characters with significant, if eccentric, substance while often relegating Anglo characters to stereotype. Particularly amusing is the Anglo in-law character, Ross, in *The Year of the Dragon* who as a "sincerely interested student of all things Chinese" fancies himself "more Chinese" than his Chinese American wife (Chin 78–79). Further, Chin's portrayal of domestic tensions in Chinatown in *The Year of the Dragon* disfigures the colorful touristic perception of a community that in reality is often a deadend economic ghetto for many of its inhabitants. Such uncompromising portrayals did not meet with success on the popular American stage. Chin's lack of success in the face of *M.Butterfly*'s subsequent popularity clearly confirms the need for the reinscription of stereotype if a playwright is to be accepted by Anglo-American audiences.

Indeed as the film/TV media has taken over the lead in the creation of mediated representational desire it becomes clear that realistic portrayals of domestic Asian American life will continue to have difficulty finding an audience while projects featuring Asians involved in violence and death will command the popular consciousness. Accordingly, films like *An Unremarkable Life* (1989), a quiet piece relating problems in interracial love relations in retirement years; *The Wash* (1988), a film that examines the disintegration of an Asian American family; *Eat a Bowl of Tea* (1989), which offers a glimpse of Chinese American domestic life in the years following World War II; *Dim Sum* (1985), which places filial piety in tension with a Chinese daughter's self-actualization; and *Chan Is Missing* (1982), a breakthrough independent production that spoofs traditional Hollywood film noir practice while providing a look at Chinese attitudes as they impact on a search for a missing person, continue to be relegated to positions of very limited release due to low audience interest. Pieces centering on violence and death, like *Year of the Dragon* (1985), *China Girl* (1987), and *Casualties of War* (1989) maintain relatively high visibility. Thus, the extent to which the popular stereotypes shape audience expectations becomes visible through the box office.

Less clear is the extent to which this same popular consciousness finally shapes Asian American racial desire as well. Arthur Dong's recent film *Forbidden City* (1989) treats this subject. And, it is awkward to admit that after watching the many interviews with Asian American dancers who wished for all the world to be Las Vegas show girls, one can come away with the uneasy conclusion that Asian American desire often coincides with Anglo-American expectations. This desire for complicity is troubling and is perhaps most clearly seen in the current controversy surrounding the proposed Broadway production of *Miss Saigon*. Even the producers admit that the piece is merely an updating of *Madama Butterfly*. Though David Henry Hwang has attacked the opera as a racist myth, he was one of the strongest voices advocating the casting of an Asian American in the lead role of the Engineer (played in London by Jonathan Pryce, an Anglo made up to look Eurasian). The desire for greater Asian American complicity in racist projects is at best confusing. In any case, it is clear that in the popular consciousness Asianness has fled from the real into the realm of representational desire. Unfortunately, in a piece like *Miss Saigon* the representational Asia carries with it a requirement of self destruction. Indeed, as Catherine Clement says, only through its death, or representational self-effacement, does Asia become real for Western audiences.

NOTES

1. Indeed, this touristic agenda was still being played out as late as 1927 in O'Neill's *Marco Millions*. See my "Eugene O'Neill's *Marco Millions*: Desiring Marginality and the Dematerialization of the Orient," in *O'Neill in China*, ed. Lui Haiping and Lowell Swortzell (Westport, Conn.: Greenwood Press, forthcoming).

2. Mark Twain and Bret Harte, *Ah Sin*, ed. Frederick Anderson (San Francisco: Book Club of California, 1961), 10–11, 87.

3. See my "David Henry Hwang's *M.Butterfly* and Philip Kan Gotanda's *Yankee Dawg You Die*: repositioning Chinese American Marginality on the American Stage," *Theatre Journal* 42 (March 1990), 48–56.

WORKS CITED

Bogdan, Robert. *Freak Show: Presenting Human Oddities for Amusement and Profit*. Chicago: University of Chicago Press, 1988.

Chin, Frank. *Chickencoop Chinaman/The Year of the Dragon: Two Plays by Frank Chin*. Seattle: University of Washington Press, 1988.

Clement, Catherine. *Opera, Or the Undoing of Women*. Minneapolis: University of Minnesota Press, 1988.

Fessler, Loren W., ed. *Chinese in America*. New York: Vantage Press, 1983.

Gotanda, Philip Kan. *Yankee Dawg You Die*. Chicago: Wisdom Bridge Theatre Company, 1988.

Harte, Bret. "John Chinaman." In *Writings of Bret Harte*, vol. 14. Boston: Houghton Mifflin, 1896.

———. "Wan Lee, The Pagan." In *Writings of Bret Harte*, vol. 2. Boston: Houghton Mifflin, 1896.

———. "See Yup." In *Writings of Bret Harte*, vol. 16. Boston: Houghton Mifflin, 1896.

Hwang, David Henry. *M.Butterfly*. New York: New American Library, 1988.

McCloskey, James J. *Across the Continent; Or Scenes from New York Life, and the Pacific Railroad*. In *America's Lost Plays*, vol. 16, ed. Barret H. Clark. Bloomington: Indiana University Press, 1963.

Moy, James S. "David Henry Hwang's *M.Butterfly* and Philip Kan Gotanda's *Yankee Dawg You Die*: Repositioning Chinese American Marginality on the American Stage." *Theatre Journal* 42 (March 1990).

———. "Eugene O'Neill's *Marco Millions*: Desiring Marginality and the Dematerialization of the Orient." In *O'Neill in China*, ed. Lui Haiping and Lowell Swortzell. Westport, Conn.: Greenwood Press, forthcoming.

O'Neill, Eugene. *Marco Millions*. London: Jonathan Cape, 1927.

Twain, Mark, and Bret Harte. *Ah Sin*, ed. Frederick Anderson. San Francisco: Book Club of California, 1961.

20

Ping Chong's Terra In/Cognita: Monsters on Stage

Suzanne R. Westfall

> Describing my work, I have always used the metaphor of traveling to a foreign country, where you might have unexpected experiences or see something you don't understand. But like visiting a foreign country, the more you see it, the more familiar it gets.
>
> —Ping Chong

MOST PEOPLE are familiar with the early maps from which I take my title. Highly colored and ornate, they chart a geography more of the imagination than of the real world. Europe appears in detail, while exotic locales such as the Americas, Africa, and Asia appear as fairly accurate outlines, their interiors labeled "Terra Incognita" to reflect the mystery and terror that the land at the "heart of darkness" holds for the colonial explorer. Caligraphed on the nearby sea—"Here be dragons."

With this image in mind, I discuss the work of theater artist Ping Chong, whose pieces (or "Ping things," as his actors tend to call them) are at once strange and disturbingly familiar. A product of his own unique sensibilities as well as of his Asian American experience, these theater pieces often reflect our twisted world through the distorted mirrors of monsters, creatures, outsiders—producing finally, almost though *verfremdungseffekt*, a truthful image. Here I intend to describe and discuss the method by which Ping produces these landscapes and how he attempts to construct audience reception by stretching its expectation horizons. In addition, I examine the functions of the aliens that appear on these horizons. For this geography is a "figurative spatialization or literalization of the notion that what horrifies is that which lies *outside* cultural categories and is, perforce, unknown" (Carroll, *Philosophy* 35).

Part of what makes Ping's work *terra incognita* to a Western audience accustomed to straightforward narrative and traditional realism is Ping's theatrical style, which relies on Asian aesthetics, nonlinear structures, and themes, plots and characters that are surreal rather than realistic, appealing to the subconscious rather than the rational mind. Although Ping Chong does not always resort to the free associative and synchronic methodology of the surrealists, his notion of reality is similar, and audiences usually intuit the meaning of his enigmatic images before they can logically integrate them.

Like our ancient map, the works provide a mere outline of dramatic conventions: we sit in a theater, lights go up and down, costumed performers move, speak, dance, and sing. While the paradigms are familiar, however, the syntagms are not; because these signs are highly motivated, unconstrained by popular conventions and social codes, the works initially appear confusing, and audiences must trust that Ping will fill in the blanks that will allow them to construct meaningful responses. Until the audience becomes familiar with Ping's method of signification, however, the kernel, as Conrad put it, remains elusive and allusive and must often be reconstructed in retrospect, after the theatrical experience has ended, after the voyage has been made.

Ping Chong's work is largely unknown in most of the United States, although Europeans are quite familiar with his accomplishments. Ping has spent over twenty years as an author, director, designer, filmmaker, and artistic director of the Fiji Company in New York City. He is a two-time recipient of the Creative Artist Public Service Fellowship, an Obie-Award winner, twice received an National Endowment of the Arts Grant, and twice a Guggenheim. With his company, he has toured all over the United States, Europe, Eastern Europe, and Asia. In collaboration with Meredith Monk, he wrote *The Games* (recognized for outstanding achievement by the National Institute of Music Theatre) to open the 1984 season at the

Brooklyn Academy of Music. For television they produced "Paris" and "Turtle Dreams," which won the grand prize for video at the Toronto Video Festival. In New York he is most frequently produced at La Mama, where almost all of his pieces have premiered, and where the Fiji Company presently resides.

The son of Chinese, opera-trained immigrants, Ping grew up in Toronto's and New York's Chinatowns, speaking Chinese and generally protected from American popular culture. When he began to study visual art at Pratt Institute, he absorbed American pop culture from fast food to B-movies quickly, without preconceived value judgments, and also without a priori niches to categorize impressions.

This "stranger in a strange land" biography informs and explains many aspects of his work. Ping's assistant in Amsterdam for the tour of *Angels of Swedenborg* probably put it best: "Mr. Chong, you're a strange man; you're part popcorn and part Chinese."[1] Ping relishes that image, for he believes that Asian and American art should mix. In fact, his play *Kind Ness* begins with a split-screen slide show that contemplates analogy, playing with our notions of similarity and difference:

> Slide 16: Ante up. Auntie Mame.
> Slide 17: Woman from Este Lauder Ad. Woman from Algeria.
> [voiceover] "The image on the right is of a woman who had to remove her veil in order for this picture to be taken."
> Slide 18: A designer chair. A masked terrorist.
> [voiceover] "Germany."
> Slide 19: Tupperwear. Elizabeth Taylor and Richard Burton in *Cleopatra*.
> [voiceover] "Images of Nesting."
> Slide 29: "Think tank." "Tank top."
> Slide 39: "George Raft." "George Sand." (*Kind Ness* 61–63)[2]

At the very start of the play, such word games and juxtapositions begin to manipulate audience expectation horizons; they "make strange" by recontextualizing the concepts, images, and ideas that we take for granted, thus moving us from the known to the unknown, from the coastline to the interior, initiating us into the idiolectic world by questioning our conventional significations and generating new associations. Most highly original art forms demand that the receivers stretch their aesthetic expectations, that they abandon the familiar to focus on the unknown (Pavis 75), and such art requires that a spectator perform virtuoso hermeneutics, a function most audiences do not anticipate or desire.

Worse yet, this particular world is multicultural, multilingual and multimedial, automatically casting the average American theater patron as the outsider. Believing that "a cross-cultural perspective demands a cross-disciplinary approach," (Hulser 13), Ping creates theater that blends text, sound, light, movement, and idea in innovative ways.

Just as *terra incognita* lacks definition beyond its fringes, Ping's "works" defy generic classification; his nontraditional method of creating the work invites us to question authority and intentionality. Trained originally as a visual artist, dancer, and filmmaker (he still contracts to make "installations" for major museums), Ping "makes" theater collaboratively, concentrating on process, with the available artists from his troupe, a methodology that again reflects his Asian sensibility. Frequently he alternates what he calls a "text" piece with a dance piece; even more frequently he alternates textual interests with movement interests within one piece.

This "bricolage"[3] approach and effect has led Actors Equity to categorize his work as "performance art," a label with which Ping does not precisely agree, but which he prefers to being classified "mainstream." As Ping expresses it:

> There's nothing I can say about what people want to call my work. It's out of my control. Anyway, people don't say multimedia that much anymore. They say performance art, although that term seems to be fading away too—thank God. That term represented a lot of terrible work. Viewers can call my work whatever they want since I'm hard to pin down anyway. I deal with theatre or live media more as a visual artist than as playwright or director. I always want to experiment. Being a 20th-century artist is to experiment. There is no final form. (Sandla 33)

People who search out Ping Chong's work generally know what to expect, at least within certain limits. In a sense they expect the unexpected; they desire to be baffled, to exercise their interpretive abilities, to enjoy the free play of images without immediately adding up the numbers to figure out the "plot" or "meaning," to play the detective looking for clues. Ping's audiences are less interested in

Aristotelian catharsis than in Brechtian *verfremdungseffekt*, are less interested in text than in the unity and beauty of the multimedial or intramedial effects, are less interested in reaffirmation of their ideology than in social and political satire and criticism. They are advocates of "fashionable cultural consumption." As Stephen Holden of the *New York Times* puts it, audiences "tend to share a bohemian disregard for convention and a sensualist's attitude that art need not be understood to be enjoyed" (Holden 1).

Ping begins to produce his terra incognita by his lighting palette, most frequently highly saturated and monochromatic for successive scenes, a technique that lends the pieces what I call hyper-realism, a heightened vividness inappropriate to realism, an acuteness echoed by the intensity of each "scene." Steep raking and backlighting increase the alienation. Aural elements—stylistic mixtures of simple sound effects, jazz, nonwestern strains, classical and original music by Brian Hallas (Howard 26–32)—are as significant and as uniquely blended as any other element of the show.

Proxemically,[4] traditional stage blocking is often confuted, as actors move and gesture with unexpected, unnatural angles and durations, using body positions outside the habitual "personal sphere"—positions on the floor, gestures above the shoulders, facing upstage, half visible. Frequently silhouette, tableaux, and mime convey a contemplative mood just before or after or even sometimes during a scene of frenetic movement. Although precisely designed and executed, movement appears awkward and unnatural. Ping's choreography, sometimes rhythmic, sometimes cacophonous, sometimes contrapuntal, if often repetitious, periodically sustained for abnormal lengths of time, generally interrupting or commenting upon a scene that appears to be traditionally constructed dialogue. Movement, light, and sound provide an intriguing subtext for dialogue and plot.

Text is similarly alienating. Ping likens his "text pieces" or subversive comedies (such as *Kind Ness, 4 A.M. America*, and *Elephant Memories*) to prose, and his movement pieces (such as *Brightness* and *Skin*) to poetry, all the while stressing that always "the intent is more metaphorical and open. I like things to be evocative and have possible multiple meanings" (Sandla 27). Through parallel and simultaneous dialogue, time and logic sequences become skewed. The pieces tend to provide an audience with flashes that are recalled or echoed later, with scenes whose meaning emerges slowly from context rather than from content, since Ping stresses the individual scene over the sequence of scenes. What passes for plot is elliptical, fragmentary. Cognitive dissonance is the order of the evening, and the resulting unexpected contrasts illuminate the everyday.

Ping, like Jacques Lacan, strives to explicate and imitate the unconscious simultaneously. In addition, the psychological and linguistic structures that Lacan delineates bear a remarkable resemblance to Ping's theatrical techniques. The plays are rebuses, tempting audiences to rearrange and order scenes in order to make meaning, to create narrative. In *Kind Ness*, for example, the scenes are:

1. A slide lecture (neutral time and space)
2. Daphne's Garden (high school age)
3. First Day of School
4. Slapstick #1 (A white hunter-ape routine)
   [stagehand crosses with rock]
5. Chez Buzz (college age)
6. Introductions (second grade through summer)
7. Slapstick #2
8. Questions and answers (late teenage)
9. Bus stop (second grade)
   [rain slide show of Buzz in Rwanda, years before the main action of the play]
10. Prom night
    [stagehand crosses with rock]
11. Testimonials (ten years later, topic: "the last time I saw Buzz . . .)
    [stagehand sets rock]
12. At the zoo (Buzz and Daphne married with child, though in the previous scene she speaks of the last time she saw him.)

Time and space do not obey Newton's laws here, and plot does not obey Aristotle's. Not only must the audience retrospectively reorder the scenes if they want to create a linear account, but also they must account for stylistic, thematic, and narrative interruptions (rather like Robert Wilson and Philip Glass's notion of "knee plays" or entre acts) in which unidentified and motiveless characters perform enigmatic business. Many of the theater works follow this form.

Lacan's concept of the *corps morcele*, or nontotalized body image, is also helpful in understanding Ping's work. Lacan maintains that a sense of unity follows from viewing the body in various pieces over time, then reconstituting "sense" retrospectively. Ping's unconnected "scenes" allow us glimpses of the "body" of the work, a gestalt which will ultimately provide a view of the symbolic.

Ping's aesthetic is also unique. He claims that his "sensibility is really Asian, because it's about subtlety. . . . it's formal—it's not brash and American, though sometimes it is, since I am a mixture." In addition to the Asian nuance, refinement, form, and strong sense of mood, Ping often selects Asian themes. *Maraya: Acts of Nature in Geological Time* is almost liturgical, a Buddhist meditation on time; most of the works mourn our loss of spirituality, and almost every play includes some representation of the outsider, the foreigner.

For western audiences, these techniques provide an alienation effect that prevents suspension of disbelief. Within this landscape aliens and monsters are neither unexpected nor unacceptable; rather these strange creatures hold the mirror up to human nature by forcing us to question our cultural and personal presuppositions and assumptions. Rather than viewing the Other as monster, Ping forces us to see the Other as self.

Armed with this sketchy map of the world, I'd like now to focus on the dragons. Here I will concentrate on four works, or rather on characters within four works, to illustrate and analyze Ping's use of the monster, which I am for the moment defining rather loosely as the "alien," "other," or "outsider." This character is usually nonanthropomorphic, sometimes partaking of human physiognomy, but always a reflection of the human psyche. Since the monster does not ascribe to ideas or processes that are familiar to us, our cultural codes dictate that it must be evil or insane. Along these ethnocentric lines, deviance is to be feared, and must be made to conform or be expelled. A whole slew of fifties science fiction movies and more contemporary horror movies attest to the strength of this xenophobic concept. Clearly we dehumanize and detest any figure, particularly one unlike us, who may rob us of something.

Some psychoanalysts believe that when these shapeless and amorphous fears are made flesh (or in Ping's worlds, feather, fin, fur, or fang), they may be confronted, fought, beaten, and integrated by the ego. As Freud noted of dream images, we tend to externalize our inexpressible fears by projecting or displacing them onto figures foreign to ourselves. Rather than signifying ill health, these confrontations are natural and productive, as Bruno Bettelheim has pointed out in the process of rescuing our grotesque fairy tales from pop-psyche do-gooders who would make childhood a bland and "safe" idyll. In the postmodern world of the anti-hero we must realize that we frequently valorize the monster, attempting to empathize with his deprivations and therefore to forgive his trespasses, assuming his guilt ourselves. Ping is more complicit with John Gardner's *Grendel* than with the eighth-century *Beowulf.*

To a certain extent, Ping's gallery of monsters enacts these psychological processes. Frequently he presents a grotesque in order to explore some aspect of the darker side of our culture, to expose the inflamed nerve of racism, sexism, ethnocentricity, and down-home ignorance so that the infection may be observed and treated.

For example, the early work *Fear and Loathing in Gotham* reflects perhaps most directly the phobic hatred of the Anglo for the Asian. Based on the movie *M*, the play concerns a Chinese immigrant, a serial killer of white children. The work is Ping's most overt statement about the issue of biculturalism; a Chinese critic compared it to Eldridge Cleaver's *Soul on Ice* (Carroll, "Select" 72). But Ping exposes the tormented and human heart of the monster in a scene in which the murderer futilely attempts to keep up with an English-language teaching record. He cannot maintain the pace of the tutor, and the scene builds to a nightmarish howl, reflecting the frustration of the alien. Murder becomes his only way of "relating." As Ping's monster dwindles from the mythic to the personalized particular, so in direct proportion does the audience come to recognize itself in the portrait of an extraordinary creature in an ordinary world, or an ordinary creature in an extraordinary world.

In spite of such emotionally credible abreactions, Ping is not a psychologist, he is not a patient presenting his dreams publicly to a therapist/audience, he is an artist and therefore concerned with aesthetics as well as psychosis. Consequently, his monsters metamorphose from work to work, even from scene to scene, as they reflect new insights, new angles on the subject in question. "The monster," he says, "has always existed in my work—whether he's called the outsider, the scapegoat, or the symbol on which you can throw all your negatives."

Perhaps the best example of such an ambiguous attitude toward the monster, the classic cthonic figure, is *Nosferatu*, inspired by the Murnau film of the same name, which employs a particularly rich symbol, the vampire. A blending of eros and thanatos, the bringer of death cannot die. Yet in Ping's play this figure of the id incarnate ironically offers salvation from the sterile yuppie lifestyle of dinner parties, health clubs, power lunches and "style."

One of the most riveting scenes in the play, foregrounded by lively choreography and vibrant color (in contrast to the monochromatic grey and black palette of the rest of the play) is the "dance of death." Dressed in skeleton costumes reminiscent of the Mexican "day of the dead," a number of lively characters cavort onstage: skeletons in Reboks jog, a skeletal nurse juggles three skeletal babies, a skeletal bride waltzes with a skeletal groom.[5] Even dead, these figures are alive, engaged, and emotional, in contrast to the central characters, the yuppies who will eventually be invaded by giant hairballs and delivered from their limbo by the kiss of the vampire.

Here is a perfect example of how Ping Chong manipulates audience response. Tradition dictates that we should be repulsed and disgusted by such monstrosities, which Carroll calls "interstitial and contradictory"—incomplete representatives of either the living or the dead (Carroll, *Philosophy* 32, 51). Yet we remain neutral. In the traditional work of horror, audience response is guided either by the disgusting appearance of the monster or by the reactions of other characters within the fictive frame toward the monster. Another guide, "horrific metonymy," would associate the vampire with nauseating surroundings such as rats, body fluids, and boneyards. Yet here, Nosferatu is designed to be striking in movement and costume, placed in a designer apartment with beautiful people, and skeletal dancers are grotesquely comic. In addition, the onstage audience, the characters, are utterly oblivious to the creatures and overly horrified by the rather everyday terror of overflowing drains. Consequently, we in the theater have no cues, or rather contradictory cues, for the construction of our response.

The monster is oxymoronic and paradoxical, cognitively threatening, challenging to common knowledge and cultural order. As such, Nosferatu represents the side of our personalities, of our culture, that we refuse to deal with, the dark side. Nosferatu is not evil—he is morally neutral, like any reflection—but the cultural and aesthetic echoes are horrifying.

In *The Angels of Swedenborg* we have a number of otherworldly characters, some metaphysical, some monstrous. The "fishhead" monster manipulates the philosopher/scientist like a marionette; his stage-right movements echo the cavorting angels in their stage-left pen of feathers. Enter the stranger, who seduces the angel and literally clips his wings; the stranger/monster here represents the sophisticate, the internationalist; he is urbane, sumptuously dressed. He speaks cliches in multiple languages, beginning with the innocent "Got a dime?" "Je pense qu'il va pleuvoir?" disintegrating to "I'm forever blowing bubbles" to the threatening chaos of:

> I have wings too.
> I'll show you.
> Come.
> Komminzee mein kinnan.
> Come to daddy.
> Come fly with me.
> We fly the friendly skies.
> Come'ere sugar booger.
> Moo Goo Gai Pan, Kawasaki.
> Peek-a-boo.

Once again the familiar is by context made strange.

Like the Asian murderer in *Fear and Loathing*, this monster also has a double meaning, depending upon how the audience chooses to respond to the beleaguered angel. On the one hand, the stranger is certainly a lethal threat to the individual. On the other, as a "foreigner" he represents American xenophobia, the stereotypic outsider we always fear: a real threat and therefore out of our control, or one we ourselves create by our fear? The dark irony is that regardless of the origin of the monster, the clipping is nevertheless fatal.

In *Kind Ness* Ping creates the "monster" by the process of fusion, which "unites distinct attributes in one unambiguous entity." Such attributes may be life and death, as in Nosferatu, or male and female, or Eastern and Western, or any aggregate contradictory qualities (Carroll, *Philosophy* 16, 43–51).[6] Buzz is a teenager who happens to be a gorilla. Most of his friends—a blind girl, an impoverished Canuck, a WASP debutante—do not seem to notice, but the audience is constantly forced to contemplate how Buzz is like and unlike his human buddies. Although various characters are available to model audience response, the wild divergence of their reactions prevents an "ideal" character from guiding audience reaction. Buzz's obliviousness to his difference provokes explosive actions on the part of observers, who engage the Other in opposition, negation, ostentation, and lies in order to define themselves. The product of such explosion is, ultimately, change in the *weltanschauung* of the observers. Whether the change is positive or negative, Ping refuses to decide.

At times Buzz represents the African American, at times the vaudeville monkey, at times the threatening King Kong, at times the typical teenager. "Buzz," claims Ping, "is not any different than the way Americans feel about Iranians." But rather than resisting, Buzz excels at the human trivial pursuits; in the long run he is thoroughly assimilated—financially successful, cultured, eventually marrying the debutante. But in the end he does not really accept himself. The last scene of the play drives home Ping's irony: Buzz, pushing his son in a stroller through the zoo, barely acknowledges his double—a monster created by fission. Brother gorilla swings in a cage, and Buzz fails to recognize his own cage.

But how should the audience react? Do we applaud his integration? Denounce him for abandoning his heritage? Feel compassion for the terrible decision he is forced to make? In Buzz we see all the strains of identity and allegience that torment any assimilating ethnic group or subculture—Asian, female, Black, Jew, or Amerindian. Buzz serves as a sounding board for everyone's prejudices. He is the wonderful naive innocent simian-American, yet at the same time he is the savage creature of the jungle.

In the most moving scene of the play, Buzz stands alone in the rain, maintaining otherness while he recalls his home in the jungle of Rwanda and the deaths of his parents by poachers. Ping, like most artists, claims to present, not to judge; he is not critical of anyone's choice, but wishes us to observe the pain involved in the choosing. Buzz's predicament naturally throws light on the ways we treat anyone who is "different;" at one point a blind character, who has been harassed and tormented all her life, explodes:

> I've had it! I'm sick and tired of the way you've been treating me all these years! You've made fun of me, played tricks on me. . . . You've treated me

> like I'm a freak! Well, what about Buzz?? He's a fucking monkey and you don't give him half the shit you give me!

We may choose, based on the fads of society, our bigotries.

For Lacan, as for Ping, text or style is a rebus and enacts the process of explication. By continually postponing closure, by repeatedly interrupting the "forward" motion of the "plot," Ping endows his signifiers with the power of suspense and implies rather than states the sense (Lacan 153–59, Lemaire 43–44). By indulging in word play, riddles, and obfuscation, the works make us attribute intentionality to their creators, and thus to try to solve the mystery of meaning about which we have been given so many cryptic clues. The process is rather like dream interpretation.

Ping's theatrical product, like his method of creation, is continually a moment in process, which must be anticipatory and retroactive (Gallop 79–84, Lacan 1–7). The effect of anticipation is usually anxiety, which explains audience uneasiness with such performance art. We are in the habit of reading discursively, and when Ping demands that we read his work recursively by presenting us with nonlinear form, we are frustrated.

When we further complicate matters by adding the multidimensionality and multimediality of performance, we may become even more frustrated, for we are unused to articulating our interpretations of nontextual signs, which we frequently assume to be iconic. *Witz*, or visual puns must be integrated; movement provides subtext.

When it comes to multimediality, Roman Jakobson's notion of metonymy and metaphor as well as Lacan's concept of algorithms assist us in "reading" these performance texts (Lacan 154–66, Lemaire 38–40). Like a musical score or an architect's blueprint, a performance text must be read both horizontally and vertically to acknowledge its many dimensions. After Saussure, Lacan and Jakobson associated the horizontal dimension of language with metonymy, with the Western tradition of writing, with the syntagmatic, with the diachronic. The vertical or metaphoric, in contrast, represents non-Western, paradigmatic, and synchronic impulses (Gallop 122–26). As an Asian American artist and as a creator of theater, Ping unquestionably demands that both axes be contemplated simultaneously. Only then can we sit back and enjoy both the *terra* and the terror.

Ping's works are full of potentially terrifying outsiders, yet these characters almost always turn out to be awesome and symbolic creatures of myth rather than the repellant monsters of horror. For if any one quality unites his productions it is his concern with the outside point of view, or the insider's point of view of the outsider, or the other way around, or simultaneously. Since we cannot see ourselves so clearly, we must rely on Ping's aliens to tell us more accurately who we really are.

In many ways Ping is himself an outsider not only to white American society but also to his own Asian American community. He complains that the director of Asian Cine-vision claims "he doesn't really do Chinese things. . . . he's not really part of the Asian American aesthetic." He has always resisted talking about the specific problems of Asian Americans as, for example, David Henry Hwang does in *FOB* and *Dance and the Railroad*. In a sense, Ping is in a position like his monsters'—in order to continue to present his visions he must maintain a careful cultural balance.

However, it is possible to discern some sort of "progression" in Ping's use of the monster. The figures, from the serial killer to Buzz, become less and less "evil," less and less "Asian"; they also succeed and assimilate more and more fully. I hate to even suggest that these changing monsters are reflections of the changing artist, who is also becoming more successful and assimilating more easily into the world of contemporary art. Yet Ping's "otherness" and refusal to become a "commodity" for Broadway theater or television make his financial survival continually precarious.

Aesthetically, and perhaps as a consequence of his twenty years' experience with the artistic and financial woes of the mainstream theater, Ping's treatment of monsters is becoming more sophisticated, more heavily ironic. The figures become simultaneously frightening and frightened, embodiments of our fears and saviors from our fears. These monsters serve as context, as a form of psychic release for people who ignore or cannot recognize their needs. On a cultural level, monsters speak to the fears of the group. In addition, they provide an innovative viewpoint:

> when you're not part of something, the world is not a given, it is always new and different, and you may be punished or rewarded but it's a gift and a curse. . . . You will come up with magic that no one else has thought of because you don't know any better; because you're never quite sure of yourself you're always reverent, you always have some degree of humility. This is absolutely integral to my existence and I feel as put upon as I feel praised.

Ping's *terra* is much more *cognita* that we might first suppose, for once we get beyond race, gender, species, and culture, we are all human. These works of the avant garde also tell us that we have met the monsters, and they are us.

NOTES

1. From an interview I conducted with Ping Chong at the Noho Star in New York City on November 24, 1989. Quotations without attribution are drawn from this interview.

2. The complete text of *Kind Ness* is printed in *New Plays: USA*, ed. James Leverett and Gillian Richards (New York: Theatre Communications Group, 1988), 53–94.

3. I first noticed this term in Ping's notes for *Maraya*, when he had been reading Claude Levi-Strauss. Bricolage is a process whereby the primal craftsman creates an artifact out of objects "at hand," rearranging and reassembling objects that have a particular function in order to produce another object which has no identification with its source materials. See Noel Carroll, "A Select View of Earthlings: Ping Chong," *Drama Review* 27.1 (1983): 72–81 and Mel Gussow's review of *Nuit Blanche* in *The New York Times*, January 23, 1981, 3:8.

4. Proxemics, a term coined by Edward T. Hall, studies spatial codes, "the interrelated observations and theories of man's use of space as a specialized elaboration of culture" (*The Hidden Dimension* [New York: Doubleday, 1966], 1). Scrutiny of stage proxemics is crucial to thorough theatrical scholarship, since it provides a language and means of analysis for one of the most ephemeral (and therefore most neglected by literary scholars), aspects of performance.

5. Ping remade *Nosferatu* in April 1991 on a Lila Wallace Grant for Lafayette College in Easton, Penn. For the new version, the company added many references to contemporary plagues—Exxon signs, AIDS references, right-wing death squads, nuclear symbols—to stress our responsibility for the creation of political and ecological "monsters."

6. Carroll delineates four tropes for creating monsters: (1) fusion (Freud's collective figure or condensation), opposing characteristics in one body, such as vampires and werewolves; (2) fission, contradicting elements spread between two bodies, such as dopplegangers, Jekyll and Hyde; (3) magnification or massing, larger-than-natural creatures or hoards that act together, such as killer ants and bees; and (4) horrific metonymy, seemingly innocent entities whose surroundings or attendants are offensive.

WORKS CITED

Bettleheim, Bruno. *The Uses of Enchantment*. New York: Alfred A. Knopf, 1976.

Carroll, Noel. *The Philosophy of Horror: Or Paradoxes of the Heart*. New York: Routledge, 1990.

———. "A Select View of Earthlings: Ping Chong." *The Drama Review* 27.1 (1983): 72–81.

Gallop, Jane. *Reading Lacan*. Ithaca and London: Cornell University Press, 1985.

Gussow, Mel. "*Nuit Blanche*." *New York Times*, 23 January 1981: C8.

Hall, Edward T. *The Hidden Dimension*. New York: Doubleday, 1966.

Holden, Stephen. "When Avant-Garde Meets the Mainstream." *New York Times*, 29 September 1985: B1.

Howard, Beth. "Ping Chong: Creating a Visual and Aural Feast." *Theatre Crafts*, March 1990: 26–32.

Hulser, Kathleen. "Electric Language." *American Theatre* 4.3 (June 1987): 10–16.

Lacan, Jacques. *Ecrits: A Selection*. Ed. and trans. Alan Sheridan. New York: W. W. Norton and Co., 1977.

Lemaire, Anika. *Jacques Lacan*. Trans. David Macey. London: Routledge and Kegan Paul, 1977.

Pavis, Patrice. *Languages of the Stage: Essays in the Semiology of Theatre*. New York: Performing Arts Journal Publications, 1982.

Sandla, Robert. "Practical Visionary: Ping Chong." *Theater Week*, January 1989: 26–33.

NOTES ON THE CONTRIBUTORS

King-Kok Cheung is Associate Professor of English and Asian American Studies at the University of California, Los Angeles.

Renny Christopher is writing her Ph.D. dissertation on Vietnamese/American literature with the Literature Board, University of California, Santa Cruz.

Cheng Lok Chua is Professor of English at California State University, Fresno.

Oscar V. Campomanes is completing his Ph.D. in the Department of American Civilization, Brown University.

Donald C. Goellnicht is Associate Professor of English at McMaster University, Ontario, Canada.

Ruth Hsiao teaches in the English department at Tufts University, Boston.

Elaine H. Kim is Professor of Asian American Studies in the Ethnic Studies Department, University of California, Berkeley.

David Leiwei Li is Assistant Professor in the English department, University of Southern California.

Shirley Geok-lin Lim is Professor of Asian American Studies at the University of California, Santa Barbara.

Patricia Lin is Associate Professor of Ethnic and Women's Studies at California State Polytechnic University, Pomona.

Amy Ling is Associate Professor of English and Director of the Asian American Studies program at the University of Wisconsin, Madison.

James S. Moy is Associate Professor of Theatre Arts at the University of Wisconsin, Madison.

Gayle K. Fujita Sato is Assistant Professor in the Economics Department at Keio University, Yokohama, Japan.

Stephen H. Sumida is Associate Professor of English at the University of Michigan, Ann Arbor.

Craig Tapping is Professor of Third World Studies in Malaspina College, Gabriola Island, British Columbia, Canada.

Qui-Phiet Tran is Associate Professor of English at Schreiner University, Kerrville, Texas.

George Uba is Associate Professor of English at California State University, Northridge.

Stan Yogi is presently coordinator of the California Council for the Humanities, Berkeley.

Suzanne R. Westfall is Associate Professor of English and Director of Theatre at Lafayette College, Easton, Pennsylvania.

Sau-ling Cynthia Wong is Associate Professor of Asian American Studies in the Ethnic Studies Department, University of California, Berkeley.

Chung-Hei Yun is Assistant Professor of English and Humanities at Shawnee State University, Portsmouth, Ohio.